ESSAYS OF JOHN DRYDEN

W. P. KER

ESSAYS

OF

JOHN DRYDEN

SELECTED AND EDITED

BY

W. P. KER

VOLUME I

New York
RUSSELL & RUSSELL
1961

PREFACE

THE present work is a collection of Dryden's principal Essays on literary subjects, with a short commentary, and an introduction intended to explain his position as a critic. It is not a complete edition of Dryden's prose. The more ponderous works have been left out, and those not concerned with literature, such as the *History of the League* ; also some of the lighter Prefaces and Dedications, chiefly complimentary in their substance. This selection is not meant to take the place of Scott or of Malone, but may serve as a convenient book for reference, to be used especially by such readers as are interested in criticism and the history of criticism, and who may be glad to have Dryden's critical opinions put before them in a form adapted for ready consultation and comparison.

The text has been throughout collated with the original editions except in one case, the *Trans-*

lations from Ovid (1680), where the earliest edition accessible was the third, of 1683.

In the *Essay of Dramatic Poesy* the text is that of the first edition (1668), without the grammatical amendments introduced by Dryden in his revision (1684). The excuse for this choice of a text is that the edition of 1668 gives Dryden's own authentic mode of speech at that epoch of his life, and is therefore preferable in a collection which presents the essays in order of time as they were composed. Besides, the revised version has been often reprinted, and is easily accessible,—e. g. in Mr. Arnold's edition in this series,—while the text of 1668 has only once been re-published, in the edition of Mr. W. H. Low.

The spelling has been modernized. It would have been a pleasure to give the essays in old spelling, but the difficulties were too great. It is hardly possible to separate the old spelling from the old type and from the original shape of the page ; it comes to be an alternative between *facsimile* reproduction and modern spelling. If the original spelling had been kept, it would have represented, not Dryden's own way of writing, but the caprices of various printers between 1664 and 1700. An appearance of quaintness and confusion would have been the result, and this was not convenient ; Dryden, who was absolutely without concern in such matters, did not seem to be a good subject for this sort of antiquarian curiosity. It might have been possible to frame a conventional uniform seventeenth-century spelling for the whole book; but it was easier to adopt the modern convention, which will be found to have been recognized in most points somewhere or other in Dryden's works. Thus, the principal differences between the old and the new spellings are exemplified in the title *An Essay of Dramatick Poesie*; but there is nothing in the spelling *Dramatic Poesy* which Dryden would have disapproved. The Preface to *Troilus and Cressida*, 1679, which is printed in italics, and in the Italian manner, with few capitals, is generally modern in spelling, and gives *Dramatic Poetry, critic*, not *critique* nor *critick, choleric, phlegmatic, virtuous* not *vertuous*. *Extream* is the common spelling in Dryden's time, but *extreme* is allowed; so is *horror* besides *horrour*. *Shock'd* is the spelling in the *Essay of Dramatic Poesy*; so that there is no need to recall to active service the experimental *chocqu'd* of the *Indian Emperor*. *Then* for *than* is common in the earlier books, but *than* is used as well; and so it is possible to find authority for most modern ways of spelling in Dryden. Modernization of course must stop short of organic change in the word. Dryden's word is *interess'd*, not *interested*, and he does not recognize the spelling *fund* for his *fond*.

The punctuation is generally careless and irrational in the original editions. ' The printer has enough to answer for in false pointings,' says the author himself in the *Second Miscellany*. It is not always easy to find the best correction of the points. The colon (:) is often used for the end of a sentence, the next phrase after the colon beginning with a capital letter. The full stop is not infrequently used, especially in Tonson's books, the *Virgil*, for example, where a colon or semicolon would be more suitable. One instance of difficult punctuation may be noted at the beginning of the *Dramatic Essay* (p. 28, l. 6). All the three original editions are agreed about the first period ; in all, the second sentence begins at *While*, with a capital. But this has not hitherto been permitted to stand by any editor, except Mr. Low.

A list of Dryden's writings is given ; it was not necessary to write another biography of Dryden. After Johnson, Malone, and Scott, after Mr. Saintsbury's *Dryden* in the *English Men of Letters*, after Mr. Churton Collins's essay on *Dryden* (*Essays and Studies*, 1895), and Mr. Christie's biographical notices in the *Globe* Edition, and in the *Selected Poems* for the Clarendon Press, there is little room and little need for another account of Dryden's life without fresh materials and documents. What his quality as a critic was, the Introduction makes an attempt to explain ; it is superfluous to speak in praise of Dryden, but there are some things in the circumstances of his time, and in the conditions of literary taste, that require to be examined as a preliminary to the study of his discourses.

On many points I have received most welcome assistance, by which I hope this book may have profited ; and I desire especially to record my obligations to Mr. Saintsbury, Mr. Gosse, Mr. C. H. Firth, and Mr. Oliver Elton, for the interest they have taken in the problems submitted to them.

W. P. KER.

September, 1899.

CONTENTS

INTRODUCTION

I.

DRYDEN'S critical writings have been less damaged by the lapse of time and have kept their original freshness better than any literary discourses which can be compared with them, even taking the next century into consideration. He has suffered much less from changes of literary fashion than Addison or Dr. Johnson. Although there are many things that are antiquated or conventional in his discussion of literary principles, although he had his share of the literary pedantries of his age, there is an inexhaustible liveliness and spirit in his essays which has given them an advantage over many more laborious and philosophical pieces of criticism. Every one of his essays contains some independent judgment. His love of literature was instinctive ; his mind answered at once to the touch of poetry, and gave in return his estimate of it, in ' the other harmony of prose.' It is true that his opinions are sometimes encumbered by the respect which he feels himself bound to pay to established authorities, and sometimes he condescends to hackwork and compilation, as, for instance, in much of the essays on *Satire* and on *Epic Poetry*. But even when he is tired of this business he keeps his ease of manner, and it is in the manner of his discourses that he shows his power as a critic. There is nothing in literary criticism more satisfactory, merely as a display of literary strength and skill, than the essays in which Dryden's mind is expatiating freely, as in the *Dramatic Poesy* and the Preface to the *Fables*, where he faces his adversaries, personal and impersonal, with the security of a man who has confidence in his own powers, and in the clearness of his eye. He is at his best when he has set himself to try the value of dogmatic rules and principles ; cautious, respectful, seeming to comply with them, till the time comes for the stroke that ends the encounter, and leaves the arena to be cleared for the next anta- gonist. ' Now what, I beseech you, is more easy than to write a regular French play, or more difficult than to write an irregular English one, like those of Fletcher or of Shakespeare ? ' The natural grace and the readiness of his style in explanation and controversy have never been surpassed. His language is a creature moving at its own will, in its proper element.

The other great critic of Dryden's time, St. Evremond, had found it to be the fault of the English that they dug too deep, and lost themselves in the windings of their own thoughts before they could bring anything to the surface, to be made available for the common sense of mankind ; as, on the other hand, the defect of the French was that they would not follow an argument home, and were too easily contented with the sound of their own voices. It would be good for each nation to learn from the other ; for the English to acquire the art of human conversation ; for the French to go deeper in their studies. This balance of faculties is secured in Dryden more completely than in any other English writer, and there is no better account of the excel- lences of his prose than is given in these phrases of

St. Evremond : ' A la vérité, je n'ai point vu de gens de meilleur entendement que les Français qui considèrent les choses avec attention, et les Anglais qui peuvent se détacher de leurs trop grandes méditations pour revenir à la facilité du discours et à certaine liberté d'esprit qu'il faut posséder toujours, s'il est possible. Les plus honnêtes gens du monde, ce sont les Français qui pensent, et les Anglais qui parlent.'

Dryden's power as a writer of criticism does not depend upon his definite judgments. He is not to be refuted, though he may be proved to have thought too highly of Rapin and Bossu among critics, of Fairfax and Waller among English poets. Many little critics, like Dick Minim in the *Idler*, lived on Dryden's traditional utterances after they had hardened into dogmas ; Idols of the Coffee-house. ' *Denham* and *Waller* he held the first reformers of English numbers.' But the separate positive sentences of Dryden are of small account in his work as a critic. His virtue is that in a time when literature was pestered and cramped with formulas he found it impossible to write otherwise than freely. He is sceptical, tentative, disengaged, where most of his contemporaries, and most of his successors for a hundred years, are pledged to certain dogmas and principles.

II. THE HEROIC POEM.

Dryden's Essays belong to the history of the Renaissance. They are part of the general effort of the world to come to an understanding with itself about the ideals of literature which had been imposed upon it by the learning of the classical scholars. There were exact patterns of different kinds of poetry laid up in some heaven to which the true scholar might rise

in his contemplations, and from which he might bring
down his knowledge for the instruction of modern
poetical artificers. The patterns of Epic (commonly
called the 'Heroic Poem') and of Tragedy, or the
Heroic Play, are those that chiefly concern Dryden.
What influence those ideal patterns had, what reverence
they evoked, is scarcely conceivable now, and is seldom
thought of by historians. The 'Heroic Poem' is not
commonly mentioned in histories of Europe as a matter
of serious interest : yet from the days of Petrarch and
Boccaccio to those of Dr. Johnson, and more especially
from the sixteenth century onward, it was a subject that
engaged some of the strongest intellects in the world
(among them, Hobbes, Gibbon, and Hume) [1] ; it was
studied and discussed as fully and with as much thought
as any of the problems by which the face of the world
was changed in those centuries. There might be
difference of opinion about the essence of the Heroic
Poem or the Tragedy, but there was no doubt about their
value. Truth about them was ascertainable, and truth
about them was necessary to the intellect of man, for they
were the noblest things belonging to him [2].

About the middle of the seventeenth century there
was an increased activity in the business of epic poetry,
especially in France and England ; owing, no doubt, to

---

[1] See 'The Answer of Mr. Hobbes to Sir William Davenant's Preface
before Gondibert,' 1650, and 'The Iliads and Odysses of Homer, translated out of Greek into English by Thomas Hobbes, of Malmesbury.
With a large Preface concerning the virtues of an Heroic Poem, written
by the translator,' 1676 ; Hume, 'Letter to the authors of the *Critical
Review* concerning the *Epigoniad* of Wilkie,' April 1759 ; Gibbon, 'An
Inquiry whether a Catalogue of the Armies sent into the Field is an
essential part of an Epic Poem,' Dec. 23, 1763.

[2] 'A Heroic Poem, truly such, is undoubtedly the greatest work
which the soul of man is capable to perform' (*Dedication of the
Æneis*).

the accumulation of testimony on the subject by the older generations. It was discussed between Hobbes and Davenant ; it was meditated by the French poets ; and Davenant in England, Chapelain and others in France, undertook to show by their example how the rules and principles of the Heroic Poem might be carried out in practice. *Paradise Lost* is one of those experiments. It is easy to pass by *Gondibert*, and to accept the unanimous judgment which disposes of Chapelain's *Pucelle* ; but Milton's work was begun and carried out under the same critical principles, and no small part of his motive was the same learned ambition to embody the abstract form of Epic in a modern vernacular work. Like Ronsard and Tasso before him, like Davenant, like Chapelain, Desmarests, Scudéry, and Father Le Moyne, he was under the spell of the phantom Epic, the pure idea of a Virgilian poem. The heroic poem was an unbodied ghost that might choose for the habit of its earthly life either the story of Paradise or that of the Round Table ; just as the tragedy which is *Samson Agonistes* might have been *Samson Hybristes* or *Pursophorus*, or even *Solomon Gynæcocratumenus*, or any other of the inventions noted by Milton in his list of subjects in the Trinity MS. The abstract inspiration of the Virgilian form of Epic, or of the Euripidean form of Tragedy, before the subject was determined at all, must count for more than a little in the history of Milton's poetry ; to realize the importance of these abstract ideas is one of the first requisites in coming to the study of Dryden's critical essays. His freedom cannot be rightly estimated except in relation to the potent authorities with which he had to deal.

Dryden's attitude towards the pure abstract Forms of Poetry is not very difficult to understand when once their character has been appreciated. He had read and admired the Latin poets. He appreciated clear reasoning and exposition, such as he found in Rapin and Bossu, and he was not by nature inclined to dissent from established opinion without sufficient cause. He shows respect to the orthodox views wherever he can. The worship of the pure form and the ambition to realize it affected him strongly ; for example, in his theory of Heroic Plays, and in his contemplated Epic on King Arthur. But he will not make it a point of honour or of faith to enforce the principles of Heroic Poetry. His original work is determined by present conditions of taste (among which of course a respect for orthodox literary canons must count for something), and his general criticism, having always a reference to his own present undertakings, follows his judgment of what is desirable and feasible for him (or for contemporary English authors) at the moment. The patterns of literature have to demean themselves accordingly. Dryden is willing to pay reverence to the Heroic Poem and to the ideal of Tragedy : it never occurs to him to hesitate. But he does not ' believe what he knows to be untrue,' and nothing is further from his thoughts than to impose on his fellows a bondage like that of Trissino in Italy or Gabriel Harvey in England —two similar spirits in their flat, uncompromising zeal for the purity of classical example, and in their abhorrence of anything like modern novelty. The rules of the pedants are a different thing from the genial influence of the great ancient poets, and they are treated by Dryden in a different way. He felt strongly the conventional obligation to admire the classical poets ; but this element of convention or duty was corrected by his natural liking for good literature wherever he found it, and he was able to think of Virgil and Ovid without prejudice when he came to close quarters with their works.

III. DRYDEN AND CORNEILLE.

Dryden's position in criticism is very like that of two of his forerunners, Tasso and Corneille, both of whom felt themselves obliged on the one hand to pay reverence to the Ancients, and on the other hand to consider their own genius and the claims of contemporary fashion. With Tasso's critical opinions, as stated in the book of 1587, *Discorsi e Lettere Poetiche*, Dryden was well acquainted, though they do not seem to have taught him anything that he did not know before ; from Corneille's essays in the 1660 edition of his plays, Dryden seems to have got, if not the original impulse to write freely about his literary opinions, at any rate a quickening of interest in critical discussion which left its effects on all his later writings.

The history of Corneille's original work, and of his relation to literary ideals and criticism, is very like that of Dryden. He began writing before the Unities were much thought of, as Dryden began in the older ' metaphysical ' manner, before the complete establishment of the reforms of Waller. He saw the progress of ' correct ' ideas, and felt himself obliged to conform to them, as Dryden was obliged to withdraw from the variegated pattern of *Annus Mirabilis*, which is full of ' metaphysical ' conceits, in favour of a more coherent and less capricious mode of poetical elocution, that of *Absalom and Achitophel*. Like Dryden, Corneille had to come to an understanding with himself about the meaning and the authority of the rules of Poetry ; like Dryden, he had an original love of freedom ; it was his business as a critic to find some compromise between freedom and authority, to explain the laws of Poetry in such a way as to reserve for himself the faculty of doing his own work without undue sacrifices. The great difference between Corneille and Dryden is that Corneille in his criticism was limited to the Drama, to the kind of composition in which he was at home, for which he had a natural gift. It detracts somewhat from the value of Dryden's essays that so many of them are concerned with kinds of work for which he was not suited. Corneille is at the centre ; he has made the province of Tragedy his own before he begins to write about it as an expositor. Dryden began to write as a critic of the Drama while he was still finding his way, and, unhappily, where there was no satisfactory way to be found. The difference in situation between Corneille and Dryden is that Corneille is a master reviewing the work he has already done and explaining it ; Dryden is a master of forms of poetry not dramatic, trying in his dramatic essays to find his way into provinces not his own, to plant a new dramatic colony, by artifice if not by violence, in place of the older kinds of drama which he sees to be exhausted. The fault of his prefaces is that they make one disappointed with his plays, when one comes to them after his criticisms. This is not the case with his non-dramatic work ; there the drawback is of another kind, namely, that so much of his Discourses on Satire (the Preface to *Juvenal*) and on Epic (the Dedication of the *Æneis*) is mere unoriginal learning, without the freshness of the earlier essays. For this, however, there is compensation, and something more, in the glorious Preface to the *Fables*, written more than thirty years after the *Essay of Dramatic Poetry*, and fully its equal in liveliness and vigour. The earlier essays are generally concerned with Drama, the later with other forms of composition. It may be remarked, however, that the distinction is rather a superficial one, for various reasons, and principally on account of that worship of the *Heroic Poem* already referred to. The ' Heroic Plays ' of the sixties and early seventies in that century had their origin in the *Epic Poem* : they were to transfer the ideal of Epic, as far as might be, to the stage. They were not from the beginning dramatic ; the Heroic Plays were in their origin narrative, and the points most considered by their authors were not dramatic, but moral, such as the character of the Hero, or rhetorical, such as the proper sort of verse. Hence the Preface to *Annus Mirabilis*, with its notes on heroic poetry and on poetical expression, is not out of place among the dramatic criticisms, for much of Dryden's dramatic criticism is taken up with these non-dramatic subjects ; the essay *Of Heroic Plays* is an essay on Epic Poetry. Hence, quite naturally, the Preface to the *State of Innocence* (Dryden's dramatic version of *Paradise Lost*) is *An Apology for Heroic Poetry and Poetic Licence*, with hardly a reference to Drama. Thus if Dryden's interest in the Drama is at times half-hearted, and different from the single-minded devotion of Corneille, he makes up for it by his digressions into the other kinds where he feels himself more at home. And also in another way : for if he cannot explain the secrets of the dramatic workshop with the same confidence and intimate knowledge as Corneille, he has more to admire in the authors of the previous generation, and more power of admiring them. Dryden on Shakespeare is unlike any other critic : there are as yet no commentators, there is no general opinion on the subject, or none worth considering : ' thought is free ' ; and what Dryden thinks about Shakespeare is, like Ben Jonson's estimate, on this side idolatry. But if Dryden speaks about Shakespeare with little anticipation of the vast multitude and the many voices that were to follow him with their praises, his judgment is none the worse for that. The isolation of his point of view, the simplicity of his statement (one mortal man and good writer talking happily about another), the enthusiastic tone, and at the same time the want of reverence, all bring out the individual genius of Dryden as a critic, the directness and truth of his answer when he is appealed to by good poetry. No critic has ever given so convincing an account of his own poetical likings with so little display, so little expense of rhetoric.

IV. ANCIENTS AND MODERNS.

In the *Battle of the Books* Dryden is one of the Moderns. His critical work cannot be fully understood without some reference to this long debate, which had several new beginnings and no end during his lifetime. There was more reason in the debate, and it was conducted, at times, with more good sense than might be gathered either from Swift's allegory or from some of the impertinences on either side that preceded it. It was the inevitable result of the Revival of Learning ; it had gone on for centuries ; the splutter of Perrault's fireworks being a minor incident in the contention. What was the right way to think of the Ancients ? What was the right way to make use of their example ? These were questions that were asked long before the times to which the name *Renaissance* is generally given. They were questions that might be made inconvenient by any pedant to any poet, as by Gabriel Harvey to Spenser. Tasso's *Discourses* are an attempt to make a compromise without giving up either respect for the Ancients or any rights of the Moderns. If Aristotle left *Romance* out of his *Poetics* he was not the less Aristotle : if Romance had existed, it would have come into his

system. Tasso in this way tried to reconcile the two
sides, and he is followed by Corneille and by Dryden
with similar attempts at a compromise. But in Dryden's
time the debate between Ancients and Moderns was not
merely between classical precedent and modern liberty :
there was a cross-debate, with a different motive. In
the *Battle of the Books* the Moderns are not on the side
of liberty ; they are not for romance against classical
authority. The superstition of classical authority brought
its own Nemesis in the most singular way, almost as
soon as the French Academy was founded to provide
an audience for the new views. The champion of the
Moderns claims a hearing, like Boisrobert in the French
Academy in 1635 [1], and Perrault later, not because the
Moderns want more freedom, but because they are more
correct than the Ancients, more classical than Homer.
This new claim for the Moderns is quite unlike Tasso's
gentle plea for the realm of the Fairy Queen, for the
elements of chivalry. These new Moderns are really
more ancient and more pedantic than Gabriel Harvey.
The Revival of ancient Learning has succeeded so well
that the ancient poets are disqualified and treated with
disrespect.

Dryden's attitude in this *Battle of the Books* is
throughout consistent and honourable. As, with
Corneille and even beyond Corneille, he vindicates the
freedom of modern art against the positive laws derived
from the Classics, so against the more furious and ultra-
classical Moderns he stands up for the honour of Greek
and Latin poetry. He was one man at any rate in the
seventeenth century to whom the shocks of literary
conflict brought advantage. Between the classically-
minded, who would have imposed the Ancients on the

---

[1] See Rigault, *Histoire de la querelle des Anciens et des Modernes,* 1856.

world as infallible lawgivers, and the modern precisians, in whose sight the *Iliad* itself was a shocking example of licence, Dryden kept his head and his own opinions. The soundness of his judgment saved him from the classical vanity, as is sufficiently proved in his comparison of Ovid and Chaucer ; the sensitive appreciation and the unfailing *gusto* with which he applauded the good things of poetry secured him from all risks of doing injustice to either side. Out of all the contradictions and paradoxes of the *Battle of the Books* Dryden seems to have taken nothing but a further strengthening of his natural habit of criticism, which led him instinctively to recognize what was good, and to praise it. Between the ancient and the modern pedants Dryden found it natural to see things with his own eyes, and the effect of the charges and counter-charges in the literary tumult was if anything to make him all the more resolved that neither Ovid nor Chaucer should suffer wrong, either from ignorance on the one hand or pedantry on the other.

V. ' NATURE.'

There is one idea common to Dryden and all his contemporaries which, in spite of its ambiguity, is seldom misleading ; that is the idea of Nature : ' At once the source, and end, and test of Art.' Pope could not help himself in the *Essay on Criticism* ; he had to say ' first follow Nature,' because all the critics and poets had been saying the same thing for generations past, and it was not his business to disagree with them. Nor was it Dryden's wish in this respect to avoid conforming with the rest of the guild. ' Nature ' means whatever the author thinks right ; sometimes it is the reality that is copied by the artist ; sometimes, and much more commonly, it is the principles of sound

reason in poetry ; and sometimes it is the Ideal. Thus
Dryden refers to Nature to justify heroic couplets in
serious drama ; ' heroic rhyme is nearest Nature, as
being the noblest kind of modern verse.' It might
seem as if there were little value in a conception so
vague, so mutable, so easily turned to sophistry and
fallacy. Yet it would be a mistake to think so. ' Nature '
made many writers say good things by way of criticism
who were unsuccessful in their original works. The
French heroic romances have long been fair game for
satirists, but Scudéry's preface to *Ibrahim ou l'Illustre
Bassa* (1641) is by no means ridiculous : ' Pour moy je
tiens que plus les avantures sont naturelles, plus elles
donnent de satisfaction : et le cours ordinaire du soleil
me semble plus merveilleux, que les estranges et
funestes rayons des comettes.' Chapelain's epic poem
has been a byword since it was printed, but his motives
were good : ' Je me suis plus attaché aux sentimens de
la Nature, qu'aux subtilités de la Déclamation.' These
are commonplaces, no doubt, and they would not carry
one very far in the composition of the Epic Poem or
the Heroic Play. But as commonplaces they had their
value ; they discouraged the invention of conceits, they
made young authors think of the arrangement of their
work, of that *ordonnance* which the critics of those days
picked up from the schools of painting. Dryden by his
adoption of these commonplaces did much to strengthen
the hold of ' Nature ' on English criticism without doing
much to explain it. One correction indeed he made.
When he found ' Nature ' turned into an excuse for
dulness he spoke out, in the *Apology for Heroic
Poetry*. For though he grew out of the ' Metaphysical '
School, and repented of *Maximin* and *Almanzor*, he
would make no terms with correct insipidity.

In the *Parallel of Poetry and Painting* he gives a

clear statement of the current idealist theory of Art and Nature, which was taken up afterwards and taught more fully, not without reference to Dryden, in the *Discourses* of Sir Joshua Reynolds.

VI. Style.

Dryden's prose has been described by Dr. Johnson in one of the pleasantest passages in the *Lives* : ' Criticism, either didactic or defensive, occupies almost all his prose, except those pages which he has devoted to his patrons ; but none of his prefaces were ever thought tedious. They have not the formality of a settled style, in which the first half of the sentence betrays the other. The clauses are never balanced, nor the periods modelled : every word seems to drop by chance, though it falls into its proper place. Nothing is cold or languid ; the whole is airy, animated, and vigorous ; what is little, is gay ; what is great, is splendid. He may be thought to mention himself too frequently ; but while he forces himself upon our esteem, we cannot refuse him to stand high in his own. Every thing is excused by the play of images and the spriteliness of expression. Though all is easy, nothing is feeble ; though all seems careless, there is nothing harsh ; and though since his earlier works more than a century has passed, they have nothing yet uncouth or obsolete.'

To this account of Dryden's style there is little to be added except in the way of illustration. It is a paragraph in which the great master of formal periods has taken occasion to salute the master of the other sort of prose, and in so doing to pay honour to both styles. Nowhere has the grace of Dryden's free elocution been better described. Dryden's sentences are like sentences of good conversation, in which it is not necessary that every point should be deliberated. They run on easily, clauses are added to qualify the chief proposition, and in one case at least there is so much freedom and exuberance in the dependent clauses that the grammar of the sentence is left helpless in the tangle and thicket of relative pronouns [1].

In his revision of the *Essay of Dramatic Poesy*, Dryden came to believe that he ought to put some restraint on his tendency to leave hanging phrases at the end of his sentences. As he tells us himself, he noted as a fault the preposition left at the end of a clause and belonging to a relative understood ; and in the revised version of his Essay he carefully corrected ' the end he aimed at ' into ' the end at which he aimed,' and ' the age I live in ' to ' the age in which I live,' and so on [2]. But this correction and restriction, though it was a move towards greater propriety of language, was very far short of conversion to the periodic structure of sentences, and Dryden's prose remains in the Preface to the *Fables* in 1700 essentially what it was in the Essay of 1668 ; no less ' airy and animated,' and no more stately and dignified.

Dryden's prose, which is intended for the greatest number, which is meant to be popular, loses nothing of its value by being compared with his contemporaries, though it may be found to be not altogether exceptional nor new in character. Dryden himself, according to Congreve's well-known evidence, acknowledged Tillotson as his master in the art of familiar discourse [3] ; and

---

[1] Preface to *Juvenal*, vol. ii. p. 38, l. 4.

[2] See p. 168 below, and note there.

[3] ' I have heard him frequently own with pleasure that if he had any talent for English prose, it was owing to his having often read the writings of the great Archbishop Tillotson.' Congreve Dedication of *Dryden's Dramatic Works*.

there were others ; before all, there was Cowley, whose
stylé obtains from Dr. Johnson little less than the
praise given to the *Essays* of Dryden for their light-
ness, grace, and ease. There were also the French
authors. However much the influence of France may
have been abused by historians as an explanation of
the new fashions of literature at the accession of
Charles II, there is no reason why it should be dis-
allowed or refused its due in accounting for the changes
of taste. French criticism, French talk about literature,
had already found the right kind of expression thirty
years and more before the *Essay of Dramatic Poesy*.
The ancestors of Dryden's prose are to be traced in
Chapelain's Preface to the *Adone* of Marino, in Mesnardière's *Poëtique*, in the Dialogues and Essays of
Sarrasin, in the Prefaces of Scudéry, in the Discourses
and *Examens* of Corneille. In all these different authors,
and in others, there was to be found, with different
faculties, the same common quality of clearness in
exposition and argument, which even without genius
may be pleasing, and with genius is the most valuable
auxiliary, as in the essays of Dryden and Corneille.
What criticism might be without the example of the
French is shown in the Preface to *Samson Agonistes*.
In date it is some years later than Dryden's *Essay* ; in
temper it belongs to the Italy of a hundred years
before ; it is like one of the solemn sermons before an
Italian learned society, in which the doctrine of Poetry
used to be expounded more gravely than any text of
St. Thomas. The difference between an Italian and
a French education in their influence on prose may
be seen by comparing Milton and Chapelain, authors
much alike in ambition, self-respect, and solemnity of
mind ; in everything but poetical genius and the circumstances of their lives. Milton writing his opinions

about Tragic Poetry writes like an Italian contemporary of Tasso, with grave magnificence ; Chapelain, by nature no less grave, and as much inclined as Milton to walk with the gait of ' the magnanimous man,' is obliged by his associates to let his dignity go and to speak like other people.   Between the scholar who was also a wit—Ménage—and the man of the world who was also a student—Sarrasin—there was no more room for declamation than there is in a reading party in summer. Chapelain the pedant has written a dialogue with Ménage and Sarrasin the wits taking part in it, and it is as easy and pleasant as the writing of the wits themselves, as fresh as anything of Dryden's ; a defence of Lancelot and the library of Don Quixote, a delightful apology for Romance, by the great champion of literary authority, the patron if not the inventor of the Unities.   It is no small part of the attraction of Dryden's *Essays* that they bring their readers into acquaintance with that new world of France in the age of Louis XIII, when all the world and the Dramatic Unities were young, when Corneille at the Hôtel de Bourgogne scarcely knew himself as yet for anything different from Hardy, when Scaramouche and Jodelet were getting things ready for Molière, and when the cloak and sword of Madrid, and the Castilian Point of Honour, were mingled in the visions of the dramatic poet with an idea of some unattained perfection, a sort of inaudible dramatic music, a harmony partly moral, partly imaginative, which should constitute the absolutely faultless play.   It is from this world, so adventurous yet so decorous, so strangely mixed of ' Gothic ' traditions and pedantic authority, Spanish comedies and classical learning, and through all of it the zest and interest of a society which sees a long day before it and much to be won, that the spirit of Dryden's Essays is in great measure derived.

Much also is native to them in England ; they inherit from Ben Jonson's *Discoveries* as well as from the Discourses of Corneille. But it is from the language and the manners of Corneille and his fellows that the *Essays* of Dryden have caught their style and accent.

There is little that is peculiarly French in the details of Dryden's prose. In a well-known passage of *Marriage à la Mode*, Act iii. sc. 1, there is a satire on the importation of French phrases and their use in the warfare of conversation. ' They began at *sottises* and ended *en ridicule* ' ; they include *foible, chagrin, grimace, embarrasse, double entendre, equivoque, eclaircissement, suitte, beveue, façon, penchant, coup d'etourdy, languissant*. Dryden does not allow himself to be led very far on this way in his own practice. In the *Dedication of the Rival Ladies* (p. 5) he protests against the abuse of foreign terms, and in the Preface to the *Second Miscellany* (p. 266) he even seems to note the word *diction* as not completely naturalized. But Dryden was not the man to make any fanatical opposition to a prevailing fashion, and he uses French words as they come convenient.

If there is anything old-fashioned in his style it is perhaps that liking for conceits which fortunately never disappears from his verse nor from his prose. He is indeed more temperate than the men *moribus antiquis*, such as Butler must be reckoned in spite of Butler's affection for lucidity and good sense. But there are many places where Dryden seems to be writing for a sentence or two in the manner of Butler or Cleveland. So in the Dedication of *Love in a Nunnery* :—

' For this reason I have often laughed at the ignorant and ridiculous descriptions which some Pedants have given of the Wits, as they are pleased to call them, which are a generation of men as unknown to them as the people of Tartary or the *Terra Australis* are to us.

And therefore as we draw giants and anthropophagi in those vacancies of our maps, where we have not travelled to draw better, so these wretches paint lewdness, atheism, folly, ill-reasoning, and all manner of extravagancies amongst us, from want of understanding what we are.'

Other aspects of Dryden's criticism may be noted under the separate headings that follow.

DEDICATION OF THE RIVAL LADIES (1664).

AT the end of his answer to Sir Robert Howard (*Defence of the Essay*, p. 133) Dryden explains how the argument about dramatic verse began in the dedication of the *Rival Ladies*, and led to the *Essay of Dramatic Poesy*, and further. Lord Orrery had written rhyming plays before Dryden took up the fashion (' yet I must remember it is your Lordship to whom I speak, who have much better commended this way by your writing in it, than I can do by writing for it,' p. 9). The example followed by Lord Orrery is found by Dryden in D'Avenant's *Siege of Rhodes*. More important, however, than the dramatic criticism in this preface is the acknowledgement of the authority of Waller as the founder of the new school of English verse, and the coupling of his name with that of Sir John Denham. That ' the excellence and dignity of rhyme were never fully known till Mr. Waller taught it,' and that Waller in this reform was seconded by Denham, became a dogma in the schools of criticism. Though opinions have changed about the value of Waller's verse, his influence as the master of Dryden and Pope is still recognized in the history of English poetry. Dryden's early reference to him here is the expression of an opinion from which he never altered, and he repeats his homage at the end of his life, in the Preface to the *Fables* (vol. ii. p. 259).

None of Lord Orrery's plays seem as yet to have been published in 1664. Dryden perhaps had seen *Henry the Fifth*, which was acted in this year. His praise of Lord Orrery's dramatic genius may be compared with Pepys's estimate (Dec. 8, 1668) : ' and so went home to dinner, where my wife tells me of my Lord Orrery's new play *Tryphon* at the Duke of York's house, which, however, I would see, and therefore put a bit of meat in our mouths, and went thither, where with much ado, at half-past one, we got into a blind hole in the 18*d.* place, above stairs, where we could not hear well, but the house infinite full, but the prologue most silly, and the play, though admirable, yet no pleasure almost in it, because just the very same design, and words, and sense, and plot, as every one of his plays have, any one of which alone would be held admirable, whereas so many of the same design and fancy do but dull one another ; and this, I perceive, is the sense of everybody else, as well as myself, who therefore showed but little pleasure in it.'

PREFACE TO *ANNUS MIRABILIS* (1667).

The ' Account of the ensuing Poem ' breaks the sequence of dramatic criticism, but more in form than in substance. Dryden's interest in the theatre was always connected with a stronger interest in non-dramatic forms of poetry : his ' Heroic Drama ' is professedly founded on the ' Heroic Poem.' Here, for once, he has an opportunity of speaking about the Heroic Poem apart from the distractions of the stage. If this essay is compared with the *Dedication of the Æneis* it will be found to display the same literary tastes, with some differences of judgment. In *Annus Mirabilis* Dryden had not yet fully appropriated the lessons of Waller. The poem is a series of fragments, with no more than an accidental unity : it is not organic, it is not, like the poems of 1681 and 1682, an argument secure of itself and directing its own progress from beginning to end ; it has to keep to the events of the year, under a constraint which Dryden, later, would have refused to submit to. In another respect *Annus Mirabilis* shows clearly its comparatively old-fashioned character, namely in the use of technical details. The *Preface* states the principle without hesitation : ' We hear indeed among our poets of the thundering of guns, the smoke, the disorder, and the slaughter, but all these are common notions. And certainly, as those who, in a logical dispute, keep in general terms, would hide a fallacy, so those who do it in any poetical description would veil their ignorance ' (p. 13). The *Dedication of the Æneis* contradicts this—' I will not give the reasons why I writ not always in the proper terms of navigation, land-service, as in the cant of any profession. I will only say that Virgil has avoided those proprieties, because he writ not to mariners, soldiers, astronomers, gardeners, peasants, &c., but to all in general, and in particular to men and ladies of the first quality, who have been better bred than to be too nicely knowing in the terms' (vol. ii. p. 236). In *Annus Mirabilis* Dryden agrees with Ronsard :—' Tu practiqueras bien souvent les artisans de tous mestiers, comme de *Marine, Venerie, Fauconnerie*, et principalement les artisans de feu, *Orfévres, Fondeurs, Marechaux, Minerailliers* ; et de là tireras maintes belles et vives comparaisons avecques les noms propres des mestiers, pour enrichir ton œuvre et le rendre plus agreable et parfait ' (*Abrégé de l'Art Poëtique François*). In 1697 Dryden has given up the technical dictionary and gone over to the school of general terms, whose principles were formulated by Buffon in his *Discourse on Style*[1]; he has become more ' classical.' Nevertheless the preface to *Annus Mirabilis* takes up a position which, with all its concessions to the older fashions, is definitely opposed to the vanities, the ' trimmings slight,' of the poetical art : ' 'Tis not the jerk or sting of an epigram, nor the seeming contradiction of a poor antithesis ' : it is ' lively and apt description ' with one's eye upon the object, in which the ' proper wit ' of an Heroic Poem consists.   Dryden never wrote anything so definite, in his critical works, as the account of the three functions of the poetical imagination in this preface.   He never again committed himself to anything so nearly resembling philosophical analysis as his distinction between *Invention, Fancy,* and *Elocution,* the three modes of *Imagination.*   ' Fancy,' which might be thought to have more than its due share in the ' ensuing poem,' is in this critical preface duly restrained, by the authority of Nature and Virgil. It is true that Virgil here is chiefly admired for separate passages of description, and that not enough consideration is given to the *unities* of the Heroic Poem.   This is characteristic of Dryden's earlier point of view, and of the older fashion of richly figurative details which he was following in the *Annus Mirabilis.*   At the same time the preface, as criticism, goes beyond the poem in recognizing more kinds of poetical work than the poem itself contains.   The praise of the dramatic imagination of Ovid leads naturally on to the essays immediately following, in which the Drama is the principal theme,

---

[1] ' A cette première règle, dictée par le génie, si l'on joint de la délicatesse et du goût, du scrupule sur le choix des expressions, *de l'attention à ne nommer les choses que par les termes les plus généraux,* le style aura de la noblesse ' (Buffon, *Discours sur le Style,* 1753).

and the Historical and Heroic Poem is brought in
only for purposes of illustration.

AN ESSAY OF DRAMATIC POESY (1668).

The argument for rhyme in the Dedication of the
Rival Ladies (1664) was answered by Sir Robert Howard
in the preface to his Plays (1665) ; ' that,' says Dryden,
' occasioned my reply in my *Essay* ' (see p. 133, below).
The *Essay* is, however, much more than an argument
on behalf of rhyming plays : the four friends in their
dialogue are led to discuss the question of Ancients
against Moderns, of French against English, the Three
Unities, the *liaison des scènes*, the plots of Terence, the
art of Ben Jonson, and many other things besides the
original problem of rhyme. It is Dryden's most elaborate piece of criticism, and the most careful of his prose
works, while at the same time it is the liveliest and
freshest till the incomparable Preface to the *Fables*, in
the last year of his life.

The Dialogue was a favourite form of composition in
all the languages after the revival of learning, through
the examples of Plato and Cicero. It was common in
French among authors whom Dryden had probably
read. Sometimes the persons appeared under their
own names, like Ménage, Chapelain, and Sarrasin in
Sarrasin's Dialogue, *S'il faut qu'un jeune homme soit
amoureux* (*Œuvres*, ed. G. Ménage, Paris, 1656) [1].
Sometimes the names were allegorical, like Eusèbe
and Philédon in Desmarests' *Délices de l'Esprit* (1658).
It is not impossible that Dryden may have known,
though he does not mention, the *Cigarrales de Toledo*

---

[1] The same persons take part in Chapelain's remarkable Dialogue,
De la Lecture des Vieux Romans, which, however, seems to have remained in manuscript till 1870 (ed. A. Feillet).

(Madrid, 1624) of Tirso de Molina, the author of the
original *Don Juan*, who reports conversations about the
nature of Comedy, the Unities, the authority of the
Ancients, and other subjects in which Dryden was
interested, in something like Dryden's liberal manner.
' Dryden has assured me that he got more from the
Spanish critics alone than from the Italian and French
and all other critics put together ' is the evidence of
Bolingbroke in Spence's *Anecdotes*, and the Spanish
conversations of Tirso de Molina may claim to be
considered among the possible sources of the *Essay—*
' a little discourse in dialogue, for the most part borrowed from the observations of others ' (*Defence of the
Essay*, p. 112). The principal source, however, as
Dryden plainly indicates, is not a dialogue, but the
series of Discourses prefixed by Corneille to the three
volumes of his collected Dramas in 1660, with the
Examens attached, in the same edition, to each of his
plays.

Martin Clifford accused Dryden of pilfering from
' Monsieur Hédelin, Mesnardière, and Corneille.' Dryden
had not professed to be original, and made no secret
of his obligations to Corneille. It does not appear
that he owed much to the others, but he had probably
read them. ' Monsieur Hédelin,' the Abbé d'Aubignac,
whose *Pratique du Théâtre* appeared in 1657, though it
was written long before, is one of the most wearisome
of all the righteous critics. St. Evremond has disposed
of him :—' On n'a jamais vu tant de règles pour faire
des belles tragédies ; et on en fait si peu, qu'on est obligé
de représenter les vieilles. Il me souvient que l'abbé
d'Aubignac en composa une, selon toutes les lois qu'il
avait impérieusement données pour le théâtre. Ella ne
réussit point ; et comme il se vantait partout d'être le
seul de nos auteurs qui eût bien suivi les préceptes

d'Aristote : " Je sais bon gré à M. d'Aubignac," dit
M. le Prince, " d'avoir si bien suivi les règles d'Aristote ;
mais je ne pardonne point aux règles d'Aristote d'avoir
fait faire une si méchante tragédie à M. d'Aubignac." '
His book was translated into English (*The whole Art of
the Stage*, 1684) and had some reputation in England.

Mesnardière is much livelier in his *Poëtique* (1640),
and by no means scrupulous.   Dryden probably also
knew Sarrasin's *Discours de la Tragédie ou Remarques
sur l'Amour Tyrannique*, a Preface written in 1639 for
G. de Scudéry's drama of that name, printed in 1640.

The persons of Dryden's dialogue are EUGENIUS,
that is, Charles, Lord Buckhurst (Earl of Dorset, 1677) ;
CRITES, Sir Robert Howard ; LISIDEIUS, Sir Charles
Sedley ; and NEANDER, who is Dryden.

The Dialogue is Socratic, or Platonic, in its arrangement [1] ; beginning by an account of the circumstances,
and leading gradually, and by easy and natural
stages, to a restriction of the talk with a view to the
definition and description of one *species*, the Drama.
The polemic motives, as they might be called, the rally-
ing cries which lead to the debate, are those of *Ancients*
against *Moderns* ; the *last generation* against the *present*,
and *French* against *English*.   The issue of the debate,
to which it is guided by Neander, is a compromise.
The conventional admiration of the classical dramatists
(Crites) and the superstition of the French stage
(Lisideius) are challenged by Eugenius and Neander
and shown not to bear examination.   The dramatists of
the last generation, Shakespeare, Jonson, and Fletcher

---

[1] Cf. *Defence of Essay*, p. 124 : ' My whole discourse was sceptical,
according to that way of reasoning which was used by Socrates, Plato,
and all the Academics of old, which Tully and the best of the Ancients
followed, and which is imitated by the modest inquisitions of the Royal
Society.'

(*theirs was the giant age before the Flood*), are vindicated by Dryden against the ' mechanic ' view of dramatic art ; while in the case of Jonson, and by means of a detailed *Examen* of one of his plays, the *Silent Woman*, it is shown that he had little to learn from the French in the way of exact construction. On the other hand, the Ancients and the French are not treated with any disrespect. Dryden's mind is working on lines of its own, but not so as to cut across the lines of the Ancients or of Corneille. The Unities, which give him a good deal of anxiety, are not adopted by him because they are ancient, or because they are French, but still they are adopted, because to a great extent they seem to agree with his own judgment of what is requisite in a play.

Corneille was a great help to him in getting through his perplexities. Although Dryden saw that a good deal of the French ' correct ' drama was pretence, and that the French symmetry and neatness were obtained by throwing away some of the most essential elements of a play, still he could not help admiring their protest against slovenly and ill-braced Drama, and he was attracted by sympathy with Corneille's frank and unaffected confession of his difficulties in his *Discours* and *Examens*. The Unities had been, and were still for some pedants, authoritative principles, positive laws. Corneille had begun his dramatic work in years of freedom, when the French popular stage was scarcely more restrained than the English stage when Sir Philip Sidney criticized it. He had gradually come under the influence of formal criticism, but the formal principles had to prove themselves reasonable before they were accepted : they were not to be accepted under the authority of Aristotle or Horace. Dryden was going through a similar progress in his own views about his work, and Corneille's discussion of principles must have seemed to him in many places the echo of his own thoughts.

THE UNITIES.   1. *Action*.

The Unity of Action was interpreted in different ways by different dramatists. As a decree excluding disconnected episodes and separate secondary plots, it was not the peculiar property of any classical school : as a strict rule, requiring no more than one single theme of interest in a play, ' single and separate, not composed of parts [1],' it was generally too severe for even very correct authors, and Jonson had rejected it with a solemnity more impressive than the curses of Ernulphus or of Milton. ' Which thing out of antiquity itself hath deceived many, and more this day it doth deceive.' Corneille does not refuse to allow subordinate actions, working into the main plot, and Dryden accepts this as sufficient : ' Eugenius has already shown us, from the confession of the French poets, that the Unity of Action is sufficiently preserved, if all the imperfect actions of the play are conducing to the main design.' (*Essay*, p. 71.)

It is in the *liaison des scènes* that Corneille exhibits the efficient working of this Unity of Action, and it is here that Dryden follows him with least reserve. The Unity of Action is proved to be valid when the exits and entrances explain and justify themselves, when each successive grouping of the *dramatis personae* is seen to follow naturally out of what went before, when there is no sudden break in the middle of the act to introduce new actors and a change of interest. That the action should be continuous is a rule for the practical dramatist ; with the ' scenes unbroken ' the play gets hold upon the attention of the audience, and the art of the playwright has its reward. By calling attention to this rule

[1] Ben Jonson, *Discoveries*. See below, note on p. 41, l. 10

of the working dramatist (which he had been rather late in discovering, as he confesses), Corneille not only gave practical and much needed help to beginners, but saved the stage from some of the afflictions of pedantry, especially from some of the exhaustion and depletion which were sure to follow from too pertinacious observance of the Unity of Action. Dryden, and the English generally, felt that the French plays were apt to be rather thin and abstract. Dryden must have felt that Corneille's account of his plots allowed too little room for movement and variety :—

'Il faut donc qu'une action, pour être d'une juste grandeur, ait un commencement, un milieu et une fin. Cinna conspire contre Auguste, et rend compte de sa conspiration à Emilie, voilà le commencement ; Maxime en fait avertir Auguste, voilà le milieu ; Auguste lui pardonne, voilà la fin. Ainsi, dans les comédies, j'ai presque toujours établi deux amans en bonne intelligence, je les ai brouillés ensemble par quelque fourbe, et les ai réunis par l'éclaircissement de cette même fourbe qui les séparait.'—*Premier Discours.*

Simplicity of this sort appeared to an English observer and to St. Evremond in England rather dearly purchased. But the *liaison des scènes* was some compensation, for if there was not the variety and substance of the English romantic drama or of Jonson's *Comedy of Humours*, there might at any rate be the life and speed of a well constructed play, and the want of body might be made up by neatness, elegance of design, and a clear and reasonable sequence in the action and the dialogue. In England, with all the difference between French and English taste in drama, there was no reason why the *liaison des scènes* should be neglected, why, with greater weight of argument, the dramatists should be slovenly about the arrangement of the exits and entrances. The English Drama was fuller of body and more substantial than the French; but there was no reason why it should not be improved, and it might be improved by not trusting wholly to its weight. The French device of skilfully mortised scenes—*Ce nouvel usage qui passe en précepte,* as Corneille calls it—was available for dramatists of different schools. This is what Dryden points out, and this is the most important part of his dealings with the Unity of Action.

THE UNITIES. 2. *Time.*

Everywhere in the sixteenth and seventeenth centuries there was to be heard the protest of scholars against the loose ways of the popular drama in regard to the time supposed to be covered by the action. Sir Philip Sidney's well-known description in the *Apology for Poetry* is to be found, with very little difference, in Spanish and French, in Cervantes and Boileau.

Boileau (*L'Art Poétique,* iii. 39 sq.) refers to the licence of the Spanish stage almost in the same terms as Sidney speaking of the English—

> ' Un rimeur, sans péril, delà les Pyrénées,
> Sur la scène en un jour renferme des années :
> Là souvent le héros d'un spectacle grossier,
> Enfant au premier acte, est barbon au dernier.
> Mais nous, que la raison à ses règles engage,
> Nous voulons qu'avec art l'action se ménage ;
> Qu'en un lieu, qu'en un jour, un seul fait accompli
> Tienne jusqu'à la fin le théâtre rempli.'

Boileau did not think it necessary to say that the French popular drama had been within a generation as rude in this respect as the Spanish, and that the audiences of the Hôtel de Bourgogne about 1630 might have deserved what Lope in his apology for his comedies said of his spectators in Madrid : that they thought themselves ill provided for unless they were shown in two hours from Genesis to the Day of Judgment :—

> ' la cólera
> De un Español sentado no se templa
> Si no le representen en dos horas
> Hasta el final juicio desde el Genesis [1].'

The Unities which had been exemplified (though not always strictly) by the authors of correct Tragedy, such as Jodelle, Garnier, and Montchrestien, were neglected in the popular drama of the Hôtel de Bourgogne, in the tragicomedies of Alexandre Hardy and his contemporaries. For tragedy they were still requisite ; for the popular drama they were unnecessary. The correct tragedies were for the popular dramatist in France what *Gorboduc* was to Marlowe and his companions ; something to be taken into consideration by the practical playwright, not something to be followed religiously as an authority, unless he chose for his own purposes to commit himself to the stricter and more learned kind of composition. But the same thing happened with the Unity of Time as with the Unity of Action. The popular practice came to approximate to the learned ideal : practice in dramatic writing taught the playwright to work for concentration, and without pedantry his natural instincts led him to restrict the time of his story. This spontaneous concentration and compression led to increased respect for the critical theory of the Unities. The success of Mairet's *Sophonisbe* does not seem to have been due to pedantry, but to the genuine satisfaction of the audience in neat workmanship. The process of approximation may be partly traced in the *Examens* of Corneille's early comedies, which show how the French dramatist about 1635,

---

[1] *El Nuevo Arte de hacer Comedias.*

like the English forty years before, had shortened the time of the action, because it was convenient and effective to have it so. Corneille goes further than the English, and comes under the influence of the revival of the learned rules, but his treatment of the Unity of Time in his *Discourses* is generally free enough. It helps the effect of the Drama to have the imaginary action taking up no more than the two hours required to play it. But more time may be taken, if necessary.

Dryden follows in Corneille's spirit, and goes further. He was evidently touched with sympathy for Corneille's struggles against the pedants ; he quotes with approval as a full expression of his own opinion the concluding words of Corneille in his *Discourse of the Unities* :—
' 'Tis easy for speculative persons to judge severely ; but if they would produce to public view ten or twelve pieces of this nature, they would perhaps give more latitude to the rules than I have done, when by experience they had known how much we are bound up and constrained by them, and how many beauties of the stage they banished from it ' (p. 75). Dryden thought of the Unity of Time in the same general way as Corneille, and in the same way as he thought of the Unity of Action : both of them were good negative or corrective rules, prohibiting waste of time, prohibiting incoherent plots ; but they were not to be allowed to fix any positive limit for the dramatic poet ; and the English poet (this is Dryden's main contention) will take more liberty than the French. He will require more time for his story, as he puts more into it than the French authors, and embraces more subordinate actions under the control of his *primum mobile*, his principal dramatic theme.

THE UNITIES. 3. *Place.*

Dryden found comfort in Corneille's explicit refusal to accept the Unity of Place as one of the ancient rules. Crites had spoken, in the usual manner, of the Unity of Place as one of the rules derived from Aristotle. Eugenius, following Corneille, will not accept this conventional pedigree : ' in the first place give me leave to tell you that the Unity of Place, however it might be practised by them, was never any of their rules ; we neither find it in Aristotle, Horace, or any who have written of it, till in our age the French poets first made it a precept of the stage ' (p. 48).

The Unity of Place is in a different class from the other two. Action and Time were to be considered by the dramatist in shaping and proportioning his story ; Place was naturally restricted along with Time and Action, and did not need special consideration until it came to be a question of the decoration of the stage, a matter for the scene-painter. Here came in an organic difference between French and English customs which led to a great deal of confusion when the French critics were studied in England.

The Elizabethan stage, not being hampered with scenery, made no unnecessary difficulty or absurdity for the audience in changing the scene. It all depended on the story ; if the story required it, the change was all right ; if the change was wrong, it was not on account of any absurdity in pretending to move from Venice to Cyprus, or from Sicily to Bohemia ; it was as easy to make the scene in one place as in another ; the change must be criticized, and approved or condemned, by reference to the standards of Time and of Action, not of Place ; *Place* was not an independent category but a subordinate species dependent on the other two. The introduction of painted scenery made no difference in this respect. Whether and how often the scene should be changed, must be determined by the structure of the play, by the manner in which the plot was developed.

In France things were different, and the Unity of Place meant a different thing, something scarcely intelligible to an untravelled Englishman. Considerations of Place were forced upon the French dramatists not only by the arrangement of their stories but more forcibly by the mechanical conditions of their stage.

The popular stage of the Hôtel de Bourgogne at the beginning of the seventeenth century was more antique in its appliances than anything in London in the time of Marlowe or Shakespeare. The Hôtel de Bourgogne had inherited the goodwill of the Confraternity of the Passion, and the stage devices of the medieval religious drama. The Elizabethan Drama, by a ' divine chance,' had got rid of the medieval stage management, except for incidental purposes, as in Peter Quince's entertainment. The French stage, when Corneille began to write, was still faithful to the old traditions, in accordance with which all the different scenes required in the play were represented on the stage at once. Some compromises had indeed been made ; a kind of shorthand or symbolic representation. The old *mansions* of the *Mystères* were placed side by side on a long stage which might have seven or eight different places represented on it, as in the Mystery of the Passion described by M. Petit de Julleville, where the *mansions* represent (1) Paradise ; (2) Nazareth ; (3) the Temple ; (4) Jerusalem ; (5) the Palace ; (6) the Golden Gate ; (7) the Sea of Galilee ; and (8) Limbo and Hell [1].

[1] Cf. Eugène Rigal, *Alexandre Hardy*, p. 70, and *Histoire de la*

In the Hôtel de Bourgogne there was more art : the decoration was often in the form of a perspective view, which could give beside the central picture two or more different places on each side, one behind the other. The commonly accepted theory of the scenes is represented in a passage quoted by M. Rigal [1] from *La Poëtique* of Jules de La Mesnardière (c. xi. *La Disposition du Théâtre*) :—

'Si l'Avanture s'est passée moitié dans le Palais d'un Roy en plusieurs appartemens, et moitié hors de la Maison en beaucoup d'endroits différens ; il faut que le grand du Théâtre, le προσκήνιον des Grecs, je veux dire *cette largeur qui limite le parterre*, serve pour tous les dehors où ces choses ont été faites ; et que les Renfondremens soient divisez en plusieurs Chambres, par les divers Frontispices, Portaux, Colonnes ou Arcades. Car il faut que les Spectateurs distinguent, par ces différences, la diversité des endroits où les particularitez que le Poëte aura démeslées, seront exactement depeintes, et que les Distinctions de Scene empeschent que l'on ne treuve de la confusion en ces Lieux, qui

---

Littérature Français, ed. Petit de Julleville, t. ii., where a reproduction of the original picture of the stage is given.

[1] *ibid.* p. 173. M. Rigal gives illustrations—pictures as well as descriptions—from the MS. notebook of Laurent Mahelot, head of the scenery and properties department at the Hôtel de Bourgogne about 1630. Perhaps the most interesting of all the notes is that of the scene required for Hardy's *Pandoste, Première Journée* (*A Winter's Tale*) : 'Au milieu du théâtre il faut un beau palais ; à un des côtés, une grande prison où l'on paraît tout entier ; à l'autre côté, un temple ; au-dessous, une pointe de vaisseau, une mer basse, des roseaux, et marches de degrés ; un réchaud, une aiguière, un chapeau de fleurs, une fiole pleine de vins, un cornet d'encens, un tonnerre, des flammes ; au quatrième acte, il faut un enfant ; il faut aussi deux chandeliers et des trompettes.' Compare also the chapters on the Drama by M. Rigal and M. Lemaître in Petit de Julleville, *Hist. Litt. Fr.* t. iv.

embarrasse l'Auditeur, et qui seule soit capable de gaster le plus bel Ouvrage, et de le rendre ridicule.'

Corneille is hard driven by the Unity of Place. In 1660, in his critical essays, he still kept a good deal of the old conventions of the Hôtel de Bourgogne. According to these, the different scenes required in the play were all indicated in the decoration of the stage. Corneille spoke of *cet horrible dérèglement qui mettait Paris, Rome et Constantinople sur le même théâtre* ; but while he gave up this freedom of the old Comedy, he kept the convention of supposing the actors to change their place without a change of the scene ; the actors were to move in a *lieu théâtral*, an abstract conventional space, about which the spectators were not to ask too many questions. Dryden, of course, feels no temptation to accept this, and he dismisses the French Unity of Place without ceremony, and perhaps not quite fairly, in Neander's description of the ' regular ' French play, where ' the street, the window, the houses, and the closet are made to walk about, and the persons to stand still.'

Although Neander's wit is not quite just to the French plays of that time, there is a passage in Corneille's *Examen* of the *Cid* which goes far to bear it out in sober earnest. In the first Act of the *Cid* you may pretend, if you like, that the houses walk about, while the Count and Don Diego stand still. Or else you must suppose that the place is purely abstract, and that Don Diego may cry aloud in his distress without moving from the place where he has been struck the shameful blow, and without attracting any notice except of his son, who is to avenge him :—' Tout s'y passe donc en Séville, et garde ainsi quelque espèce d'unité de lieu en général : mais le lieu particulier change de scène en scène ; et tantôt c'est le palais du Roi, tantôt l'appartement de l'Infante, tantôt la maison de Chimène, et tantôt une rue ou place publique. On la détermine aisément pour les scènes détachées ; mais pour celles qui ont leur liaison ensemble, comme les quatre dernières du premier acte, il est malaisé d'en choisir une qui convienne à toutes. Le Comte et Don Diegue se querellent au sortir du palais, cela se peut passer dans une rue ; mais, après le soufflet reçu, Don Diegue ne peut pas demeurer dans cette rue à faire ses plaintes en attendant que son fils survienne, qu'il ne soit aussitôt environné de peuple et ne reçoive l'offre de quelques amis. Ainsi il seroit plus à propos qu'il se plaignît dans sa maison où le met l'Espagnol, pour laisser aller ses sentimens en liberté ; mais en ce cas il faudroit délier les scènes comme il a fait. En l'état où elles sont ici, on peut dire qu'il faut quelquefois aider au théâtre, et suppléer favorablement ce qui ne s'y peut représenter. Deux personnes s'y arrêtent pour parler, et quelquefois il faut présumer qu'ils marchent, ce qu'on ne peut exposer sensiblement à la vue, parce qu'ils échapperoient aux yeux avant que d'avoir pu dire ce qu'il est nécessaire qu'ils fassent savoir à l'auditeur. Ainsi, par une fiction de théâtre, on peut s'imaginer que Don Diegue et le Comte, sortant du palais du roi, avancent toujours en se querellant, et sont arrivés devant la maison de ce premier lorsqu'il reçoit le soufflet qui l'oblige à y entrer pour y chercher du recours. Si cette fiction poëtique ne vous satisfait point, laissons-le dans la place publique, et disons que le concours du peuple autour de lui, après cette offense et les offres de service que lui font les premiers amis qui s'y rencontrent, sont des circonstances que le roman ne doit pas oublier, mais que, ces mêmes actions ne servant de rien à la principale, il n'est pas besoin que le poëte s'en embarrasse sur la scène.' Remembering that this was written in 1660, when Corneille had long given up his early freedom, one may be surprised at the leniency with which he speaks of his licentious ways of 1636 ; especially in comparison with his careful apology for a much smaller irregularity in *Cinna*.

The Unity of Place offered few temptations to the English dramatist. When Addison in *Cato* went out of his way to copy the French pattern, Dennis waited upon him and showed up his contradictions in the passage of criticism preserved by Dr. Johnson (*Life of Addison*) ; Dennis's method and point of view are those of Neander in the *Essay of Dramatic Poesy* [1].

The first Prologue to the *Maiden Queen* is an epilogue to the *Essay*, and a summing up of the whole matter. Dryden's aim is to make as much as possible out of the teaching and example of his predecessors ; he takes what he can :

> ' The Unities of Action, Place, and Time,
> The Scenes unbroken, and a mingled chime
> Of *Jonson's* humour and *Corneille's* rhyme.'

But he has no fallacious views about the things that may be borrowed or learned from others ; these are mechanical things [2], not ' the living beauties of a play.' With that phrase the learning of the critics is assigned to its proper subsidiary place.

A DEFENCE OF AN ESSAY OF DRAMATIC POESY (1668).   RHYMING PLAYS.

The argument about rhyme is now the least important part of Dryden's *Essay* ; at the time it was more exciting,

---

[1] The history of the Unities is stated with admirable clearness by H. Breitinger, *Les Unités d'Aristote avant le Cid de Corneille*. See also Jules Lemaître, *Corneille et la Poétique d'Aristote*.

[2] ' The mechanic beauties of the plot, which are the observation of the three Unities, Time, Place, and Action.'—*Preface to Troilus and Cressida*, v. inf. p. 212.

and led to more debate than anything else in the work. Crites in the *Essay* had proved that rhyme was inconvenient for dramatic composition ; shortly after the publication of the *Essay*, Sir Robert Howard, the original of Dryden's *Crites*, continued the argument, and answered Neander in his Preface to his play of *The Great Favourite, or, the Duke of Lerma* (printed for H. Herringman, in the Savoy, 1668, 4°). Dryden replied in a short paper prefixed to the second edition of his *Indian Emperor*— a defence of his *Essay*. It is written with spirit ; the phrasing is effective for debate : ' the Muses have lost him, but the Commonwealth gains by it ; the corruption of a Poet is the generation of a Statesman.' Sometimes, too, the phrase is ennobled above the immediate purpose of the dispute : ' Rhyme (for I will deal clearly) has something of the usurper in him ; but he is brave and generous, and his dominion pleasing.' It is for sentences like this that the occasional papers of Dryden are worth reading. This present *Defence* was read by Pepys apparently with some satisfaction at the way Sir Robert Howard was treated in it, but it seemed to Dryden too severe ; he was reconciled to his brother-in-law, and the Defence of the Essay was dropped out of later editions of the *Indian Emperor*.

The dispute about rhyming plays was decided as time went on, when Dryden came to discover that what had really attracted him in rhyme was something different from its suitability for dramatic purposes. The *Defence* contains one of his rather sad confessions of the uncongenial nature of some of the dramatic work he had to do. Comedy is not for him : ' I want that gaiety of humour which is required to it ; my conversation is slow and dull, my humour saturnine and reserved.' For the other kind, for heroic drama in rhyme, he seemed to find more affinity in his genius. It is easy to see now, after *Absalom and Achitophel*, that it was the rhyme itself to which he felt himself drawn, rather than the heroic play.

Among the sayings in the *Defence* that illustrate the general position of Dryden is the remark on the end of poetry as principally *delight*, and only in the second place *instruction* : ' Delight is the chief, if not the only end of poetry : instruction can be admitted but in the second place, for poesy only instructs as it delights.' The combination of pleasure and instruction in poetry was one of the inherited commonplaces of criticism which every author had to face ; Corneille had met it before, and very much in the same manner. It is touched on in the Preface to the *Mock Astrologer* ; it reappears again, and more formidable, in the *Dedication of the Æneis*.

The *Defence* goes over again some of the ground of the Unities of Time and Place, without adding much to the conclusions of the *Essay*. The Unities are good and useful in so far as they save the spectator from too much distraction and interruption ; that is the upshot of it all. The observance of them may, as Dennis put it, ' add grace and clearness and comeliness to the representation,' if they can be observed without breach of the probabilities.

PREFACE TO AN EVENING'S LOVE, OR THE MOCK ASTROLOGER.

The Mock Astrologer, taken from the *Feint Astrologue* of Thomas Corneille, which was from *El Astrólogo Fingido* of Calderon, was acted in 1668 [1], and published by Herringman in 1671. The Preface begins with an

[1] See Pepys's *Diary*, June 19–21, 1668.

account of Dryden's interests and intentions with regard
to literary history ; promises which were not left un-
fulfilled. For the present, however, he left over a
number of subjects : among them Heroic Plays, in
which the age had something to boast of as against
Fletcher and Shakespeare. The theme of the Preface
is Comedy. Dryden declares for a different ideal of
Comedy than that of Ben Jonson. He was aiming
at something more refined ; whatever his own tempera-
ment might be, however he might want that ' gaiety
of humour ' which is the spirit of Comedy, he saw
that the old-fashioned English Comedy was played
out ; something more elegant must surely be within
reach. The preface to the *Mock Astrologer*, like the
Defence of the Epilogue to the Conquest of Granada, is
a cry for a new artist in Comedy ; it places the Siege
Perilous for Congreve to occupy later.

OF HEROIC PLAYS : AN ESSAY (1672).

The Conquest of Granada (two parts), published in
1672, was accompanied by two pieces of Dryden's
prose : the Essay *Of Heroique Plays* prefixed, and at
the end of the volume the *Defence of the Epilogue, or an
Essay on the Dramatique Poetry of the last Age*.

The Essay on *Heroic Plays* is an explanation of that
part of Dryden's work in which he was most in agreement with contemporary and transient literary modes.
The difference from the *Essay of Dramatic Poesy* or
the *Preface to the Fables* is felt at once by every reader,
and it is easy to point out where the difference lies.
Dryden in this present work has submitted himself to
the idols of his time much more fully than in most of
his essays : although he can never get rid of the accent
of freedom in his voice, he has here professed obedience

to certain literary conventions which he was quite able,
if he had chosen, to treat in his sceptical manner,
' according to that way of reasoning which was used
by Socrates, Plato, and all the Academics of old.' The
Essay *Of Heroic Plays* is Dryden's profession of faith
in that ideal of the Heroic Poem, whose authority in
the seventeenth century was so great and unquestioned.
It explains the origin and aim of the English heroic plays.
They were attempts to realize upon the stage that
superhuman grandeur which was the soul of epic poetry.
They were still another of the speculative enterprises of
the modern world to rival the divinities of Greece and
Rome, and to employ for modern purposes and in a
modern language the grand style of which the example
had been set by the classical authors—not, in this case,
the ancient tragic poets particularly, or even in any
considerable measure, but rather the epic poets. Homer
and Virgil are the masters of Dryden in his heroic plays ;
that is his own account of the matter. *The Conquest of
Granada* has its origin, like so much Renaissance work,
in a literary appreciation and admiration ; and the origin
of the *Conquest of Granada* is the same as the origin of
Paradise Lost. Almanzor belongs in one limb of his
pedigree to the English stage ; his ancestors are among
the Elizabethans ; he derives from Tamburlaine. But
it was not that relationship which seemed important to
Dryden, even if he had ever noticed it. Almanzor is
a pattern of heroic virtue, and the ambition which led
Dryden to think of Almanzor is the same as that which
led Spenser to his epic scheme of virtuous and gentle
discipline, and Tasso to his didactic poem of Godfrey
and Rinaldo. ' I must therefore avow in the first place
from whence I took the character. The first image I
had of him was from the *Achilles* of Homer ; the next
from Tasso's *Rinaldo* (who was a copy of the former),

and the third from the *Artaban* of Monsieur Calprenède, who has imitated both.'

The mention of *Artaban* brings to view another of the many effects and manifestations of the idea of the heroic poem. The French heroic romances of the seventeenth century, the *Grand Cyrus* and all the rest, were descended in one line from *Amadis of Gaul*, as Dryden's *Almanzor* descended in one line from the Elizabethan Tragedy. On the other side, the French romances are an emanation of the Abstract Epic Poem ; like Tasso's and Trissino's poems, like *Gondibert* and *Clovis*, like *Paradise Lost* again, they are rivals of the *Aeneid* for the crown of pure epic imagination. Even before *Cyrus* it had been not unusual to think of romances as epics in prose ; so Sidney seems to think of Heliodorus (*Theagenes and Chariclea*), and so Tasso of Heliodorus and of *Amadis of Gaul*. Scudéry in the preface to his epic poem of *Alaric* (1654) takes the relationship for granted ; in the preface to his sister's romance of the *Illustrious Bashaw* he had cited Homer, Virgil, Tasso, and Heliodorus as the authorities for that kind of fiction [1]. Thus there did not appear to Dryden

---

[1] ' Comme le Poëme Epique a beaucoup de raport quant à la constitution avec ces ingenieuses Fables que nous apellons des Romans, il est presques superflu que i'en parle icy : puisque i'en ay traitté assez amplement, dans l'Auant-propos de mon Illustre Bassa : et que d'ailleurs l'heureux succès de ce Grand Visir, et celuy du Grand Cyrus qui l'ont suiuy, ont assez fait voir, ce me semble, que ie n'ignore pas absolument ce genre d'escrire dont ie me mesle quelquefois.'—From Preface to *Alaric ou Rome Vaincuë, Poëme heroïque, dedié a la serenissime Reyne de Suede par Monsieur de Scudery, Gouverneur de Nostre Dame de la Garde,* M DC LIV.

Ibrahim ou l'Illustre Bassa was published in 1641 under the name of M. de Scudéry. The preface is briskly written : it takes the Romance as a kind of Epic : ' I'ay creu que pour dresser le plan de cet ouvrage il faloit consulter les Grecs, qui ont esté nos premiers maistres ; suivre la route qu'ils ont tenuë,' &c.

or his readers to be anything particularly incongruous
or absurd in the combination of Achilles and Artaban.
There was no mixture, no discord, for the heroes of the
French romances were not regarded by their authors as
' Gothic ' or unclassical personages ; Artaban, like the
Illustrious Bashaw and the Grand Cyrus, could boast
of belonging to the pure heroic strain of the Greek
Epic. Dryden, however, it will be observed, does not
make very much of the French romances in his estimate
of his hero : ' For my own part I declare myself for
Homer and Tasso, and am more in love with Achilles
and Rinaldo than with Cyrus and Oroondates. I shall
never subject my characters to the French standard
where love and honour are to be weighed by drachms
and scruples.' The heroic point of honour had been
treated with disrespect in the *Rehearsal* ; and Dryden
wished to safeguard himself as far as possible from
association with the exaggerated virtue of the ' faultless
monster.'

Among the properties or, at any rate, the almost
inseparable accidents of the heroic poem in Dryden's
time was the interest of the love story ; Love and
Valour were the two motives. The heroic poem of
the modern authors was not purely classical, for all
their boasts. The tradition, the vogue, of chivalrous
sentiment was too strong for all but one or two of the
graver poets, and a few of the extreme classical pedants.
One of Tasso's leading motives in his laboured arguments about epic poetry was to find a satisfactory
compromise between Homer and Amadis of Gaul.
Dryden takes for granted, without any hesitation, that
this is the right kind of theme for an heroic poet ; he
has his key from Ariosto. ' For the very next reflexion which I made was this, that an heroic play
ought to be an imitation, in little, of an heroic poem ;

and consequently that love and valour ought to be the subject of it.' Corneille had protested against the excessive importance of the love story in tragedies, and had chosen other interests by preference for his own dramas, but not till he had written the *Cid*, the one great and unrivalled heroic play of love and valour, the play that shows how much there was of reason behind all the confused and tedious formulas of the poetical theorists. The heroic ideal of love and valour and honour was not utterly abstract and sterile.

One of the passages in this essay of Dryden's may appear rather oddly irrelevant : the note upon the ' enthusiastic parts of poetry,' by which he means the magical or supernatural episodes. He instances the Ghost of Polydorus in Virgil, the Enchanted Wood in Tasso, and the Bower of Bliss in Spenser. The bearing of all this is rather difficult to understand in connexion with a play like the *Conquest of Granada*. It is partly a defence of the astral spirits in the play of *Tyrannic Love* (1670) which had been burlesqued in the *Rehearsal*. There is a sting in Dryden's language here (in touching on the ' phlegmatic heavy gownman,' the adversary of the poet) which is not accounted for by the scientific interest of the problem. At the same time this passage is not merely polemical or meant for the occasion ; it is an outbreak from Dryden's meditations upon the right use of ' machines ' in an epic poem, such as he afterwards explained more particularly in his *Preface to Juvenal* (below, vol. ii. p. 34 seq.). He is not really much interested in dramatic form, and though his present theme is Almanzor, it may be suspected that his heart is with the unwritten epic for which the right time never came.

The Defence of the Epilogue to the Second Part of the

Conquest of Granada belongs, like the *Epilogue* itself, to a different point of view from the *Essay of Dramatic Poesy*, and is generally in agreement with the Preface to the *Feigned Astrologer*. The difference in eloquence between the present age and the age of Ben Jonson is what Dryden has in his mind. His *Essay on the Dramatic Poetry of the Last Age* is an explanation of the superiority of the present times in *Wit, Language, and Conversation*.

As to Language, Dryden selects a number of examples from the older dramatists, and points out their irregularities. In Wit he finds himself obliged to make distinctions. The definition of Wit engaged Dryden's attention, and he finally arrived at a statement which satisfied him, and by which he was content to abide. In this *Essay* he comes near his later account of Wit as adequacy or propriety of language; but he distinguishes farther between two senses of the term: Wit in the larger sense is propriety of language; Wit in the narrower and stricter sense is *sharpness of conceit*. Jonson's Wit in the larger sense is unquestioned: ' he always writ *properly*, and as the character required '; his fault was that his subjects were too uniformly low. In sharpness of conceit he was not admirable; Dryden expresses the natural aversion of a later generation for the Elizabethan taste in epigrams. He remarks on the extremes between which the careless genius of Shakespeare has its range, and on the luxuriance of Fletcher; ' he is a true Englishman; he knows not when to give over.' Conversation, the third head of Dryden's discourse, brings him to the summary of his argument. His age is better than Shakespeare's because it has better manners, a more refined society, a more affable monarch. Hence the change in the dramatic ideal, as already explained in the *Mock Astrologer*. It is

an ideal of refined comedy ; for though the Epilogue
had spoken of the heroic motives of Love and Honour,
both the Epilogue and this Essay defending it take
Comedy as the form of Drama to be most thought of.
The Comedy of Jonson is still an example and a standard
as far as concerns the virtues of construction, of arrangement, of coherence. But, ' the poets of this age will be
more wary than to imitate the meanness of his persons.
Gentlemen will now be entertained with the follies of
each other ; and though they allow Cobb and Tib to
speak properly, yet they are not much pleased with their
tankard or with their rags.'

THE AUTHOR'S APOLOGY FOR HEROIC POETRY AND POETIC LICENCE (1677).

This Essay was prefixed to *The State of Innocence and
Fall of Man, an Opera in Heroic Verse,* Dryden's version
of *Paradise Lost.* The Essay has nothing very particular
to do either with the Epic or the Opera. It is an
expansion of one of Dryden's views about poetry which
he had already expressed in the *Essay of Heroic Plays* ;
it defends the magnificent language proper to the
noblest kind of poetry, and is to some extent reactionary. Dryden had acknowledged the reforms of
Waller and Denham, but he was not prepared to go
all lengths with the new order of things. There was
too much of the Elizabethan in him, and he could not
accept the common sense of his contemporaries as an
adequate test of good and bad poetry. ' What fustian,
as they call it, have I heard these gentlemen find out
in Mr. Cowley's *Odes* ! ' ' All that is dull, insipid,
languishing, and without sinews in a poem, they call an
imitation of Nature.' Dryden, like Tasso before him,

is compelled to stand up against the scholars who have learned their lesson too well ; it is as if he foresaw the sterilizing influence of the prose understanding, and the harm that might be done by correctness if the principles of correctness were vulgarized.

Imitation of Nature was no new catchword of art criticism. It came from Aristotle, and was one of the chief formulas in the endless talk about Poetry which grew out of the rhetorical and grammatical studies of the Revival of Learning. It was made the guiding principle in all sorts of literary undertakings : even the French Heroic Romances professed to be imitations of Nature, if we may trust the preface to the *Illustrious Bashaw*. Butler, in his *Character of a Small Poet*, puts the same formula in his mouth—' a nasty, flat description he calls *great Nature*.' Pope, in the *Essay on Criticism*, made this his text, and found an easy way out of it by recommending the Ancients as an equivalent. *To follow Nature is to follow them.* Nature in these discussions generally implied, as it did for Aristotle, the right conception of the true character of the subject by the reason of the poet ; hence due subordination of details ; hence abstraction from the manifold details of reality, a selective and logical method of treatment, in opposition both to the realistic accumulation of particulars (' nasty, flat description ') and to the fantastic licence of conceits.

Sir Joshua Reynolds in his *Discourses* expressed the mind of many previous generations when he explained the derivation of the grand style from that ideal beauty which is Nature. The painter must transcend reality ; ' and what may seem a paradox, he learns to design naturally by drawing his figures unlike to any one object. The idea of the perfect state of Nature, which the artist calls the ideal beauty, is the great leading

principle by which works of genius are conducted. By
this Phidias acquired his fame. He wrought upon a
sober principle what has so much excited the enthusiasm of the world ; and by this method you, who have
courage to tread the same path, may acquire equal
reputation.'

This lofty ideal was one to which Dryden, like Corneille before him, had given his homage in many passages of his criticism. It was, however, capable of being
misunderstood, and the *Apology for Heroic Poetry* is
directed against the conventional admiration of reasonable art, the conventional depreciation of everything
fantastic and capricious, which, as Dryden saw, was apt
to condemn as fustian everything that was not respectable prose. Dryden defends Fantasy in the name of
Reason, and concludes his *Apology* with the definition
of Wit (which here means the faculty of poetical style),
as *a propriety of thoughts and words.* He had already
shown that this definition was in his mind, and he
repeats it afterwards. Thus his apology, although it
is in fact reactionary, and generally in favour of the
Elizabethans and the ' metaphysical ' poets, is not one-
sided, like the later romantic rebellion against Pope.
It is comprehensive, a claim for poetical freedom,
a protest in the name of Reason and Common Sense
against a narrow and trivial misuse of Common Sense
to the detriment of Imagination.

As in the *Essay of Heroic Plays*, so also here the
question of supernatural ' machinery ' is important, and
Dryden repeats his dissent from the critics who objected
to the agency of gods or fairies. Boileau and Rapin
are referred to as among the chief of modern critics
(p. 181), and Dryden had probably attentively studied the
deliverances on the subject of ' machinery ' in Boileau's
Art Poétique. The critical authorities to which he

attaches himself in this *Apology for Poetic Licence* are not specially romantic or extravagant. It is not a factious or partisan composition, though it moves in the thick of the most dangerous matters of debate.

About this time Dryden was growing tired of his heroic plays ; the last of them, *Aureng-zebe*, was published in 1676, and contained in its *Prologue* the author's farewell to that kind of drama.

PREFACE TO ALL FOR LOVE (1678).

Aureng-zebe, the last of the rhyming heroic plays, was published in 1676. The tragedy of *All for Love* (written to please himself, as Dryden afterwards tells us) was meant to follow both Shakespeare and the classical rules. ' I have endeavoured in this play to follow the practice of the Ancients, who, as Mr. Rymer has judiciously observed, are and ought to be our masters.' But the Ancients are not to be followed to the disparagement of the English genius : ' though their models are regular they are too little for English Tragedy, which requires to be built in a larger compass.' Shakespeare is acknowledged by Dryden as his master in dramatic style ; the play is in blank verse, rhyme is abandoned ; ' not that I condemn my former way, but that this is more proper to my present purpose.'

The Preface further touches upon those themes of ignorant and malicious criticism which were provided for Dryden in his feuds with Settle and others, and most recently in Rochester's imitation of Horace (*An Allusion to the Tenth Satire of his First Book*).

THE GROUNDS OF CRITICISM IN TRAGEDY.
(Preface to *Troilus and Cressida*, 1679).

Dryden was still interested by the problems of regularity which had been discussed in the *Essay of Dra-*

matic Poesy ; he had since been reading some of the more recent critics, and they had some influence on his ideas. None of them are equal to Corneille, his master in the *Dramatic Essay*, and it is with some depression of spirits that one finds oneself obliged to listen instead to Rapin, Bossu ' the best of modern critics,' and ' my friend Mr. Rymer.' Among the changes of view is the greater tolerance shown to the moral formula : ' to lay down to yourself what that precept of morality shall be which you would insinuate into the people ' is the first rule of the heroic and not less of the dramatic poet : in his earlier essays Dryden had followed Corneille in taking the instructive part of poetry more lightly. The ' fable is the example built upon the moral, which confirms the truth of it to our experience,' and so on. There are few things more wonderful in history than the way in which this allegorical theory of poetry survived through all the most enlightened modern ages, and was not only accepted but cherished and honoured as a vital truth by authors who prided themselves on nothing so much as their modern taste and their freedom from Gothic darkness. ' The allegorical fable ' is not merely a necessary part of the seventeenth-century professional epic (Chapelain's *Pucelle*, Scudéry's *Alaric*, &c.), it is one of the headings in Pope's Preface to his *Iliad* (1715), and there is no limit to the range of its worship in the age of Dryden. It survived all the humanist attacks on the medieval allegorizing method ; the ' Renaissance ' left the allegorical theory of Poetry to be honoured by philosophers who kept no other relic of the Middle Ages.

There is rather more constraint in this essay, more obsequious respect for authorities, than is common with Dryden ; the tone of it recalls the *Essay of Heroic Plays*. He goes further than usual in submitting Shakespeare and Fletcher to the authority of the Ancients : the plots of Shakespeare and Fletcher are to be followed ' so far only as they have copied the excellencies of those who invented and brought to perfection dramatic poetry.' Yet in this case again as in so many others, after he has made concessions to his friend Mr. Rymer, and to the standards of correct writing, he saves himself by speaking out before the end, and lets it be seen that all his apparent depreciation of Shakespeare is only on the surface. ' I cannot leave this subject before I do justice to that divine poet.' There is some resemblance in details between Dryden and Voltaire in their criticism of Shakespeare ; they condemn and praise the same things. The difference is that the praise always appears to be extorted from Voltaire, while Dryden has difficulty in keeping back his admiration long enough to put in his censures upon the faults of Shakespeare.

PREFACE TO OVID'S EPISTLES (1680).

There are many passages in which Dryden speaks of Ovid between the *Essay of Dramatic Poesy* and the *Preface to the Fables*. There was an affinity between the two poets in the inexhaustible readiness of their elocution ; and, further, Dryden was able to detect and half admire in Ovid some of the rhetorical excesses which he recognized in his own work. The account of Ovid in this Preface is, however, subordinate to the discussion of the principles of translation, a subject of much importance then, as it was also in the succeeding generation. Dryden's references to Cowley and Denham explain sufficiently the current opinions and tastes.

DEDICATION OF THE SPANISH FRIAR, OR
THE DOUBLE DISCOVERY (1681).

The *Spanish Friar* was a return, on Dryden's part,
from different attempts at dramatic correctness to the
old English irregularity ; it is an Elizabethan play,
with its double plot, and its blending of tragedy and
comedy.   The Dedication is one of the liveliest of
Dryden's Prefaces, especially in its confessions of his
changes of taste, his early admiration for Du Bartas,
his repentance for some of the rhetoric of his heroic
plays, the sublimities of Maximin and Almanzor, ' those
Delilahs of the theatre.'   In none of Dryden's prose is
the language more vigorous, or less affected by the
superstitions of polite literature.   It was written when
Dryden was warming to his work in his best year ; it
has some of the glow of his great satirical poems, and
all their self-possession and security of tone.

PREFACE TO SYLVAE (1685).

The Preface to the *Second Miscellany* is a good deal
like that to Ovid's *Epistles* ; it discusses the problems
of translation, and contains some of Dryden's opinions
about the classical poets, chiefly Virgil, Ovid, Lucretius,
Theocritus, Horace, and about other matters.   Among
the rest it states, what ought to have been in those days
a commonplace, but was pretty generally neglected, the
rule of ' Pindaric ' verse in English.   It was generally
written in those days as if the object were merely to
make irregular patterns of lines different in length ; it
was a variation on the old game of writing poems in
the shape of altars, wings, and diamonds.   Dryden
knows better, and takes the opportunity of pointing out
that in English free verse each line must be justified

by its relation to the line preceding, ' the cadency of one line must be a rule to that of the next.' What he meant he demonstrated in the *Ode on Mrs. Anne Killigrew*, one of the few poems of its order which it is not absurd to compare with the free verse of Milton. Pindarics were at their height in that year, as may be seen in Hearne's collection of the poems on the death of King Charles, preserved in the Bodleian.

PREFACE TO ALBION AND ALBANIUS :
AN OPERA (1685).

Dryden, like Corneille and Molière, was led to try his hand at the new form of entertainment which was brought from Italy to Paris by Mazarin, and which came to take the place of the older Masques. The difference between the seventeenth-century Opera and the Masques and Pastoral Plays of the previous generation is not very great, and Dryden in this Preface refers to the *Pastor Fido* of Guarini as one of the ancestors of Opera. These matters, however, belong rather to the history of Dryden's poetry than of his criticism, and he does not go very deeply into the nature and origin of this kind of Drama. It was first introduced into England by Sir William D'Avenant, and the Preface to *Albion and Albanius* describes the relation of that Opera to the adaptation of the *Tempest*, in which D'Avenant had been Dryden's helper. The old conception of Opera, as properly a mythological pageant, with music, dancing, and tableaux, is affirmed by Dryden, in agreement with Corneille, whose *Andromède* and *Toison d'Or* were among the most famous examples of Opera in their day. The *Machines* were as essential to Opera as the music and the poetry, and the artist of the scenery and dresses was at least the equal of the poet and the musical composer, like Inigo Jones in his rivalry with Ben Jonson. Dryden leaves these topics in his Preface, and discusses questions of prosody, or rather the general subject of melody of language, a subject to which he afterwards returned, though his treatise on English Prosody was never completed.

At the opening of the Preface he repeats his account of poetical Wit—' a propriety of thoughts and words.'

King Charles died before the Opera was published, and the Postscript records this change for the worse in Dryden's fortunes.

PREFACE TO THIRD MISCELLANY
(EXAMEN POETICUM, 1693).

This Preface opens with one of the most vigorous of Dryden's assaults on his critical adversaries, for whose benefit an old epigram, used long before in the controversy with Sir Robert Howard, is revived and sharpened into the final and perfect form : *thus the corruption of a poet is the generation of a critic.* This is meant for Rymer, by whom Dryden had been ' seemingly courted and secretly undermined ' in the *Short View of Tragedy* then recently published.

The Preface goes on to defend the English Drama against those who would depreciate it by comparison with the Ancients ; and it also makes a stand for the honour of Dryden's own generation against those who use the names of Shakespeare and Ben Jonson to vilify their own contemporaries. It is in this way a supplement to the *Essay of Dramatic Poesy*, and repeats some of the former positions, e. g. as to the thinness of French dramatic plots, and their too servile following of the ' mechanic rules.' The question between Ancients and Moderns has taken new forms since the *Essay* of 1668, and has been brought to a head by Perrault's demonstrations in France ; Dryden is careful to guard himself against misconstruction ; it will not do to be associated too closely with the French advocates of the Moderns, and he points out that ' there is a vast difference betwixt arguing like Perrault on behalf of the French poets against Homer and Virgil, and betwixt giving the English poets their undoubted due of excelling Æschylus, Euripides, and Sophocles.' From these controversies Dryden passes to the contents of the present *Miscellany*, and says something about the poets there translated, and about his own principles of versification, a subject on which one would gladly have heard him longer.

A DISCOURSE CONCERNING THE ORIGINAL AND PROGRESS OF SATIRE
(1693).

The Preface to Juvenal addressed to the Earl of Dorset (Eugenius of the *Essay on Dramatic Poesy*) is not one of the best of Dryden's critical papers, as a great part of it is little more than an adaptation from Dacier's account of Satiric Poetry, in his translation of Horace. But the style, for all Dryden's references to the failings of ' an old man's memory,' and to ' the tattling quality of age,' is not much depressed by the amount of learning which has to be packed into the discourse, and made intelligible and palatable to the studious reader. The themes, apart from the main one, are old favourites with Dryden. The nature of Epic is discussed again, and again the problem of ' machines ' is brought up, in relation to Dryden's own plans for the poem that never was written, either about King Arthur or about the Black Prince ; while the abstract of the history of Satire leads to some less formal passages of literary history in which Dryden is left free from the cumbersome authority of Casaubon, Heinsius, and Dacier.

PARALLEL OF POETRY AND PAINTING
(1695).

The Latin poem *De Arte Graphica* of the French painter Charles Alphonse Du Fresnoy (1611–1665) was first published in 1668, with a French translation in prose ; it was dedicated to Colbert.

Dryden's *Parallel of Poetry and Painting* is in the main a statement of the case for Idealism in Art, with the implication that the true following of Nature in Art is to discover the ideal and to neglect the distractions of the manifold particulars of experience. Thus Dryden's *Parallel* is the forerunner of Sir Joshua Reynolds's *Discourses*, and indeed Reynolds associates himself with Du Fresnoy and Dryden in the notes which he contributed to Mason's version of the Latin poem in 1782. ' There is an absolute necessity for the Painter to generalize his notions ; to paint particulars is not to paint Nature, it is only to paint circumstances. When the Artist has conceived in his imagination the image of perfect beauty, or the abstract idea of forms, he may be said to be admitted into the great Council of Nature, and to

> Trace Beauty's beam to its eternal spring,
> And pure to Man the fire celestial bring.—v. 19.[1] '

Dryden supports himself in the arduous study of the Ideal with the help of a long quotation from Bellori, the Italian critic, in which the commonplaces of the Platonic theory, as accepted by Italian artists, are

---

[1] Reynolds on Du Fresnoy, Note iii.

expounded with an eloquence rather too florid for Dryden's taste. 'But in short, this is the present genius of Italy.' The subject was not altogether new to Dryden ; long before this, in his studies for the Heroic Drama, he had pondered on the ideal character of the Hero, and had found that in poetic diction the style which was most noble was at the same time most truly in accordance with Nature. But it had not previously occurred to him to work out a demonstration of the principles that were involved in his earlier dogmas. Hitherto his furthest point in this direction was in the *Apology for Heroic Poetry* (1677). Now when he takes up the subject again, it is not altogether of his own initiative ; it is part of a task required by the booksellers, and there are signs in his *Parallel*, e. g. in the quotation from Bellori, that he is compelled to take the same devices for eking out his tale of work as are to be found, more lavishly employed, in the Prefaces to *Juvenal* and to *Virgil*. Nevertheless this Essay, though one of the less lively of Dryden's critical works, is kept from flagging, and from showing signs of fatigue, until something like a fair and consistent exposition of the general principles of composition has been attained, and then, judiciously, Dryden breaks off his theme without labouring it out to the conclusion of Du Fresnoy's argument.

DEDICATION OF THE ÆNEIS (1697).

The *Dedication of the Æneis*, like the *Preface to Juvenal* four years earlier, is one of the less original of Dryden's Essays, a remarkable contrast to such free and spirited passages as the *Dedication of the Spanish Friar*. It repeats the commonplaces of the respectable Fathers of Criticism for whom the Epic Poem was all

but a matter of religion. It goes deep into the moral
functions of Epic as compared with Tragedy, and into
the defence of the character of Æneas. Great part of
it is borrowed, to save trouble, from Segrais's Preface
to his translation of the *Æneid*, including the question
whether Virgil, when he spoke of Orion, meant the
heliacal or the achronical rising of the constellation.
But the good sense of Dryden is clearly manifest
throughout the essay, and there are not wanting passages of his livelier manner, e. g. in the account of the
modern epic poets, concluding with the note on *Paradise Lost* : ' if the giant had not foiled the knight and
driven him out of his stronghold, to wander through
the world with his lady errant.' And the last pages,
a series of remarks on prosody and on poetical rhetoric,
' the turn on thoughts and words,' &c., are completely
free from the depressing influence of the French authors.

   Dryden's Virgil was published by Tonson in a magnificent folio, with many engravings, by Hollar and
Lambert, after Cleyn, which had already appeared in
Ogilby's folio Virgil of 1654. Æneas in these ' sculptures ' was, however, not quite the same personage as in
their previous state in Ogilby. His nose in Tonson's
impressions is more Roman, and sometimes he bears
also something like the wig of King William ; a circum-
stance which must have given additional point to certain malign allusions in Dryden's preface. ' Æneas,
though he married the heiress of the crown, yet claimed
no title to it during the life of his father-in-law.'

   In spite of the publisher's magnificence, the book
was carelessly printed : ' the printer is a beast, and
understands nothing I can say to him of correcting the
press.' One considerable error was allowed to remain
in all the editions till Malone's : *Aristotle* as an author
of ' novels.'

Probably the printer's obstinacy showed itself most in the punctuation, which looks capricious, and which seems generally to have been a difficulty. ' The printer has enough to answer for in the false pointings,' as Dryden puts it in the *Preface to the Second Miscellany*.

PREFACE TO THE FABLES (1700).

The *Preface to the Fables*, addressed to the Duke of Ormond, is a piece of work of which it is hard to speak except in some such terms as those which Dryden himself employs in it when he has to write about Chaucer. There is no need here for any such apologies for the failings of old age as are made by the author in the *Preface to Juvenal*. The *Preface to the Fables* is more full of life than anything else in Dryden's prose ; not inferior even to the *Essay of Dramatic Poesy* ; while nothing, either in prose or verse, brings out more admirably or to better advantage the qualities of Dryden as the great English man of letters. For this is what he was, rather than essentially a poet ; his genius is one that commands both vehicles of expression, it is not one that is specially inclined to verse ; and the free movement of his mind and speech is scarely less wonderful in a prose tract like this Preface than in the verse of *Absalom and Achitophel*. ' *His chariot wheels grow hot with driving,*' and this vehemence and speed are of the same kind whatever chariot he may happen to have selected. In this present case, he is absolutely at home in the work he has undertaken, and it brings out all his best qualities both of mind and character, from the generous, unenvying spirit in which he converses with the great masters, to the humorous correction of Milbourne and Blackmore, and the straightforward answer to Collier.

POSTSCRIPT

For the belief in ' Nature ' (*supra*, p. xxiv) the following verses of Chapman may be quoted, from the
address *To the Reader* prefixed to the *Iliads* ; speaking
of Homer—

> ' Whose right not all those great learn'd men have done,
> In some main parts, that were his commentars :
> But as the illustration of the sun
> Should be attempted by the erring stars,
> They fail'd to search his deep and treasurous heart ;
> The cause was, since they wanted the fit key
> Of Nature, in their downright strength of Art
> With Poesy to open Poesy.'

WORKS OF JOHN DRYDEN

(1631–1700).

1649. *Upon the Death of the Lord Hastings* in *Lachrymæ Musarum*, pp. 88–92, signed *Johannes Dryden, Scholæ Westm. Alumnus.* 8°. Printed by Tho. Newcomb.

1650. Poem prefixed to John Hoddesdon's *Sion and Parnassus* (*To his friend the Author on his divine Epigrams*).

1659. *A Poem upon the Death of his late Highness Oliver, Lord Protector of England, Scotland and Ireland.* 4°. (William Wilson.)

Another edition in the same year, *Three Poems upon the Death of His late Highnesse, &c. Written by Mr. Edm. Waller, Mr. Jo. Dryden, Mr. Sprat, of Oxford.* 4°. (William Wilson.) This was frequently reprinted by Dryden's enemies : in a single folio sheet, 1681 (*An Elegy on the Usurper*) ; along with the poems of Waller and Sprat in 1682 ; in 1687 (*A Poem upon the Death of the late Usurper Oliver Cromwel. By the Author of the H——d and the P——r*) ; et al.

1660. *Astræa Redux : a Poem on the happy Restoration and Return of his Sacred Majesty Charles II.* fol. (H. Herringman.)

1661. *To His Sacred Majesty : a Panegyrick on his Coronation.* fol. (Herringman.)

1662. *To My Lord Chancellor, presented on New-Years Day.* fol.

1664. *The Rival Ladies ; a Tragi-Comedy.* 4°. (Herringman.) Other editions 1669, 1675, 1693.

1667. *Annus Mirabilis : the Year of Wonders*, MDCLXVI. 8⁰. (Herringman.) Also 1688 with other poems. 4⁰.

1667. *The Indian Emperour, or the Conquest of Mexico by the Spaniards, being the Sequel of the Indian Queen.* 4⁰. (Herringman.)

1668. *An Essay of Dramatick Poesie.* 4⁰. (Herringman : second edition 1684, third 1693.)

1668. *Secret Love, or the Maiden Queen.* 4⁰. (Herringman.) Also 1669, 1679, 1691.

1668. *Sir Martin Mar-all, or the Feign'd Innocence ; a Comedy.* 4⁰. (Herringman.) Also 1678, 1691, 1697.

1668. *The Indian Emperor*, second edition, with *A Defence of an Essay of Dramatique Poesie, being an Answer to the Preface of The Great Favourite, or the Duke of Lerma.* 4⁰. (Herringman.) The *Defence* was not reprinted in the later editions (1670, 1686) of *The Indian Emperor.*

1669. *The Wild Gallant.* 4⁰. (Herringman.) Dryden's first play, acted 1663 : another edition 1684.

1670. *The Tempest, or the Enchanted Island ; a Comedy : by John Dryden and Sir Will. Davenant.* (Herringman.) Acted 1667 ; republished 1674, 1676, 1690, 1695.

1670. *Tyrannic Love, or the Royal Martyr ; a Tragedy.* 4⁰. (Herringman.) Acted 1669 ; second edition revised 1672, third ' review'd by the Author ' 1677 ; later editions 1686, 1695.

1671. *An Evening's Love, or the Mock-Astrologer.* 4⁰. (Herringman.) Acted 1668 ; republished 1680 and 1691.

1672. *The Conquest of Granada by the Spaniards* (two parts). *Of Heroique Playes ; an Essay. Defence of the Epilogue, or an Essay on the Dramatique Poetry of the last Age.* 4⁰. (Herringman.) Second edition 1673, third 1678, fourth 1687, fifth 1695. The *Defence* was omitted in some copies of the second edition, and in later editions.

1673. *Marriage à la Mode ; a Comedy.* 4⁰. (Herringman.) Republished 1691.

1673. *The Assignation, or Love in a Nunnery.* 4⁰. (Herringman.) Second edition 1678, third 1692.

1673. *Amboyna ; a Tragedy.* 4⁰. (Herringman.) Republished 1691.

1674. *Notes and Observations on the Empress of Morocco.* 4⁰.

1676. *Aureng-zebe ; a Tragedy.* 4⁰. (Herringman.) Other editions 1685, 1692, 1694, 1699.

1677. *The State of Innocence and Fall of Man ; an Opera in Heroique Verse. With the Author's Apology for Heroique Poetry and Poetique Licence.* 4⁰. (Herringman.) Other editions 1684, 1690, 1692. Entered at Stationers' Hall April 17, 1674, as *The Fall of Angels and of Man in Innocence.*

1678. *All for Love, or the World Well Lost ; a Tragedy.* 4⁰. (Herringman.) Other editions 1692, 1696.

1678. *The Kind Keeper, or Mr. Limberham.* (For R. Bentley and M. Magnes.) Other editions 1680, 1690.

1679. *Œdipus, a Tragedy : the Authors, Mr. Dryden and Mr. Lee.* 4⁰. (For R. Bentley and M. Magnes.) Other editions 1682, 1687, 1692, 1696.

1679. *Troilus and Cressida, or Truth found too late ; a Tragedy : with a Preface containing the Grounds of Criticism in Tragedy.* 4⁰. (Jacob Tonson and Abel Small.) Another edition 1695.

1680. *Ovid's Epistles Translated.*

1681. *The Spanish Friar or the Double Discovery.* 4⁰. (Richard and Jacob Tonson.) Other editions 1686, 1690, 1695.

1681. (November 17.) *Absalom and Achitophel.* Printed for J. T., and are to be sold by W. Davies in Amen Corner. fol. Second and third editions Dec. 1681, 4⁰. Fourth 1682, 4⁰.

1682. (March.) *The Medall ; a Satyre against Sedition.* 4⁰. (Jacob Tonson.) Reprinted at Edinburgh 1682, 4⁰.

1682. (October.) *Mac Flecknoe, or a Satyr upon the True-Blew Protestant Poet, T. S.* 4⁰. (Printed for D. Green.)

1682. (November 11.) *Absalom and Achitophel,* Part II. fol. By Dryden and Tate. (Jacob Tonson.)

1682. (November 30.) *Religio Laici, or a Layman's Faith ; a Poem.* 4⁰. (Tonson.) Second edition 1682 ; third 1683.

1683. (Feb.)   *The Duke of Guise; a Tragedy : by Mr. Dryden and Mr. Lee.* (For R. Bentley and J. Tonson.) Other editions 1687, 1699.

1683. *The Vindication : or the Parallel of the French Holy League, and the English League and Covenant, turn'd into a seditious Libell against the King and Duke of York by Tho. Hunt and the Authors of the Reflections upon the Pretended Parallel in the Play called the Duke of Guise.* 4°. (Jacob Tonson.)

1683. *Life of Plutarch.*

1684. *Miscellany Poems.* 8°. (Tonson.)

N.B.—There was no Preface to this volume.

1684. (April.)   *Translation of Maimbourg's History of the League.*

1685. *Sylvæ : or the second Part of Poetical Miscellanies.* 8°.

1685. (March 14.)   *Threnodia Augustalis ; a Funeral Pindarique Poem, sacred to the happy Memory of King Charles II.* 4°. (Jacob Tonson.)   Second edition March 25, 1685.

1685. (June.)   *Albion and Albanius ; an Opera.* fol. (Jacob Tonson.)   Other editions 1687 fol., 1691 4°.

1686. *To the Pious Memory of the Accomplisht Young Lady, Mrs. Anne Killigrew, excellent in the two Sister-Arts of Poësie and Painting. An Ode.* In *Poems by Mrs. Anne Killigrew.* 4°.

1686. *Defence of Papers written by the late King and the Duchess of York.* 4°.

1687. (April.)   *The Hind and the Panther ; a Poem in three Parts.* 4°. (Jacob Tonson.)   Second and third editions, 1687 ; also reprinted by James Watson, Holy-Rood-House, 1687, 4°.

1687. (November.)   *A Song for St. Cecilia's Day, 1687. Written by John Dryden, Esq., and compos'd by Mr. John Baptist Draghi,* fol. single sheet. (Printed for T. Dring.)

1688. *Britannia Rediviva ; a Poem on the Birth of the Prince.* fol. (J. Tonson : also reprinted at Holy-Rood-House 1688, 4°.)

1688. (July.) *Translation of Life of Xavier, by Father Bouhours.* 8°. (Jacob Tonson.) Dedicated to the Queen.

1690. (Jan.) *Don Sebastian, King of Portugal ; a Tragedy.* 4°. (For Jo. Hindmarsh.) Another edition 1692.

1690. (Oct.) *Amphitryon or the two Sosia's ; a Comedy.* 4°. (For J. Tonson and M. Tonson.) Issued with new title-page 1691 ; second edition 1694.

1691. (Feb.) *King Arthur, or the British Worthy ; a Dramatick Opera.* 4°. (Jacob Tonson.) Another edition 1695.

1691. *Preface to A Dialogue concerning Women* [by W. Walsh]. 8°.

1692. (March.) *Eleonora : a panegyrical Poem dedicated to the Memory of the late Countess of Abingdon.* 4°. (Jacob Tonson.)

1692. (May.) *Cleomenes, the Spartan Hero ; a Tragedy ; to which is prefixt the Life of Cleomenes.* (Jacob Tonson.) The Life was translated by Creech.

1692. *Character of St. Evremond.* In *Miscellaneous Essays : by Monsieur St. Euremont. Translated out of French with a Character by a Person of Honour here in England ; continued by Mr. Dryden.* 8°. (John Everingham.)

1693. *Examen Poeticum.* Third Miscellany. 8°. (Tonson.)

1693. *The Satires of Decimus Junius Juvenalis. Translated into English Verse by Mr. Dryden, and several other Eminent Hands. Together with the Satires of A. Persius Flaccus. Made English by Mr. Dryden. With Explanatory Notes at the end of each Satire.*
To which is prefix'd a Discourse concerning the Original and Progress of Satire. fol. (Jacob Tonson.) Another edition in 1697, 8°.

1693. *The Character of Polybius and his Writings* (prefixed to Sir Henry Sheer's translation of Polybius). 8°.

1694. (March.) *Love Triumphant, or Nature will prevail ; a Tragi-Comedy.* 4°. (Tonson.)

1694. *The Annual Miscellany for the Year 1694.* 8°. (Tonson.)

1695. (June.) *De Arte Graphicâ. The Art of Painting, by C. A. Du Fresnoy, with Remarks. Translated into English,*

Together with an original Preface, containing a Parallel betwixt Painting and Poetry. By Mr. Dryden. 4º. (W. Rogers.)

1696. Letters upon several occasions, written by and between Mr. Dryden, Mr. Wycherley, Mr. ——, Mr. Congreve and Mr. Dennis. Published by Mr. Dennis. With a new Translation of select Letters of Monsieur Voiture. . . . The First, translated by Mr. Dryden, and the rest by Mr. Dennis. 8º.

1697. (July.) The Works of Virgil: containing his Pastorals, Georgics and Æneis. Translated into English Verse; By Mr. Dryden. Adorn'd with a Hundred Sculptures. fol. (Tonson.)

1697. (November.) Alexander's Feast, or the Power of Musique: an Ode in Honour of St. Cecilia's Day. fol. (Tonson.)

1700. Fables, Ancient and Modern, translated into verse from Homer, Ovid, Boccace, and Chaucer, with Original Poems. fol. (Tonson.)

1700. A Dialogue and Secular Masque in Fletcher's Pilgrim (with Prologue and Epilogue to The Pilgrim). 4º.

1710–11. Life of Lucian, in Lucian's Works; translated by several Eminent Hands. 4 vols. 8º.

The Comedies, Tragedies and Operas, written by John Dryden, Esq. Now first collected together, and corrected from the Originals. In Two Volumes. London, 1701. fol. (Tonson.)

The Dramatick Works of John Dryden, Esq., in six volumes (edited by Congreve). London, 1717, 8º. (Tonson.)

DRYDEN'S ESSAYS

EPISTLE DEDICATORY OF

THE RIVAL LADIES

A Tragi-Comedy

[1664]

TO THE RIGHT HONOURABLE
ROGER, EARL OF ORRERY

MY LORD,

THIS worthless present was designed you, long before
it was a play; when it was only a confused mass
of thoughts, tumbling over one another in the dark;
when the fancy was yet in its first work, moving the
sleeping images of things towards the light, there to be 5
distinguished, and then either chosen or rejected by
the judgment; it was yours, my Lord, before I could
call it mine. And, I confess, in that first tumult of my
thoughts, there appeared a disorderly kind of beauty
in some of them, which gave me hope, something 10
worthy my Lord of Orrery might be drawn from them:
but I was then in that eagerness of imagination, which,
by overpleasing fanciful men, flatters them into the
danger of writing; so that, when I had moulded it
into that shape it now bears, I looked with such disgust 15
upon it, that the censures of our severest critics are
charitable to what I thought (and still think) of it
myself: 'tis so far from me to believe this perfect,
that I am apt to conclude our best plays are scarcely

so. For the stage being the representation of the world,
and the actions in it, how can it be imagined, that the
picture of human life can be more exact than life itself
is ? He may be allowed sometimes to err, who under-
5 takes to move so many characters and humours, as are
requisite in a play, in those narrow channels which are
proper to each of them ; to conduct his imaginary
persons through so many various intrigues and chances,
as the labouring audience shall think them lost under
10 every billow ; and then at length to work them so
naturally out of their distresses, that when the whole
plot is laid open, the spectators may rest satisfied that
every cause was powerful enough to produce the effect
it had ; and that the whole chain of them was with such
15 due order linked together, that the first accident would
naturally beget the second, till they all rendered the
conclusion necessary.

These difficulties, my Lord, may reasonably excuse
the errors of my undertaking ; but for this confidence
20 of my dedication, I have an argument, which is too
advantageous for me not to publish it to the world.
'Tis the kindness your lordship has continually shown
to all my writings. You have been pleased, my Lord,
they should sometimes cross the Irish seas, to kiss
25 your hands ; which passage (contrary to the experience
of others) I have found the least dangerous in the
world. Your favour has shone upon me at a remote
distance, without the least knowledge of my person ;
and (like the influence of the heavenly bodies) you have
30 done good, without knowing to whom you did it. 'Tis
this virtue in your lordship, which emboldens me to
this attempt ; for, did I not consider you as my patron,
I have little reason to desire you for my judge ; and
should appear with as much awe before you in the
35 reading, as I had when the full theatre sat upon the

action. For who could so severely judge of faults as
he, who has given testimony he commits none ? Your
excellent poems having afforded that knowledge of it to
the world, that your enemies are ready to upbraid you
with it, as a crime for a man of business to write so 5
well. Neither durst I have justified your Lordship in
it, if examples of it had not been in the world before
you ; if Xenophon had not written a romance, and
a certain Roman, called Augustus Caesar, a tragedy,
and epigrams. But their writing was the entertainment 10
of their pleasure ; yours is only a diversion of your
pain. The Muses have seldom employed your thoughts,
but when some violent fit of the gout has snatched
you from affairs of state ; and like the priestess of
Apollo, you never come to deliver his oracles, but un- 15
willingly, and in torment. So that we are obliged to
your Lordship's misery for our delight : you treat us
with the cruel pleasure of a Turkish triumph, where
those who cut and wound their bodies, sing songs of
victory as they pass, and divert others with their own 20
sufferings. Other men endure their diseases ; your
Lordship only can enjoy them. Plotting and writing
in this kind are certainly more troublesome employments than many which signify more, and are of greater
moment in the world : the fancy, memory, and judg- 25
ment, are then extended (like so many limbs) upon the
rack ; all of them reaching with their utmost stress at
Nature ; a thing so almost infinite and boundless, as
can never fully be comprehended, but where the images
of all things are always present. Yet I wonder not 30
your Lordship succeeds so well in this attempt ; the
knowledge of men is your daily practice in the world ;
to work and bend their stubborn minds, which go not
all after the same grain, but each of them so particular
a way, that the same common humours, in several 35

persons, must be wrought upon by several means.
Thus, my Lord, your sickness is but the imitation of
your health ; the Poet but subordinate to the Statesman
in you ; you still govern men with the same address,
5 and manage business with the same prudence ; allowing
it here (as in the world) the due increase and growth,
till it comes to the just height ; and then turning it when
it is fully ripe, and Nature calls out, as it were, to be
delivered. With this only advantage of ease to you
10 in your poetry, that you have fortune here at your command ; with which wisdom does often unsuccessfully
struggle in the world. Here is no chance, which you
have not foreseen ; all your heroes are more than your
subjects, they are your creatures ; and though they
15 seem to move freely in all the sallies of their passions,
yet you make destinies for them, which they cannot
shun. They are moved (if I may dare to say so) like
the rational creatures of the Almighty Poet, who walk
at liberty, in their own opinion, because their fetters are
20 invisible ; when, indeed, the prison of their will is the
more sure for being large ; and instead of an absolute
power over their actions, they have only a wretched
desire of doing that which they cannot choose but do.

I have dwelt, my Lord, thus long upon your writing,
25 not because you deserve not greater and more noble
commendations, but because I am not equally able to
express them in other subjects. Like an ill swimmer,
I have willingly stayed long in my own depth ; and
though I am eager of performing more, yet am loth to
30 venture out beyond my knowledge : for beyond your
poetry, my Lord, all is ocean to me. To speak of you
as a soldier, or a statesman, were only to betray my own ·
ignorance ; and I could hope no better success from it
than that miserable rhetorician had, who solemnly
35 declaimed before Hannibal, of the conduct of armies,

and the art of war. I can only say, in general, that the souls of other men shine out at little crannies; they understand some one thing, perhaps, to admiration, while they are darkened on all the other parts; but your Lordship's soul is an entire globe of light, breaking 5 out on every side; and, if I have only discovered one beam of it, 'tis not that the light falls unequally, but because the body, which receives it, is of unequal parts.

The acknowledgment of which is a fair occasion offered me, to retire from the consideration of your 10 Lordship to that of myself. I here present you, my Lord, with that in print, which you had the goodness not to dislike upon the stage; and account it happy to have met you here in England; it being, at best, like small wines, to be drunk out upon the place, and has not 15 body enough to endure the sea. I know not whether I have been so careful of the plot and language as I ought; but, for the latter, I have endeavoured to write English, as near as I could distinguish it from the tongue of pedants, and that of affected travellers. 20 Only I am sorry, that (speaking so noble a language as we do) we have not a more certain measure of it, as they have in France, where they have an Academy erected for that purpose, and endowed with large privileges by the present king. I wish we might at length 25 leave to borrow words from other nations, which is now a wantonness in us, not a necessity; but so long as some affect to speak them, there will not want others, who will have the boldness to write them.

But I fear, lest, defending the received words, I shall 30 be accused for following the new way; I mean, of writing scenes in verse. Though, to speak properly, 'tis not so much a new way amongst us, as an old way new revived; for many years before Shakspeare's plays, was the tragedy of Queen *Gorboduc*, in English 35

verse, written by that famous Lord Buckhurst, afterwards Earl of Dorset, and progenitor to that excellent
person, who (as he inherits his soul and title) I wish
may inherit his good fortune. But supposing our
5 countrymen had not received this writing till of late ;
shall we oppose ourselves to the most polished and
civilized nations of Europe ? Shall we, with the same
singularity, oppose the world in this, as most of us do
in pronouncing Latin ? Or do we desire that the brand,
10 which Barclay has (I hope unjustly) laid upon the
English, should still continue ? *Angli suos ac sua
omnia impensè mirantur ; cæteras nationes despectui
habent.* All the Spanish and Italian tragedies I have
yet seen, are writ in rhyme. For the French, I do
15 not name them, because it is the fate of our countrymen
to admit little of theirs among us, but the basest of
their men, the extravagancies of their fashions, and
the frippery of their merchandise. Shakspeare (who,
with some errors not to be avoided in that age, had
20 undoubtedly a larger soul of poesy than ever any of our
nation) was the first who, to shun the pains of continual
rhyming, invented that kind of writing which we call
blank verse, but the French, more properly, *prose
mesurée ;* into which the English tongue so naturally
25 slides, that, in writing prose, it is hardly to be avoided.
And therefore, I admire some men should perpetually
stumble in a way so easy, and inverting the order of
their words, constantly close their lines with verbs,
which though commended sometimes in writing Latin,
30 yet we were whipt at Westminster if we used it twice
together. I know some, who, if they were to write in
blank verse, *Sir, I ask your pardon*, would think it
sounded more heroically to write, *Sir, I your pardon
ask.* I should judge him to have little command of
35 English, whom the necessity of a rhyme should force

often upon this rock ; though sometimes it cannot
easily be avoided ; and indeed this is the only inconvenience with which rhyme can be charged. This is
that which makes them say, rhyme is not natural, it
being only so, when the poet either makes a vicious 5
choice of words, or places them, for rhyme sake, so
unnaturally as no man would in ordinary speaking ; but
when 'tis so judiciously ordered, that the first word in
the verse seems to beget the second, and that the next,
till that becomes the last word in the line, which, in 10
the negligence of prose, would be so ; it must then be
granted, rhyme has all the advantages of prose, besides
its own. But the excellence and dignity of it were
never fully known till Mr. Waller taught it ; he first
made writing easily an art ; first showed us to conclude 15
the sense most commonly in distichs, which, in the
verse of those before him, runs on for so many lines
together, that the reader is out of breath to overtake it.
This sweetness of Mr. Waller's lyric poesy was afterwards followed in the epic by Sir John Denham, in his 20
Cooper's Hill, a poem which your Lordship knows for
the majesty of the style, is, and ever will be, the exact
standard of good writing. But if we owe the invention
of it to Mr. Waller, we are acknowledging for the
noblest use of it to Sir William D'Avenant, who at once 25
brought it upon the stage, and made it perfect, in the
Siege of Rhodes.
   The advantages which rhyme has over blank verse
are so many, that it were lost time to name them.
Sir Philip Sidney, in his *Defence of Poesy*, gives us 30
one, which, in my opinion, is not the least considerable ;
I mean the help it brings to memory, which rhyme so
knits up, by the affinity of sounds, that, by remembering
the last word in one line, we often call to mind both the
verses. Then, in the quickness of reparties (which in 35

discoursive scenes fall very often), it has so particular
a grace, and is so aptly suited to them, that the sudden
smartness of the answer, and the sweetness of the
rhyme, set off the beauty of each other. But that
5 benefit which I consider most in it, because I have not
seldom found it, is, that it bounds and circumscribes the
fancy. For imagination in a poet is a faculty so wild
and lawless, that like an high-ranging spaniel, it must
have clogs tied to it, lest it outrun the judgment. The
10 great easiness of blank verse renders the poet too
luxuriant ; he is tempted to say many things, which
might better be omitted, or at least shut up in fewer
words ; but when the difficulty of artful rhyming is
interposed, where the poet commonly confines his sense
15 to his couplet, and must contrive that sense into such
words, that the rhyme shall naturally follow them, not
they the rhyme ; the fancy then gives leisure to the
judgment to come in, which, seeing so heavy a tax
imposed, is ready to cut off all unnecessary expenses.
20 This last consideration has already answered an objection which some have made, that rhyme is only an
embroidery of sense, to make that which is ordinary in
itself pass for excellent with less examination. But
certainly, that which most regulates the fancy, and
25 gives the judgment its busiest employment, is like to
bring forth the richest and clearest thoughts. The
poet examines that most, which he produceth with the
greatest leisure, and which he knows, must pass the
severest test of the audience, because they are aptest to
30 have it ever in their memory ; as the stomach makes
the best concoction when it strictly embraces the
nourishment, and takes account of every little particle
as it passes through. But as the best medicines may
lose their virtue by being ill applied, so is it with verse,
35 if a fit subject be not chosen for it. Neither must the

argument alone, but the characters and persons be great and noble ; otherwise (as Scaliger says of Claudian) the poet will be *ignobiliore materiâ depressus.* The scenes which in my opinion most commend it, are those of argumentation and discourse, on the result of 5 which the doing or not doing some considerable action should depend.

But, my Lord, though I have more to say upon this subject, yet I must remember, it is your Lordship to whom I speak ; who have much better commended this 10 way by your writing in it, than I can do by writing for it. Where my reasons cannot prevail, I am sure your Lordship's example must. Your rhetoric has gained my cause ; at least the greatest part of my design has already succeeded to my wish, which was to interest so 15 noble a person in the quarrel, and withal to testify to the world how happy I esteem myself in the honour of being,

MY LORD,

Your Lordship's most humble,

and most obedient Servant,

JOHN DRIDEN.

ANNUS MIRABILIS:

THE YEAR OF WONDERS MDCLXVI

PREFACE

(AN ACCOUNT OF THE ENSUING POEM, IN A LETTER
TO THE HONORABLE SIR ROBERT HOWARD)

SIR,

I AM so many ways obliged to you, and so little
able to return your favours, that, like those who owe too
much, I can only live by getting farther into your debt.
You have not only been careful of my fortune, which
5 was the effect of your nobleness, but you have been
solicitous of my reputation, which is that of your kindness.   It is not long since I gave you the trouble of
perusing a play for me, and now, instead of an acknowledgment, I have given you a greater, in the correction
10 of a poem.   But since you are to bear this persecution,
I will at least give you the encouragement of a martyr,
—you could never suffer in a nobler cause.   For I have
chosen the most heroic subject, which any poet could
desire : I have taken upon me to describe the motives,
15 the beginning, progress, and successes, of a most just
and necessary war ; in it, the care, management, and prudence of our King ; the conduct and valour of a Royal
Admiral, and of two incomparable Generals ; the invincible courage of our captains and seamen, and three
20 glorious victories, the result of all.   After this, I have

in the Fire, the most deplorable, but withal the greatest
argument that can be imagined ; the destruction being
so swift, so sudden, so vast and miserable, as nothing
can parallel in story. The former part of this Poem,
relating to the war, is but a due expiation for my not 5
serving my King and country in it. All gentlemen are
almost obliged to it ; and I know no reason we should
give that advantage to the commonalty of England, to
be foremost in brave actions, which the noblesse of
France would never suffer in their peasants. I should 10
not have written this but to a person, who has been
ever forward to appear in all employments, whither his
honour and generosity have called him. The latter
part of my Poem, which describes the Fire, I owe, first,
to the piety and fatherly affection of our Monarch to his 15
suffering subjects ; and, in the second place, to the
courage, loyalty, and magnanimity of the City ; both
which were so conspicuous, that I have wanted words
to celebrate them as they deserve. I have called my
poem *historical*, not *epic*, though both the actions and 20
actors are as much heroic as any poem can contain.
But since the action is not properly one, nor that
accomplished in the last successes, I have judged it
too bold a title for a few stanzas, which are little more
in number than a single *Iliad*, or the longest of the 25
Æneids. For this reason (I mean not of length, but
broken action, tied too severely to the laws of history),
I am apt to agree with those who rank Lucan rather
among historians in verse, than epic poets ; in whose
room, if I am not deceived, Silius Italicus, though a worse 30
writer, may more justly be admitted. I have chosen to
write my poem in quatrains, or stanzas of four in alter-
nate rhyme, because I have ever judged them more noble,
and of greater dignity, both for the sound and number,
than any other verse in use amongst us ; in which I am 35

sure I have your approbation. The learned languages
have certainly a great advantage of us, in not being tied
to the slavery of any rhyme ; and were less constrained
in the quantity of every syllable, which they might vary
5 with spondees or dactyls, besides so many other helps
of grammatical figures, for the lengthening or abbrevia-
tion of them, than the modern are in the close of that
one syllable, which often confines, and more often cor-
rupts, the sense of all the rest. But in this necessity
10 of our rhymes, I have always found the couplet verse
most easy (though not so proper for this occasion), for
there the work is sooner at an end, every two lines
concluding the labour of the poet ; but in quatrains he
is to carry it farther on, and not only so, but to bear
15 along in his head the troublesome sense of four lines
together. For those who write correctly in this kind
must needs acknowledge, that the last line of the stanza
is to be considered in the composition of the first.
Neither can we give ourselves the liberty of making
20 any part of a verse for the sake of rhyme, or concluding
with a word which is not current English, or using the
variety of female rhymes, all which our fathers practised ; and for the female rhymes, they are still in use
amongst other nations ; with the Italian in every line,
25 with the Spaniard promiscuously, with the French
alternately, as those who have read the *Alaric*, the
Pucelle, or any of their later poems, will agree with
me. And besides this, they write in Alexandrines, or
verses of six feet ; such as, amongst us, is the old
30 translation of Homer by Chapman : all which, by
lengthening of their chain, makes the sphere of their
activity the larger.

I have dwelt too long upon the choice of my stanza,
which you may remember is much better defended in the
35 preface to *Gondibert* ; and therefore I will hasten to ac-

quaint you with my endeavours in the writing. In general
I will only say, I have never yet seen the description of
any naval fight in the proper terms which are used at
sea ; and if there be any such, in another language, as
that of Lucan in the third of his *Pharsalia*, yet I could 5
not prevail myself of it in the English ; the terms of
art in every tongue bearing more of the idiom of it than
any other words. We hear indeed among our poets, of
the thundering of guns, the smoke, the disorder, and
the slaughter, but all these are common notions. And 10
certainly, as those who, in a logical dispute, keep in
general terms, would hide a fallacy ; so those, who
do it in any poetical description, would veil their
ignorance :—

> *Descriptas servare vices, operumque colores,*   15
> *Cur ego, si nequeo ignoroque, poeta salutor ?*

For my own part, if I had little knowledge of the
sea, yet I have thought it no shame to learn ; and if
I have made some few mistakes, it is only, as you can
bear me witness, because I have wanted opportunity to 20
correct them ; the whole poem being first written, and
now sent you from a place, where I have not so much
as the converse of any seaman. Yet though the trouble
I had in writing it was great, it was more than recompensed by the pleasure ; I found myself so warm in 25
celebrating the praises of military men, two such especially as the Prince and General, that it is no wonder if
they inspired me with thoughts above my ordinary level.
And I am well satisfied, that, as they are incomparably
the best subject I ever had, excepting only the Royal 30
Family, so also, that this I have written of them is
much better than what I have performed on any other.
I have been forced to help out other arguments, but
this has been bountiful to me ; they have been low

and barren of praise, and I have exalted them, and
made them fruitful ; but here—*Omnia sponte sua reddit
justissima tellus.* I have had a large, a fair, and a
pleasant field ; so fertile, that, without my cultivating,
5 it has given me two harvests in a summer, and in both
oppressed the reaper. All other greatness in subjects
is only counterfeit ; it will not endure the test of danger ;
the greatness of arms is only real. Other greatness
burdens a nation with its weight ; this supports it with
10 its strength. And as it is the happiness of the age, so
it is the peculiar goodness of the best of Kings, that we
may praise his subjects without offending him. Doubtless it proceeds from a just confidence of his own virtue,
which the lustre of no other can be so great as to
15 darken in him ; for the good or the valiant are never
safely praised under a bad or a degenerate Prince.

But to return from this digression to a farther account
of my poem ; I must crave leave to tell you, that as
I have endeavoured to adorn it with noble thoughts, so
20 much more to express those thoughts with elocution.
The composition of all poems is, or ought to be, of wit ;
and wit in the poet, or *Wit writing*, (if you will give me
leave to use a school-distinction), is no other than the
faculty of imagination in the writer, which, like a nimble
25 spaniel, beats over and ranges through the field of
memory, till it springs the quarry it hunted after ; or,
without metaphor, which searches over all the memory
for the species or ideas of those things which it designs
to represent. *Wit written* is that which is well defined,
30 the happy result of thought, or product of imagination.
But to proceed from wit, in the general notion of it, to
the proper wit of an Heroic or Historical Poem, I judge
it chiefly to consist in the delightful imagining of persons, actions, passions, or things. 'Tis not the jerk or
35 sting of an epigram, nor the seeming contradiction of

a poor antithesis (the delight of an ill-judging audience
in a play of rhyme), nor the jingle of a more poor paronomasia ; neither is it so much the morality of a grave
sentence, affected by Lucan, but more sparingly used
by Virgil ; but it is some lively and apt description, 5
dressed in such colours of speech, that it sets before
your eyes the absent object, as perfectly, and more
delightfully than nature. So then the first happiness
of the poet's imagination is properly invention, or finding of the thought ; the second is fancy, or the variation, 10
deriving, or moulding, of that thought, as the judgment
represents it proper to the subject ; the third is elocution, or the art of clothing and adorning that thought,
so found and varied, in apt, significant, and sounding
words : the quickness of the imagination is seen in the 15
invention, the fertility in the fancy, and the accuracy in
the expression. For the two first of these, Ovid is
famous amongst the poets ; for the latter, Virgil. Ovid
images more often the movements and affections of the
mind, either combating between two contrary passions, 20
or extremely discomposed by one. His words therefore are the least part of his care ; for he pictures nature
in disorder, with which the study and choice of words
is inconsistent. This is the proper wit of dialogue or
discourse, and consequently of the Drama, where all 25
that is said is supposed to be the effect of sudden
thought ; which, though it excludes not the quickness
of wit in repartees, yet admits not a too curious election
of words, too frequent allusions, or use of tropes, or, in
fine, anything that shows remoteness of thought, or 30
labour in the writer. On the other side, Virgil speaks
not so often to us in the person of another, like Ovid,
but in his own : he relates almost all things as from
himself, and thereby gains more liberty than the other,
to express his thoughts with all the graces of elocution, 35

to write more figuratively, and to confess as well the
labour as the force of his imagination. Though he
describes his *Dido* well and naturally, in the violence
of her passions, yet he must yield in that to the *Myrrha,*
5 the *Byblis,* the *Althæa,* of Ovid ; for, as great an admirer of him as I am, I must acknowledge that if I see
not more of their souls than I see of Dido's, at least
I have a greater concernment for them : and that convinces me that Ovid has touched those tender strokes
10 more delicately than Virgil could. But when action or
persons are to be described, when any such image is to
be set before us, how bold, how masterly, are the strokes
of Virgil ! We see the objects he presents us with in
their native figures, in their proper motions ; but so we
15 see them, as our own eyes could never have beheld
them so beautiful in themselves. We see the soul of
the poet, like that universal one of which he speaks,
informing and moving through all his pictures—

> *. . . Totamque infusa per artus*
20 > *Mens agitat molem, et magno se corpore miscet :*

we behold him embellishing his images, as he makes
Venus breathing beauty upon her son Æneas—

> *. . . . lumenque juventæ*
> *Purpureum, et lætos oculis afflarat honores :*
25 > *Quale manus addunt ebori decus, aut ubi flavo*
> *Argentum, Pariusve lapis, circumdatur auro.*

See his *Tempest,* his *Funeral Sports,* his *Combat of
Turnus and Æneas* : and in his *Georgics,* which I esteem
the divinest part of all his writings, the *Plague,* the
30 *Country,* the *Battle of Bulls,* the labour of the *Bees,* and
those many other excellent images of Nature, most
of which are neither great in themselves, nor have any
natural ornament to bear them up ; but the words
wherewith he describes them are so excellent, that it
35 might be well applied to him, which was said by Ovid,

Materiam superabat opus: the very sound of his words have often somewhat that is connatural to the subject; and while we read him, we sit, as in a play, beholding the scenes of what he represents. To perform this, he made frequent use of tropes, which you know change the nature of a known word, by applying it to some other signification; and this is it which Horace means in his *Epistle to the Pisos*—

> *Dixeris egregie, notum si callida verbum*
> *Reddiderit junctura novum.*

But I am sensible I have presumed too far, to entertain you with a rude discourse of that art, which you both know so well, and put into practice with so much happiness. Yet before I leave Virgil, I must own the vanity to tell you, and by you the world, that he has been my master in this poem. I have followed him everywhere, I know not with what success, but I am sure with diligence enough; my images are many of them copied from him, and the rest are imitations of him. My expressions also are as near as the idioms of the two languages would admit of in translation. And this, Sir, I have done with that boldness, for which I will stand accomptable to any of our little critics, who, perhaps, are not better acquainted with him than I am. Upon your first perusal of this poem, you have taken notice of some words, which I have innovated (if it be too bold for me to say refined) upon his Latin; which, as I offer not to introduce into English prose, so I hope they are neither improper, nor altogether unelegant in verse; and in this Horace will again defend me—

> *Et nova, fictaque nuper, habebunt verba fidem, si*
> *Græco fonte cadant, parce detorta.*

The inference is exceeding plain; for, if a Roman poet might have liberty to coin a word, supposing only

that it was derived from the Greek, was put into a
Latin termination, and that he used this liberty but
seldom, and with modesty ; how much more justly may
I challenge that privilege to do it with the same pre-
5 requisites, from the best and most judicious of Latin
writers ?   In some places, where either the fancy or
the words were his, or any other's, I have noted it in
the margin, that I might not seem a plagiary ; in others
I have neglected it, to avoid as well tediousness, as the
10 affectation of doing it too often.   Such descriptions or
images, well wrought, which I promise not for mine,
are, as I have said, the adequate delight of Heroic Poesy ;
for they beget admiration, which is its proper object ;
as the images of the Burlesque, which is contrary to
15 this, by the same reason beget laughter : for the one
shows nature beautified, as in the picture of a fair
woman, which we all admire ;   the other shows her
deformed, as in that of a Lazar, or of a fool with dis-
torted face and antic gestures, at 'which we cannot
20 forbear to laugh, because it is a deviation from Nature.
But though the same images serve equally for the epic
poesy, and for the historic and panegyric, which are
branches of it, yet a several sort of sculpture is to be
used in them :   if some of them are to be like those of
25 Juvenal, *stantes in curribus Aemiliani*, heroes drawn in
their triumphal chariots, and in their full proportion ;
others are to be like that of Virgil, *spirantia mollius
æra* :   there is somewhat more of softness and tenderness to be shown in them.   You will soon find I write
30 not this without concern.   Some, who have seen a
paper of verses, which I wrote last year to her Highness the Duchess, have accused them of that only thing
I could defend in them.   They said, I did *humi serpere*,
—that I wanted not only height of fancy, but dignity
35 of words, to set if off.   I might well answer with that of

Horace, *Nunc non erat his locus*; I knew I addressed
them to a lady, and accordingly I affected the softness
of expression, and the smoothness of measure, rather
than the height of thought; and in what I did endeavour, it is no vanity to say I have succeeded. I 5
detest arrogance; but there is some difference betwixt
that and a just defence. But I will not farther bribe
your candour, or the reader's. I leave them to speak
for me; and, if they can, to make out that character,
not pretending to a greater, which I have given them. 10

[*Here follow in the original edition the verses to the
Duchess.*]

And now, Sir, 'tis time I should relieve you from the
tedious length of this account. You have better and
more profitable employment for your hours, and I 15
wrong the public to detain you longer. In conclusion,
I must leave my poem to you with all its faults, which
I hope to find fewer in the printing by your emendations. I know you are not of the number of those, of
whom the younger Pliny speaks; *Nec sunt parum multi*, 20
qui carpere amicos suos judicium vocant: I am rather
too secure of you on that side. Your candour in par-
doning my errors may make you more remiss in correcting them; if you will not withal consider that they
come into the world with your approbation, and through 25
your hands. I beg from you the greatest favour you
can confer upon an absent person, since I repose upon
your management what is dearest to me, my fame and
reputation; and therefore I hope it will stir you up to
make my poem fairer by many of your blots; if not, 30
you know the story of the gamester who married the
rich man's daughter, and when her father denied the
portion, christened all the children by his sirname, that
if, in conclusion, they must beg, they should do so by

one name, as well as by the other. But, since the
reproach of my faults will light on you, 'tis but reason
I should do you that justice to the readers, to let them
know, that, if there be anything tolerable in this poem,
5 they owe the argument to your choice, the writing to
your encouragement, the correction to your judgment,
and the care of it to your friendship, to which he must
ever acknowledge himself to owe all things, who is,

SIR,

10 The most obedient, and most

faithful of your Servants,

JOHN DRYDEN.

From Charlton, *in* Wiltshire,
Novem. 10, 1666.

OF
Dramatick Poesie,
AN
ESSAY.

By *JOHN DRYDEN* Esq;

—————*Fungar vice cotis, acutum*
Reddere quæ ferrum valet, exors ipsa secandi.

Horat. De Arte Poet.

LONDON,

Printed for *Henry Herringman*, at the Sign of the
Anchor, on the Lower-walk of the New-
Exchange. 1668.

TO THE RIGHT HONOURABLE

CHARLES, LORD BUCKHURST [1]

My Lord,

As I was lately reviewing my loose papers, amongst the rest I found this Essay, the writing of which, in this rude and indigested manner wherein your Lordship now sees it, served as an amusement to me in the country, when the violence of the last plague 5 had driven me from the town. Seeing then our theatres shut up, I was engaged in these kind of thoughts with the same delight with which men think upon their absent mistresses. I confess I find many things in this discourse which I do not now approve ; my judgment 10 being a little altered [2] since the writing of it ; but whether for the better or the worse, I know not : neither indeed is it much material, in an Essay where all I have said is problematical. For the way of writing plays in verse, which I have seemed to favour, I have, 15 since that time, laid the practice of it aside, till I have more leisure, because I find it troublesome and slow. But I am no way altered from my opinion of it, at least

A= Ed. 1668.   B= Ed. 1684.   C= Ed. 1693.

[1] C has, 'Charles Earl of Dorset and Middlesex, Lord Chamberlain of Their Majesties Houshold, Knight of the most Noble Order of the Garter, &c.'
[2] not a little alter'd, BC.

with any reasons which have opposed it. For your Lordship may easily observe, that none are very violent against it, but those who either have not attempted it, or who have succeeded ill in their attempt. 'Tis
5 enough for me to have your Lordship's example for my excuse in that little which I have done in it ; and I am sure my adversaries can bring no such arguments against verse, as the fourth act of *Pompey* will furnish me with [1] in its defence. Yet, my Lord, you
10 must suffer me a little to complain of you, that you too soon withdraw from us a contentment, of which we expected the continuance, because you gave it us so early. 'Tis a revolt, without occasion, from your party, where your merits had already raised you to the
15 highest commands, and where you have not the excuse of other men, that you have been ill used, and therefore laid down arms. I know no other quarrel you can have to verse, than that which Spurina had to his beauty, when he tore and mangled the features of his
20 face, only because they pleased too well the lookers on [2]. It was an honour which seemed to wait for you, to lead out a new colony of writers from the mother nation : and upon the first spreading of your ensigns, there had been many in a readiness to have followed so fortunate
25 a leader ; if not all, yet the better part of writers [3] :

> . . . *pars, indocili melior grege ; mollis et expes
> Inominata perprimat cubilia.*

I am almost of opinion, that we should force you to accept of the command, as sometimes the Praetorian
30 bands have compelled their captains to receive the Empire. The Court, which is the best and surest judge of writing, has generally allowed of verse ; and in the town it has found favourers of wit and quality. As for

---

[1] as those with which the fourth Act of *Pompey* will furnish me, BC.
[2] the sight, BC.   [3] Poets, BC.

your own particular, my Lord, you have yet youth and
time enough to give part of it [1] to the divertisement
of the public, before you enter into the serious and
more unpleasant business of the world. That which
the French poet said of the temple of Love, may be as [5]
well applied to the temple of the Muses. The words,
as near as I can remember them, were these :

> *Le jeune homme* [2] *a* [3] *mauvaise grace,*
> *N'ayant pas adoré dans le Temple d'Amour ;*
> *Il faut qu'il entre ; et pour le sage,*   [10]
> *Si ce n'est pas son vray* [4] *sejour,*
> *C'est un giste sur son passage.*

I leave the words to work their effect upon your
Lordship in their own language, because no other can
so well express the nobleness of the thought ; and wish [15]
you may be soon called to bear a part in the affairs of
the nation, where I know the world expects you, and
wonders why you have been so long forgotten ; there
being no person amongst our young nobility, on whom
the eyes of all men are so much bent. But in the mean [20]
time, your Lordship may imitate the course of Nature,
who gives us the flower before the fruit : that I may
speak to you in the language of the Muses, which I have
taken from an excellent poem to the King :

> As Nature, when she fruit designs, thinks fit   [25]
> By beauteous blossoms to proceed to it ;
> And while she does accomplish all the spring,
> Birds to her secret operations sing.

I confess I have no greater reason, in addressing this
Essay to your Lordship, than that it might awaken in [30]
you the desire of writing something, in whatever kind
it be, which might be an honour to our age and country.
And me thinks it might have the same effect on you,

of them, BC.   [2] La jeunesse, A.
à BC.   [4] Si ce nest son vray, A.

which Homer tells us the fight of the Greeks and
Trojans before the fleet had on the spirit of Achilles ;
who, though he had resolved not to engage, yet found
a martial warmth to steal upon him at the sight of
5 blows, the sound of trumpets, and the cries of fighting
men. For my own part, if, in treating of this subject,
I sometimes dissent from the opinion of better wits,
I declare it is not so much to combat their opinions,
as to defend my own, which were first made public.
10 Sometimes, like a scholar in a fencing-school, I put
forth myself, and show my own ill play, on purpose
to be better taught. Sometimes I stand desperately to
my arms, like the foot when deserted by their horse ;
not in hope to overcome, but only to yield on more
15 honourable terms. And yet, my Lord, this war of
opinions, you well know, has fallen out among the
writers of all ages, and sometimes betwixt friends.
Only it has been prosecuted by some like pedants,
with violence of words, and managed by others like
20 gentlemen, with candour and civility. Even Tully had
a controversy with his dear Atticus ; and in one of his
Dialogues, makes him sustain the part of an enemy in
philosophy, who, in his letters, is his confident of state,
and made privy to the most weighty affairs of the
25 Roman Senate. And the same respect which was paid
by Tully to Atticus, we find returned to him afterwards
by Caesar on a like occasion, who answering his book
in praise of Cato, made it not so much his business to
condemn Cato, as to praise Cicero.
30   But that I may decline some part of the encounter
with my adversaries, whom I am neither willing to
combat, nor well able to resist ; I will give your Lordship the relation of a dispute betwixt some of our wits
upon this subject [1], in which they did not only speak

[1] on the same subject, BC.

of plays in verse, but mingled, in the freedom of discourse, some things of the ancient, many of the modern ways of writing ; comparing those with these, and the wits of our nation with those of others : 'tis true, they differed in their opinions, as 'tis probable they would : 5 neither do I take upon me to reconcile, but to relate them ; and that as Tacitus professes of himself, *sine studio partium, aut irâ*, without passion or interest ; leaving your Lordship to decide it in favour of which part you shall judge most reasonable, and withal, to 10 pardon the many errors of

Your Lordship's

Most obedient humble servant,

JOHN DRYDEN.

TO THE READER

THE drift of the ensuing Discourse was chiefly to vindicate the honour of our English writers, from the censure of those who unjustly prefer the French before them. This I intimate, lest any should think me so 15 exceeding vain, as to teach others an art which they understand much better than myself. But if this incorrect Essay, written in the country without the help of books, or advice of friends, shall find any acceptance in the world, I promise to myself a better 20 success of the second part, wherein the virtues and faults of the English poets, who have written either in this, the epic, or the lyric way, will be more fully treated of, and their several styles impartially imitated [1].

---

[1] BC, ' wherein I shall more fully treat of the virtues and faults of the English poets who have written either in this, the epic, or the lyric way.'

AN ESSAY

OF

DRAMATIC POESY

It was that memorable day, in the first summer of the
late war, when our navy engaged the Dutch ; a day
wherein the two most mighty and best appointed fleets
which any age had ever seen, disputed the command
5 of the greater half of the globe, the commerce of
nations, and the riches of the universe. While these
vast floating bodies, on either side, moved against each
other in parallel lines, and our countrymen, under the
happy conduct of his Royal Highness, went breaking,
10 by little and little, into the line of the enemies ; the
noise of the cannon from both navies reached our ears
about the City, so that all men being alarmed with it,
and in a dreadful suspense of the event which we [1]
knew was then deciding, every one went following the
15 sound as his fancy led him ; and leaving the town
almost empty, some took towards the park, some cross
the river, others down it ; all seeking the noise in the
depth of silence.

Among the rest, it was the fortune of Eugenius,
20 Crites, Lisideius, and Neander, to be in company
together ; three of them persons whom their wit and

---

[1] they BC.

quality have made known to all the town ; and whom
I have chose to hide under these borrowed names, that
they may not suffer by so ill a relation as I am going to
make of their discourse.

Taking then a barge which a servant of Lisideius 5
had provided for them, they made haste to shoot the
bridge, and left behind them that great fall of waters
which hindered them from hearing what they desired :
after which, having disengaged themselves from many
vessels which rode at anchor in the Thames, and almost 10
blocked up the passage towards Greenwich, they ordered
the watermen to let fall their oars more gently ; and
then, every one favouring his own curiosity with a strict
silence, it was not long ere they perceived the air
break [1] about them like the noise of distant thunder, or 15
of swallows in a chimney : those little undulations of
sound, though almost vanishing before they reached
them, yet still seeming to retain somewhat of their
first horror, which they had betwixt the fleets. After
they had attentively listened till such time as the sound 20
by little and little went from them, Eugenius, lifting up
his head, and taking notice of it, was the first who
congratulated to the rest that happy omen of our
Nation's victory : adding, we had [2] but this to desire
in confirmation of it, that we might hear no more of 25
that noise, which was now leaving the English coast.
When the rest had concurred in the same opinion,
Crites, a person of a sharp judgment, and somewhat
too delicate a taste in wit, which the world have mistaken
in him for ill-nature, said, smiling to us, that if the 30
concernment of this battle had not been so exceeding
great, he could scarce have wished the victory at the
price he knew he must pay for it, in being subject to
the reading and hearing of so many ill verses as he

---

[1] to break, BC.   [2] that we had, BC.

was sure would be made upon it [1]. Adding, that no
argument could scape some of those eternal rhymers,
who watch a battle with more diligence than the ravens
and birds of prey ; and the worst of them surest to be
5 first in upon the quarry : while the better able either
out of modesty writ not at all, or set that due value
upon their poems, as to let them be often called for [2]
and long expected ! ' There are some of those imper-
tinent people you speak of [3],' answered Lisideius, ' who
10 to my knowledge are already so provided, either way,
that they can produce not only a Panegyric upon the
victory, but, if need be, a Funeral Elegy on the Duke ;
and [4] after they have crowned his valour with many
laurels, at last [5] deplore the odds under which he fell,
15 concluding that his courage deserved a better destiny.'
All the company smiled at the conceit of Lisideius ; but
Crites, more eager than before, began to make particular
exceptions against some writers, and said, the public
magistrate ought to send betimes to forbid them ; and
20 that it concerned the peace and quiet of all honest
people, that ill poets should be as well silenced as
seditious preachers. ' In my opinion,' replied Eugenius,
you pursue your point too far ; for as to my own
particular, I am so great a lover of poesy, that I could
25 wish them all rewarded, who attempt but to do well ;
at least, I would not have them worse used than Sylla
the Dictator [6] did one of their brethren heretofore :—
Quem in concione vidimus (says Tully) *cum ei libellum
malus poeta de populo subjecisset, quod epigramma in eum
30 fecisset tantummodo alternis versibus longiusculis, statim
ex iis rebus quas tunc vendebat jubere ei præmium tribui,*

---

[1] on that subject, BC.

[2] desired, BC.

[3] of whom you speak, BC.

[4] wherein, BC.

[5] they will at last, BC.

[6] than one of their brethren was by Sylla the Dictator, BC.

sub ea conditione ne quid postea scriberet.' ' I could wish
with all my heart,' replied Crites, ' that many whom we
know were as bountifully thanked upon the same condition,—that they would never trouble us again. For
amongst others, I have a mortal apprehension of two 5
poets, whom this victory, with the help of both her
wings, will never be able to escape.' ' 'Tis easy to
guess whom you intend,' said Lisideius ; ' and without
naming them, I ask you, if one of them does not perpetually pay us with clenches upon words, and a certain 10
clownish kind of raillery ? if now and then he does not
offer at a catachresis or Clevelandism, wresting and
torturing a word into another meaning : in fine, if he
be not one of those whom the French would call *un
mauvais buffon* ; one that [1] is so much a well-willer to 15
the satire, that he spares [2] no man ; and though he
cannot strike a blow to hurt any, yet ought [3] to be
punished for the malice of the action, as our witches are
justly hanged, because they think themselves so [4] ; and
suffer deservedly for believing they did mischief, because 20
they meant it.' ' You have described him,' said Crites,
' so exactly, that I am afraid to come after you with my
other extremity of poetry. He is one of those who,
having had some advantage of education and converse,
knows better than the other what a poet should be, but 25
puts it into practice more unluckily than any man ; his
style and matter are everywhere alike : he is the most
calm, peaceable writer you ever read : he never dis-
quiets your passions with the least concernment, but
still leaves you in as even a temper as he found you ; 30
he is a very Leveller in poetry : he creeps along with
ten little words in every line, and helps out his numbers
with *For to*, and *Unto*, and all the pretty expletives he

[1] who, BC.
[2] intends at least to spare, BC.
[3] he ought, BC.
[4] think themselves to be such, BC.

can find, till he drags them to the end of another line ;
while the sense is left tired half way behind it : he
doubly starves all his verses, first for want of thought,
and then of expression ; his poetry neither has wit in it,
5 nor seems to have it ; like him in Martial :

Pauper videri Cinna *vult, et est pauper.*

' He affects plainness, to cover his want of imagination : when he writes the serious way, the highest
flight of his fancy is some miserable antithesis, or
10 seeming contradiction ; and in the comic he is still
reaching at some thin conceit, the ghost of a jest, and
that too flies before him, never to be caught ; these
swallows which we see before us on the Thames are
the just resemblance of his wit : you may observe
15 how near the water they stoop, how many proffers
they make to dip, and yet how seldom they touch it ;
and when they do, 'tis but the surface : they skim over
it but to catch a gnat, and then mount into the air and
leave it.'

20 ' Well, gentlemen,' said Eugenius, ' you may speak
your pleasure of these authors ; but though I and some
few more about the town may give you a peaceable
hearing, yet assure yourselves, there are multitudes
who would think you malicious and them injured :
25 especially him whom you first described ; he is the
very Withers of the city : they have bought more
editions of his works than would serve to lay under
all their pies at the Lord Mayor's Christmas. When
his famous poem first came out in the year 1660, I have
30 seen them reading it in the midst of 'Change time ; nay
so vehement they were at it, that they lost their bargain
by the candles' ends ; but what will you say, if he has
been received amongst the great ones [1] ? I can assure

---

[1] amongst great persons, BC.

you he is, this day, the envy of a great Person [1] who is
lord in the art of quibbling ; and who does not take it
well, that any man should intrude so far into his province.' ' All I would wish,' replied Crites, ' is that they
who love his writings, may still admire him, and his 5
fellow poet : *Qui Bavium non odit, &c.*, is curse sufficient.' ' And farther,' added Lisideius, ' I believe
there is no man who writes well, but would think
himself very hardly dealt with [2], if their admirers should
praise anything of his : *Nam quos contemnimus, eorum* 10
quoque laudes contemnimus.' ' There are so few who
write well in this age,' says Crites, ' that methinks any
praises should be welcome ; they neither rise to the
dignity of the last age, nor to any of the Ancients :
and we may cry out of the writers of this time, with 15
more reason than Petronius of his, *Pace vestrâ liceat*
dixisse, primi omnium eloquentiam perdidistis : you have
debauched the true old poetry so far, that Nature,
which is the soul of it, is not in any of your writings.'

' If your quarrel,' said Eugenius, ' to those who now 20
write, be grounded only on your reverence to antiquity,
there is no man more ready to adore those great Greeks
and Romans than I am : but on the other side, I cannot
think so contemptibly of the age I live in [3], or so dis-
honourably of my own country, as not to judge we equal 25
the Ancients in most kinds of poesy, and in some
surpass them ; neither know I any reason why I may
not be as zealous for the reputation of our age, as we
find the Ancients themselves [4] in reference to those
who lived before them. For you hear your Horace 30
saying,

Indignor quidquam reprehendi, non quia crasse
Compositum, illepidève putetur, sed quia nuper.

[1] one, BC.   [2] think he had hard measure, BC.
[3] in which I live, BC.   [4] themselves were, BC,

And after :

Si meliora dies, ut vina, poemata reddit,
Scire velim, pretium chartis quotus arroget annus?

'But I see I am engaging in a wide dispute, where
5 the arguments are not like to reach close on either
side ; for Poesy is of so large an extent, and so many
both of the Ancients and Moderns have done well in
all kinds of it, that in citing one against the other, we
shall take up more time this evening than each man's
10 occasions will allow him : therefore I would ask Crites
to what part of Poesy he would confine his arguments,
and whether he would defend the general cause of the
Ancients against the Moderns, or oppose any age of the
Moderns against this of ours ? '

15   Crites, a little while considering upon this demand,
told Eugenius he approved his propositions, and if he
pleased [1], he would limit their dispute to Dramatic Poesy ;
in which he thought it not difficult to prove, either that
the Ancients were superior to the Moderns, or the last
20 age to this of ours.

Eugenius was somewhat surprised, when he heard
Crites make choice of that subject. ' For ought I see,'
said he, ' I have undertaken a harder province than
I imagined ; for though I never judged the plays of the
25 Greek or Roman poets comparable to ours, yet, on the
other side, those we now see acted come short of many
which were written in the last age : but my comfort is,
if we are o'ercome, it will be only by our own countrymen : and if we yield to them in this one part of poesy,
30 we more surpass them in all the other : for in the epic
or lyric way, it will be hard for them to show us one
such amongst them, as we have many now living, or
who lately were so [2] : they can produce nothing so courtly

---

[1] told Eugenius that if he pleased, BC.   [2] *om.* so, BC.

writ, or which expresses so much the conversation of a gentleman, as Sir John Suckling ; nothing so even, sweet, and flowing, as Mr. Waller ; nothing so majestic, so correct, as Sir John Denham ; nothing so elevated, so copious, and full of spirit, as Mr. Cowley ; as for 5 the Italian, French, and Spanish plays, I can make it evident, that those who now write surpass them ; and that the Drama is wholly ours.'

All of them were thus far of Eugenius his opinion, that the sweetness of English verse was never under- 10 stood or practised by our fathers ; even Crites himself did not much oppose it : and every one was willing to acknowledge how much our poesy is improved by the happiness of some writers yet living ; who first taught us to mould our thoughts into easy and significant 15 words ; to retrench the superfluities of expression, and to make our rime [1] so properly a part of the verse, that it should never mislead the sense, but itself be led and governed by it.

Eugenius was going to continue this discourse, when 20 Lisideius told him it was [2] necessary, before they proceeded further, to take a standing measure of their controversy ; for how was it possible to be decided who writ the best plays, before we know what a play should be ? But, this once agreed on by both parties, each 25 might have recourse to it, either to prove his own advantages, or to discover the failings of his adversary.

He had no sooner said this, but all desired the favour of him to give the definition of a play ; and they were the more importunate, because neither Aristotle, nor 30 Horace, nor any other, who writ [3] of that subject, had ever done it.

Lisideius, after some modest denials, at last confessed

---

[1] so AB ; rhyme, C.   [2] that it was, BC.
[3] had writ, BC.

he had a rude notion of it ; indeed, rather a description than a definition ; but which served to guide him in his private thoughts, when he was to make a judgment of what others writ : that he conceived a play ought to
5 be, *A just and lively image of human nature, representing its passions and humours, and the changes of fortune to which it is subject, for the delight and instruction of mankind.*

This definition, though Crites raised a logical objec-
10 tion against it ; that it was only *a genere et fine,* and so not altogether perfect ; was yet well received by the rest : and after they had given order to the watermen to turn their barge, and row softly, that they might take the cool of the evening in their return, Crites, being
15 desired by the company to begin, spoke on behalf of the Ancients, in this manner :

'If confidence presage a victory, Eugenius, in his own opinion, has already triumphed over the Ancients : nothing seems more easy to him, than to overcome
20 those whom it is our greatest praise to have imitated well ; for we do not only build upon their foundation [1], but by their models. Dramatic Poesy had time enough, reckoning from Thespis (who first invented it) to Aristophanes, to be born, to grow up, and to flourish in
25 maturity. It has been observed of arts and sciences, that in one and the same century they have arrived to a great [2] perfection ; and no wonder, since every age has a kind of universal genius, which inclines those that live in it to some particular studies : the work then
30 being pushed on by many hands, must of necessity go forward.

'Is it not evident, in these last hundred years (when the study of philosophy has been the business of all the Virtuosi in Christendom), that almost a new Nature has

---

[1] foundations, BC.   [2] to great, BC.

been revealed to us ?—that more errors of the school have been detected, more useful experiments in philosophy have been made, more noble secrets in optics, medicine, anatomy, astronomy, discovered, than in all those credulous and doting ages from Aristotle to us ?— 5 so true is it, that nothing spreads more fast than science, when rightly and generally cultivated.

'Add to this, the more than common emulation that was in those times of writing well ; which though it be found in all ages and all persons that pretend 10 to the same reputation, yet Poesy, being then in more esteem than now it is, had greater honours decreed to the professors of it, and consequently the rivalship was more high between them ; they had judges ordained to decide their merit, and prizes to reward it ; and his- 15 torians have been diligent to record of Eschylus, Euripides, Sophocles, Lycophron, and the rest of them, both who they were that vanquished in these wars of the theatre, and how often they were crowned : while the Asian kings and Grecian commonwealths scarce 20 afforded them a nobler subject than the unmanly luxuries of a debauched court, or giddy intrigues of a factious city. *Alit æmulatio ingenia,* (says Paterculus,) *et nunc invidia, nunc admiratio incitationem accendit* : Emulation is the spur of wit ; and sometimes envy, sometimes 25 admiration, quickens our endeavours.

'But now, since the rewards of honour are taken away, that virtuous emulation is turned into direct malice ; yet so slothful, that it contents itself to condemn and cry down others, without attempting to do 30 better : 'tis a reputation too unprofitable, to take the necessary pains for it ; yet, wishing they had it [1] is incitement enough to hinder others from it. And this, in short, Eugenius, is the reason why you have now so

---

[1] wishing they had it, that desire, BC.

few good poets, and so many severe judges. Certainly,
to imitate the Ancients well, much labour and long study
is required ; which pains, I have already shown, our
poets would want encouragement to take, if yet they
5 had ability to go through with it [1]. Those Ancients
have been faithful imitators and wise observers of that
Nature which is so torn and ill represented in our
plays ; they have handed down to us a perfect resemblance of her ; which we, like ill copiers, neglecting to
10 look on, have rendered monstrous, and disfigured. But,
that you may know how much you are indebted to those
your masters, and be ashamed to have so ill requited
them, I must remember you, that all the rules by which
we practise the Drama at this day, (either such as relate to
15 the justness and symmetry of the plot, or the episodical
ornaments, such as descriptions, narrations, and other
beauties, which are not essential to the play,) were
delivered to us from the observations which Aristotle
made, of those poets, which [2] either lived before him,
20 or were his contemporaries : we have added nothing of
our own, except we have the confidence to say our wit
is better ; of which none boast in this our age, but such
as understand not theirs. Of that book which Aristotle
has left us, περὶ τῆς Ποιητικῆς, Horace his *Art of Poetry* is
25 an excellent comment, and, I believe, restores to us
that Second Book of his concerning *Comedy*, which is
wanting in him.

‘ Out of these two have [3] been extracted the famous
Rules, which the French call *Des Trois Unitez*, or, the
30 Three Unities, which ought to be observed in every
regular play ; namely, of Time, Place, and Action.

‘ The Unity of Time they comprehend in twenty-four
hours, the compass of a natural day, or as near as it
can be contrived ; and the reason of it is obvious to

[1] through the work, BC.   [2] who, BC.   [3] has, A.

every one,—that the time of the feigned action, or fable
of the play, should be proportioned as near as can be to
the duration of that time in which it is represented :
since therefore, all plays are acted on the theatre in
a space of time much within the compass of twenty-four 5
hours, that play is to be thought the nearest imitation
of nature, whose plot or action is confined within that
time ; and, by the same rule which concludes this
general proportion of time, it follows, that all the parts
of it are [1] to be equally subdivided ; as namely [2], that 10
one act take not up the supposed time of half a day,
which is out of proportion to the rest ; since the other
four are then to be straitened within the compass of the
remaining half : for it is unnatural that one act, which
being spoke or written is not longer than the rest, 15
should be supposed longer by the audience ; 'tis therefore the poet's duty, to take care that no act should be
imagined to exceed the time in which it is represented
on the stage ; and that the intervals and inequalities of
time be supposed to fall out between the acts.   20

' This rule of time, how well it has been observed
by the Ancients, most of their plays will witness ; you
see them in their tragedies, (wherein to follow this rule,
is certainly most difficult,) from the very beginning of
their plays, falling close into that part of the story which 25
they intend for the action or principal object of it, leaving
the former part to be delivered by narration : so that
they set the audience, as it were, at the post where the
race is to be concluded ; and, saving them the tedious
expectation of seeing the poet set out and ride the 30
beginning of the course, you behold him not [3] till he is
in sight of the goal, and just upon you.

' For the second Unity, which is that of Place, the

---

[1] are (as near as may be), BC.   [2] *om.* as BC.
[3] they suffer you not to behold him, BC.

Ancients meant by it, that the scene ought to be continued through the play, in the same place where it
was laid in the beginning : for the stage on which it is
represented being but one and the same place, it is un-
5 natural to conceive it many ; and those far distant from
one another. I will not deny but, by the variation of
painted scenes, the fancy, which in these cases will
contribute to its own deceit, may sometimes imagine it
several places, with some appearance of probability ;
10 yet it still carries the greater likelihood of truth, if those
places be supposed so near each other, as in the same
town or city ; which may all be comprehended under
the larger denomination of one place ; for a greater
distance will bear no proportion to the shortness of
15 time which is allotted in the acting, to pass from one
of them to another ; for the observation of this, next to
the Ancients, the French are to be most commended.
They tie themselves so strictly to the Unity of Place,
that you never see in any of their plays, a scene changed
20 in the middle of an act : if the act begins in a garden,
a street, or chamber, 'tis ended in the same place ; and
that you may know it to be the same, the stage is so
supplied with persons, that it is never empty all the
time : he that enters the second [1], has business with him
25 who was on before ; and before the second quits the
stage, a third appears who has business with him. This
Corneille [2] calls *la liaison des scenes*, the continuity or
joining of the scenes ; and 'tis a good mark of a well-
contrived play, when all the persons are known to each
30 other, and every one of them has some affairs with all
the rest.

' As for the third Unity, which is that of Action, the
Ancients meant no other by it than what the logicians
do by their *finis*, the end or scope of any action ; that

---

[1] who enters second, BC.   [2] Corneil, A.

which is the first in intention, and last in execution :
now the poet is to aim at one great and complete
action, to the carrying on of which all things in his
play, even the very obstacles, are to be subservient ;
and the reason of this is as evident as any of the 5
former.

' For two actions, equally laboured and driven on by
the writer, would destroy the unity of the poem ; it
would be no longer one play, but two : not but that
there may be many actions in a play, as Ben Johnson 10
has observed in his *Discoveries* ; but they must be all
subservient to the great one, which our language happily
expresses in the name of *under-plots* : such as in
Terence's *Eunuch* is the difference and reconcilement
of Thais and Phædria, which is not the chief business 15
of the play, but promotes the marriage of Chærea and
Chremes's sister, principally intended by the poet.
There ought to be but one action, says Corneille, that
is, one complete action which leaves the mind of the
audience in a full repose ; but this cannot be brought 20
to pass but by many other imperfect actions, which
conduce to it, and hold the audience in a delightful
suspense of what will be.

' If by these rules (to omit many other drawn from
the precepts and practice of the Ancients) we should 25
judge our modern plays, 'tis probable that few of them
would endure the trial : that which should be the business of a day, takes up in some of them an age ; instead
of one action, they are the epitomes of a man's life ;
and for one spot of ground (which the stage should 30
represent) we are sometimes in more countries than the
map can show us.

' But if we will allow the Ancients to have contrived
well, we must acknowledge them to have writ [1] better ;

[1] written, BC.

questionless we are deprived of a great stock of wit in
the loss of Menander among the Greek poets, and of
Cæcilius, Afranius, and Varius, among the Romans ;
we may guess at Menander's excellency by the plays
5 of Terence, who translated some of his [1] ; and yet
wanted so much of him, that he was called by C. Caesar
the half-Menander ; and may judge [2] of Varius, by the
testimonies of Horace, Martial, and Velleius Paterculus.
'Tis probable that these, could they be recovered, would
10 decide the controversy ; but so long as Aristophanes in
the old Comedy, and Plautus in the new [3] are extant,
while the tragedies of Euripides, Sophocles, and Seneca,
are to be had [4], I can never see one of those plays which
are now written, but it increases my admiration of the
15 Ancients. And yet I must acknowledge farther, that to
admire them as we ought, we should understand them
better than we do. Doubtless many things appear flat
to us, whose wit [5] depended on some custom or story,
which never came to our knowledge ; or perhaps on
20 some criticism in their language, which being so long
dead, and only remaining in their books, 'tis not possible
they should make us know it perfectly [6]. To read
Macrobius, explaining the propriety and elegancy of
many words in Virgil, which I had before passed over
25 without consideration, as common things, is enough to
assure me that I ought to think the same of Terence ;
and that in the purity of his style (which Tully so much
valued that he ever carried his works about him) there
is yet left in him great room for admiration, if I knew
30 but where to place it. In the mean time I must desire
you to take notice, that the greatest man of the last

[1] them, BC.   [2] A *om.* may judge.
[3] ' in the old Comedy,' ' in the new,' *om.* BC.
[4] are in our hands, BC.   [5] the wit of which, BC.
[6] understand perfectly, BC.

age (Ben Johnson) was willing to give place to them in all things : he was not only a professed imitator of Horace, but a learned plagiary of all the others ; you track him every where in their snow : if Horace, Lucan, Petronius Arbiter, Seneca, and Juvenal, had their own 5 from him, there are few serious thoughts which are new in him : you will pardon me, therefore, if I presume he loved their fashion, when he wore their clothes. But since I have otherwise a great veneration for him, and you, Eugenius, prefer him above all 10 other poets, I will use no farther argument to you than his example : I will produce Father Ben to you [1], dressed in all the ornaments and colours of the Ancients ; you will need no other guide to our party, if you follow him ; and whether you consider the bad plays of our age, or 15 regard the good ones [2] of the last, both the best and worst of the modern poets will equally instruct you to esteem [3] the Ancients.'

Crites had no sooner left speaking, but Eugenius, who had [4] waited with some impatience for it, thus 20 began :

' I have observed in your speech, that the former part of it is convincing as to what the Moderns have profited by the rules of the Ancients ; but in the latter you are careful to conceal how much they have excelled 25 them ; we own all the helps we have from them, and want neither veneration nor gratitude while we acknowledge that to overcome them we must make use of the advantages we have received from them : but to these assistances we have joined our own industry ; for, had 30 we sat down with a dull imitation of them, we might then have lost somewhat of the old perfection, but never acquired any that was new. We draw not therefore

[1] before you Father Ben, BC.

[2] good plays, BC.

[3] admire, BC.

[4] A *om.* had.

after their lines, but those of Nature ; and having the
life before us, besides the experience of all they knew,
it is no wonder if we hit some airs and features which
they have missed. I deny not what you urge of arts
5 and sciences, that they have flourished in some ages
more than others ; but your instance in philosophy
makes for me : for if natural causes be more known
now than in the time of Aristotle, because more studied,
it follows that poesy and other arts may, with the same
10 pains, arrive still nearer to perfection ; and, that granted,
it will rest for you to prove that they wrought more
perfect images of human life than we ; which seeing in
your discourse you have avoided to make good, it shall
now be my task to show you some part of their defects,
15 and some few excellencies of the Moderns. And I think
there is none among us can imagine I do it enviously,
or with purpose to detract from them ; for what interest
of fame or profit can the living lose by the reputation of
the dead ? On the other side, it is a great truth
20 which Velleius Paterculus affirms : *Audita visis libentius
laudamus ; et præsentia invidia, præterita admiratione
prosequimur ; et his nos obrui, illis instrui credimus :* that
praise or censure is certainly the most sincere, which
unbribed posterity shall give us.

25   ' Be pleased then in the first place to take notice,
that the Greek poesy, which Crites has affirmed to
have arrived to perfection in the reign of the Old
Comedy, was so far from it, that the distinction of
it into acts was not known to them ; or if it were, it
30 is yet so darkly delivered to us that we cannot make
it out.

   ' All we know of it is, from the singing of their
Chorus ; and that too is so uncertain, that in some of
their plays we have reason to conjecture they sung
35 more than five times. Aristotle indeed divides the

integral parts of a play into four. First, the *Protasis,*
or entrance, which gives light only to the characters
of the persons, and proceeds very little into any part of
the action. Secondly, the *Epitasis,* or working up of
the plot ; where the play grows warmer, the design 5
or action of it is drawing on, and you see something
promising that it will come to pass. Thirdly, the
Catastasis, or counterturn [1], which destroys that expectation, imbroils the action in new difficulties, and leaves
you far distant from that hope in which it found you ; 10
as you may have observed in a violent stream resisted
by a narrow passage,—it runs round to an eddy, and
carries back the waters with more swiftness than it
brought them on. Lastly, the *Catastrophe,* which the
Grecians called λύσις [2], the French *le denouement,* and 15
we the discovery or unravelling of the plot : there you
see all things settling again upon their first foundations ; and, the obstacles which hindered the design
or action of the play once removed, it ends with that
resemblance of truth and nature, that the audience 20
are satisfied with the conduct of it. Thus this great
man delivered to us the image of a play ; and I must
confess it is so lively, that from thence much light has
been derived to the forming it more perfectly into acts
and scenes : but what poet first limited to five the 25
number of the acts, I know not ; only we see it so
firmly established in the time of Horace, that he gives
it for a rule in comedy ; *Neu brevior quinto, neu sit productior actu.* So that you see the Grecians cannot be
said to have consummated this art ; writing rather by 30
entrances, than by acts, and having rather a general

---

[1] Thirdly, the *Catastasis,* called by the Romans *Status,* the height
and full growth of the play : we may call it properly the counterturn, BC.

[2] δέσις, A.

indigested notion of a play, than knowing how and
where to bestow the particular graces of it.

' But since the Spaniards at this day allow but three
acts, which they call *Jornadas*, to a play, and the
5 Italians in many of theirs follow them, when I condemn the Ancients, I declare it is not altogether
because they have not five acts to every play, but
because they have not confined themselves to one
certain number : it is building an house without a
10 model ; and when they succeeded in such undertakings,
they ought to have sacrificed to Fortune, not to the
Muses.

' Next, for the plot, which Aristotle called τὸ μῦθος,
and often τῶν πραγμάτων σύνθεσις, and from him the
15 Romans *Fabula*, it has already been judiciously observed by a late writer, that in their tragedies it was
only some tale derived from Thebes or Troy, or at least
something that happened in those two ages ; which was
worn so threadbare by the pens of all the epic poets,
20 and even by tradition itself of the talkative Greeklings,
(as Ben Johnson calls them,) that before it came upon
the stage, it was already known to all the audience :
and the people, so soon as ever they heard the name of
Œdipus, knew as well as the poet, that he had killed
25 his father by a mistake, and committed incest with his
mother, before the play ; that they were now to hear of
a great plague, an oracle, and the ghost of Laius : so
that they sat with a yawning kind of expectation, till he
was to come with his eyes pulled out, and speak a hun-
30 dred or two of verses [1] in a tragic tone, in complaint of
his misfortunes. But one Œdipus, Hercules, or Medea,
had been tolerable : poor people, they scaped not so
good cheap ; they had still the *chapon bouillé* set before
them till their appetites were cloyed with the same

---

[1] hundred or more verses, BC.

dish, and, the novelty being gone, the pleasure vanished ;
so that one main end of Dramatic Poesy in its definition, which was to cause delight, was of consequence
destroyed.

' In their comedies, the Romans generally borrowed 5
their plots from the Greek poets ; and theirs was commonly a little girl stolen or wandered from her parents,
brought back unknown to the same city [1], there got with
child by some lewd young fellow, who, by the help of
his servant, cheats his father ; and when her time comes, 10
to cry *Juno Lucina, fer opem*, one or other sees a little
box or cabinet which was carried away with her, and so
discovers her to her friends, if some god do not prevent
it, by coming down in a machine, and take [2] the thanks
of it to himself.   15

' By the plot you may guess much of the characters
of the persons. An old father, who would willingly,
before he dies, see his son well married ; his debauched
son, kind in his nature to his wench [3], but miserably
in want of money ; a servant or slave, who has so 20
much wit to strike in with him, and help to dupe his
father ; a braggadochio captain, a parasite, and a lady of
pleasure.

' As for the poor honest maid, whom all the story is
built upon [4], and who ought to be one of the principal 25
actors in the play, she is commonly a mute in it : she
has the breeding of the old Elizabeth way [5], for maids
to be seen and not to be heard ; and it is enough you
know she is willing to be married, when the fifth act
requires it.   30

' These are plots built after the Italian mode of
houses ; you see through them all at once : the characters are indeed the imitations of Nature, but so

---

[1] *om.* same, BC.   [2] taking, BC.   [3] Mistres, B ; Mistress, C.
[4] on whom the story is built, BC.   [5] way, which was, BC.

narrow, as if they had imitated only an eye or an hand, and did not dare to venture on the lines of a face, or the proportion of a body.

' But in how strait a compass soever they have bounded
5 their plots and characters, we will pass it by, if they have regularly pursued them, and perfectly observed those three Unities of Time, Place, and Action ; the knowledge of which you say is derived to us from them. But in the first place give me leave to tell you, that the
10 Unity of Place, however it might be practised by them, was never any of their rules : we neither find it in Aristotle, Horace, or any who have written of it, till in our age the French poets first made it a precept of the stage. The Unity of Time, even Terence himself (who
15 was the best and most regular of them) has neglected : his *Heautontimorumenos*, or *Self-Punisher*, takes up visibly two days ; therefore, says Scaliger, the two first acts concluding the first day were acted overnight ; the three last on the ensuing day [1] ; and Euripides, in tying
20 himself to one day, has committed an absurdity never to be forgiven him ; for in one of his tragedies he has made Theseus go from Athens to Thebes, which was about forty English miles, under the walls of it to give battle, and appear victorious in the next act ; and yet,
25 from the time of his departure to the return of the Nuntius, who gives the relation of his victory, Æthra and the Chorus have but thirty-six verses ; that [2] is not for every mile a verse.

' The like error is as evident in Terence his *Eunuch*,
30 when Laches, the old man, enters in a mistake the house [3] of Thais ; where, betwixt his exit and the entrance of Pythias, who comes to give an ample relation

---

[1] ' two days, says Scaliger, the two first acts concluding the first day, the three last the day ensuing,' BC.

[2] which, BC.   by mistake into the house, BC.

of the garboyles [1] he has raised within, Parmeno, who was left upon the stage, has not above five lines to speak. *C'est bien employer* [2] *un temps si court*, says the French poet, who furnished me with one of the observations : and almost all their tragedies will afford us 5 examples of the like nature.

' 'Tis true, they have kept the continuity, or, as you called it, *liaison des scenes*, somewhat better : two do not perpetually come in together, talk, and go out together ; and other two succeed them, and do the same through- 10 out the act, which the English call by the name of single scenes ; but the reason is, because they have seldom above two or three scenes, properly so called, in every act ; for it is to be accounted a new scene, not every time [3] the stage is empty ; but every person who 15 enters, though to others, makes it so ; because he introduces a new business. Now the plots of their plays being narrow, and the persons few, one of their acts was written in a less compass than one of our well-wrought scenes ; and yet they are often deficient even 20 in this. To go no further than Terence ; you find in the *Eunuch* Antipho entering single in the midst of the third act, after Cremes and Pythias were gone off ; in the same play you have likewise Dorias beginning the fourth act alone ; and after she had made a relation of 25 what was done at the Soldier's entertainment (which by the way was very inartificial, because she was presumed to speak directly to the audience, and to acquaint them with what was necessary to be known, but yet should have been so contrived by the poet as to have 30 been told by persons of the drama to one another, and so by them to have come to the knowledge of the people), she quits the stage, and Phædria enters next, alone

---

[1] give ample relation of the disorders, BC.   employé, A.

[3] not only every time, BC.

likewise : he also gives you an account of himself, and
of his returning from the country, in monologue ; to
which unnatural way of narration Terence is subject in
all his plays.   In his *Adelphi*, or Brothers, Syrus and
5 Demea enter after the scene was broken by the departure of Sostrata, Geta, and Canthara ; and indeed you
can scarce look into any of his comedies, where you will
not presently discover the same interruption.

' But as they have failed both in laying of their plots,
10 and managing of them [1], swerving from the rules of
their own art by misrepresenting Nature to us, in which
they have ill satisfied one intention of a play, which was
delight ; so in the instructive part they have erred
worse : instead of punishing vice and rewarding virtue,
15 they have often shown a prosperous wickedness, and an
unhappy piety : they have set before us a bloody image
of revenge in Medea, and given her dragons to convey
her safe from punishment ; a Priam and Astyanax mur-
dered, and Cassandra ravished, and the lust and murder
20 ending in the victory of him who acted them : in short,
there is no indecorum in any of our modern plays,
which if I would excuse, I could not shadow with some
authority from the Ancients.

' And one farther note of them let me leave you :
25 tragedies and comedies were not writ then as they are
now, promiscuously, by the same person ; but he who
found his genius bending to the one, never attempted
the other way.   This is so plain, that I need not instance
to you, that Aristophanes, Plautus, Terence, never any
30 of them writ a tragedy ; Æschylus, Euripides, Sophocles, and Seneca, never meddled with comedy : the sock
and buskin were not worn by the same poet.   Having
then so much care to excel in one kind, very little is to
be pardoned them, if they miscarried in it ; and this

[1] in the management, BC.

would lead me to the consideration of their wit, had not Crites given me sufficient warning not to be too bold in my judgment of it ; because, the languages being dead, and many of the customs and little accidents on which it depended lost to us, we are not competent judges of 5 it. But though I grant that here and there we may miss the application of a proverb or a custom, yet a thing well said will be wit in all languages ; and though it may lose something in the translation, yet to him who reads it in the original, 'tis still the same : he has an 10 idea of its excellency, though it cannot pass from his mind into any other expression or words than those in which he finds it. When Phædria, in the *Eunuch*, had a command from his mistress to be absent two days, and, encouraging himself to go through with it, said, 15 *Tandem ego non illa caream, si sit opus* [1], *vel totum triduum ?*—Parmeno, to mock the softness of his master, lifting up his hands and eyes, cries out, as it were in admiration, *Hui ! universum triduum !* the elegancy of which *universum*, though it cannot be rendered in our 20 language, yet leaves an impression on our souls : but this happens seldom in him ; in Plautus oftener, who is infinitely too bold in his metaphors and coining words, out of which many times his wit is nothing ; which questionless was one reason why Horace falls upon 25 him so severely in those verses :—

> *Sed proavi nostri Plautinos et numeros et*
> *Laudavere sales, nimium patienter utrumque,*
> *Ne dicam stolidè.*

For Horace himself was cautious to obtrude a new word 30 on his readers, and makes custom and common use the best measure of receiving it into our writings :

> *Multa renascentur quae nunc cecidere, cadentque*
> *Quae nunc sunt in honore vocabula, si volet usus,*
> *Quem penes arbitrium est, et jus, et norma loquendi.* 35

[1] si opus sit, A.

' The not observing this rule is that which the world has blamed in our satyrist, Cleveland : to express a thing hard and unnaturally, is his new way of elocution. 'Tis true, no poet but may sometimes use a catachresis : 5 Virgil does it—

> *Mistaque ridenti colocasia fundet acantho—*

in his eclogue of *Pollio* ; and in his 7th *Æneid.*

> *. . . mirantur et undae,*
> *Miratur nemus insuetum fulgentia longe*
> 10 *Scuta virum fluvio pictasque innare carinas.*

And Ovid once so modestly, that he asks leave to do it :

> *. . . quem, si verbo audacia detur,*
> *Haud metuam summi dixisse Palatia caeli :*

calling the court of Jupiter by the name of Augustus 15 his palace ; though in another place he is more bold, where he says,—*et longas visent Capitolia pompas.* But to do this always, and never be able to write a line without it, though it may be admired by some few pedants, will not pass upon those who know that wit 20 is best conveyed to us in the most easy language ; and is most to be admired when a great thought comes dressed in words so commonly received, that it is understood by the meanest apprehensions, as the best meat is the most easily digested : but we cannot read 25 a verse of Cleveland's without making a face at it, as if every word were a pill to swallow : he gives us many times a hard nut to break our teeth, without a kernel for our pains. So that there is this difference betwixt his *Satires* and doctor Donne's ; that the one gives 30 us deep thoughts in common language, though rough cadence ; the other gives as common thoughts in abstruse words : 'tis true, in some places his wit is independent of his words, as in that of the *Rebel Scot* :

> Had *Cain* been *Scot*, God would have chang'd his doom ;
> 35   Not forc'd him wander, but confin'd him home.

' *Si sic omnia dixisset!* This is wit in all languages :
'tis like Mercury, never to be lost or killed :—and so
that other—

> For beauty, like white powder, makes no noise,
> And yet the silent hypocrite destroys. 5

You see, the last line is highly metaphorical, but it is
so soft and gentle, that it does not shock us as we
read it.

' But, to return from whence I have digressed, to the
consideration of the Ancients' writing, and their wit ; of 10
which by this time you will grant us in some measure to
be fit judges. Though I see many excellent thoughts
in Seneca, yet he of them who had a genius most proper
for the stage, was Ovid ; he had a way of writing so fit
to stir up a pleasing admiration and concernment, which 15
are the objects of a tragedy, and to show the various
movements of a soul combating betwixt two different
passions, that, had he lived in our age, or in his own
could have writ with our advantages, no man but must
have yielded to him ; and therefore I am confident the 20
Medea is none of his : for, though I esteem it for the
gravity and sententiousness of it, which he himself
concludes to be suitable to a tragedy,—*Omne genus
scripti gravitate tragaedia vincit,*—yet it moves not my
soul enough to judge that he, who in the epic way wrote 25
things so near the drama as the story of Myrrha, of
Caunus and Biblis, and the rest, should stir up no more
concernment where he most endeavoured it. The
master-piece of Seneca I hold to be that scene in the
Troades, where Ulysses is seeking for Astyanax to kill 30
him ; there you see the tenderness of a mother so
represented in Andromache, that it raises compassion
to a high degree in the reader, and bears the nearest
resemblance of any thing in their tragedies [1] to the

---

[1] in the tragedies of the ancients, BC.

excellent scenes of passion in Shakespeare, or in
Fletcher : for love-scenes, you will find few among
them ; their tragic poets dealt not with that soft passion,
but with lust, cruelty, revenge, ambition, and those
5 bloody actions they produced ; which were more capable
of raising horror than compassion in an audience :
leaving love untouched, whose gentleness would have
tempered them, which is the most frequent of all the
passions, and which being the private concernment of
10 every person, is soothed by viewing its own image in
a public entertainment.

' Among their comedies, we find a scene or two of
tenderness, and that where you would least expect it,
in Plautus ; but to speak generally, their lovers say
15 little, when they see each other, but *anima mea, vita
mea :* ζωη καὶ ψυχη, as the women in Juvenal's time
used to cry out in the fury of their kindness : then indeed
to speak sense were an offence [1]. Any sudden gust of
passion (as an extasy of love in an unexpected meeting)
20 cannot better be expressed than in a word and a sigh,
breaking one another. Nature is dumb on such occasions ; and to make her speak, would be to represent
her unlike herself. But there are a thousand other
concernments of lovers, as jealousies, complaints, con-
25 trivances, and the like, where not to open their minds
at large to each other, were to be wanting to their own
love, and to the expectation of the audience ; who
watch the movements of their minds, as much as the
changes of their fortunes. For the imaging of the first
30 is properly the work of a poet ; the latter he borrows
of [2] the historian.'

Eugenius was proceeding in that part of his discourse,
when Crites interrupted him. ' I see,' said he, ' Eugenius
and I are never like to have this question decided

---

[1] ' then indeed ' &c. *om.* BC.   [2] from, BC.

betwixt us ; for he maintains the Moderns have acquired a new perfection in writing ; I can only grant they have altered the mode of it. Homer described his heroes men of great appetites, lovers of beef broiled upon the coals, and good fellows ; contrary to the practice of the French Romances, whose heroes neither eat, nor drink, nor sleep, for love. Virgil makes Æneas a bold avower of his own virtues :

Sum pius Æneas, fama super aethera notus ;

which in the civility of our poets is the character of a fanfaron or Hector : for with us the knight takes occasion to walk out, or sleep, to avoid the vanity of telling his own story, which the trusty squire is ever to perform for him. So in their love-scenes, of which Eugenius spoke last, the Ancients were more hearty, we more talkative : they writ love as it was then the mode to make it ; and I will grant thus much to Eugenius, that perhaps one of their poets, had he lived in our age, *si foret hoc nostrum fato delapsus in ævum* (as Horace says of Lucilius), he had altered many things ; not that they were not as natural [1] before, but that he might accommodate himself to the age he lived in [2]. Yet in the mean time, we are not to conclude any thing rashly against those great men, but preserve to them the dignity of masters, and give that honour to their memories, *quos Libitina sacravit*, part of which we expect may be paid to us in future times.'

This moderation of Crites, as it was pleasing to all the company, so it put an end to that dispute ; which Eugenius, who seemed to have the better of the argument, would urge no farther : but Lisideius, after he had acknowledged himself of Eugenius his opinion concerning the Ancients, yet told him, he had forborne,

---

[1] as, *om.* BC.   [2] age in which he liv'd, BC.

till his discourse were ended, to ask him why he preferred the English plays above those of other nations ?
and whether we ought not to submit our stage to the
exactness of our next neighbours ?

5 ' Though,' said Eugenius, I am at all times ready to
defend the honour of my country against the French,
and to maintain, we are as well able to vanquish them
with our pens, as our ancestors have been with their
swords ; yet, if you please,' added he, looking upon
10 Neander, ' I will commit this cause to my friend's
management ; his opinion of our plays is the same with
mine : and besides, there is no reason, that Crites and
I, who have now left the stage, should re-enter so
suddenly upon it ; which is against the laws of comedy.'

15 ' If the question had been stated,' replied Lisideius,
' who had writ best, the French or English, forty years
ago, I should have been of your opinion, and adjudged
the honour to our own nation ; but since that time '
(said he, turning towards Neander) ' we have been so
20 long tôgether bad Englishmen, that we had not leisure
to be good poets. Beaumont, Fletcher, and Johnson
(who were only capable of bringing us to that degree of
perfection which we have) were just then leaving the
world ; as if (in an age of so much horror) wit, and those
25 milder studies of humanity, had no farther business
among us. But the Muses, who ever follow peace, went
to plant in another country : it was then that the great
Cardinal of Richelieu began to take them into his protection ; and that, by his encouragement, Corneille, and
30 some other Frenchmen, reformed their theatre, which
before was as much below ours, as it now surpasses it
and the rest of Europe. But because Crites in his
discourse for the Ancients has prevented me, by touching upon [1] many rules of the stage which the Moderns

[1] observing, BC.

have borrowed from them, I shall only, in short, demand
of you, whether you are not convinced that of all nations
the French have best observed them ?   In the Unity of
Time you find them so scrupulous, that it yet remains
a dispute among their poets, whether the artificial day 5
of twelve hours, more or less, be not meant by Aristotle,
rather than the natural one of twenty-four ; and consequently, whether all plays ought not to be reduced into
that compass.   This I can testify, that in all their
dramas writ within these last twenty years and upwards, 10
I have not observed any that have extended the time to
thirty. hours : in the Unity of Place they are full as
scrupulous ; for many of their critics limit it to that very
spot of ground where the play is supposed to begin ;
none of them exceed the compass of the same town or 15
city.   The Unity of Action in all plays is yet more conspicuous ; for they do not burden them with underplots,
as the English do : which is the reason why many
scenes of our tragi-comedies carry on a design that is
nothing of kin to the main plot ; and that we see two 20
distinct webs in a play, like those in ill-wrought stuffs ;
and two actions, that is, two plays, carried on together,
to the confounding of the audience ; who, before they
are warm in their concernments for one part, are
diverted to another ; and by that means espouse the 25
interest of neither.   From hence likewise it arises, that
the one half of our actors are not known to the other.
They keep their distances, as if they were Mountagues
and Capulets, and seldom begin an acquaintance till the
last scene of the fifth act, when they are all to meet 30
upon the stage.   There is no theatre in the world has
any thing so absurd as the English tragi-comedy ; 'tis
a drama of our own invention, and the fashion of it is
enough to proclaim it so ; here a course of mirth, there
another of sadness and passion, a third of honour, and 35

fourth a duel [1] : thus, in two hours and a half, we run
through all the fits of Bedlam. The French affords
you as much variety on the same day, but they do it
not so unseasonably, or *mal à propos*, as we : our poets
5 present you the play and the farce together ; and our
stages still retain somewhat of the orginal civility of
the *Red Bull* :

Atque ursum et pugiles media inter carmina poscunt.

The end of tragedies or serious plays, says Aristotle, is
10 to beget admiration, compassion, or concernment ; but
are not mirth and compassion things incompatible ?
and is it not evident that the poet must of necessity
destroy the former by intermingling of the latter ?   that
is, he must ruin the sole end and object of his tragedy,
15 to introduce somewhat that is forced in [2], and is not of
the body of it. Would you not think that physician
mad, who, having prescribed a purge, should immediately order you to take restringents upon it [3] ?

' But to leave our plays, and return to theirs. I have
20 noted one great advantage they have had in the plotting
of their tragedies ; that is, they are always grounded
upon some known history : according to that of Horace,
Ex noto fictum carmen sequar ; and in that they have so
imitated the Ancients, that they have surpassed them.
25 For the Ancients, as was observed before, took for the
foundation of their plays some poetical fiction, such as
under that consideration could move but little concernment in the audience, because they already knew the
event of it. But the French goes farther :

30   *Atque ita mentitur, sic veris falsa remiscet,*
        Primo ne medium, medio ne discrepet imum.

He so interweaves truth with probable fiction, that he

---

[1] and a third of honour, and a duel, BC.
[2] into it, BC.   [3] upon it, *om.* BC.

puts a pleasing fallacy upon us ; mends the intrigues of fate, and dispenses with the severity of history, to reward that virtue which has been rendered to us there unfortunate. Sometimes the story has left the success so doubtful, that the writer is free, by the privilege of [5] a poet, to take that which of two or more relations will best suit with his design : as for example, the [1] death of Cyrus, whom Justin and some others report to have perished in the Scythian war, but Xenophon affirms to have died in his bed of extreme old age. Nay more, [10] when the event is past dispute, even then we are willing to be deceived, and the poet, if he contrives it with appearance of truth, has all the audience of his party ; at least during the time his play is acting : so naturally we are kind to virtue, when our own interest is not in [15] question, that we take it up as the general concernment of mankind. On the other side, if you consider the historical plays of Shakespeare, they are rather so many chronicles of kings, or the business many times of thirty or forty years, cramped into a representation of [20] two hours and an half ; which is not to imitate or paint Nature, but rather to draw her in miniature, to take her in little ; to look upon her through the wrong end of a perspective, and receive her images not only much less, but infinitely more imperfect than the life : [25] this, instead of making a play delightful, renders it ridiculous :—

Quodcunque ostendis mihi sic, incredulus odi.

For the spirit of man cannot be satisfied but with truth, or at least verisimility ; and a poem is to contain, if not [30] τὰ ἔτυμα, yet ἐτύμοισιν ὁμοῖα, as one of the Greek poets has expressed it.

‘ Another thing in which the French differ from us

---

[1] in the death, BC.

and from the Spaniards, is, that they do not embarrass, or cumber themselves with too much plot ; they only represent so much of a story as will constitute one whole and great action sufficient for a play ; we, who
5 undertake more, do but multiply adventures ; which, not being produced from one another, as effects from causes, but barely following, constitute many actions in the drama, and consequently make it many plays.

' But by pursuing close [1] one argument, which is not
10 cloyed with many turns, the French have gained more liberty for verse, in which they write ; they have leisure to dwell on a subject which deserves it ; and to represent the passions (which we have acknowledged to be the poet's work), without being hurried from one
15 thing to another, as we are in the plays of Calderon, which we have seen lately upon our theatres, under the name of Spanish plots. I have taken notice but of one tragedy of ours, whose plot has that uniformity and unity of design in it, which I have commended in
20 the French ; and that is *Rollo*, or rather, under the name of Rollo, the story of Bassianus and Geta in Herodian : there indeed the plot is neither large nor intricate, but just enough to fill the minds of the audience, not to cloy them. Besides, you see it founded
25 upon the truth of history, only the time of the action is not reduceable to the strictness of the rules ; and you see in some places a little farce mingled, which is below the dignity of the other parts ; and in this all our poets are extremely peccant : even Ben Johnson himself, in
30 *Sejanus* and *Catiline*, has given us this oleo of a play, this unnatural mixture of comedy and tragedy ; which to me sounds just as ridiculously as the history of David with the merry humours of Golias [2]. In *Sejanus* you may take notice of the scene betwixt Livia and the

[1] closely, BC.   [2] Golia's, AB ; Goliah's, C.

physician, which is a pleasant satire upon the artificial helps of beauty : in *Catiline* you may see the parliament of women ; the little envies of them to one another ; and all that passes betwixt Curio and Fulvia : scenes admirable in their kind, but of an ill mingle with the rest. 5

'But I return again to the French writers, who, as I have said, do not burden themselves too much with plot, which has been reproached to them by an *ingenious person* of our nation as a fault ; for, he says, they commonly make but one person considerable in a play ; 10 they dwell on him, and his concernments, while the rest of the persons are only subservient to set him off. If he intends this by it, that there is one person in the play who is of greater dignity than the rest, he must tax, not only theirs, but those of the Ancients, and which 15 he would be loth to do, the best of ours ; for it is impossible but that one person must be more conspicuous in it than any other, and consequently the greatest share in the action must devolve on him. We see it so in the management of all affairs ; even in the most equal 20 aristocracy, the balance cannot be so justly poised, but some one will be superior to the rest, either in parts, fortune, interest, or the consideration of some glorious exploit ; which will reduce the greatest part of business into his hands. 25

'But, if he would have us to imagine, that in exalting one character the rest of them are neglected, and that all of them have not some share or other in the action of the play, I desire him to produce any of Corneille's tragedies, wherein every person, like so many servants 30 in a well-governed family, has not some employment, and who is not necessary to the carrying on of the plot, or at least to your understanding it.

'There are indeed some protatick persons in the Ancients, whom they make use of in their plays, either 35 to hear or give the relation : but the French avoid this with great address, making their narrations only to, or by such, who are some way interested in the main design. And now I am speaking of relations, I cannot 5 take a fitter opportunity to add this in favour of the French, that they often use them with better judgment and more *à propos* than the English do. Not that I commend narrations in general,—but there are two sorts of them. One, of those things which are ante- 10 cedent to the play, and are related to make the conduct of it more clear to us. But 'tis a fault to choose such subjects for the stage as will force us on that rock, because we see they are seldom listened to by the audience, and that is many times the ruin of the play ; 15 for, being once let pass without attention, the audience can never recover themselves to understand the plot : and indeed it is somewhat unreasonable that they should be put to so much trouble, as that, to comprehend what passes in their sight, they must have recourse to what 20 was done, perhaps, ten or twenty years ago.

'But there is another sort of relations, that is, of things happening in the action of the play, and supposed to be done behind the scenes ; and this is many times both convenient and beautiful ; for by it the French 25 avoid the tumult which we are subject to [1] in England, by representing duels, battles, and the like ; which renders our stage too like the theatres where they fight prizes. For what is more ridiculous than to represent an army with a drum and five men behind it ; all which 30 the hero of the other side is to drive in before him ; or to see a duel fought, and one slain with two or three thrusts of the foils, which we know are so blunted, that we might give a man an hour to kill another in good earnest with them.

[1] to which we are subject, BC.

' I have observed that in all our tragedies, the audience cannot forbear laughing when the actors are to die ; it is the most comic part of the whole play. All *passions* may be lively represented on the stage, if to the well-writing of them the actor supplies a good commanded voice, and limbs that move easily, and without stiffness ; but there are many *actions* which can never be imitated to a just height : dying especially is a thing which none but a Roman gladiator could naturally perform on the stage, when he did not imitate or represent, but naturally do it [1] ; and therefore it is better to omit the representation of it.

' The words of a good writer, which describe it lively, will make a deeper impression of belief in us than all the actor can persuade us to [2], when he seems to fall dead before us ; as a poet in the description of a beautiful garden, or a meadow, will please our imagination more than the place itself can please our sight. When we see death represented, we are convinced it is but fiction ; but when we hear it related, our eyes, the strongest witnesses, are wanting, which might have undeceived us ; and we are all willing to favour the sleight, when the poet does not too grossly impose on us. They therefore who imagine these relations would make no concernment in the audience, are deceived, by confounding them with the other, which are of things antecedent to the play : those are made often in cold blood, as I may say, to the audience ; but these are warmed with our concernments, which were before awakened in the play. What the philosophers say of motion, that, when it is once begun, it continues of itself, and will do so to eternity, without some stop put to it, is clearly true on this occasion : the soul, being already moved with the characters and fortunes of those

[1] naturally *om*, BC.　　　　[2] insinuate into us, BC.

imaginary persons, continues going of its own accord;
and we are no more weary to hear what becomes of
them when they are not on the stage, than we are to
listen to the news of an absent mistress.   But it is
5 objected, that if one part of the play may be related,
then why not all ?   I answer, some parts of the action
are more fit to be represented, some to be related.
Corneille says judiciously, that the poet is not obliged
to expose to view all particular actions which conduce
10 to the principal : he ought to select such of them to be
seen, which will appear with the greatest beauty, either
by the magnificence of the show, or the vehemence of
passions which they produce, or some other charm
which they have in them ; and let the rest arrive to
15 the audience by narration.   'Tis a great mistake in us
to believe the French present no part of the action
on the stage ; every alteration or crossing of a design,
every new-sprung passion, and turn of it, is a part
of the action, and much the noblest, except we conceive
20 nothing to be action till they come [1] to blows ; as if the
painting of the hero's mind were not more properly
the poet's work than the strength of his body.   Nor
does this anything contradict the opinion of Horace,
where he tells us,

25
> *Segnius irritant animos demissa per aurem,*
> *Quam quæ sunt oculis subjecta fidelibus.*

For he says immediately after,

> .   .   .   .   . *Non tamen intus*
> *Digna geri promes in scenam;* multaque *tolles*
> 30 *Ex oculis, quae mox narret facundia præsens.*

Among which many he recounts some :

> *Nec pueros coram populo Medea trucidet,*
> *Aut in avem Progne mutetur, Cadmus in anguem;* &c.

[1] the players come, BC.

That is, those actions which by reason of their cruelty will cause aversion in us, or by reason of their impossibility, unbelief, ought either wholly to be avoided by a poet, or only delivered by narration. To which we may have leave to add such as to avoid tumult (as was before hinted), or to reduce the plot into a more reasonable compass of time, or for defect of beauty in them, are rather to be related than presented to the eye. Examples of all these kinds are frequent, not only among all the Ancients, but in the best received of our English poets. We find Ben Johnson using them in his *Magnetick Lady*, where one comes out from dinner, and relates the quarrels and disorders of it, to save the undecent appearance of them on the stage, and to abbreviate the story; and this in express imitation of Terence, who had done the same before him in his *Eunuch*, where Pythias makes the like relation of what had happened within at the Soldier's entertainment. The relations likewise of Sejanus's death, and the prodigies before it, are remarkable; the one of which was hid from sight, to avoid the horror and tumult of the representation; the other, to shun the introducing of things impossible to be believed. In that excellent play, *The King and no King*, Fletcher goes yet farther; for the whole unravelling of the plot is done by narration in the fifth act, after the manner of the Ancients; and it moves great concernment in the audience, though it be only a relation of what was done many years before the play. I could multiply other instances, but these are sufficient to prove that there is no error in choosing a subject which requires this sort of narrations; in the ill managing [1] of them, there may.

'But I find I have been too long in this discourse, since the French have many other excellencies not

[1] management, BC.

common to us ; as that you never see any of their
plays end with a conversion, or simple change of will,
which is the ordinary way which our poets use to
end theirs. It shows little art in the conclusion of
5 a dramatic poem, when they who have hindered the
felicity during the four acts, desist from it in the fifth,
without some powerful cause to take them off [1] ; and
though I deny not but such reasons may be found, yet
it is a path that is cautiously to be trod, and the poet is
10 to be sure he convinces the audience that the motive
is strong enough. As for example, the conversion of
the Usurer in *The Scornful Lady*, seems to me a little
forced ; for, being an Usurer, which implies a lover of
money to the highest degree of covetousness (and such
15 the poet has represented him), the account he gives for
the sudden change is, that he has been duped by the
wild young fellow ; which in reason might render him
more wary another time, and make him punish himself with harder fare and coarser clothes, to get it up
20 again [2] : but that he should look on it as a judgment,
and so repent, we may expect to hear of [3] in a sermon,
but I should never endure it in a play.

' I pass by this ; neither will I insist on the care they
take, that no person after his first entrance shall ever
25 appear, but the business which brings him upon the
stage shall be evident ; which [4], if observed, must needs
render all the events in the play more natural ; for
there you see the probability of every accident, in the
cause that produced it ; and that which appears chance
30 in the play, will seem so reasonable to you, that you
will there find it almost necessary : so that in the exits
of the actors [5] you have a clear account of their [6] purpose

---

[1] off their design, BC.   [2] to get up again what he had lost, BC.

[3] of, *om.* BC.   [4] which rule, BC.

[5] exit of the actor, BC.   [6] his, BC.

and design in the next entrance (though, if the scene be
well wrought, the event will commonly deceive you),
for there is nothing so absurd, says Corneille, as for
an actor to leave the stage, only because he has no
more to say.   5
'I should now speak of the beauty of their rhyme,
and the just reason I have to prefer that way of writing
in tragedies before ours in blank-verse ; but because it
is partly received by us, and therefore not altogether
peculiar to them, I will say no more of it in relation 10
to their plays. For our own, I doubt not but it will
exceedingly beautify them ; and I can see but one
reason why it should not generally obtain, that is,
because our poets write so ill in it. This indeed may
prove a more prevailing argument than all others which 15
are used to destroy it, and therefore I am only troubled
when great and judicious poets, and those who are
acknowledged such, have writ or spoke against it : as
for others, they are to be answered by that one sentence
of an ancient author :—*Sed ut primo ad consequendos* 20
eos quos priores ducimus, accendimur, ita ubi aut præte-
riri, aut æquari eos posse desperavimus, studium cum spe
senescit : quod, scilicet, assequi non potest, sequi desinit ;
. . . præteritoque eo in quo eminere non possumus, aliquid
in quo nitamur, conquirimus.'   25
Lisideius concluded in this manner ; and Neander,
after a little pause, thus answered him :
'I shall grant Lisideius, without much dispute, a great
part of what he has urged against us ; for I acknowledge
that the French contrive their plots more regularly, and 30
observe the laws of comedy, and decorum of the stage
(to speak generally), with more exactness than the
English. Farther, I deny not but he has taxed us justly
in some irregularities of ours, which he has mentioned ;
yet, after all, I am of opinion that neither our faults 35

nor their virtues are considerable enough to place them
above us.

‘ For the lively imitation of Nature being in the definition of a play, those which best fulfil that law ought to
5 be esteemed superior to the others. 'Tis true, those
beauties of the French poesy are such as will raise perfection higher where it is, but are not sufficient to give
it where it is not : they are indeed the beauties of
a statue, but not of a man, because not animated with
10 the soul of Poesy, which is imitation of humour and
passions : and this Lisideius himself, or any other,
however biassed to their party, cannot but acknowledge, if he will either compare the humours of our
comedies, or the characters of our serious plays, with
15 theirs. He that [1] will look upon theirs which have
been written till these last ten years, or thereabouts,
will find it an hard matter to pick out two or three
passable humours amongst them. Corneille himself,
their arch-poet, what has he produced except *The Liar*,
20 and you know how it was cried up in France ; but
when it came upon the English stage, though well
translated, and that part of Dorant acted to so much
advantage by Mr. Hart [2] as I am confident it never
received in its own country, the most favourable to it
25 would not put it [3] in competition with many of Fletcher's
or Ben Johnson's. In the rest of Corneille's comedies
you have little humour ; he tells you himself, his way
is, first to show two lovers in good intelligence with
each other ; in the working up of the play to embroil
30 them by some mistake, and in the latter end to clear it,
and reconcile them [4]

‘ But of late years Molière [5], the younger Corneille,
Quinault, and some others, have been imitating afar

[1] He who, BC.   [2] ‘ by Mr. Hart,’ *om.* BC.
[3] A *om.* it.   [4] to clear it up, A.   [5] de Molière, A.

off [1] the quick turns and graces of the English stage. They have mixed their serious plays with mirth, like our tragi-comedies, since the death of Cardinal Richelieu ; which Lisideius and many others not observing, have commended that in them for a virtue which they them- 5 selves no longer practice. Most of their new plays are, like some of ours, derived from the Spanish novels. There is scarce one of them without a veil, and a trusty Diego, who drolls much after the rate of the *Adventures*. But their humours, if I may grace them with that name, 10 are so thin-sown, that never above one of them comes up in any play. I dare take upon me to find more variety of them in some one play of Ben Johnson's, than in all theirs together ; as he who has seen *The Alchymist, The Silent Woman*, or *Bartholomew-Fair*, 15 cannot but acknowledge with me.

' I grant the French have performed what was possible on the ground-work of the Spanish plays ; what was pleasant before, they have made regular : but there is not above one good play to be writ on all those plots; 20 they are too much alike to please often ; which we need not the experience of our own stage to justify. As for their new way of mingling mirth with serious plot, I do not, with Lisideius, condemn the thing, though I cannot approve their manner of doing it. He tells us, we 25 cannot so speedily recollect ourselves after a scene of great passion and concernment, as to pass to another of mirth and humour, and to enjoy it with any relish : but why should he imagine the soul of man more heavy than his senses ? Does not the eye pass from an un- 30 pleasant object to a pleasant in a much shorter time than is required to this ? and does not the unpleasantness of the first commend the beauty of the latter ? The old rule of logic might have convinced him, that

[1] of afar off, A.

contraries, when placed near, set off each other. A continued gravity keeps the spirit too much bent ; we must refresh it sometimes, as we bait in a journey, that we may go on with greater ease. A scene of mirth, mixed
5 with tragedy, has the same effect upon us which our music has betwixt the acts ; and that we find [1] a relief to us from the best plots and language of the stage, if the discourses have been long. I must therefore have stronger arguments, ere I am convinced that compassion
10 and mirth in the same subject destroy each other ; and in the mean time cannot but conclude, to the honour of our nation, that we have invented, increased, and perfected a more pleasant way of writing for the stage, than was ever known to the ancients or moderns of any
15 nation, which is tragi-comedy.

' And this leads me to wonder why Lisideius and many others should cry up the barrenness of the French plots, above the variety and copiousness of the English. Their plots are single ; they carry on
20 one design, which is pushed forward by all the actors, every scene in the play contributing and moving towards it. Our plays [2], besides the main design, have underplots or by-concernments, of less considerable persons and intrigues, which are carried on with the motion of
25 the main plot : just as [3] they say the orb of the fixed stars, and those of the planets, though they have motions of their own, are whirled about by the motion of the *Primum Mobile*, in which they are contained. That similitude expresses much of the English stage ; for if
30 contrary motions may be found in nature to agree ; if a planet can go east and west at the same time, one way by virtue of his own motion, the other by the force of the First Mover, it will not be difficult to imagine how the under-plot, which is only different, not contrary to

---

[1] which we find, BC.   [2] Ours, A.   [3] just, *om.* BC.

the great design, may naturally be conducted along with it.

' Eugenius has already shown us, from the confession of the French poets, that the Unity of Action is sufficiently preserved, if all the imperfect actions of 5 the play are conducing to the main design ; but when those petty intrigues of a play are so ill ordered, that they have no coherence with the other, I must grant that Lisideius has reason to tax that want of due connexion ; for co-ordination in a play is as dangerous and 10 unnatural as in a state. In the mean time he must acknowledge, our variety, if well ordered, will afford a greater pleasure to the audience.

' As for his other argument, that by pursuing one single theme they gain an advantage to express and 15 work up the passions, I wish any example he could bring from them would make it good ; for I confess their verses are to me the coldest I have ever read. Neither, indeed, is it possible for them, in the way they take, so to express passion, as that the effects of 20 it should appear in the concernment of an audience, their speeches being so many declamations, which tire us with the length ; so that instead of persuading us to grieve for their imaginary heroes, we are concerned for our own trouble, as we are in the tedious [1] visits of 25 bad company ; we are in pain till they are gone. When the French stage came to be reformed by Cardinal Richelieu, those long harangues were introduced, to comply with the gravity of a churchman. Look upon the *Cinna* and the *Pompey* ; they are not 30 so properly to be called plays, as long discourses of reason of state ; and *Polieucte* in matters of religion is as solemn as the long stops upon our organs. Since that time it is grown into a custom, and their actors

[1] the, *om.* BC.

speak by the hour-glass, as our parsons do [1] ; nay,
they account it the grace of their parts, and think
themselves disparaged by the poet, if they may not
twice or thrice in a play entertain the audience with
5 a speech of an hundred or two hundred lines [2]. I deny
not but this may suit well enough with the French ; for
as we, who are a more sullen people, come to be
diverted at our plays, so they, who are of an airy
and gay temper, come thither to make themselves
10 more serious : and this I conceive to be one reason
why comedy is [3] more pleasing to us, and tragedies
to them. But to speak generally : it cannot be denied
that short speeches and replies are more apt to move
the passions and beget concernment in us, than the
15 other ; for it is unnatural for any one in a gust of
passion to speak long together, or for another in the
same condition to suffer him, without interruption.
Grief and passion are like floods raised in little
brooks by a sudden rain ; they are quickly up ; and
20 if the concernment be poured unexpectedly in upon
us, it overflows us : but a long sober shower gives
them leisure to run out as they came in, without
troubling the ordinary current. As for Comedy, repartee is one of its chiefest graces ; the greatest pleasure
25 of the audience is a chace of wit, kept up on both sides,
and swiftly managed. And this our forefathers, if
not we, have had in Fletcher's plays, to a much
higher degree of perfection than the French poets
can arrive at [4].
30   ' There is another part of Lisideius his discourse,
in which he has rather excused our neighbours, than
commended them ; that is, for aiming only to make

---

[1] like our parsons, BC.   [2] or two hundred, *om.* BC.
            [3] Comedy's are, B ; Comedies are, C.
            [4] can, reasonably, hope to reach, BC.

one person considerable in their plays. 'Tis very true
what he has urged, that one character in all plays, even
without the poet's care, will have advantage of all the
others ; and that the design of the whole drama will
chiefly depend on it. But this hinders not that there 5
may be more shining characters in the play : many
persons of a second magnitude, nay, some so very near,
so almost equal to the first, that greatness may be
opposed to greatness, and all the persons be made
considerable, not only by their quality, but their action. 10
'Tis evident that the more the persons are, the greater
will be the variety of the plot. If then the parts are
managed so regularly, that the beauty of the whole be
kept entire, and that the variety become not a perplexed
and confused mass of accidents, you will find it infinitely 15
pleasing to be led in a labyrinth of design, where you
see some of your way before you, yet discern not the
end till you arrive at it. And that all this is practicable,
I can produce for examples many of our English plays :
as *The Maid's Tragedy, The Alchymist, The Silent* 20
Woman : I was going to have named *The Fox*, but
that the unity of design seems not exactly observed in
it ; for there appear [1] two actions in the play ; the first
naturally ending with the fourth act ; the second forced
from it in the fifth : which yet is the less to be con- 25
demned in him, because the disguise of Volpone, though
it suited not with his character as a crafty or covetous
person, agreed well enough with that of a voluptuary ;
and by it the poet gained the end he aimed at [2], the
punishment of vice, and the reward of virtue, which [3] 30
that disguise produced. So that to judge equally of it,
it was an excellent fifth act, but not so naturally proceeding from the former.

[1] appears, A.   [2] the end at which he aym'd, BC.
[3] both which, BC.

'But to leave this, and pass to the latter part of Lisideius his discourse, which concerns relations : I must acknowledge with him, that the French have reason when they hide [1] that part of the action which
5 would occasion too much tumult on the stage, and choose [2] rather to have it made known by narration to the audience. Farther, I think it very convenient, for the reasons he has given, that all incredible actions were removed ; but, whether custom has so insinuated
10 itself into our countrymen, or nature has so formed them to fierceness, I know not ; but they will scarcely suffer combats and other objects of horror to be taken from them. And indeed, the indecency of tumults is all which can be objected against fighting : for why may
15 not our imagination as well suffer itself to be deluded with the probability of it, as with any other thing in the play ? For my part, I can with as great ease persuade myself that the blows which are struck [3], are given in good earnest, as I can, that they who strike them are
20 kings or princes, or those persons which they represent. For objects of incredibility, I would be satisfied from Lisideius, whether we have any so removed from all appearance of truth, as are those of Corneille's *Andromede* ; a play which has been frequented the most of
25 any he has writ. If the Perseus, or the son of an heathen god, the Pegasus, and the Monster, were not capable to choke a strong belief, let him blame any representation of ours hereafter. Those indeed were objects of delight ; yet the reason is the same as to the
30 probability : for he makes it not a Ballette [4] or masque, but a play, which is to resemble truth. But for death, that it ought not to be represented, I have, besides the arguments alleged by Lisideius, the authority of

---

[1] to hide, BC.

[2] and to choose, BC.

[3] BC *om.* which are struck.

[4] Balette, C.

Ben Johnson, who has forborn it in his tragedies ; for both the death of Sejanus and Catiline are related : though in the latter I cannot but observe one irregularity of that great poet ; he has removed the scene in the same act from Rome to Catiline's army, and from thence 5 again to Rome ; and besides, has allowed a very inconsiderable time, after Catiline's speech, for the striking of the battle, and the return of Petreius, who is to relate the event of it to the senate : which I should not animadvert on him, who was otherwise 10 a painful observer of τὸ πρέπον, or the *decorum* of the stage, if he had not used extreme severity in his judgment on the incomparable Shakespeare for the same fault.—To conclude on this subject of relations ; if we are to be blamed for showing too much of the action, 15 the French are as faulty for discovering too little of it : a mean betwixt both should be observed by every judicious writer, so as the audience may neither be left unsatisfied by not seeing what is beautiful, or shocked by beholding what is either incredible or 20 undecent.

'I hope I have already proved in this discourse, that though we are not altogether so punctual as the French, in observing the laws of Comedy, yet our errors are so few, and little, and those things wherein 25 we excel them so considerable, that we ought of right to be preferred before them. But what will Lisideius say, if they themselves acknowledge they are too strictly tied up[1] by those laws, for breaking which he has blamed the English ? I will allege Corneille's words, 30 as I find them in the end of his Discourse of the Three Unities :—*Il est facile aux speculatifs d'estre severes, &c.* " 'Tis easy for speculative persons to judge severely ; but if they would produce to public view ten or twelve

---

[1] bounded, BC.

pieces of this nature, they would perhaps give more
latitude to the rules than I have done, when, by experience, they had known how much we are bound up [1]
and constrained by them, and how many beauties of the
5 stage they banished from it." To illustrate a little what
he has said : by their servile observations of the Unities
of Time and Place, and integrity of scenes, they have
brought on themselves that dearth of plot, and narrowness of imagination, which may be observed in all their
10 plays. How many beautiful accidents might naturally
happen in two or three days, which cannot arrive with
any probability in the compass of twenty-four hours ?
There is time to be allowed also for maturity of design,
which, amongst great and prudent persons, such as are
15 often represented in Tragedy, cannot, with any likelihood of truth, be brought to pass at so short a warning.
Farther ; by tying themselves strictly to the Unity of
Place, and unbroken scenes, they are forced many times
to omit some beauties which cannot be shown where
20 the act began ; but might, if the scene were interrupted,
and the stage cleared for the persons to enter in another
place ; and therefore the French poets are often forced
upon absurdities ; for if the act begins in a chamber, all
the persons in the play must have some business or
25 other to come thither, or else they are not to be shown
that act ; and sometimes their characters are very un-
fitting to appear there. As, suppose it were the king's
bed-chamber ; yet the meanest man in the tragedy must
come and dispatch his business there, rather than in
30 the lobby or courtyard (which is fitter for him), for fear
the stage should be cleared, and the scenes broken.
Many times they fall by it in a greater inconvenience ;
for they keep their scenes unbroken, and yet change
the place ; as in one of their newest plays, where the

[1] limited, BC.

act begins in the street. There a gentleman is to meet his friend ; he sees him with his man, coming out from his father's house ; they talk together, and the first goes out : the second, who is a lover, has made an appointment with his mistress ; she appears at the window, and 5 then we are to imagine the scene lies under it. This gentleman is called away, and leaves his servant with his mistress ; presently her father is heard from within ; the young lady is afraid the servingman should be discovered, and thrusts him in through a door [1], which 10 is supposed to be her closet. After this, the father enters to the daughter, and now the scene is in a house ; for he is seeking from one room to another for this poor Philipin, or French Diego, who is heard from within, drolling and breaking many a miserable conceit upon 15 his sad [2] condition. In this ridiculous manner the play goes on [3], the stage being never empty all the while : so that the street, the window, the houses, and the closet, are made to walk about, and the persons to stand still. Now what, I beseech you, is more easy than to 20 write a regular French play, or more difficult than write an irregular English one, like those of Fletcher, or of Shakespeare ?

' If they content themselves, as Corneille did, with some flat design, which, like an ill riddle, is found out 25 ere it be half proposed, such plots we can make every way regular, as easily as they ; but whene'er they endeavour to rise to any quick turns and counterturns of plot, as some of them have attempted, since Corneille's plays have been less in vogue, you see they write as 30 irregularly as we, though they cover it more speciously. Hence the reason is perspicuous, why no French plays, when translated, have, or ever can succeed on the

---

[1] for ' in through a door,' BC have ' into a place of safety.'
[2] on the subject of his sad, BC.   [3] goes forward, BC.

English stage. For, if you consider the plots, our own are fuller of variety; if the writing, ours are more quick and fuller of spirit; and therefore 'tis a strange mistake in those who decry the way of writing plays in
5 verse, as if the English therein imitated the French. We have borrowed nothing from them; our plots are weaved in English looms: we endeavour therein to follow the variety and greatness of characters which are derived to us from Shakespeare and Fletcher; the
10 copiousness and well-knitting of the intrigues we have from Johnson; and for the verse itself we have English precedents[1] of elder date than any of Corneille's plays. Not to name our old comedies before Shakespeare, which were all writ in verse of six feet, or
15 Alexandrines, such as the French now use, I can show in Shakespeare, many scenes of rhyme together, and the like in Ben Johnson's tragedies: in *Catiline* and *Sejanus* sometimes thirty or forty lines, I mean besides the Chorus, or the monologues; which, by the
20 way, showed Ben no enemy to this way of writing, especially if you look upon[2] his *Sad Shepherd*, which goes sometimes on rhyme, sometimes on blank verse, like an horse who eases himself on trot and amble. You find him likewise commending Fletcher's pastoral of
25 *The Faithful Shepherdess*, which is for the most part rhyme, though not refined to that purity to which it hath since been brought. And these examples are enough to clear us from a servile imitation of the French.
30   ' But to return from[3] whence I have digressed: I dare boldly affirm these two things of the English drama;— First, that we have many plays of ours as regular as any of theirs, and which, besides, have more variety of plot and characters; and secondly, that in most of the

[1] Presidents, AB.   [2] read, BC.   [3] BC. *om.* from.

irregular plays of Shakespeare or Fletcher (for Ben Johnson's are for the most part regular) there is a more masculine fancy and greater spirit in the writing, than there is in any of the French. I could produce, even in Shakespeare's and Fletcher's works, some plays which are almost exactly formed ; as *The Merry Wives of Windsor*, and *The Scornful Lady* : but because (generally speaking) Shakespeare, who writ first, did not perfectly observe the laws of Comedy, and Fletcher, who came nearer to perfection, yet through carelessness made many faults ; I will take the pattern of a perfect play from Ben Johnson, who was a careful and learned observer of the dramatic laws, and from all his comedies I shall select *The Silent Woman* ; of which I will make a short examen, according to those rules which the French observe.'

As Neander was beginning to examine *The Silent Woman*, Eugenius, looking earnestly upon him[1] ; ' I beseech you, Neander,' said he, ' gratify the company, and me in particular, so far, as before you speak of the play, to give us a character of the author ; and tell us frankly your opinion, whether you do not think all writers, both French and English, ought to give place to him.'

' I fear,' replied Neander, ' that in obeying your commands I shall draw a little envy [2] on myself. Besides, in performing them, it will be first necessary to speak somewhat of Shakespeare and Fletcher, his rivals in poesy ; and one of them, in my opinion, at least his equal, perhaps his superior.

' To begin, then, with Shakespeare. He was the man who of all modern, and perhaps ancient poets, had the largest and most comprehensive soul. All the images of Nature were still present to him, and he drew

---

[1] earnestly regarding him, BC.   [2] some envy, BC.

them, not laboriously, but luckily ; when he describes
any thing, you more than see it, you feel it too. Those
who accuse him to have wanted learning, give him the
greater commendation : he was naturally learn'd ; he
5 needed not the spectacles of books to read Nature ; he
looked inwards, and found her there. I cannot say
he is every where alike ; were he so, I should do him
injury to compare him with the greatest of mankind.
He is many times flat, insipid ; his comic wit degene-
10 rating into clenches, his serious swelling into bombast.
But he is always great, when some great occasion is
presented to him ; no man can say he ever had a fit
subject for his wit, and did not then raise himself as
high above the rest of poets,

15   *Quantum lenta solent inter viburna cupressi.*

The consideration of this made Mr. Hales of Eaton say,
that there was no subject of which any poet ever writ, but
he would produce it much better treated of [1] in Shakespeare ; and however others are now generally preferred
20 before him, yet the age wherein he lived, which had
contemporaries with him Fletcher and Johnson, never
equalled them to him in their esteem : and in the last
King's court, when Ben's reputation was at highest, Sir
John Suckling, and with him the greater part of the
25 courtiers, set our Shakespeare far above him.
  ' Beaumont and Fletcher, of whom I am next to
speak, had, with the advantage of Shakespeare's wit,
which was their precedent, great natural gifts, improved
by study : Beaumont especially being so accurate a
30 judge of plays, that Ben Johnson, while he lived, submitted all his writings to his censure, and, 'tis thought,
used his judgment in correcting, if not contriving, all
his plots. What value he had for him, appears by the

----

[1] better done, BC.

verses he writ to him ; and therefore I need speak no
farther of it. The first play that brought Fletcher and
him in esteem was their *Philaster* : for before that, they
had written two or three very unsuccessfully, as the
like is reported of Ben Johnson, before he writ *Every* 5
Man in his Humour. Their plots were generally more
regular than Shakespeare's, especially those which were
made before Beaumont's death ; and they understood
and imitated the conversation of gentlemen much better ;
whose wild debaucheries, and quickness of wit in re- 10
partees, no poet can ever paint [1] as they have done.
Humour, which [2] Ben Johnson derived from particular
persons, they made it not their business to describe :
they represented all the passions very lively, but above
all, love. I am apt to believe the English language in 15
them arrived to its highest perfection : what words have
since been taken in, are rather superfluous than ornamental [3]. Their plays are now the most pleasant and
frequent entertainments of the stage ; two of theirs
being acted through the year for one of Shakespeare's 20
or Johnson's : the reason is, because there is a certain
gaiety in their comedies, and pathos in their more
serious plays, which suits generally with all men's
humours. Shakespeare's language is likewise a little
obsolete, and Ben Johnson's wit comes short of theirs. 25
 ' As for Johnson, to whose character I am now arrived,
if we look upon him while he was himself (for his last
plays were but his dotages), I think him the most
learned and judicious writer which any theatre ever
had. He was a most severe judge of himself, as well 30
as others. One cannot say he wanted wit, but rather
that he was frugal of it. In his works you find little to
retrench or alter. Wit, and language, and humour

---

[1] for ' can ever paint ' BC have ' before them could paint.'
[2] This Humour of which, A.   [3] necessary, A.

also in some measure, we had before him ; but something of art was wanting to the Drama, till he came.
He managed his strength to more advantage than any
who preceded him. You seldom find him making love
5 in any of his scenes, or endeavouring to move the
passions ; his genius was too sullen and saturnine to
do it gracefully, especially when he knew he came after
those who had performed both to such an height.
Humour was his proper sphere ; and in that he de-
10 lighted most to represent mechanic people. He was
deeply conversant in the Ancients, both Greek and Latin,
and he borrowed boldly from them : there is scarce a
poet or historian among the Roman authors of those
times whom he has not translated in *Sejanus* and
15 *Catiline*. But he has done his robberies so openly,
that one may see he fears not to be taxed by any law.
He invades authors like a monarch ; and what would
be theft in other poets, is only victory in him. With
the spoils of these writers he so represents old Rome
20 to us, in its rites, ceremonies, and customs, that if one
of their poets had written either of his tragedies, we
had seen less of it than in him. If there was any fault
in his language, 'twas that he weaved it too closely
and laboriously, in his serious plays [1] : perhaps too, he
25 did a little too much Romanize our tongue, leaving the
words which he translated almost as much Latin as he
found them : wherein, though he learnedly followed the
idiom of their [2] language, he did not enough comply with
the idiom of ours. If I would compare him with Shake-
30 speare, I must acknowledge him the more correct poet,
but Shakespeare the greater wit. Shakespeare was the
Homer, or father of our dramatic poets ; Johnson was
the Virgil, the pattern of elaborate writing ; I admire

---

[1] for ' serious Playes ' BC have ' comedies especially.'
[2] the idiom of, *om.* BC.

him, but I love Shakespeare. To conclude of him ; as he has given us the most correct plays, so in the precepts which he has laid down in his *Discoveries*, we have as many and profitable rules for perfecting the stage, as any wherewith the French can furnish us. 5

' Having thus spoken of the author, I proceed to the examination of his comedy, *The Silent Woman*.

' *Examen of the* SILENT WOMAN.

' To begin first with the length of the action ; it is so far from exceeding the compass of a natural day, that it 10 takes not up an artificial one. 'Tis all included in the limits of three hours and an half, which is no more than is required for the presentment on the stage. A beauty perhaps not much observed ; if it had, we should not have looked on the Spanish translation of *Five Hours* 15 with so much wonder. The scene of it is laid in London ; the latitude of place is almost as little as you can imagine ; for it lies all within the compass of two houses, and after the first act, in one. The continuity of scenes is observed more than in any of our plays, except his own *Fox* and 20 *Alchymist*. They are not broken above twice or thrice at most in the whole comedy ; and in the two best of Corneille's plays, the *Cid* and *Cinna*, they are interrupted once apiece [1]. The action of the play is entirely one ; the end or aim of which is the settling Morose's estate 25 on Dauphine. The intrigue of it is the greatest and most noble of any pure unmixed comedy in any language ; you see in it many persons of various characters and humours, and all delightful : as first, Morose, or an old man, to whom all noise but his own talking is 30 offensive. Some who would be thought critics, say this humour of his is forced : but to remove that objection,

---

[1] apiece, *om.* BC.

we may consider him first to be naturally of a delicate
hearing, as many are, to whom all sharp sounds are
unpleasant ; and secondly, we may attribute much of it
to the peevishness of his age, or the wayward authority
5 of an old man in his own house, where he may make
himself obeyed ; and this the poet seems to allude to [1]
in his name Morose. Besides this, I am assured from
divers persons, that Ben Johnson was actually acquainted
with such a man, one altogether as ridiculous as he is
10 here represented. Others say, it is not enough to find
one man of such an humour ; it must be common to
more, and the more common the more natural. To prove
this, they instance in the best of comical characters,
Falstaff : there are many men resembling him ; old, fat,
15 merry, cowardly, drunken, amorous, vain, and lying.
But to convince these people, I need but tell them, that
humour is the ridiculous extravagance of conversation,
wherein one man differs from all others. If then it be
common, or communicated to many, how differs it from
20 other men's ? or what indeed causes it to be ridiculous
so much as the singularity of it ? As for Falstaff, he is
not properly one humour, but a miscellany of humours
or images, drawn from so many several men : that
wherein he is singular is his wit, or those things he
25 says *præter expectatum*, unexpected by the audience ;
his quick evasions, when you imagine him surprised,
which, as they are extremely diverting of themselves,
so receive a great addition from his person ; for the
very sight of such an unwieldy old debauched fellow is
30 a comedy alone. And here, having a place so proper
for it, I cannot but enlarge somewhat upon this subject
of humour into which I am fallen. The ancients had
little of it in their comedies ; for the τὸ γελοῖον of the

---

[1] to this the poet seems to allude, BC.

Old Comedy, of which Aristophanes was chief, was not
so much to imitate a man, as to make the people laugh
at some odd conceit, which had commonly somewhat of
unnatural or obscene in it. Thus, when you see Socrates
brought upon the stage, you are not to imagine him 5
made ridiculous by the imitation of his actions, but
rather by making him perform something very unlike
himself ; something so childish and absurd, as by comparing it with the gravity of the true Socrates, makes
a ridiculous object for the spectators. In their New 10
Comedy which succeeded, the poets sought indeed to
express the ἦθος, as in their tragedies the πάθος of
mankind. But this ἦθος contained only the general
characters of men and manners ; as old men, lovers,
serving-men, courtezans, parasites, and such other per- 15
sons as we see in their comedies ; all which they made
alike : that is, one old man or father, one lover, one
courtezan, so like another, as if the first of them had
begot the rest of every sort : *Ex homine hunc natum
dicas.* The same custom they observed likewise in their 20
tragedies. As for the French, though they have the
word *humeur* among them, yet they have small use of
it in their comedies or farces ; they being but ill imitations of the *ridiculum*, or that which stirred up laughter
in the Old Comedy. But among the English 'tis other- 25
wise : where by humour is meant some extravagant
habit, passion, or affection, particular (as I said before)
to some one person, by the oddness of which, he is
immediately distinguished from the rest of men ; which
being lively and naturally represented, most frequently 30
begets that malicious pleasure in the audience which is
testified by laughter ; as all things which are deviations
from common customs [1] are ever the aptest to produce it :

[1] common *om.* BC.

though by the way this laughter is only accidental, as the
person represented is fantastic or bizarre ; but pleasure
is essential to it, as the imitation of what is natural. The
description of these humours, drawn from the knowledge
5 and observation of particular persons, was the peculiar
genius and talent of Ben Johnson ; to whose play I now
return.

' Besides Morose, there are at least nine or ten different characters and humours in *The Silent Woman* ; all
10 which persons have several concernments of their own,
yet are all used by the poet, to the conducting of the
main design to perfection. I shall not waste time in
commending the writing of this play ; but I will give you
my opinion, that there is more wit and acuteness of fancy
15 in it than in any of Ben Johnson's. Besides, that he
has here described the conversation of gentlemen in the
persons of True-Wit, and his friends, with more gaiety,
air, and freedom, than in the rest of his comedies. For
the contrivance of the plot, 'tis extreme elaborate, and
20 yet withal easy ; for the $\lambda \acute{v} \sigma \iota s$ [1], or untying of it, 'tis so
admirable, that when it is done, no one of the audience
would think the poet could have missed it ; and yet it
was concealed so much before the last scene, that any
other way would sooner have entered into your thoughts.
25 But I dare not take upon me to commend the fabric
of it, because it is altogether so full of art, that I must
unravel every scene in it to commend it as I ought.
And this excellent contrivance is still the more to be
admired, because 'tis comedy, where the persons are
30 only of common rank, and their business private, not
elevated by passions or high concernments, as in serious
plays. Here every one is a proper judge of all he sees,
nothing is represented but that with which he daily
converses : so that by consequence all faults lie open

[1] $\delta \acute{\epsilon} \sigma \iota s$, A.

to discovery, and few are pardonable. 'Tis this which Horace has judiciously observed :

> *Creditur, ex medio quia res arcessit, habere*
> *Sudoris minimum ; sed habet Comedia tanto*
> *Plus oneris, quanto veniæ minus.*   5

But our poet who was not ignorant of these difficulties, had prevailed himself [1] of all advantages ; as he who designs a large leap takes his rise from the highest ground. One of these advantages is that which Corneille has laid down as the greatest which can arrive 10 to any poem, and which he himself could never compass above thrice in all his plays ; viz. the making choice of some signal and long-expected day, whereon the action of the play is to depend. This day was that designed by Dauphine for the settling of his uncle's estate upon 15 him ; which to compass, he contrives to marry him. That the marriage had been plotted by him long beforehand, is made evident by what he tells True-Wit in the second act, that in one moment he had destroyed what he had been raising many months.   20

' There is another artifice of the poet, which I cannot here omit, because by the frequent practice of it in his comedies he has left it to us almost as a rule ; that is, when he has any character or humour wherein he would show a *coup de Maistre*, or his highest skill, he recom- 25 mends it to your observation by a pleasant description of it before the person first appears. Thus, in *Bartholomew Fair* he gives you the pictures of Numps and Cokes, and in this those of Daw, Lafoole, Morose, and the Collegiate Ladies ; all which you hear described before you 30 see them. So that before they come upon the stage, you have a longing expectation of them, which prepares you to receive them favourably ; and when they are there, even from their first appearance you are so far

---

[1] has made use, BC.

acquainted with them, that nothing of their humour is lost to you.

' I will observe yet one thing further of this admirable plot ; the business of it rises in every act. The second
5 is greater than the first ; the third than the second ; and so forward to the fifth. There too you see, till the very last scene, new difficulties arising to obstruct the action of the play ; and when the audience is brought into despair that the business can naturally be effected, then,
10 and not before, the discovery is made. But that the poet might entertain you with more variety all this while, he reserves some new characters to show you, which he opens not till the second and third act. In the second Morose, Daw, the Barber, and Otter ; in the third the
15 Collegiate Ladies : all which he moves afterwards in by-walks, or under-plots, as diversions to the main design, lest it should grow tedious, though they are still naturally joined with it, and somewhere or other subservient to it. Thus, like a skilful chess-player, by little and little
20 he draws out his men, and makes his pawns of use to his greater persons.

' If this comedy and some others of his were trans-lated into French prose (which would now be no wonder to them, since Molière has lately given them plays out
25 of verse, which have not displeased them), I believe the controversy would soon be decided betwixt the two nations, even making them the judges. But we need not call our heroes to our aid ; be it spoken to the honour of the English, our nation can never want in
30 any age such who are able to dispute the empire of wit with any people in the universe. And though the fury of a civil war, and power for twenty years together abandoned to a barbarous race of men, enemies of all good learning, had buried the Muses under the
35 ruins of monarchy ; yet, with the restoration of our

happiness, we see revived Poesy lifting up its head, and
already shaking off the rubbish which lay so heavy on
it. We have seen since his Majesty's return, many
dramatic poems which yield not to those of any foreign
nation, and which deserve all laurels but the English. 5
I will set aside flattery and envy : it cannot be denied
but we have had some little blemish either in the plot
or writing of all those plays which have been made
within these seven years (and perhaps there is no
nation in the world so quick to discern them, or so 10
difficult to pardon them, as ours) : yet if we can persuade ourselves to use the candour of that poet, who,
though the most severe of critics, has left us this
caution by which to moderate our censures—

> . . . *ubi plura nitent in carmine, non ego paucis* 15
> *Offendar maculis ;—*

if, in consideration of their many and great beauties,
we can wink at some slight and little imperfections,
if we, I say, can be thus equal to ourselves, I ask no
favour from the French. And if I do not venture upon 20
any particular judgment of our late plays, 'tis out of the
consideration which an ancient writer gives me : *vivorum, ut magna admiratio, ita censura difficilis* : betwixt
the extremes of admiration and malice, 'tis hard to
judge uprightly of the living. Only I think it may be 25
permitted me to say, that as it is no lessening to us to
yield to some plays, and those not many, of our own
nation in the last age, so can it be no addition to
pronounce of our present poets, that they have far
surpassed all the Ancients, and the modern writers of 30
other countries.'

This, my Lord [1], was the substance of what was then
spoke on that occasion ; and Lisideius, I think, was

---

[1] my Lord, *om.* BC

going to reply, when he was prevented thus by Crites :
' I am confident,' said he, ' that the most material things
that can be said have been already urged on either
side ; if they have not, I must beg of Lisideius that he
5 will defer his answer till another time : for I confess
I have a joint quarrel to you both, because you have
concluded, without any reason given for it, that rhyme
is proper for the stage. I will not dispute how ancient
it hath been among us to write this way ; perhaps our
10 ancestors knew no better till Shakespeare's time. I will
grant it was not altogether left by him, and that Fletcher
and Ben Johnson used it frequently in their Pastorals,
and sometimes in other plays. Farther, I will not
argue whether we received it originally from our own
15 countrymen, or from the French ; for that is an inquiry
of as little benefit, as theirs who, in the midst of the
great Plague [1], were not so solicitous to provide against
it, as to know whether we had it from the malignity
of our own air, or by transportation from Holland.
20 I have therefore only to affirm, that it is not allowable
in serious plays ; for comedies, I find you already concluding with me. To prove this, I might satisfy myself
to tell you, how much in vain it is for you to strive
against the stream of the people's inclination ; the
25 greatest part of which are prepossessed so much with
those excellent plays of Shakespeare, Fletcher, and
Ben Johnson, which have been written out of rhyme,
that except you could bring them such as were written
better in it, and those too by persons of equal reputa-
30 tion with them, it will be impossible for you to gain
your cause with them, who will still be judges. This
it is to which, in fine, all your reasons must submit.
The unanimous consent of an audience is so powerful,
that even Julius Cæsar (as Macrobius reports of him),

---

[1] the late plague, BC.

when he was perpetual dictator, was not able to balance
it on the other side. But when Laberius, a Roman
Knight, at his request contended in the Mime with
another poet, he was forced to cry out, *Etiam favente
me victus es, Laberi.* But I will not on this occasion 5
take the advantage of the greater number, but only
urge such reasons against rhyme, as I find in the
writings of those who have argued for the other way.
First then, I am of opinion, that rhyme is unnatural
in a play, because dialogue there is presented as the 10
effect of sudden thought : for a play is the imitation of
Nature ; and since no man without premeditation speaks
in rhyme, neither ought he to do it on the stage. This
hinders not but the fancy may be there elevated to an
higher pitch of thought than it is in ordinary discourse ; 15
for there is a probability that men of excellent and
quick parts may speak noble things *ex tempore* : but
those thoughts are never fettered with the numbers or
sound of verse without study, and therefore it cannot
be but unnatural to present the most free way of speak- 20
ing in that which is the most constrained. For this
reason, says Aristotle, 'tis best to write tragedy in that
kind of verse which is the least such, or which is
nearest prose : and this amongst the Ancients was the
iambic, and with us is blank verse, or the measure of 25
verse kept exactly without rhyme. These numbers
therefore are fittest for a play ; the others for a paper
of verses, or a poem ; blank verse being as much below
them, as rhyme is improper for the Drama. And if it
be objected that neither are blank verses made *ex tem-* 30
pore, yet, as nearest nature, they are still to be preferred.—But there are two particular exceptions, which
many besides myself have had to verse ; by which it
will appear yet more plainly how improper it is in
plays. And the first of them is grounded on that very 35

reason for which some have commended rhyme ; they say, the quickness of repartees in argumentative scenes receives an ornament from verse. Now what is more unreasonable than to imagine that a man should not
5 only light upon the wit [1], but the rhyme too, upon the sudden ? This nicking of him who spoke before both in sound and measure, is so great an happiness, that you must at least suppose the persons of your play to be born poets : *Arcades omnes, et cantare pares, et*
10 *respondere parati* : they must have arrived to the degree of *quicquid conabar dicere* ;—to make verses almost whether they will or no. If they are any thing below this, it will look rather like the design of two, than the answer of one : it will appear that your actors hold
15 intelligence together ; that they perform their tricks like fortune-tellers, by confederacy. The hand of art will be too visible in it, against that maxim of all professions, *Ars est celare artem*, that it is the greatest perfection of art to keep itself undiscovered. Nor will
20 it serve you to object, that however you manage it, 'tis still known to be a play ; and, consequently, the dialogue of two persons understood to be the labour of one poet. For a play is still an imitation of Nature ; we know we are to be deceived, and we desire to be so ;
25 but no man ever was deceived but with a probability of truth ; for who will suffer a gross lie to be fastened on him ? Thus we sufficiently understand, that the scenes which represent cities and countries to us are not really such, but only painted on boards and canvas ; but shall
30 that excuse the ill painture or designment of them ? Nay, rather ought they not to be laboured with so much the more diligence and exactness, to help the imagination ? since the mind of man does naturally tend to, and seek after [2] truth ; and therefore the nearer

---

[1] not only imagine the Wit, BC.   [2] and seek after, *om.* BC

any thing comes to the imitation of it, the more it pleases.

' Thus, you see, your rhyme is uncapable of expressing the greatest thoughts naturally, and the lowest it cannot with any grace : for what is more unbefitting 5 the majesty of verse, than to call a servant, or bid a door be shut in rhyme ? And yet this miserable necessity you are forced upon [1]. But verse, you say, circumscribes a quick and luxuriant fancy, which would extend itself too far on every subject, did not the labour 10 which is required to well-turned and polished rhyme, set bounds to it. Yet this argument, if granted, would only prove that we may write better in verse, but not more naturally. Neither is it able to evince that ; for he who wants judgment to confine his fancy in blank 15 verse, may want it as much in rhyme : and he who has it will avoid errors in both kinds. Latin verse was as great a confinement to the imagination of those poets, as rhyme to ours ; and yet you find Ovid saying too much on every subject. *Nescivit* (says Seneca) *quod* 20 *bene cessit relinquere* : of which he gives you one famous instance in his description of the deluge :

> *Omnia pontus erat, deerant quoque litora ponto.*
> Now all was sea, nor had that sea a shore.

Thus Ovid's fancy was not limited by verse, and Virgil 25 needed not verse to have bounded his.

' In our own language we see Ben Johnson confining himself to what ought to be said, even in the liberty of blank verse ; and yet Corneille, the most judicious of the French poets, is still varying the same sense an 30 hundred ways, and dwelling eternally on the same subject, though confined by rhyme. Some other exceptions I have to verse ; but being these [2] I have named

---

[1] you are often forced on this miserable necessity, BC.

[2] but since these, BC.

are for the most part already public, I conceive it
reasonable they should first be answered.'

' It concerns me less than any,' said Neander (seeing
he had ended), ' to reply to this discourse ; because
5 when I should have proved that verse may be natural
in plays, yet I should always be ready to confess, that
those which I have written in this kind come short of
that perfection which is required. Yet since you are
pleased I should undertake this province, I will do it,
10 though with all imaginable respect and deference, both
to that person from whom you have borrowed your
strongest arguments, and to whose judgment, when
I have said all, I finally submit. But before I proceed
to answer your objections, I must first remember you,
15 that I exclude all Comedy from my defence ; and next
that I deny not but blank verse may be also used ; and
content myself only to assert, that in serious plays
where the subject and characters are great, and the plot
unmixed with mirth, which might allay or divert these
20 concernments which are produced, rhyme is there as
natural and more effectual than blank verse.

' And now having laid down this as a foundation,—
to begin with Crites, I must crave leave to tell him,
that some of his arguments against rhyme reach no
25 farther than, from the faults or defects of ill rhyme, to
conclude against the use of it in general. May not
I conclude against blank verse by the same reason ?
If the words of some poets who write in it, are either
ill chosen, or ill placed, which makes not only rhyme,
30 but all kind of verse in any language unnatural, shall
I, for their vicious affectation, condemn those excellent
lines of Fletcher, which are written in that kind ? Is
there any thing in rhyme more constrained than this
line in blank verse, *I heaven invoke, and strong resistance*
35 *make ?* where you see both the clauses are placed

unnaturally, that is, contrary to the common way of speaking, and that without the excuse of a rhyme to cause it : yet you would think me very ridiculous, if I should accuse the stubbornness of blank verse for this, and not rather the stiffness of the poet. Therefore, 5 Crites, you must either prove that words, though well chosen, and duly placed, yet render not rhyme natural in itself ; or that, however natural and easy the rhyme may be, yet it is not proper for a play. If you insist on the former part, I would ask you, what other conditions 10 are required to make rhyme natural in itself, besides an election of apt words, and a right disposing [1] of them ? For the due choice of your words expresses your sense naturally, and the due placing them adapts the rhyme to it. If you object that one verse may be made for the 15 sake of another, though both the words and rhyme be apt, I answer, it cannot possibly so fall out ; for either there is a dependance of sense betwixt the first line and the second, or there is none : if there be that connection, then in the natural position of the words the 20 latter line must of necessity flow from the former ; if there be no dependance, yet still the due ordering of words makes the last line as natural in itself as the other : so that the necessity of a rhyme never forces any but bad or lazy writers to say what they would not 25 otherwise. 'Tis true, there is both care and art required to write in verse. A good poet never concludes upon [2] the first line, till he has sought out such a rhyme as may fit the sense, already prepared to heighten the second : many times the close of the sense falls into 30 the middle of the next verse, or farther off, and he may often prevail himself of the same advantages in English which Virgil had in Latin ; he may break off in the hemistich, and begin another line. Indeed, the not

---

[1] disposition, BC.   [2] establishes, BC .

observing these two last things, makes plays which are
writ in verse so tedious : for though, most commonly,
the sense is to be confined to the couplet, yet nothing
that does *perpetuo tenore fluere*, run in the same channel,
5 can please always. 'Tis like the murmuring of a stream,
which not varying in the fall, causes at first attention,
at last drowsiness. Variety of cadences is the best
rule ; the greatest help to the actors, and refreshment to
the audience.

10 ' If then verse may be made natural in itself, how
becomes it improper to [1] a play ? You say the stage
is the representation of Nature, and no man in ordinary
conversation speaks in rhyme. But you foresaw when
you said this, that it might be answered—neither does
15 any man speak in blank verse, or in measure without
rhyme. Therefore you concluded, that which is nearest
Nature is still to be preferred. But you took no notice
that rhyme might be made as natural as blank verse, by
the well placing of the words, &c. All the difference
20 between them, when they are both correct, is, the sound
in one, which the other wants ; and if so, the sweetness
of it, and all the advantage resulting from it, which are
handled in the Preface to *The Rival Ladies*, will yet
stand good. As for that place of Aristotle, where he
25 says, plays should be writ in that kind of verse which
is nearest prose, it makes little for you ; blank verse
being properly but measured prose. Now measure
alone, in any modern language, does not constitute
verse ; those of the Ancients in Greek and Latin con-
30 sisted in quantity of words, and a determinate number
of feet. But when, by the inundation of the Goths and
Vandals into Italy, new languages were brought in [2],
and barbarously mingled with the Latin, of which the
Italian, Spanish, French, and ours (made out of them

---

[1] unnatural in, BC.   [2] introduced, BC.

and the Teutonic) are dialects, a new way of poesy was
practised ; new, I say, in those countries, for in all probability it was that of the conquerors in their own nations[1].
This new way consisted in measure or number of feet,
and rhyme ; the sweetness of rhyme, and observation of 5
accent, supplying the place of quantity in words, which
could neither exactly be observed by those Barbarians,
who knew not the rules of it, neither was it suitable to
their tongues, as it had been to the Greek and Latin.
No man is tied in modern poesy to observe any 10
farther rule in the feet of his verse, but that they be
dissyllables ; whether spondee, trochee, or iambic, it
matters not ; only he is obliged to rhyme. Neither
do the Spanish, French, Italian, or Germans, acknowledge at all, or very rarely, any such kind of poesy as 15
blank verse amongst them. Therefore, at most 'tis but
a poetic prose, a *sermo pedestris* ; and as such, most
fit for comedies, where I acknowledge rhyme to be
improper. Farther ; as to that quotation of Aristotle,
our couplet verses may be rendered as near prose as 20
blank verse itself, by using those advantages I lately
named, as breaks in a[2] hemistich, or running the sense
into another line, thereby making art and order appear
as loose and free as nature : or not tying ourselves to
couplets strictly, we may use the benefit of the Pindaric 25
way practised in *The Siege of Rhodes* ; where the
numbers vary, and the rhyme is disposed carelessly,
and far from often chiming. Neither is that other
advantage of the Ancients to be despised, of changing
the kind of verse when they please, with the change of 30
the scene, or some new entrance ; for they confine not
themselves always to iambics, but extend their liberty

---

[1] BC *add* 'at least we are able to prove, that the eastern people
have used it from all antiquity. *Vid.* Dan. his *Defence of Rhyme.*'

[2] an, BC.

to all lyric numbers, and sometimes even to hexameter.
But I need not go so far to prove that rhyme, as it
succeeds to all other offices of Greek and Latin verse,
so especially to this of plays, since the custom of all [1]
5 nations at this day confirms it, all [2] the French, Italian,
and Spanish tragedies are generally writ in it ; and
sure the universal consent of the most civilized parts of
the world ought in this, as it doth in other customs, to [3]
include the rest.

10   ' But perhaps you may tell me, I have proposed such
a way to make rhyme natural, and consequently proper
to plays, as is unpracticable ; and that I shall scarce
find six or eight lines together in any play, where the
words are so placed and chosen as is required to make
15 it natural. I answer, no poet need constrain himself at
all times to it. It is enough he makes it his general
rule ; for I deny not but sometimes there may be
a greatness in placing the words otherwise ; and sometimes they may sound better, sometimes also the variety
20 itself is excuse enough. But if, for the most part, the
words be placed as they are in the negligence of prose,
it is sufficient to denominate the way practicable ; for
we esteem that to be such, which in the trial oftener
succeeds than misses. And thus far you may find the
25 practice made good in many plays : where you do not,
remember still, that if you cannot find six natural
rhymes together, it will be as hard for you to produce
as many lines in blank verse, even among the greatest
of our poets, against which I cannot make some reason-
30 able exception.

    ' And this, Sir, calls to my remembrance the begin-
ning of your discourse, where you told us we should
never find the audience favourable to this kind of
writing, till we could produce as good plays in rhyme,

[1] all, *om.* BC.   [2] all, *om.* BC.   [3] A *om.* to.

as Ben Johnson, Fletcher, and Shakespeare, had writ
out of it. But it is to raise envy to the living, to compare them with the dead. They are honoured, and
almost adored by us, as they deserve ; neither do I
know any so presumptuous of themselves as to con- 5
tend with them. Yet give me leave to say thus much,
without injury to their, ashes ; that not only we shall
never equal them, but they could never equal themselves,
were they to rise and write again. We acknowledge
them our fathers in wit ; but they have ruined their 10
estates themselves, before they came to their children's
hands. There is scarce an humour, a character, or any
kind of plot, which they have not blown upon [1]. All
comes sullied or wasted to us : and were they to entertain this age, they could not make [2] so plenteous treat- 15
ments out of such decayed fortunes. This therefore
will be a good argument to us, either not to write at all,
or to attempt some other way. There is no bays to be
expected in their walks : *tentanda via est, qua me quoque*
possum tollere humo.   20
' This way of writing in verse they have only left free
to us ; our age is arrived to a perfection in it, which
they never knew ; and which (if we may guess by
what of theirs we have seen in verse, as *The Faithful*
Shepherdess, and *Sad Shepherd*) 'tis probable they never 25
could have reached. For the genius of every age is
different ; and though ours excel in this, I deny not but
that to imitate Nature in that perfection which they did
in prose, is a greater commendation than to write in
verse exactly. As for what you have added, that the 30
people are not generally inclined to like this way ; if
it were true, it would be no wonder, that betwixt the
shaking off an old habit, and the introducing of a new,
there should be difficulty. Do we not see them stick to

[1] used, BC.   [2] could not now make, BC.

Hopkins' and Sternhold's psalms, and forsake those of
David, I mean Sandys his translation of them ? If by
the people you understand the multitude, the οἱ πολλοί,
'tis no matter what they think ; they are sometimes in
5 the right, sometimes in the wrong : their judgment is
a mere lottery. *Est ubi plebs recte putat, est ubi peccat.*
Horace says it of the vulgar, judging poesy. But if
you mean the mixed audience of the populace and the
noblesse, I dare confidently affirm that a great part of
10 the latter sort are already favourable to verse ; and that
no serious plays written since the King's return have
been more kindly received by them, than *The Siege of
Rhodes*, the *Mustapha*, *The Indian Queen*, and *Indian
Emperor.*

15   ' But I come now to the inference of your first argument. You said [1] the dialogue of plays is presented as
the effect of sudden thought, but no man speaks suddenly, or *ex tempore*, in rhyme ; and you inferred from
thence, that rhyme, which you acknowledge to be
20 proper to epic poesy, cannot equally be proper to
dramatic, unless we could suppose all men born so
much more than poets, that verses should be made in
them, not by them.

   ' It has been formerly urged by you, and confessed
25 by me, that since no man spoke any kind of verse *ex
tempore*, that which was nearest Nature was to be preferred. I answer you, therefore, by distinguishing
betwixt what is nearest to the nature of Comedy, which
is the imitation of common persons and ordinary speak-
30 ing, and what is nearest the nature of a serious play :
this last is indeed the representation of Nature, but 'tis
Nature wrought up to an higher pitch. The plot, the
characters, the wit, the passions, the descriptions, are
all exalted above the level of common converse, as high

[1] said that, BC.

as the imagination of the poet can carry them, with
proportion to verisimility. Tragedy, we know, is wont
to image to us the minds and fortunes of noble persons,
and to portray these exactly ; heroic rhyme is nearest
Nature, as being the noblest kind of modern verse.   5

Indignatur enim privatis et prope socco
Dignis carminibus narrari cœna Thyestæ,

says Horace : and in another place,

Effutire leves indigna tragœdia versus.

Blank verse is acknowledged to be too low for a poem, 10
nay more, for a paper of verses ; but if too low for an
ordinary sonnet, how much more for Tragedy, which is
by Aristotle, in the dispute betwixt the epic poesy and
the dramatic, for many reasons he there alleges, ranked
above it ?   15
' But setting this defence aside, your argument is
almost as strong against the use of rhyme in poems as
in plays ; for the epic way is every where interlaced
with dialogue, or discoursive scenes ; and therefore you
must either grant rhyme to be improper there, which is 20
contrary to your assertion, or admit it into plays by
the same title which you have given it to poems. For
though Tragedy be justly preferred above the other,
yet there is a great affinity between them, as may easily
be discovered in that definition of a play which Lisi- 25
deius gave us. The *genus* of them is the same, a just and
lively image of human nature, in its actions, passions,
and traverses of fortune : so is the end, namely, for the
delight and benefit of mankind. The characters and
persons are still the same, viz. the greatest of both 30
sorts ; only the manner of acquainting us with those
actions, passions, and fortunes, is different. Tragedy
performs it *viva voce*, or by action, in dialogue ;
wherein it excels the Epic Poem, which does it chiefly

by narration, and therefore is not so lively an image of human nature. However, the agreement betwixt them is such, that if rhyme be proper for one, it must be for the other. Verse, 'tis true, is not the effect of sudden
5 thought ; but this hinders not that sudden thought may be represented in verse, since those thoughts are such as must be higher than Nature can raise them without premeditation, especially to a continuance of them, even out of verse ; and consequently you cannot
10 imagine them to have been sudden either in the poet or in the actors. A play, as I have said, to be like Nature, is to be set above it ; as statues which are placed on high are made greater than the life, that they may descend to the sight in their just proportion.
15   ' Perhaps I have insisted too long on this objection ; but the clearing of it will make my stay shorter on the rest. You tell us, Crites, that rhyme appears most unnatural in repartees, or short replies : when he who answers, it being presumed he knew not what the
20 other would say, yet makes up that part of the verse which was left incomplete, and supplies both the sound and measure of it. This, you say, looks rather like the confederacy of two, than the answer of one.
    ' This, I confess, is an objection which is in every
25 one's [1] mouth, who loves not rhyme : but suppose, I be-seech you, the repartee were made only in blank verse, might not part of the same argument be turned against you ? for the measure is as often supplied there, as it is in rhyme ; the latter half of the hemistich as commonly
30 made up, or a second line subjoined as a reply to the former ; which any one leaf in Johnson's plays will sufficiently clear to you. You will often find in the Greek tragedians, and in Seneca, that when a scene grows up into the warmth of repartees, which is the

---

[1] man's, BC.

close fighting of it, the latter part of the trimeter is supplied by him who answers ; and yet it was never observed as a fault in them by any of the ancient or modern critics. The case is the same in our verse, as it was in theirs ; rhyme to us being in lieu of quantity 5 to them. But if no latitude is to be allowed a poet, you take from him not only his licence of *quidlibet audendi*, but you tie him up in a straiter compass than you would a philosopher. This is indeed *Musas colere severiores.* You would have him follow Nature, but he must follow 10 her on foot : you have dismounted him from his Pegasus. But you tell us, this supplying the last half of a verse, or adjoining a whole second to the former, looks more like the design of two, than the answer of one. Supposing we acknowledge it : how comes this 15 confederacy to be more displeasing to you, than in a dance which is well contrived ? You see there the united design of many persons to make up one figure : after they have separated themselves in many petty divisions, they rejoin one by one into a gross : the con- 20 federacy is plain amongst them, for chance could never produce any thing so beautiful ; and yet there is nothing in it, that shocks your sight. I acknowledge the hand of art appears in repartee, as of necessity it must in all kinds of verse. But there is also the quick 25 and poynant brevity of it (which is an high imitation of Nature in those sudden gusts of passion) to mingle with it ; and this, joined with the cadency and sweetness of the rhyme, leaves nothing in the soul of the hearer to desire. 'Tis an art which appears ; but it 30 appears only like the shadowings of painture, which being to cause the rounding of it, cannot be absent ; but while that is considered, they are lost : so while we attend to the other beauties of the matter, the care and labour of the rhyme is carried from us, or at least 35

drowned in its own sweetness, as bees are sometimes
buried in their honey. When a poet has found the
repartee, the last perfection he can add to it, is to put it
into verse. However good the thought may be, how-
5 ever apt the words in which 'tis couched, yet he finds
himself at a little unrest, while rhyme is wanting : he
cannot leave it till that comes naturally, and then is at
ease, and sits down contented.

' From replies, which are the most elevated thoughts
10 of verse, you pass to the most mean ones, those
which [1] are common with the lowest of household conversation. In these, you say, the majesty of verse
suffers. You instance in the calling of a servant, or
commanding a door to be shut, in rhyme. This, Crites,
15 is a good observation of yours, but no argument : for it
proves no more but that such thoughts should be waved,
as often as may be, by the address of the poet. But
suppose they are necessary in the places where he uses
them, yet there is no need to put them into rhyme.
20 He may place them in the beginning of a verse, and
break it off, as unfit, when so debased, for any other
use ; or granting the worst,—that they require more
room than the hemistich will allow, yet still there is
a choice to be made of the best words, and least vulgar
25 (provided they be apt) to express such thoughts. Many
have blamed rhyme in general, for this fault, when the
poet with a little care might have redressed it. But
they do it with no more justice, than if English Poesy
should be made ridiculous for the sake of the Water
30 Poet's rhymes. Our language is noble, full, and significant ; and I know not why he who is master of it may
not clothe ordinary things in it as decently as the Latin,
if he use the same diligence in his choice of words.
Delectus verborum origo est eloquentiae. It was the

---

[1] to those which are most mean, and which, BC.

saying of Julius Cæsar, one so curious in his, that
none of them can be changed but for a worse.   One
would think, *unlock the door*, was a thing as vulgar as
could be spoken ; and yet Seneca could make it sound
high and lofty in his Latin :   5

> *Reserate clusos regii postes laris.*
> Set wide the palace gates [1].

' But I turn from this exception, both because it
happens not above twice or thrice in any play that
those vulgar thoughts are used ; and then too, were 10
there no other apology to be made, yet the necessity
of them, which is alike in all kind of writing, may
excuse them [2].   Besides that the great eagerness and
precipitation with which they are spoken makes us
rather mind the substance than the dress ; that for 15
which they are spoken, rather than what is spoke.   For
they are always the effect of some hasty concernment,
and something of consequence depends on them.

' Thus, Crites, I have endeavoured to answer your
objections ; it remains only that I should vindicate an 20
argument for verse, which you have gone about to overthrow.   It had formerly been said, that the easiness
of blank verse renders the poet too luxuriant, but that
the labour of rhyme bounds and circumscribes an over-
fruitful fancy ; the sense there being commonly confined 25
to the couplet, and the words so ordered that the
rhyme naturally follows them, not they the rhyme.
To this you answered, that it was no argument to the
question in hand ; for the dispute was not which way
a man may write best, but which is most proper for the 30
subject on which he writes.

[1] A *om.*
[2] For if they are little and mean in rhyme, they are of consequence
such in blank verse, *added in* BC.

'First, give me leave, Sir, to remember you, that the argument against which you raised this objection, was only secondary : it was built on this hypothesis, that to write in verse was proper for serious plays. 5 Which supposition being granted (as it was briefly made out in that discourse, by showing how verse might be made natural), it asserted, that this way of writing was an help to the poet's judgment, by putting bounds to a wild overflowing fancy. I think, therefore, 10 it will not be hard for me to make good what it was to prove [1]. But you add, that were this let pass, yet he who wants judgment in the liberty of his fancy, may as well show the defect of it when he is confined to verse ; for he who has judgment will avoid 15 errors, and he who has it not, will commit them in all kinds of writing.

'This argument, as you have taken it from a most acute person, so I confess it carries much weight in it : but by using the word judgment here indefinitely, 20 you seem to have put a fallacy upon us. I grant, he who has judgment, that is, so profound, so strong, so infallible [2] a judgment, that he needs no helps to keep it always poised and upright, will commit no faults either in rhyme or out of it. And on the other 25 extreme, he who has a judgment so weak and crazed that no helps can correct or amend it, shall write scurvily out of rhyme, and worse in it. But the first of these judgments is no where to be found, and the latter is not fit to write at all. To speak therefore of 30 judgment as it is in the best poets ; they who have the greatest proportion of it, want other helps than from it, within. As for example, you would be loth to say, that he who was [3] endued with a sound judgment had [4]

---

[1] BC *add* on that supposition.
[3] is, BC.

[2] or rather so infallible, BC.
[4] has, BC.

no need of History, Geography, or Moral Philosophy, to write correctly.   Judgment is indeed the master-workman in a play ; but he requires many subordinate hands, many tools to his assistance.   And verse I affirm to be one of these ; 'tis a rule and line by which he keeps his building compact and even, which otherwise lawless imagination would raise either irregularly or loosely.   At least, if the poet commits errors with this help, he would make greater and more without it : 'tis, in short, a slow and painful, but the surest kind of working.   Ovid, whom you accuse for luxuriancy in verse, had perhaps been farther guilty of it, had he writ in prose.   And for your instance of Ben Johnson, who, you say, writ exactly without the help of rhyme ; you are to remember, 'tis only an aid to a luxuriant fancy, which his was not : as he did not want imagination, so none ever said he had much to spare.   Neither was verse then refined so much to be an help to that age, as it is to ours.   Thus then the second thoughts being usually the best, as receiving the maturest digestion from judgment, and the last and most mature product of those thoughts being artful and laboured verse, it may well be inferred, that verse is a great help to a luxuriant fancy ; and this is what that argument which you opposed was to evince.'

Neander was pursuing this discourse so eagerly, that Eugenius had called to him twice or thrice, ere he took notice that the barge stood still, and that they were at the foot of Somerset Stairs, where they had appointed it to land.   The company were all sorry to separate so soon, though a great part of the evening was already spent ; and stood a-while looking back on the water, which the moon-beams played upon [1], and made it appear like floating quick-silver : at last they went up

[1] upon which the moon-beams played, BC.

through a crowd of French people, who were merrily dancing in the open air, and nothing concerned for the noise of guns which had alarmed the town that afternoon. Walking thence together to the Piazze, they
5 parted there ; Eugenius and Lisideius to some pleasant appointment they had made, and Crites and Neander to their several lodgings.

PROLOGUE

I.

HE who writ this, not without pains and thought,
From *French* and *English* theatres has brought
Th' exactest rules, by which a play is wrought.

II.

The Unities of Action, Place, and Time ;
The scenes unbroken ; and a mingled chime   5
Of *Johnson's* humour, with *Corneille's* rhyme.

III.

But while dead colours he with care did lay,
He fears his wit, or plot, he did not weigh,
Which are the living beauties of a play.

IV.

Plays are like towns, which howe'er fortified   10
By engineers, have still some weaker side,
By the o'erseen defendant unespied.

V.

And with that art you make approaches now,
Such skilful fury in assaults you show,
That every poet without shame may bow.   15

VI.

Ours, therefore, humbly would attend your doom,
If, soldier-like, he may have terms to come,
With flying colours, and with beat of drum.

A DEFENCE

OF AN

ESSAY OF DRAMATIC POESY

BEING AN ANSWER TO THE PREFACE OF ' THE GREAT
FAVOURITE, OR, THE DUKE OF LERMA '

(Prefixed to the Second Edition of *The Indian
Emperor*, 1668.)

THE former edition of *The Indian Emperor* being full
of faults, which had escaped the printer, I have been
willing to overlook this second with more care : and
though I could not allow myself so much time as was
5 necessary, yet by that little I have done, the press is
freed from some gross errors which it had to answer
for before. As for the more material faults of writing,
which are properly mine, though I see many of them,
I want leisure to amend them. 'Tis enough for those
10 who make one poem the business of their lives, to leave
that correct : yet, excepting Virgil, I never met with
any which was so in any language.

But while I was thus employed about this impression,
there came to my hands a new printed play, called,
15 *The Great Favourite, or the Duke of Lerma* ; the author
of which, a noble and most ingenious person, has done

me the favour to make some observations and animad-
versions upon my Dramatic Essay. I must confess he
might have better consulted his reputation, than by
matching himself with so weak an adversary. But if
his honour be diminished in the choice of his antago- 5
nist, it is sufficiently recompensed in the election of his
cause : which being the weaker, in all appearance, as
combating the received opinions of the best ancient and
modern authors, will add to his glory, if he overcome,
and to the opinion of his generosity, if he be van- 10
quished, since he engages at so great odds, and, so
like a cavalier, undertakes the protection of the weaker
party. I have only to fear, on my own behalf, that so
good a cause as mine may not suffer by my ill management, or weak defence ; yet I cannot in honour but take 15
the glove when 'tis offered me ; though I am only
a champion by succession, and no more able to defend
the right of Aristotle and Horace, than an infant Dimock
to maintain the title of a king.

For my own concernment in the controversy, it is so 20
small, that I can easily be contented to be driven from
a few notions of Dramatic Poesy ; especially by one,
who has the reputation of understanding all things :
and I might justly make that excuse for my yielding to
him, which the philosopher made to the Emperor ; why 25
should I offer to contend with him, who is master of
more than twenty legions of arts and sciences ? But
I am forced to fight, and therefore it will be no shame
to be overcome.

Yet I am so much his servant, as not to meddle with 30
anything which does not concern me in his Preface :
therefore I leave the good sense and other excellencies
of the first twenty lines, to be considered by the critics.
As for the play of *The Duke of Lerma*, having so much
altered and beautified it as he has done, it can justly 35

belong to none but him. Indeed they must be extreme
ignorant, as well as envious, who would rob him of that
honour ; for you see him putting in his claim to it, even
in the first two lines :

5   Repulse upon repulse, like waves thrown back,
               That slide to hang upon obdurate rocks.

After this, let detraction do its worst ; for if this be
not his, it deserves to be. For my part, I declare for
distributive justice ; and from this, and what follows, he
10 certainly deserves *those advantages, which he acknow-*
ledges to have received from the opinion of sober men.

In the next place, I must beg leave to observe his
great address in courting the reader to his party. For,
intending to assault all poets, both ancient and modern,
15 he discovers not his whole design at once, but seems
only to aim at me, and attacks me on my weakest side,
my defence of verse.

To begin with me, he gives me the compellation of
' The Author of *a Dramatic Essay* ' ; which is a little
20 discourse in dialogue, for the most part borrowed from
the observations of others ; therefore, that I may not
be wanting to him in civility, I return his compliment
by calling him, ' The Author of *the Duke of Lerma* '.

But (that I may pass over his salute) he takes notice
25 of my great pains to prove rhyme as natural in a serious
play, and more effectual than blank verse. Thus indeed
I did state the question ; but he tells me, *I pursue that*
which I call natural in a wrong application; for 'tis not
the question, whether rhyme, or not rhyme, be best, or most
30 *natural for a serious subject, but what is nearest the*
nature of that it represents.

If I have formerly mistaken the question, I must
confess my ignorance so far, as to say I continue still
in my mistake : but he ought to have proved that I

mistook it ; for it is yet but *gratis dictum* ; I still shall think I have gained my point, if I can prove that rhyme is best, or most natural for a serious subject. As for the question as he states it, whether rhyme be nearest the nature of what it represents, I wonder he should 5 think me so ridiculous as to dispute whether prose or verse be nearest to ordinary conversation.

It still remains for him to prove his inference ; that, since verse is granted to be more remote than prose from ordinary conversation, therefore no serious plays 10 ought to be writ in verse : and when he clearly makes that good, I will acknowledge his victory as absolute as he can desire it.

The question now is, which of us two has mistaken it ; and if it appear I have not, the world will suspect, 15 *what gentleman that was, who was allowed to speak twice in Parliament, because he had not yet spoken to the question* ; and perhaps conclude it to be the same, who, as 'tis reported, maintained a contradiction *in terminis*, in the face of three hundred persons. 20

But to return to verse ; whether it be natural or not in plays, is a problem which is not demonstrable of either side : 'tis enough for me, that he acknowledges he had rather read good verse than prose : for if all the enemies of verse will confess as much, I shall not need 25 to prove that it is natural. I am satisfied if it cause delight ; for delight is the chief, if not the only, end of poesy : instruction can be admitted but in the second place, for poesy only instructs as it delights. 'Tis true, that to imitate well is a poet's work ; but to affect the 30 soul, and excite the passions, and, above all, to move admiration (which is the delight of serious plays), a bare imitation will not serve. The converse, therefore, which a poet is to imitate, must be heightened with all the arts and ornaments of poesy ; and must be such as, 35

strictly considered, could never be supposed spoken by
any without premeditation.

As for what he urges, that *a play will still be supposed to be a composition of several persons speaking*
5 *ex tempore, and that good verses are the hardest things
which can be imagined to be so spoken* ; I must crave
leave to dissent from his opinion, as to the former part
of it : for, if I am not deceived, a play is supposed to
be the work of the poet, imitating or representing the
10 conversation of several persons : and this I think to be
as clear, as he thinks the contrary.

But I will be bolder, and do not doubt to make it
good, though a paradox, that one great reason why
prose is not to be used in serious plays, is, because it is
15 too near the nature of converse : there may be too
great a likeness ; as the most skilful painters affirm,
that there may be too near a resemblance in a picture :
to take every lineament and feature is not to make
an excellent piece, but to take so much only as will
20 make a beautiful resemblance of the whole : and, with
an ingenious flattery of nature, to heighten the beauties
of some parts, and hide the deformities of the rest.
For so says Horace,

> *Ut pictura poesis erit, etc. . . . .*
> 25 *Hæc amat obscurum, vult hæc sub luce videri,*
> *Judicis argutum quæ non formidat acumen.*
> .   .   .   .   .   . *Et quæ*
> *Desperat tractata nitescere posse, relinquit.*

In *Bartholomew Fair*, or the lowest kind of comedy,
30 that degree of heightening is used, which is proper to
set off that subject : it is true the author was not there
to go out of prose, as he does in his higher arguments
of Comedy, *The Fox* and *Alchymist* ; yet he does so
raise his matter in that prose, as to render it delight-
35 ful ; which he could never have performed, had he only

said or done those very things, that are daily spoken or practised in the fair : for then the fair itself would be as full of pleasure to an ingenious person as the play, which we manifestly see it is not. But he hath made an excellent Lazar of it ; the copy is of price, though 5 the original be vile. You see in *Catiline* and *Sejanus*, where the argument is great, he sometimes ascends to verse, which shows he thought it not unnatural in serious plays ; and had his genius been as proper for rhyme as it was for humour, or had the age 10 in which he lived attained to as much knowledge in verse as ours, it is probable he would have adorned those subjects with that kind of writing.

Thus Prose, though the rightful prince, yet is by common consent deposed, as too weak for the govern- 15 ment of serious plays : and he failing, there now start up two competitors ; one, the nearer in blood, which is Blank Verse ; the other, more fit for the ends of government, which is Rhyme. Blank Verse is, indeed, the nearer Prose, but he is blemished with the weakness 20 of his predecessor. Rhyme (for I will deal clearly) has somewhat of the usurper in him ; but he is brave, and generous, and his dominion pleasing. For this reason of delight, the Ancients (whom I will still believe as wise as those who so confidently correct them) wrote 25 all their tragedies in verse, though they knew it most remote from conversation.

But I perceive I am falling into the danger of another rebuke from my opponent ; for when I plead that the Ancients used verse, I prove not that they would have 30 admitted rhyme, had it then been written. All I can say is only this, that it seems to have succeeded verse by the general consent of poets in all modern languages ; for almost all their serious plays are written in it ; which, though it be no demonstration that therefore 35

they ought to be so, yet at least the practice first, and
then the continuation of it, shows that it attained the
end, which was to please ; and if that cannot be com-
passed here, I will be the first who shall lay it down.
5 For I confess my chief endeavours are to delight the
age in which I live. If the humour of this be for low
comedy, small accidents, and raillery, I will force my
genius to obey it, though with more reputation I could
write in verse. I know I am not so fitted by nature to
10 write comedy : I want that gaiety of humour which is
required to it. My conversation is slow and dull ; my
humour saturnine and reserved ; in short, I am none
of those who endeavour to break jests in company, or
make reparties. So that those, who decry my comedies,
15 do me no injury, except it be in point of profit : reputation in them is the last thing to which I shall pretend.
I beg pardon for entertaining the reader with so ill
a subject ; but before I quit that argument, which was
the cause of this digression, I cannot but take notice
20 how I am corrected for my quotation of Seneca, in my
defence of plays in verse. My words are these : ' Our
language is noble, full, and significant ; and I know not
why he, who is a master of it, may not clothe ordinary
things in it as decently as the Latin, if he use the
25 same diligence in his choice of words. One would
think, *unlock a door*, was a thing as vulgar as could
be spoken ; yet Seneca could make it sound high and
lofty in his Latin :

Reserate clusos regii postes laris.'

30 But he says of me, ' That being filled with the precedents of the Ancients, who writ their plays in verse,
I commend the thing, declaring our language to be full,
noble, and significant, and charging all defects upon
the *ill placing of words*, which I prove by quoting

Seneca loftily expressing such an ordinary thing as *shutting a door*.'

Here he manifestly mistakes ; for I spoke not of the placing, but of the choice of words ; for which I quoted that aphorism of Julius Caesar, *Delectus verborum est* 5 *origo eloquentiae* ; but *delectus verborum* is no more Latin for the *placing of words*, than *reserate* is Latin for *shut the door*, as he interprets it, which I ignorantly construed *unlock* or *open* it.

He supposes I was highly affected with the sound of 10 those words, and I suppose I may more justly imagine it of him ; for if he had not been extremely satisfied with the sound, he would have minded the sense a little better.

But these are now to be no faults ; for ten days after 15 his book is published, and that his mistakes are grown so famous, that they are come back to him, he sends his *Errata* to be printed, and annexed to his play ; and desires, that, instead of *shutting*, you would read *opening*, which, it seems, was the printer's fault. I wonder 20 at his modesty, that he did not rather say it was Seneca's or mine ; and that, in some authors, *reserare* was to *shut* as well as to *open*, as the word *barach*, say the learned, is both to *bless* and *curse*.

Well, since it was the printer, he was a naughty man 25 to commit the same mistake twice in six lines : I warrant you *delectus verborum*, for *placing of words*, was his mistake too, though the author forgot to tell him of it : if it were my book, I assure you I should. For those rascals ought to be the proxies of every gentleman 30 author, and to be chastised for him, when he is not pleased to own an error. Yet since he has given the *Errata*, I wish he would have enlarged them only a few sheets more, and then he would have spared me the labour of an answer : for this cursed printer is so 35

given to mistakes, that there is scarce a sentence in
the preface without some false grammar, or hard sense
in it ; which will all be charged upon the poet, because
he is so good-natured as to lay but three errors to the
5 printer's account, and to take the rest upon himself,
who is better able to support them. But he needs not
apprehend that I should strictly examine those little
faults, except I am called upon to do it : I shall return
therefore to that quotation of Seneca, and answer, not
10 to what he writes, but to what he means. I never
intended it as an argument, but only as an illustration
of what I had said before concerning the election of
words ; and all he can charge me with is only this, that
if Seneca could make an ordinary thing sound well in
15 Latin by the choice of words, the same, with the like
care, might be performed in English : if it cannot,
I have committed an error on the right hand, by commending too much the copiousness and well-sounding
of our language, which I hope my countrymen will
20 pardon me. At least the words which follow in my
Dramatic Essay will plead somewhat in my behalf ; for
I say there, that this objection happens but seldom in
a play ; and then, too, either the meanness of the expression may be avoided, or shut out from the verse by
25 breaking it in the midst.

But I have said too much in the defence of verse ;
for, after all, it is a very indifferent thing to me whether
it obtain or not. I am content hereafter to be ordered
by his rule, that is, to write it sometimes because it
30 pleases me, and so much the rather, because he has
declared that it pleases him. But he has taken his
last farewell of the Muses, and he has done it civilly, by
honouring them with the name of *his long acquain-
tances*, which is a compliment they have scarce deserved
35 from him. For my own part, I bear a share in the

public loss ; and how emulous soever I may be of his fame and reputation, I cannot but give this testimony of his style, that it is extreme poetical, even in oratory ; his thoughts elevated sometimes above common apprehension ; his notions politic and grave, and tending to 5 the instruction of Princes, and reformation of States ; that they are abundantly interlaced with variety of fancies, tropes, and figures, which the critics have enviously branded with the name of obscurity and false grammar.   10

Well, he is now fettered in business of more unpleasant nature : the Muses have lost him, but the Commonwealth gains by it ; the corruption of a poet is the generation of a statesman.

He will not venture again into the civil wars of 15 *censure, ubi—nullos habitura triumphos* : if he had not told us he had left the Muses, we might have half suspected it by that word *ubi*, which does not any way belong to them in that place : the rest of the verse is indeed Lucan's, but that *ubi*, I will answer for it, is his 20 own.   Yet he has another reason for this disgust of Poesy ; for he says immediately after, that *the manner of plays which are now in most esteem is beyond his power to perform* ; to perform the manner of a thing, I confess, is new English to me.   *However, he con-* 25 *demns not the satisfaction of others, but rather their unnecessary understanding, who, like Sancho Pança's doctor, prescribe too strictly to our appetites; for*, says he, *in the difference of Tragedy and Comedy, and of Farce itself, there can be no determination but by the* 30 *taste, nor in the manner of their composure.*

We shall see him now as great a critic as he was a poet ; and the reason why he excelled so much in poetry will be evident, for it will appear to have proceeded from the exactness of his judgment.   *In the* 35

*difference of Tragedy, Comedy, and Farce itself, there
can be no determination but by the taste.* I will not
quarrel with the obscurity of his phrase, though I justly
might ; but beg his pardon if I do not rightly under-
5 stand him. If he means that there is no essential
difference betwixt Comedy,Tragedy,and Farce, but what
is only made by the people's taste, which distinguishes
one of them from the other, that is so manifest an error,
that I need not lose time to contradict it. Were there
10 neither judge, taste, nor opinion in the world, yet they
would differ in their natures ; for the action, character,
and language of Tragedy, would still be great and
high ; that of Comedy, lower and more familiar ; admiration would be the delight of one, and satire of the
15 other.

I have but briefly touched upon these things, because,
whatever his words are, I can scarce imagine, that *he,
who is always concerned for the true honour of reason,
and would have no spurious issue fathered upon her,*
20 should mean anything so absurd as to affirm, *that there
is no difference betwixt Comedy and Tragedy but what is
made by the taste only* ; unless he would have us understand the comedies of my lord L——, where the first
act should be pottages, the second fricassees, &c., and
25 the fifth a *chère entière* of women.

I rather guess he means, that betwixt one comedy or
tragedy and another, there is no other difference but
what is made by the liking or disliking of the audience.
This is indeed a less error than the former, but yet it
30 is a great one. The liking or disliking of the people
gives the play the denomination of good or bad, but
does not really make or constitute it such. To please
the people ought to be the poet's aim, because plays are
made for their delight ; but it does not follow that they
35 are always pleased with good plays, or that the plays

which please them are always good. The humour of
the people is now for Comedy ; therefore, in hope to
please them, I write comedies rather than serious plays :
and so far their taste prescribes to me : but it does not
follow from that reason, that Comedy is to be preferred 5
before Tragedy in its own nature ; for that which is so
in its own nature cannot be otherwise, as a man cannot
but be a rational creature : but the opinion of the people
may alter, and in another age, or perhaps in this, serious
plays may be set up above comedies.   10

This I think a sufficient answer ; if it be not, he has
provided me of an excuse : it seems, in his wisdom,
he foresaw my weakness, and has found óut this expe-
dient for me, *that it is not necessary for poets to study
strict reason, since they are so used to a greater latitude* 15
*than is allowed by that severe inquisition, that they must
infringe their own jurisdiction, to profess themselves obliged
to argue well.*

I am obliged to him for discovering to me this back
door ; but I am not yet resolved on my retreat ; for 20
I am of opinion, that they cannot be good poets, who
are not accustomed to argue well. False reasonings
and colours of speech are the certain marks of one who
does not understand the stage ; for moral truth is the
mistress of the poet as much as of the philosopher ; 25
Poesy must resemble natural truth, but it must *be*
ethical. Indeed, the poet dresses truth, and adorns
nature, but does not alter them :

> *Ficta voluptatis causâ sint proxima veris.*

Therefore that is not the best poesy which resembles 30
notions of things that are not, to things that are :
though the fancy may be great and the words flowing,
yet the soul is but half satisfied when there is not truth
in the foundation. This is that which makes Virgil be

preferred before the rest of poets. In variety of fancy, and sweetness of expression, you see Ovid far above him ; for Virgil rejected many of those things which Ovid wrote. *A great wit's great work is to refuse,* as
5 my worthy friend Sir John Berkenhead has ingeniously expressed it : you rarely meet with anything in Virgil but truth, which therefore leaves the strongest impression of pleasure in the soul. This I thought myself obliged to say in behalf of Poesy ; and to declare, though
10 it be against myself, that when poets do not argue well, the defect is in the workmen, not in the art.

And now I come to the boldest part of his discourse, wherein he attacks not me, but all the Ancients and Moderns ; and undermines, as he thinks, the very
15 foundations on which Dramatic Poesy is built. I could wish he would have declined that envy which must of necessity follow such an undertaking, and contented himself with triumphing over me in my opinions of verse, which I will never hereafter dispute with him ;
20 but he must pardon me if I have that veneration for Aristotle, Horace, Ben Johnson, and Corneille, that I dare not serve him in such a cause, and against such heroes, but rather fight under their protection, as Homer reports of little Teucer, who shot the Trojans
25 from under the large buckler of Ajax Telamon :

Στῆ δ' ἄρ' ὑπ' Αἴαντος σάκεῖ Τελαμωνιάδαω, &c.

He stood beneath his brother's ample shield ;
And cover'd there, shot death through all the field.

The words of my noble adversary are these :
30 *But if we examine the general rules laid down for plays by strict reason, we shall find the errors equally gross; for the great foundation which is laid to build upon, is nothing as it is generally stated, as will appear upon the examination of these particulars.*

These particulars in due time shall be examined. In
the meanwhile, let us consider what this great foundation is, which he says is nothing, as it is generally
stated. I never heard of any other foundation of
Dramatic Poesy than the imitation of Nature ; neither 5
was there ever pretended any other by the Ancients or
Moderns, or me, who endeavour to follow them in that
rule. This I have plainly said in my definition of
a play ; that it is a just and lively image of human
nature, &c. Thus the foundation, as it is generally 10
stated, will stand sure, if this definition of a play be
true ; if it be not, he ought to have made his exception
against it, by proving that a play is not an imitation
of Nature, but somewhat else, which he is pleased to
think it.   15
But 'tis very plain, that he has mistaken the founda-
tion for that which is built upon it, though not immediately : for the direct and immediate consequence is
this ; if Nature be to be imitated, then there is a rule for
imitating Nature rightly ; otherwise there may be an end, 20
and no means conducing to it. Hitherto I have proceeded by demonstration ; but as our divines, when
they have proved a Deity, because there is order, and
have inferred that this Deity ought to be worshipped,
differ afterwards in the manner of the worship ; so, 25
having laid down, that Nature is to be imitated, and that
proposition proving the next, that then there are means
which conduce to the imitating of Nature, I dare proceed
no further positively ; but have only laid down some
opinions of the Ancients and Moderns, and of my own, 30
as means which they used, and which I thought probable for the attaining of that end. Those means are
the same which my antagonist calls the foundations,
how properly the world may judge ; and to prove that
this is his meaning, he clears it immediately to you, by 35

enumerating those rules or propositions against which
he makes his particular exceptions ; as, namely, those
of Time and Place, in these words : *First, we are told
the plot should not be so ridiculously contrived, as to crowd
5 two several countries into one stage; secondly, to cramp
the accidents of many years or days into the representation
of two hours and a half; and, lastly, a conclusion drawn,
that the only remaining dispute is, concerning time, whether
it should be contained in twelve or twenty-four hours ; and
10 the place to be limited to that spot of ground where the play
is supposed to begin: and this is called nearest Nature;
for that is concluded most natural, which is most probable,
and nearest to that which it presents.*

Thus he has only made a small mistake, of the
15 means conducing to the end for the end itself, and of
the superstructure for the foundation : but he proceeds :
*to show therefore upon what ill grounds they dictate laws
for Dramatic Poesy,* &c. He is here pleased to charge
me with being magisterial, as he has done in many
20 other places of his preface ; therefore, in vindication of
myself, I must crave leave to say, that my whole discourse was sceptical, according to that way of reasoning
which was used by Socrates, Plato, and all the Academics of old, which Tully and the best of the Ancients
25 followed, and which is imitated by the modest inquisitions of the Royal Society. That it is so, not only the
name will show, which is *an Essay*, but the frame and
composition of the work. You see it is a dialogue sus-
tained by persons of several opinions, all of them left
30 doubtful, to be determined by the readers in general ;
and more particularly deferred to the accurate judgment of my Lord Buckhurst, to whom I made a dedication of my book. These are my words in my epistle,
speaking of the persons whom I introduced in my
35 dialogue : ' 'Tis true they differed in their opinions, as

'tis probable they would ; neither do I take upon me to
reconcile, but to relate them, leaving your Lordship to
decide it in favour of that part which you shall judge
most reasonable.' And after that, in my advertisement
to the reader, I said this : ' The drift of the ensuing 5
discourse is chiefly to vindicate the honour of our English writers from the censure of those who unjustly
prefer the French before them. This I intimate, lest
any should think me so exceeding vain, as to teach
others an art, which they understand much better than 10
myself.' But this is more than necessary to clear my
modesty in that point : and I am very confident that
there is scarce any man who has lost so much time, as
to read that trifle, but will be my compurgator as to
that arrogance whereof I am accused. The truth is, if 15
I had been naturally guilty of so much vanity as to
dictate my opinions ; yet I do not find that the character
of a positive or self-conceited person is of such advantage
to any in this age, that I should labour to be publicly
admitted of that order. 20

But I am not now to defend my own cause, when
that of all the Ancients and Moderns is in question :
for this gentleman, who accuses me of arrogance, has
taken a course not to be taxed with the other extreme
of modesty. Those propositions which are laid down 25
in my discourse as helps to the better imitation of
Nature, are not mine (as I have said), nor were ever
pretended so to be, but derived from the authority of
Aristotle and Horace, and from the rules and examples
of Ben Johnson and Corneille. These are the men with 30
whom properly he contends, and against *whom he will
endeavour to make it evident, that there is no such thing
as what they all pretend.*

His argument against the Unities of Place and Time
is this : *that 'tis as impossible for one stage to present two* 35

*rooms or houses truly, as two countries or kingdoms; and
as impossible that five hours or twenty-four hours should
be two hours, as that a thousand hours or years should be
less than what they are, or the greatest part of time to be*
5 *comprehended in the less: for all of them being impossible,
they are none of them nearest the truth, or nature of what
they present; for impossibilities are all equal, and admit of
no degree.*

This argument is so scattered into parts, that it can
10 scarce be united into a syllogism; yet, in obedience to
him, *I will abbreviate*, and comprehend as much of it as
I can in few words, that my answer to it may be more
perspicuous. I conceive his meaning to be what follows,
as to the Unity of Place: (if I mistake, I beg his pardon,
15 professing it is not out of any design to play the *Argumentative Poet*). If one stage cannot properly present
two rooms or houses, much less two countries or kingdoms, then there can be no Unity of Place. But one
stage cannot properly perform this: therefore there can
20 be no Unity of Place.

I plainly deny his minor proposition; the force of
which, if I mistake not, depends on this, that the stage
being one place cannot be two. This indeed is as great
a secret, as that we are all mortal; but to requite it
25 with another, I must crave leave to tell him, that though
the stage cannot be two places, yet it may properly
represent them successively, or at several times. His
argument is indeed no more than a mere fallacy, which
will evidently appear when we distinguish place, as it
30 relates to plays, into real and imaginary. The real place
is that theatre, or piece of ground, on which the play is
acted. The imaginary, that house, town, or country
where the action of the drama is supposed to be, or,
more plainly, where the scene of the play is laid. Let
35 us now apply this to that Herculean argument, *which*

*if strictly and duly weighed, is to make it evident that
there is no such thing as what they all pretend.* 'Tis
impossible, he says, for one stage to present two rooms
or houses : I answer, 'tis neither impossible, nor improper, for one real place to represent two or more 5
imaginary places, so it be done successively ; which in
other words, is no more than this, that the imagination
of the audience, aided by the words of the poet, and
painted scenes, may suppose the stage to be sometimes
one place, sometimes another ; now a garden, or wood, 10
and immediately a camp : which I appeal to every man's
imagination, if it be not true. Neither the Ancients nor
Moderns, as much fools as he is pleased to think them,
ever asserted that they could make one place two ; but
they might hope, by the good leave of this author, that 15
the change of a scene might lead the imagination to
suppose the place altered : so that he cannot fasten those
absurdities upon this scene of a play, or imaginary
place of action, that it is one place, and yet two. And
this being so clearly proved, that 'tis past any show of 20
a reasonable denial, it will not be hard to destroy that
other part of his argument, which depends upon it,
namely, that 'tis as impossible for a stage to represent
two rooms or houses, as two countries or kingdoms :
for his reason is already overthrown, which was, because 25
both were alike impossible. This is manifestly otherwise ; for 'tis proved that a stage may properly represent two rooms or houses ; for the imagination being
judge of what is represented, will in reason be less
shocked with the appearance of two rooms in the same 30
house, or two houses in the same city, than with two
distant cities in the same country, or two remote countries in the same universe. Imagination in a man, or
reasonable creature, is supposed to participate of Reason,
and when that governs, as it does in the belief of fiction, 35

Reason is not destroyed, but misled, or blinded ; that
can prescribe to the Reason, during the time of the
representation, somewhat like a weak belief of what it
sees and hears ; and Reason suffers itself to be so hood-
5 winked, that it may better enjoy the pleasures of the
fiction : but it is never so wholly made a captive, as to
be drawn headlong into a persuasion of those things
which are most remote from probability : 'tis in that
case a free-born subject, not a slave ; it will contribute
10 willingly its assent, as far as it sees convenient, but
will not be forced. Now, there is a greater vicinity in
nature betwixt two rooms than betwixt two houses ;
betwixt two houses, than betwixt two cities ; and so of
the rest : Reason, therefore, can sooner be led by
15 imagination to step from one room into another, than
to walk to two distant houses, and yet rather to go
thither, than to fly like a witch through the air, and be
hurried from one region to another. Fancy and Reason
go hand in hand ; the first cannot leave the last behind :
20 and though Fancy, when it sees the wide gulf, would
venture over, as the nimbler, yet it is withheld by
Reason, which will refuse to take the leap, when the
distance over it appears too large. If Ben Johnson himself will remove the scene from Rome into Tuscany in
25 the same act, and from thence return to Rome, in the
scene which immediately follows, Reason will consider
there is no proportionable allowance of time to perform
the journey, and, therefore, will choose to stay at home.
So, then, the less change of place there is, the less time
30 is taken up in transporting the persons of the drama,
with analogy to reason ; and in that analogy, or resemblance of fiction to truth, consists the excellency of the
play.

  For what else concerns the Unity of Place, I have
35 already given my opinion of it in my *Essay*, that there

is a latitude to be allowed to it, as several places in the same town or city, or places adjacent to each other in the same country ; which may all be comprehended under the larger denomination of one place ; yet with this restriction, that the nearer and fewer those 5 imaginary places are, the greater resemblance they will have to truth ; and reason, which cannot make them one, will be more easily led to suppose them so.

What has been said of the Unity of Place, may easily be applied to that of Time : I grant it to be impossible, 10 that the greater part of time should be comprehended in the less, that twenty-four hours should be crowded into three : but there is no necessity of that supposition ; for as *place*, so *time* relating to a play, is either imaginary or real : the real is comprehended in those three hours, 15 more or less, in the space of which the play is represented ; the imaginary is that which is supposed to be taken up in the representation, as twenty-four hours, more or less. Now, no man ever could suppose, that twenty-four real hours could be included in the space 20 of three ; but where is the absurdity of affirming, that the feigned business of twenty-four imagined hours, may not more naturally be represented in the compass of three real hours, than the like feigned business of twenty-four years in the same proportion of real time ? 25 For the proportions are always real, and much nearer, by his permission, of twenty-four to three, than of four thousand to it.

I am almost fearful of illustrating anything by similitude, lest he should confute it for an argument ; yet 30 I think the comparison of a glass will discover very aptly the fallacy of his argument, both concerning time and place. The strength of his reason depends on this, that the less cannot comprehend the greater. I have already answered, that we need not suppose it does ; 35

I say not that the less can comprehend the greater,
but only, that it may represent it ; as in a glass, or
mirror, of half-a-yard diameter, a whole room, and many
persons in it, may be seen at once ; not that it can
5 comprehend that room, or those persons, but that it
represents them to the sight.

But the author of the *Duke of Lerma* is to be excused
for his declaring against the Unity of Time ; for, if I be
not much mistaken, he is an interested person ;—the
10 time of that play taking up so many years as the favour
of the Duke of Lerma continued ; nay, the second and
third act including all the time of his prosperity, which
was a great part of the reign of Philip the Third : for
in the beginning of the second act he was not yet a
15 favourite, and before the end of the third, was in
disgrace. I say not this with the least design of limit-
ing the stage too servilely to twenty-four hours, however
he be pleased to tax me with dogmatising on that point.
In my Dialogue, as I before hinted, several persons
20 maintained their several opinions : one of them, indeed,
who supported the cause of the French Poesy, said how
strict they were in that particular ; but he who answered,
in behalf of our nation, was willing to give more latitude to the rule, and cites the words of Corneille him-
25 self, complaining against the severity of it, and observing,
what beauties it banished from the stage, *pag.* 44 of my
Essay. In few words, my own opinion is this (and
I willingly submit it to my adversary, when he will
please impartially to consider it) that the imaginary time
30 of every play ought to be contrived into as narrow
a compass, as the nature of the plot, the quality of the
persons, and variety of accidents will allow. In Comedy,
I would not exceed twenty-four or thirty hours ; for the
plot, accidents, and persons, of Comedy are small, and
35 may be naturally turned in a little compass : but in

Tragedy, the design is weighty, and the persons great ; therefore, there will naturally be required a greater space of time in which to move them. And this, though Ben Johnson has not told us, yet it is manifestly his opinion : for you see that to his comedies he allows 5 generally but twenty-four hours ; to his two tragedies, *Sejanus* and *Catiline*, a much larger time, though he draws both of them into as narrow a compass as he can : for he shows you only the latter end of Sejanus his favour, and the conspiracy of Catiline already ripe, and 10 just breaking out into action.

But as it is an error, on the one side, to make too great a disproportion betwixt the imaginary time of the play, and the real time of its representation ; so, on the other side, 'tis an oversight to compress the accidents 15 of a play into a narrower compass than that in which they could naturally be produced. Of this last error the French are seldom guilty, because the thinness of their plots prevents them from it ; but few Englishmen, except Ben Johnson, have ever made a plot, with variety 20 of design in it, included in twenty-four hours, which was altogether natural. For this reason, I prefer the *Silent Woman* before all other plays, I think justly, as I do its author, in judgment, above all other poets. Yet, of the two, I think that error the most pardonable 25 which in too strait a compass crowds together many accidents, since it produces more variety, and, consequently, more pleasure to the audience ; and because the nearness of proportion betwixt the imaginary and real time, does speciously cover the compression of the 30 accidents.

Thus I have endeavoured to answer the meaning of his argument ; for, as he drew it, I humbly conceive that it was none,—as will appear by his proposition, and the proof of it. His proposition was this : 35

*If strictly and duly weighed, it is as impossible for one
stage to present two rooms, or houses, as two countries, or
kingdoms,* &c. And his proof this : *For all being impossible, they are none of them nearest the truth or nature of*
5 *what they present.*

Here you see, instead of proof, or reason, there is
only *petitio principii.* For, in plain words, his sense
is this : two things are as impossible as one another,
because they are both equally impossible : but he takes
10 those two things to be granted as impossible, which he
ought to have proved such before he had proceeded to
prove them equally impossible : he should have made
out first, that it was impossible for one stage to represent two houses, and then have gone forward to prove,
15 that it was as equally impossible for a stage to present
two houses, as two countries.

After all this, the very absurdity, to which he would
reduce me, is none at all : for he only drives at this,
that, if his argument be true, I must then acknowledge
20 that there are degrees in impossibilities, which I easily
grant him without dispute ; and, if I mistake not, Aristotle and the School are of my opinion. For there
are some things which are absolutely impossible, and
others which are only so *ex parte* ; as it is absolutely
25 impossible for a thing *to be,* and *not to be* at the same
time : but for a stone to move naturally upward, is only
impossible *ex parte materiæ* ; but it is not impossible
for the First Mover to alter the nature of it.

His last assault, like that of a Frenchman, is most
30 feeble ; for whereas I have observed, that none have
been violent against verse, but such only as have not
attempted it, or have succeeded ill in their attempt, he
will needs, according to his usual custom, improve my
observation to an argument, that he might have the
35 glory to confute it. But I lay my observation at his

feet, as I do my pen, which I have often employed
willingly in his deserved commendations, and now most
unwillingly against his judgment. For his person and
parts, I honour them as much as any man living, and
have had so many particular obligations to him, that 5
I should be very ungrateful, if I did not acknowledge
them to the world. But I gave not the first occasion
of this difference in opinions. In my epistle dedica-
tory, before my *Rival Ladies*, I had said somewhat in
behalf of verse, which he was pleased to answer in his 10
preface to his plays : that occasioned my reply in my
Essay ; and that reply begot this rejoinder of his, in his
preface to the *Duke of Lerma*. But as I was the last
who took up arms, I will be the first to lay them down.
For what I have here written, I submit it wholly to 15
him ; and if I do not hereafter answer what may be
objected against this paper, I hope the world will not
impute it to any other reason, than only the due respect
which I have for so noble an opponent.

AN EVENING'S LOVE ;

OR,

THE MOCK ASTROLOGER

THE PREFACE (1671)

I HAD thought, Reader, in this Preface, to have
written somewhat concerning the difference betwixt
the plays of our age and those of our predecessors on
the English stage : to have shown in what parts of
5 Dramatic Poesy we were excelled by Ben Johnson, I
mean, humour, and contrivance of Comedy ; and in
what we may justly claim precedence of Shakespeare
and Fletcher, namely in Heroic Plays : but this design
I have waved on second considerations ; at least, de-
10 ferred it till I publish *The Conquest of Granada*, where
the discourse will be more proper. I had also prepared to treat of the improvement of our language since
Fletcher's and Johnson's days, and consequently of our
refining the courtship, raillery, and conversation of
15 plays : but as I am willing to decline that envy which
I should draw on myself from some old opiniatre judges
of the stage, so likewise I am pressed in time so much
that I have not leisure, at present, to go thorough with
it. Neither, indeed, do I value a reputation gained

from Comedy, so far as to concern myself about it, any
more than I needs must in my own defence : for I think
it, in its own nature, inferior to all sorts of dramatic
writing. Low comedy especially requires, on the
writer's part, much of conversation with the vulgar, 5
and much of ill nature in the observation of their follies. But let all men please themselves according to
their several tastes : that which is not pleasant to me,
may be to others who judge better. And, to prevent an
accusation from my enemies, I am sometimes ready to 10
imagine, that my disgust of low comedy proceeds not
so much from my judgment as from my temper ;
which is the reason why I so seldom write it ; and that
when I succeed in it (I mean so far as to please the
audience), yet I am nothing satisfied with what I have 15
done ; but am often vexed to hear the people laugh,
and clap, as they perpetually do, where I intended 'em
no jest ; while they let pass the better things, without
taking notice of them. Yet even this confirms me in
my opinion of slighting popular applause, and of con- 20
temning that approbation which those very people give,
equally with me, to the zany of a mountebank ; or to
the appearance of an antic on the theatre, without wit
on the poet's part, or any occasion of laughter from the
actor, besides the ridiculousness of his habit and his 25
grimaces.

But I have descended, before I was aware, from
Comedy to Farce ; which consists principally of grimaces.
That I admire not any comedy equally with tragedy, is,
perhaps, from the sullenness of my humour ; but that 30
I detest those farces, which are now the most frequent
entertainments of the stage, I am sure I have reason on
my side. Comedy consists, though of low persons, yet
of natural actions and characters ; I mean such humours,
adventures, and designs, as are to be found and met 35

with in the world. Farce, on the other side, consists of forced humours, and unnatural events. Comedy presents us with the imperfections of human nature : Farce entertains us with what is monstrous and chime-
5 rical. The one causes laughter in those who can judge of men and manners, by the lively representation of their folly or corruption : the other produces the same effect in those who can judge of neither, and that only by its extravagances. The first works on the
10 judgment and fancy ; the latter on the fancy only : there is more of satisfaction in the former kind of laughter, and in the latter more of scorn. But, how it happens, that an impossible adventure should cause our mirth, I cannot so easily imagine. Something there may be
15 in the oddness of it, because on the stage it is the common effect of things unexpected to surprise us into a delight : and that is to be ascribed to the strange appetite, as I may call it, of the fancy ; which, like that of a longing woman, often runs out into the most extra-
20 vagant desires ; and is better satisfied sometimes with loam, or with the rinds of trees, than with the wholesome nourishments of life. In short, there is the same difference betwixt Farce and Comedy, as betwixt an empiric and a true physician : both of them may attain
25 their ends ; but what the one performs by hazard, the other does by skill. And as the artist is often unsuccessful, while the mountebank succeeds ; so farces more commonly take the people than comedies. For to write unnatural things is the most probable way of
30 pleasing them, who understand not Nature. And a true poet often misses of applause, because he cannot debase himself to write so ill as to please his audience.

After all, it is to be acknowledged, that most of those comedies, which have been lately written, have been
35 allied too much to Farce : and this must of necessity

fall out, till we forbear the translation of French plays :
for their poets, wanting judgment to make or to maintain true characters, strive to cover their defects with
ridiculous figures and grimaces. While I say this,
I accuse myself as well as others : and this very play 5
would rise up in judgment against me, if I would
defend all things I have written to be natural : but I
confess I have given too much to the people in it, and
am ashamed for them as well as for myself, that I have
pleased them at so cheap a rate. Not that there is 10
anything here which I would not defend to an ill-
natured judge (for I despise their censures, who I am
sure would write worse on the same subject) : but,
because I love to deal clearly and plainly, and to speak
of my own faults with more criticism, than I would of 15
another poet's. Yet I think it no vanity to say, that
this comedy has as much of entertainment in it, as
many others which have been lately written : and, if
I find my own errors in it, I am able, at the same time,
to arraign all my contemporaries for greater. As I 20
pretend not that I can write humour, so none of them
can reasonably pretend to have written it as they ought.
Johnson was the only man, of all ages and nations, who
has performed it well, and that but in three or four of
his comedies : the rest are but a *crambe bis cocta* ; the 25
same humours a little varied and written worse. Neither
was it more allowable in him, than it is in our present
poets, to represent the follies of particular persons ; of
which many have accused him. *Parcere personis, dicere
de vitiis*, is the rule of plays. And Horace tells you, 30
that the Old Comedy amongst the Grecians was silenced
for the too great liberties of the poets :

> . . *In vitium libertas excidit et vim*
> *Dignam lege regi : Lex est accepta, chorusque*
> *Turpiter obticuit sublato jure nocendi.* 35

Of which he gives you the reason in another place :
where, having given the precept,

Neve immunda crepent, ignominiosaque dicta,

he immediately subjoins,

5   *Offenduntur enim quibus est equus, et pater, et res.*

But Ben Johnson is to be admired for many excellencies ; and can be taxed with fewer failings than any
English poet. I know I have been accused as an
enemy of his writings ; but without any other reason,
10 than that I do not admire him blindly, and without
looking into his imperfections.   For why should he
only be exempted from those frailties, from which
Homer and Virgil are not free ?   Or why should there
be any *Ipse dixit* in our poetry, any more than there is
15 in our philosophy ?   I admire and applaud him where
I ought : those who do more, do but value themselves
in their admiration of him ; and, by telling you they
extol Ben Johnson's way, would insinuate to you that
they can practise it.   For my part, I declare that I want
20 judgment to imitate him ;   and should think it a great
impudence in myself to attempt it.   To make men appear
pleasantly ridiculous on the stage, was, as I have said,
his talent ; and in this he needed not the acumen of wit
but that of judgment.   For the characters and repre-
25 sentations of folly are only the effects of observation ;
and observation is an effect of judgment.   Some ingenious men, for whom I have a particular esteem, have
thought I have much injured Ben Johnson, when I have
not allowed his wit to be extraordinary : but they con-
30 found the notion of what is witty, with what is pleasant.
That Ben Johnson's plays were pleasant, he must want
reason who denies : but that pleasantness was not properly wit, or the sharpness of conceit, but the natural

imitation of folly ; which I confess to be excellent in its kind, but not to be of that kind which they pretend. Yet if we will believe Quintilian, in his chapter *de movendo risu,* he gives his opinion of both in these following words : *Stulta reprehendere facillimum est ;* 5 *nam per se sunt ridicula, et a derisu non procul abest risus : sed rem urbanam facit aliqua ex nobis adjectio.*

And some perhaps would be apt to say of Johnson, as it was said of Demosthenes, *non displicuisse illi jocos, sed non contigisse.* I will not deny, but that I approve 10 most the mixed way of Comedy ; that which is neither all wit, nor all humour, but the result of both. Neither so little of humour as Fletcher shows, nor so little of love and wit as Johnson ; neither all cheat, with which the best plays of the one are filled, nor all adventure, 15 which is the common practice of the other. I would have the characters well chosen, and kept distant from interfering with each other ; which is more than Fletcher or Shakespeare did : but I would have more of the *urbana, venusta, salsa, faceta,* and the rest which 20 Quintilian reckons up as the ornaments of wit ; and these are extremely wanting in Ben Johnson. As for repartie, in particular ; as it is the very soul of conversation, so it is the greatest grace of Comedy, where it is proper to the characters. There may be much of 25 acuteness in a thing well said ; but there is more in a quick reply : *sunt enim longe venustiora omnia in respondendo quam in provocando.* Of one thing I am sure, that no man ever will decry wit, but he who despairs of it himself ; and who has no other quarrel to 30 it, but that which the fox had to the grapes. Yet, as Mr. Cowley (who had a greater portion of it than any man I know) tells us in his *Character of Wit,* rather than all wit, let there be none. I think there is no folly so great in any poet of our age, as the superfluity and 35

waste of wit was in some of our predecessors : particularly we may say of Fletcher and of Shakespeare,
what was said of Ovid, *in omni ejus ingenio, facilius quod
rejici, quam quod adjici potest, invenies.* The contrary
5 of which was true in Virgil, and our incomparable
Johnson.

Some enemies of repartie have observed to us, that
there is a great latitude in their characters, which are
made to speak it : and that it is easier to write wit than
10 humour ; because, in the characters of humour, the
poet is confined to make the person speak what is only
proper to it. Whereas, all kind of wit is proper in
the character of a witty person. But, by their favour,
there are as different characters in wit as in folly.
15 Neither is all kind of wit proper in the mouth of every
ingenious person. A witty coward, and a witty brave,
must speak differently. Falstaff and the Liar speak
not like Don John in the *Chances*, and Valentine in
Wit without Money. And Johnson's Truewit in the
20 *Silent Woman*, is a character different from all of
them. Yet it appears, that this one character of wit
was more difficult to the author, than all his images
of humour in the play : for those he could describe
and manage from his observations of men ; this he
25 has taken, at least a part of it, from books : witness
the speeches in the first act, translated *verbatim* out of
Ovid *de Arte Amandi* ; to omit what afterwards he
borrowed from the sixth satire of Juvenal against
women.

30   However, if I should grant, that there were a greater
latitude in characters of wit, than in those of humour ;
yet that latitude would be of small advantage to such
poets, who have too narrow an imagination to write it.
And to entertain an audience perpetually with humour,
35 is to carry them from the conversation of gentlemen,

and treat them with the follies and extravagancies of
Bedlam.

I find I have launched out farther than I intended
in the beginning of this preface ; and that, in the heat
of writing, I have touched at something, which I thought 5
to have avoided. 'Tis time now to draw homeward ;
and to think rather of defending myself, than assaulting
others. I have already acknowledged, that this play
is far from perfect : but I do not think myself obliged
to discover the imperfections of it to my adversaries, 10
any more than a guilty person is bound to accuse
himself before his judges. It is charged upon me that
I make debauched persons (such as, they say, my
Astrologer and Gamester are) my protagonists, or the
chief persons of the drama ; and that I make them 15
happy in the conclusion of my play ; against the law
of Comedy, which is to reward virtue, and punish vice.
I answer, first, that I know no such law to have been
constantly observed in Comedy, either by the ancient or
modern poets. Chærea is made happy in the *Eunuch*, 20
after having deflowered a virgin ; and Terence generally
does the same through all his plays, where you perpetually see, not only debauched young men enjoy
their mistresses, but even the courtesans themselves
rewarded and honoured in the catastrophe. The same 25
may be observed in Plautus almost everywhere. Ben
Johnson himself, after whom I may be proud to err,
has given me more than once the example of it. That
in *The Alchemist* is notorious, where Face, after having
contrived and carried on the great cozenage of the 30
play, and continued in it without repentance to the last,
is not only forgiven by his master, but enriched, by
his consent, with the spoils of those whom he had
cheated. And, which is more, his master himself,
a grave man, and a widower, is introduced taking his 35

man's counsel, debauching the widow first, in hope to
marry her afterward. In the *Silent Woman*, Dauphine
(who, with the other two gentlemen, is of the same
character with my Celadon in the *Maiden Queen*, and
5 with Wildblood in this) professes himself in love with
all the Collegiate Ladies : and they likewise are all of
the same character with each other, excepting only
Madam Otter, who has something singular : yet this
naughty Dauphine is crowned in the end with the
10 possession of his uncle's estate, and with the hopes of
enjoying all his mistresses ; and his friend, Mr. Truewit
(the best character of a gentleman which Ben Johnson
ever made) is not ashamed to pimp for him. As for
Beaumont and Fletcher, I need not allege examples
15 out of them ; for that were to quote almost all their
comedies. But now it will be objected, that I patronize
vice by the authority of former poets, and extenuate
my own faults by recrimination. I answer, that as
I defend myself by their example, so that example
20 I defend by reason, and by the end of all dramatic
poesy. In the first place, therefore, give me leave to
show you their mistake, who have accused me. They
have not distinguished, as they ought, betwixt the rules
of Tragedy and Comedy. In Tragedy, where the actions
25 and persons are great, and the crimes horrid, the laws
of justice are more strictly observed ; and examples of
punishment to be made, to deter mankind from the
pursuit of vice. Faults of this kind have been rare
amongst the ancient poets : for they have punished in
30 Œdipus, and in his posterity, the sin which he knew
not he had committed. Medea is the only example
I remember at present, who escapes from punishment
after murder. Thus Tragedy fulfils one great part of
its institution ; which is, by example, to instruct. But
35 in Comedy it is not so ; for the chief end of it is

divertisement and delight : and that so much, that it is
disputed, I think, by Heinsius, before Horace his *Art
of Poetry*, whether instruction be any part of its employment. At least I am sure it can be but its secondary
end : for the business of the poet is to make you laugh : 5
when he writes humour, he makes folly ridiculous ;
when wit, he moves you, if not always to laughter, yet
to a pleasure that is more noble. And if he works
a cure on folly, and the small imperfections in mankind,
by exposing them to public view, that cure is not per- 10
formed by an immediate operation. For it works first
on the ill-nature of the audience ; they are moved to
laugh by the representation of deformity ; and the
shame of that laughter teaches us to amend what is
ridiculous in our manners. This being then established, 15
that the first end of Comedy is delight, and instruction
only the second ; it may reasonably be inferred, that
Comedy is not so much obliged to the punishment of
faults which it represents, as Tragedy. For the persons
in Comedy are of a lower quality, the action is little, 20
and the faults and vices are but the sallies of youth,
and the frailties of human nature, and not premeditated
crimes : such to which all men are obnoxious, not such
as are attempted only by few, and those abandoned to
all sense of virtue : such as move pity and commisera- 25
tion, not detestation and horror : such, in short, as may
be forgiven, not such as must of necessity be punished.
But, lest any man should think that I write this to
make libertinism amiable, or that I cared not to debase
the end and institution of Comedy, so I might thereby 30
maintain my own errors, and those of better poets,
I must further declare, both for them and for myself,
that we make not vicious persons happy, but only as
Heaven makes sinners so ; that is, by reclaiming them
first from vice. For so it is to be supposed they are, 35

when they resolve to marry ; for then, enjoying what they desire in one, they cease to pursue the love of many.   So Chærea is made happy by Terence, in marrying her whom he had deflowered : and so are
5 Wildblood and the Astrologer in this play.

There is another crime with which I am charged, at which I am yet much less concerned, because it does not relate to my manners, as the former did, but only to my reputation as a poet : a name of which I assure
10 the reader I am nothing proud ; and therefore cannot be very solicitous to defend it.   I am taxed with stealing all my plays, and that by some, who should be the last men from whom I would steal any part of 'em.   There is one answer which I will not make ; but it has been
15 made for me, by him to whose grace and patronage I owe all things,—

Et spes et ratio studiorum in Caesare tantum—

and without whose command they should no longer be troubled with anything of mine :—that he only desired,
20 that they, who accused me of theft, would always steal him plays like mine.   But though I have reason to be proud of this defence, yet I should waive it, because I have a worse opinion of my own comedies than any of my enemies can have.   'Tis true, that wherever
25 I have liked any story in a romance, novel, or foreign play, I have made no difficulty, nor ever shall, to take the foundation of it, to build it up, and to make it proper for the English stage.   And I will be so vain to say, it has lost nothing in my hands : but it always
30 cost me so much trouble to heighten it for our theatre (which is incomparably more curious in all the ornaments of dramatic poesy than the French or Spanish), that when I had finished my play, it was like the hulk of Sir Francis Drake, so strangely altered, that there

scarcely remained any plank of the timber which first built it. To witness this, I need go no farther than this play : it was first Spanish, and called *El Astrologo Fingido* ; then made French by the younger Corneille ; and is now translated into English, and in print, under 5 the name of *The Feigned Astrologer*. What I have performed in this will best appear by comparing it with those : you will see that I have rejected some adventures which I judged were not divertising ; that I have heightened those which I have chosen ; and that I 10 have added others, which were neither in the French nor Spanish. And, besides, you will easily discover, that the walk of the Astrologer is the least considerable in my play : for the design of it turns more on the parts of Wildblood and Jacintha, who are the chief 15 persons in it. I have farther to add, that I seldom use the wit and language of any romance or play, which I undertake to alter : because my own invention (as bad as it is) can furnish me with nothing so dull as what is there. Those who have called Virgil, Terence, 20 and Tasso, plagiaries (though they much injured them), had yet a better colour for their accusation ; for Virgil has evidently translated Theocritus, Hesiod, and Homer, in many places ; besides what he has taken from Ennius in his own language. Terence was not 25 only known to translate Menander (which he avows also in his prologues), but was said also to be helped in those translations by Scipio the African, and Lælius. And Tasso, the most excellent of modern poets, and whom I reverence next to Virgil, has taken both from 30 Homer many admirable things, which were left untouched by Virgil, and from Virgil himself, where Homer could not furnish him. Yet the bodies of Virgil's and Tasso's poems were their own ; and so are all the ornaments of language and elocution in 35

them. The same (if there were anything commendable
in this play) I could say for it. But I will come nearer
to our own countrymen. Most of Shakespeare's plays,
I mean the stories of them, are to be found in the
5 *Hecatommuthi*, or *Hundred Novels* of Cinthio. I have
myself read in his Italian, that of *Romeo and Juliet*, the
Moor of Venice, and many others of them. Beaumont
and Fletcher had most of theirs from Spanish novels :
witness *The Chances*, *The Spanish Curate*, *Rule a Wife*
10 *and have a Wife*, *The Little French Lawyer*, and so many
others of them as compose the greatest part of their
volume in folio. Ben Johnson, indeed, has designed
his plots himself ; but no man has borrowed so much
from the Ancients as he has done : and he did well in
15 it, for he has thereby beautified our language.

But these little critics do not well consider what is
the work of a poet, and what the graces of a poem :
the story is the least part of either : I mean the foundation of it, before it is modelled by the art of him who
20 writes it ; who forms it with more care, by exposing
only the beautiful parts of it to view, than a skilful
lapidary sets a jewel. On this foundation of the story,
the characters are raised : and, since no story can
afford characters enough for the variety of the English
25 stage, it follows, that it is to be altered and enlarged
with new persons, accidents, and designs, which will
almost make it new. When this is done, the forming
it into acts and scenes, disposing of actions and passions
into their proper places, and beautifying both with
30 descriptions, similitudes, and propriety of language, is
the principal employment of the poet ; as being the
largest field of fancy, which is the principal quality
required in him : for so much the word ποιητής implies.
Judgment, indeed, is necessary in him ; but 'tis fancy
35 that gives the life-touches, and the secret graces to it ;

especially in serious plays, which depend not much on observation. For, to write humour in comedy (which is the theft of poets from mankind), little of fancy is required ; the poet observes only what is ridiculous and pleasant folly, and by judging exactly what is so, 5 he pleases in the representation of it.

But in general, the employment of a poet is like that of a curious gunsmith, or watchmaker : the iron or silver is not his own ; but they are the least part of that which gives the value : the price lies wholly in 10 the workmanship. And he who works dully on a story, without moving laughter in a comedy, or raising concernment in a serious play, is no more to be accounted a good poet, than a gunsmith of the Minories is to be compared with the best workman of the town. 15

But I have said more of this than I intended ; and more, perhaps, than I needed to have done : I shall but laugh at them hereafter, who accuse me with so little reason ; and withal contemn their dulness, who, if they could ruin that little reputation I have got, and 20 which I value not, yet would want both wit and learning to establish their own ; or to be remembered in after ages for anything, but only that which makes them ridiculous in this.

OF HEROIC PLAYS

AN ESSAY

(Prefixed to *The Conquest of Granada*, 1672)

WHETHER Heroic Verse ought to be admitted into
serious plays, is not now to be disputed : 'tis already in
possession of the stage ; and I dare confidently affirm,
that very few tragedies, in this age, shall be received
5 without it. All the arguments which are formed against
it, can amount to no more than this, that it is not so
near conversation as prose, and therefore not so natural.
But it is very clear to all who understand poetry, that
serious plays ought not to imitate conversation too
10 nearly. If nothing were to be raised above that level,
the foundation of Poetry would be destroyed. And if
you once admit of a latitude, that thoughts may be
exalted, and that images and actions may be raised
above the life, and described in measure without rhyme,
15 that leads you insensibly from your own principles to
mine : you are already so far onward of your way, that
you have forsaken the imitation of ordinary converse.
You are gone beyond it ; and to continue where you
are, is to lodge in the open fields, betwixt two inns.
20 You have lost that which you call natural, and have
not acquired the last perfection of Art. But it was only

custom which cozened us so long ; we thought, because
Shakespeare and Fletcher went no farther, that there
the pillars of poetry were to be erected ; that, because
they excellently described passion without rhyme, therefore rhyme was not capable of describing it.   But time 5
has now convinced most men of that error.   'Tis indeed
so difficult to write verse, that the adversaries of it have
a good plea against many who undertake that task,
without being formed by Art or Nature for it.   Yet, even
they who have written worst in it, would have written 10
worse without it : they have cozened many with their
sound, who never took the pains to examine their sense.
In fine, they have succeeded ; though, it is true, they
have more dishonoured rhyme by their good success,
than they have done by their ill.   But I am willing to 15
let fall this argument : 'tis free for every man to write,
or not to write, in verse, as he judges it to be, or not to
be, his talent ;   or as he imagines the audience will
receive it.

For Heroic Plays (in which only I have used it without 20
the mixture of prose), the first light we had of them, on
the English theatre, was from the late Sir William
D'Avenant.   It being forbidden him in the rebellious
times to act tragedies and comedies, because they contained some matter of scandal to those good people, 25
who could more easily dispossess their lawful sovereign
than endure a wanton jest, he was forced to turn his
thoughts another way, and to introduce the examples of
moral virtue, writ in verse, and performed in recitative
music.   The original of this music, and of the scenes 30
which adorned his work, he had from the Italian operas ;
but he heightened his characters (as I may probably
imagine) from the example of Corneille and some French
poets.   In this condition did this part of poetry remain
at his Majesty's return ; when, growing bolder, as being 35

now owned by a public authority, he reviewed his *Siege
of Rhodes*, and caused it be acted as a just drama. But
as few men have the happiness to begin and finish any
new project, so neither did he live to make his design
5 perfect : there wanted the fulness of a plot, and the
variety of characters to form it as it ought ; and,
perhaps, something might have been added to the
beauty of the style. All which he would have performed with more exactness, had he pleased to have
10 given us another work of the same nature. For myself
and others, who come after him, we are bound, with
all veneration to his memory, to acknowledge what
advantage we received from that excellent groundwork
which he laid : and, since it is an easy thing to add to
15 what already is invented, we ought all of us, without
envy to him, or partiality to ourselves, to yield him the
precedence in it.

Having done him this justice, as my guide, I may do
myself so much, as to give an account of what I have
20 performed after him. I observed then, as I said, what
was wanting to the perfection of his *Siege of Rhodes* ;
which was design, and variety of characters. And in
the midst of this consideration, by mere accident,
I opened the next book that lay by me, which was an
25 Ariosto in Italian ; and the very first two lines of that
poem gave me light to all I could desire :

> *Le donne, i cavalier, l'arme, gli amori,*
> *Le cortesie, l'audaci imprese io canto,* etc.

For the very next reflexion which I made was this, that
30 an heroic play ought to be an imitation, in little, of an
heroic poem ; and, consequently, that Love and Valour
ought to be the subject of it. Both these Sir William
D'Avenant had begun to shadow ; but it was so, as first
discoverers draw their maps, with headlands, and pro-

montories, and some few outlines of somewhat taken
at a distance, and which the designer saw not clearly.
The common drama obliged him to a plot well formed
and pleasant, or, as the Ancients call it, one entire and
great action.   But this he afforded not himself in 5
a story, which he neither filled with persons, nor
beautified with characters, nor varied with accidents.
The laws of an heroic poem did not dispense with those
of the other, but raised them to a greater height, and
indulged him a further liberty of fancy, and of drawing 10
all things as far above the ordinary proportion of the
stage, as that is beyond the common words and actions
of human life ;   and, therefore, in the scanting of his
images and design, he complied not enough with the
greatness and majesty of an heroic poem.   15

I am sorry I cannot discover my opinion of this kind
of writing, without dissenting much from his, whose
memory I love and honour.   But I will do it with the
same respect to him, as if he were now alive, and over-
looking my paper while I write.   His judgment of an 20
heroic poem was this : *That it ought to be dressed in*
a more familiar and easy shape; more fitted to the
common actions and passions of human life; and, in
short, more like a glass of Nature, showing us ourselves
in our ordinary habits, and figuring a more practicable 25
virtue to us, than was done by the Ancients or Moderns.
Thus he takes the image of an heroic poem from the
Drama, or stage poetry ;   and accordingly intended to
divide it into five books, representing the same number
of acts ;   and every book into several cantos, imitating 30
the scenes which compose our acts.

But this, I think, is rather a play in narration, as
I may call it, than an heroic poem ;   if at least you
will not prefer the opinion of a single man to the
practice of the most excellent authors, both of ancient 35

and latter ages. I am no admirer of quotations ; but
you shall hear, if you please, one of the Ancients
delivering his judgment on this question ; it is Petronius
Arbiter, the most elegant, and one of the most judicious
5 authors of the Latin tongue ; who, after he had given
many admirable rules for the structure and beauties
of an epic poem, concludes all in these following
words :—

Non enim res gestæ versibus comprehendendæ sunt,
10 *quod longe melius historici faciunt: sed, per ambages,*
deorumque ministeria, præcipitandus est liber spiritus, ut
potius furentis animi vaticinatio appareat, quam religiosæ
orationis, sub testibus, fides.

In which sentence, and his own essay of a poem,
15 which immediately he gives you, it is thought he taxes
Lucan, who followed too much the truth of history,
crowded sentences together, was too full of points, and
too often offered at somewhat which had more of the
sting of an epigram, than of the dignity and state of
20 an heroic poem. Lucan used not much the help of his
heathen deities : there was neither the ministry of the
gods, nor the precipitation of the soul, nor the fury of
a prophet (of which my author speaks), in his *Pharsalia* ;
he treats you more like a philosopher than a poet, and
25 instructs you, in verse, with what he had been taught
by his uncle Seneca in prose. In one word, he walks
soberly afoot, when he might fly. Yet Lucan is not
always this religious historian. The oracle of Appius,
and the witchcraft of Erictho, will somewhat atone for
30 him, who was, indeed, bound up by an ill-chosen and
known argument, to follow truth with great exactness.
For my part, I am of opinion, that neither Homer,
Virgil, Statius, Ariosto, Tasso, nor our English Spencer,
could have formed their poems half so beautiful, without
35 those gods and spirits, and those enthusiastic parts of

poetry, which compose the most noble parts of all their writings. And I will ask any man who loves heroic poetry (for I will not dispute their tastes who do not), if the ghost of *Polydorus* in Virgil, the *Enchanted Wood* in Tasso, and the *Bower of Bliss* in Spencer 5 (which he borrows from that admirable Italian) could have been omitted, without taking from their works some of the greatest beauties in them. And if any man object the improbabilities of a spirit appearing, or of a palace raised by magic ; I boldly answer him, that an 10 heroic poet is not tied to a bare representation of what is true, or exceeding probable ; but that he may let himself loose to visionary objects, and to the representation of such things as depending not on sense, and therefore not to be comprehended by knowledge, may 15 give him a freer scope for imagination. 'Tis enough that, in all ages and religions, the greatest part of mankind have believed the power of magic, and that there are spirits or spectres which have appeared. This, I say, is foundation enough for poetry ; and I dare 20 further affirm, that the whole doctrine of separated beings, whether those spirits are incorporeal substances (which Mr. Hobbs, with some reason, thinks to imply a contradiction), or that they are a thinner or more aërial sort of bodies (as some of the Fathers have con- 25 jectured), may better be explicated by poets than by philosophers or divines. For their speculations on this subject are wholly poetical ; they have only their fancy for their guide ; and that, being sharper in an excellent poet, than it is likely it should in a phlegmatic, 30 heavy gownman, will see further in its own empire, and produce more satisfactory notions on those dark and doubtful problems.

Some men think they have raised a great argument against the use of spectres and magic in heroic poetry, 35

by saying they are unnatural; but whether they or I believe there are such things, is not material; 'tis enough that, for aught we know, they may be in Nature; and whatever is, or may be, is not properly unnatural.
5 Neither am I much concerned at Mr. Cowley's verses before *Gondibert* (though his authority is almost sacred to me) : 'tis true, he has resembled the epic poetry to a fantastic fairy-land; but he has contradicted himself by his own example. For he has himself made use of
10 angels and visions in his *Davideis*, as well as Tasso in his *Godfrey*.

What I have written on this subject will not be thought a digression by the reader, if he please to remember what I said in the beginning of this essay, that I have
15 modelled my heroic plays by the rules of an heroic poem. And if that be the most noble, the most pleasant, and the most instructive way of writing in verse, and withal the highest pattern of human life, as all poets have agreed, I shall need no other argument to justify
20 my choice in this imitation. One advantage the drama has above the other, namely, that it represents to view what the poem only does relate; and, *Segnius irritant animum demissa per aures, quam quae sunt oculis subjecta fidelibus*, as Horace tells us.

25 To those who object my frequent use of drums and trumpets, and my representations of battles, I answer, I introduced them not on the English stage : Shakespeare used them frequently; and though Johnson shows no battle in his *Catiline*, yet you hear from
30 behind the scenes the sounding of trumpets, and the shouts of fighting armies. But I add farther, that these warlike instruments, and even their presentations of fighting on the stage, are no more than necessary to produce the effects of an heroic play; that is,
35 to raise the imagination of the audience, and to per-

suade them, for the time, that what they behold on
the theatre is really performed. The poet is then to
endeavour an absolute dominion over the minds of the
spectators ; for, though our fancy will contribute to its
own deceit, yet a writer ought to help its operation : 5
and that the *Red Bull* has formerly done the same, is no
more an argument against our practice, than it would
be for a physician to forbear an approved medicine,
because a mountebank has used it with success.

Thus I have given a short account of heroic plays. 10
I might now, with the usual eagerness of an author,
make a particular defence of this. But the common
opinion (how unjust soever) has been so much to my
advantage, that I have reason to be satisfied, and to
suffer with patience all that can be urged against it. 15

For, otherwise, what can be more easy for me, than
to defend the character of Almanzor, which is one great
exception that is made against the play ? 'Tis said,
that Almanzor is no perfect pattern of heroic virtue,
that he is a contemner of kings, and that he is made to 20
perform impossibilities.

I must therefore avow, in the first place, from whence
I took the character. The first image I had of him,
was from the *Achilles* of Homer ; the next from Tasso's
Rinaldo (who was a copy of the former), and the third 25
from the *Artaban* of Monsieur Calprenède, who has
imitated both. The original of these, Achilles, is taken
by Homer for his hero ; and is described by him as
one, who in strength and courage surpassed the rest of
the Grecian army ; but withal of so fiery a temper, so 30
impatient of an injury, even from his king and general,
that when his mistress was to be forced from him by
the command of Agamemnon, he not only disobeyed it,
but returned him an answer full of contumely, and in
the most opprobrious terms he could imagine. They 35

are Homer's words which follow, and I have cited but some few amongst a multitude :

Οἰνοβαρές, κυνὸς ὄμματ' ἔχων, κραδίην δ' ἐλάφοιο—Il. A. v. 225.
Δημοβόρος βασιλεύς, etc.—Il. A. v. 231.

5 Nay, he proceeded so far in his insolence, as to draw out his sword, with intention to kill him :

Ελκετο δ' ἐκ κολεοῖο μέγα ξίφος.—Il. A. v. 194.

And, if Minerva had not appeared, and held his hand, he had executed his design ; and it was all she could
10 do to dissuade him from it. The event was, that he left the army, and would fight no more. Agamemnon gives his character thus to Nestor :

'Αλλ' ὅδ' ἀνὴρ ἐθέλει περὶ πάντων ἔμμεναι ἄλλων,
Πάντων μὲν κρατέειν ἐθέλει, πάντεσσι δ' ἀνάσσειν—Il. A. v. 287, 288.

15 and Horace gives the same description of him in his *Art of Poetry* :

Honoratum si fortè reponis Achillem,
Impiger, iracundus, inexorabilis, acer,
Jura neget sibi nata, nihil non arroget armis.

20 Tasso's chief character, Rinaldo, was a man of the same temper ; for, when he had slain Gernando in his heat of passion, he not only refused to be judged by Godfrey, his general, but threatened that if he came to seize him, he would right himself by arms upon him ;
25 witness these following lines of Tasso :

Venga egli, o mandi, io terrò fermo il piede :
Giudici fian tra noi la sorte, e l'arme ;
Fera tragedia vuol che s'appresenti,
Per lor diporto, alle nemiche genti.

30 You see how little these great authors did esteem the *point of honour,* so much magnified by the French, and so ridiculously aped by us. They made their

heroes men of honour ; but so as not to divest them quite of human passions and frailties : they contented themselves to show you, what men of great spirits would certainly do when they were provoked, not what they were obliged to do by the strict rules of moral virtue. 5 For my own part, I declare myself for Homer and Tasso, and am more in love with Achilles and Rinaldo, than with Cyrus and Oroondates. I shall never subject my characters to the French standard, where love and honour are to be weighed by drachms and scruples. 10 Yet, where I have designed the patterns of exact virtues, such as in this play are the parts of Almahide, of Ozmyn, and Benzayda, I may safely challenge the best of theirs.

But Almanzor is taxed with changing sides : and 15 what tie has he on him to the contrary ? He is not born their subject whom he serves, and he is injured by them to a very high degree. He threatens them, and speaks insolently of sovereign power ; but so do Achilles and Rinaldo, who were subjects and soldiers 20 to Agamemnon and Godfrey of Bulloigne. He talks extravagantly in his passion ; but, if I would take the pains to quote an hundred passages of Ben Johnson's Cethegus, I could easily show you, that the rodomontades of Almanzor are neither so irrational as his, nor 25 so impossible to be put in execution ; for Cethegus threatens to destroy Nature, and to raise a new one out of it ; to kill all the Senate for his part of the action ; to look Cato dead ; and a thousand other things as extravagant he says, but performs not one 30 action in the play.

But none of the former calumnies will stick : and, therefore, 'tis at last charged upon me, that Almanzor does all things ; or if you will have an absurd accusation, in their nonsense who make it, that he performs 35

impossibilities. They say, that being a stranger, he appeases two fighting factions, when the authority of their lawful sovereign could not. This is indeed the most improbable of all his actions, but 'tis far from
5 being impossible. Their king had made himself contemptible to his people, as the history of Granada tells us ; and Almanzor, though a stranger, yet was already known to them by his gallantry, in the *juego de toros*, his engagement on the weaker side, and more especially
10 by the character of his person and brave actions, given by Abdalla just before ; and, after all, the greatness of the enterprise consisted only in the daring, for he had the king's guards to second him. But we have read both of Cæsar, and many other generals, who
15 have not only calmed a mutiny with a word, but have presented themselves single before an army of their enemies ; which upon sight of them has revolted from their own leaders and come over to their trenches. In the rest of Almanzor's actions you see him for the most
20 part victorious ; but the same fortune has constantly attended many heroes, who were not imaginary. Yet, you see it no inheritance to him ; for, in the first place, he is made a prisoner ; and, in the last, defeated, and not able to preserve the city from being taken. If the
25 history of the late Duke of Guise be true, he hazarded more, and performed not less in Naples, than Almanzor is feigned to have done in Granada.

I have been too tedious in this apology ; but to make some satisfaction, I will leave the rest of my play
30 exposed to the critics, without defence.

The concernment of it is wholly passed from me, and ought to be in them who have been favourable to it, and are somewhat obliged to defend their own opinions. That there are errors in it, I deny not ;
35   *Ast opere in tanto fas est obrepere somnum.*

But I have already swept the stakes ; and, with the common good fortune of prosperous gamesters, can be content to sit quietly ; to hear my fortune cursed by some, and my faults arraigned by others, and to suffer both without reply. 5

EPILOGUE

TO THE SECOND PART OF 'THE CONQUEST OF GRANADA'

THEY, who have best succeeded on the stage,
Have still conform'd their genius to their age.
Thus *Johnson* did mechanic humour show,
When men were dull, and conversation low.
5 Then, *Comedy* was faultless, but 'twas coarse :
Cobb's tankard was a jest, and *Otter's* horse.
And, as their *Comedy*, their love was mean ;
Except, by chance, in some one labour'd scene,
Which must atone for an ill-written play :
10 They rose, but at their height could seldom stay.
Fame then was cheap, and the first comer sped ;
And they have kept it since, by being dead.
But, were they now to write, when critics weigh
Each line, and ev'ry word, throughout a play,
15 None of them, no, not *Johnson* in his height,
Could pass, without allowing grains for weight.
Think it not envy, that these truths are told :
Our poet's not malicious, though he 's bold.
'Tis not to brand 'em that their faults are shown,
20 But, by their errors, to excuse his own.
If *Love* and *Honour* now are higher rais'd,
'Tis not the poet, but the age is prais'd.

Wit 's now arriv'd to a more high degree ;
Our native language more refin'd and free.
Our ladies and our men now speak more wit
In conversation, than those poets writ.
Then, one of these is, consequently, true ;   5
That what this poet writes comes short of you,
And imitates you ill (which most he fears),
Or else his writing is not worse than theirs.
Yet, though you judge (as sure the critics will),
That some before him writ with greater skill,   10
In this one praise he has their fame surpast,
To please an age more gallant than the last.

DEFENCE OF THE EPILOGUE ;

OR,

AN ESSAY ON THE DRAMATIC POETRY
OF THE LAST AGE

THE promises of authors, that they will write again, are, in effect, a threatening of their readers with some new impertinence ; and they, who perform not what they promise, will have their pardon on easy terms.
5 It is from this consideration, that I could be glad to spare you the trouble, which I am now giving you, of a postscript, if I were not obliged, by many reasons, to write somewhat concerning our present plays, and those of our predecessors on the English stage. The
10 truth is, I have so far engaged myself in a bold *Epilogue* to this play, wherein I have somewhat taxed the former writing, that it was necessary for me either not to print it, or to show that I could defend it. Yet I would so maintain my opinion of the present age, as not to be
15 wanting in my veneration for the past : I would ascribe to dead authors their just praises in those things wherein they have excelled us ; and in those wherein we contend with them for the pre-eminence, I would acknowledge our advantages to the age, and claim no victory from
20 our wit. This being what I have proposed to myself, I hope I shall not be thought arrogant when I inquire

into their errors. For we live in an age so sceptical,
that as it determines little, so it takes nothing from
antiquity on trust ; and I profess to have no other
ambition in this *Essay*, than that poetry may not go
backward, when all other arts and sciences are ad- 5
vancing. Whoever censures me for this inquiry, let
him hear his character from Horace :

> *Ingeniis non ille favet, plauditque sepultis,*
> *Nostra sed impugnat ; nos nostraque lividus odit.*
>
> He favours not dead wits, but hates the living.   10

It was upbraided to that excellent poet, that he was
an enemy to the writings of his predecessor Lucilius,
because he had said, *Lucilium lutulentum fluere*, that he
ran muddy ; and that he ought to have retrenched from
his satires many unnecessary verses. But Horace 15
makes Lucilius himself to justify him from the imputation of envy, by telling you that he would have done
the same, had he lived in an age which was more
refined :

> *Si foret hoc nostrum fato delapsus in aevum,*   20
> *Detereret sibi multa, recideret omne quod ultra*
> *Perfectum traheretur,* etc.

And, both in the whole course of that satire, and in his
most admirable *Epistle to Augustus*, he makes it his
business to prove, that antiquity alone is no plea for 25
the excellency of a poem ; but that, one age learning
from another, the last (if we can suppose an equality of
wit in the writers) has the advantage of knowing more
and better than the former. And this, I think, is the
state of the question in dispute. It is therefore my 30
part to make it clear, that the language, wit, and conversation of our age, are improved and refined above
the last ; and then it will not be difficult to infer, that
our plays have received some part of those advantages.

In the first place, therefore, it will be necessary to state, in general, what this refinement is, of which we treat ; and that, I think, will not be defined amiss : *An improvement of our Wit, Language, and Conversation ;* 5 *or, an alteration in them for the better.*

To begin with Language. That an alteration is lately made in ours, or since the writers of the last age (in which I comprehend Shakespeare, Fletcher, and Johnson), is manifest. Any man who reads those 10 excellent poets, and compares their language with what is now written, will see it almost in every line ; but that this is an improvement of the language, or an alteration for the better, will not so easily be granted. For many are of a contrary opinion, that the English 15 tongue was then in the height of its perfection ; that from Johnson's time to ours it has been in a continual declination, like that of the Romans from the age of Virgil to Statius, and so downward to Claudian ; of which, not only Petronius, but Quintilian himself so 20 much complains, under the person of Secundus, in his famous dialogue *de Causis corruptae Eloquentiae.*

But, to show that our language is improved, and that those people have not a just value for the age in which they live, let us consider in what the refinement of a 25 language principally consists : that is, *either in rejecting such old words, or phrases, which are ill sounding, or improper ; or in admitting new, which are more proper, more sounding, and more significant.*

The reader will easily take notice, that when I speak 30 of rejecting improper words and phrases, I mention not such as are antiquated by custom only, and, as I may say, without any fault of theirs. For in this case the refinement can be but accidental ; that is, when the words and phrases, which are rejected, happen to be 35 improper. Neither would I be understood, when I

speak of impropriety of language, either wholly to
accuse the last age, or to excuse the present, and least
of all myself ; for all writers have their imperfections
and failings : but I may safely conclude in the general,
that our improprieties are less frequent, and less gross 5
than theirs. One testimony of this is undeniable, that
we are the first who have observed them ; and, certainly, to observe errors is a great step to the correcting
of them. But, malice and partiality set apart, let any
man, who understands English, read diligently the 10
works of Shakespeare and Fletcher, and I dare undertake, that he will find in every page either some solecism
of speech, or some notorious flaw in sense ; and yet
these men are reverenced, when we are not forgiven.
That their wit is great, and many times their expres- 15
sions noble, envy itself cannot deny :

> *Neque ego illis detrahere ausim*
> *Haerentem capiti multâ cum laude coronam.*

But the times were ignorant in which they lived. Poetry
was then, if not in its infancy among us, at least not 20
arrived to its vigour and maturity : witness the lameness of their plots ; many of which, especially those
which they writ first (for even that age refined itself
in some measure), were made up of some ridiculous
incoherent story, which in one play many times took 25
up the business of an age. I suppose I need not name
Pericles, Prince of Tyre, nor the historical plays of
Shakespeare : besides many of the rest, as the *Winter's
Tale, Love's Labour Lost, Measure for Measure,* which
were either grounded on impossibilities, or at least so 30
meanly written, that the comedy neither caused your
mirth, nor the serious part your concernment. If I
would expatiate on this subject, I could easily demon-
strate, that our admired Fletcher, who writ after him,
neither understood correct plotting, nor that which they 35

call *the decorum of the stage*. I would not search in
his worst plays for examples : he who will consider his
Philaster, his *Humorous Lieutenant*, his *Faithful Shepherdess*, and many others which I could name, will find
5 them much below the applause which is now given
them. He will see Philaster wounding his mistress,
and afterwards his boy, to save himself ; not to mention
the Clown, who enters immediately, and not only has the
advantage of the combat against the hero, but diverts
10 you from your serious concernment, with his ridiculous
and absurd raillery. In his *Humorous Lieutenant*, you
find his Demetrius and Leontius staying in the midst
of a routed army, to hear the cold mirth of the
Lieutenant ; and Demetrius afterwards appearing with
15 a pistol in his hand, in the next age to Alexander
the Great. And for his Shepherd, he falls twice into
the former indecency of wounding women. But these
abÈurdities, which those poets committed, may more
properly be called the age's fault than theirs : for,
20 besides the want of education and learning (which was
their particular unhappiness), they wanted the benefit
of converse : but of that I shall speak hereafter, in
a place more proper for it. Their audiences knew no
better ; and therefore were satisfied with what they
25 brought. Those, who call theirs *the Golden Age of
Poetry*, have only this reason for it, that they were
then content with acorns before they knew the use of
bread, or that ἅλις δρυὸς was become a proverb. They
had many who admired them, and few who blamed
30 them ; and certainly a severe critic is the greatest help
to a good wit : he does the office of a friend, while he
designs that of an enemy ; and his malice keeps a poet
within those bounds, which the luxuriancy of his fancy
would tempt him to overleap.
35   But it is not their plots which I meant principally to

tax ; I was speaking of their sense and language ; and I dare almost challenge any man to show me a page together which is correct in both. As for Ben Johnson, I am loath to name him, because he is a most judicious writer ; yet he very often falls into these errors : and 5 I once more beg the reader's pardon for accusing him of them. Only let him consider, that I live in an age where my least faults are severely censured ; and that I have no way left to extenuate my failings, but by showing as great in those whom we admire :   10

> *Cædimus, inque vicem præbemus crura sagittis.*

I cast my eyes but by chance on *Catiline* ; and in the three or four last pages, found enough to conclude that Johnson writ not correctly :—

> Let the long-hid seeds   15
> Of treason, in thee, now shoot forth in deeds
> Ranker than horror.

In reading some bombast speeches of Macbeth, which are not to be understood, he used to say that it was horror ; and I am much afraid that this is so.   20

> Thy parricide late on thy only son,
> After his mother, to make empty way
> For thy last wicked nuptials, worse than they
> That blaze that act of thy incestuous life,
> Which gained thee at once a daughter and a wife.   25

The sense is here extremely perplexed ; and I doubt the word *they* is false grammar.

> And be free
> Not heaven itself from thy impiety.

A *synchysis*, or ill-placing of words, of which Tully so 30 much complains in oratory.

> The waves and dens of beasts could not receive
> The bodies that those souls were frighted from.

The preposition in the end of the sentence ; a common fault with him, and which I have but lately observed in my own writings.

> What all the several ills that visit earth,
> 5   Plague, famine, fire, could not reach unto,
> The sword, nor surfeits, let thy fury do.

Here are both the former faults : for, besides that the preposition *unto* is placed last in the verse, and at the half period, and is redundant, there is the former
10 synchysis in the words *the sword, nor surfeits*, which in construction ought to have been placed before the other.

Catiline says of Cethegus, that for his sake he would

> *Go on upon* the Gods, kiss lightning, wrest
> 15   The engine from the Cyclops, and give fire
> At face of a full cloud, and stand his ire.

To *go on upon*, is only to go on twice. To *give fire at face of a full cloud*, was not understood in his own time ; *and stand his ire*, besides the antiquated word *ire*,
20 there is the article *his*, which makes false construction : and *giving fire at the face of a cloud*, is a perfect image of shooting, however it came to be known in those days to Catiline.

> Others there are,
> 25   Whom envy to the state draws and pulls on,
> For contumelies received ; and such are sure ones.

Ones, in the plural number : but that is frequent with him ; for he says, not long after,

> Cæsar and Crassus, if they be ill men,
> 30   Are mighty ones—
> Such men, they do not succour more the cause, &c.

They redundant.

> Though Heaven should speak with all his wrath at once,
> We should stand upright and unfear'd.

His is ill syntax with *Heaven* ; and by *unfeared* he means *unafraid* : words of quite a contrary signification.

The ports are open.

He perpetually uses ports for gates ; which is an affected error in him, to introduce Latin by the loss of 5 the English idiom ; as, in the translation of Tully's speeches he usually does.

Well-placing of words, for the sweetness of pronunciation, was not known till Mr. Waller introduced it ; and, therefore, it is not to be wondered if Ben Johnson has 10 many such lines as these :

But being bred up in his father's needy fortunes; brought up in 's sister's prostitution, &c.

But meanness of expression one would think not to be his error in a tragedy, which ought to be more high 15 and sounding than any other kind of poetry ; and yet, amongst others in *Catiline,* I find these four lines together :

> So Asia, thou art cruelly even
> With us, for all the blows thee given ;   20
> When we, whose virtues conquered thee,
> Thus by thy vices ruin'd be.

Be there is false English for *are* ; though the rhyme hides it.

But I am willing to close the book, partly out of 25 veneration to the author, partly out of weariness to pursue an argument which is so fruitful, in so small a compass. And what correctness, after this, can be expected from Shakespeare or from Fletcher, who wanted that learning and care which Johnson had ? I will, there- 30 fore, spare my own trouble of inquiring into their faults ; who, had they lived now, had doubtless written more correctly. I suppose it will be enough for me to affirm (as I think I safely may), that these, and the like errors, which I taxed in the most correct of the last age, are 35

such into which we do not ordinarily fall. I think few
of our present writers would have left behind them such
a line as this :

Contain your spirit in more stricter bounds.

5   But that gross way of two comparatives was then
ordinary ; and, therefore, more pardonable in Johnson.

As for the other part of refining, which consists in
receiving new words and phrases, I shall not insist
much on it. It is obvious that we have admitted many,
10 some of which we wanted, and therefore our language
is the richer for them, as it would be by importation of
bullion : others are rather ornamental than necessary ;
yet, by their admission, the language is become more
courtly, and our thoughts are better drest. These are
15 to be found scattered in the writers of our age, and it is
not my business to collect them. They, who have lately
written with most care, have, I believe, taken the rule of
Horace for their guide ; that is, not to be too hasty in
receiving of words, but rather to stay till custom has
20 made them familiar to us :

Quem penes arbitrium est, et jus, et norma loquendi.

For I cannot approve of their way of refining, who
corrupt our English idiom by mixing it too much with
French : that is a sophistication of language, not an
25 improvement of it ; a turning English into French, rather
than a refining of English by French. We meet daily
with those fops, who value themselves on their travelling, and pretend they cannot express their meaning in
English, because they would put off to us some French
30 phrase of the last edition ; without considering, that, for
aught they know, we have a better of our own. But
these are not the men who are to refine us ; their talent
is to prescribe fashions, not words : at best, they are
only serviceable to a writer, so as Ennius was to Virgil.

He may *aurum ex stercore colligere* : for 'tis hard if,
amongst many insignificant phrases, there happen not
something worth preserving ; though they themselves,
like Indians, know not the value of their own commodity.

There is yet another way of improving language, which 5
poets especially have practised in all ages ; that is, by
applying received words to a new signification ; and this,
I believe, is meant by Horace, in that precept which is
so variously construed by expositors :

> *Dixeris egregie, notum si callida verbum*   10
> *Reddiderit junctura novum.*

And, in this way, he himself had a particular happiness ;
using all the tropes, and particular metaphors, with that
grace which is observable in his *Odes*, where the beauty
of expression is often greater than that of thought ; as, 15
in that one example, amongst an infinite number of
others, *Et vultus nimium lubricus aspici.*

And therefore, though he innovated little, he may
justly be called a great refiner of the Roman tongue.
This choice of words, and heightening of their natural 20
signification, was observed in him by the writers of the
following ages ; for Petronius says of him, *et Horatii
curiosa felicitas.* By this graffing, as I may call it, on
old words, has our tongue been beautified by the three
fore-mentioned poets, Shakespeare, Fletcher, and John- 25
son, whose excellencies I can never enough admire ; and
in this they have been followed, especially by Sir John
Suckling and Mr. Waller, who refined upon them.
Neither have they, who succeeded them, been wanting
in their endeavours to adorn our mother tongue : but 30
it is not so lawful for me to praise my living contemporaries, as to admire my dead predecessors.

I should now speak of the refinement of Wit ; but
I have been so large on the former subject, that I am
forced to contract myself in this. I will therefore only 35

observe to you, that the wit of the last age was yet more
incorrect than their language. Shakespeare, who many
times has written better than any poet, in any language,
is yet so far from writing wit always, or expressing that
5 wit according to the dignity of the subject, that he writes,
in many places, below the dullest writer of ours, or any
precedent age. Never did any author precipitate himself
from such height of thought to so low expressions, as he
often does. He is the very Janus of poets ; he wears
10 almost everywhere two faces ; and you have scarce begun
to admire the one, ere you despise the other. Neither
is the luxuriance of Fletcher (which his friends have
taxed in him) a less fault than the carelessness of Shakespeare. He does not well always ; and, when he does,
15 he is a true Englishman ; he knows not when to give
over. If he wakes in one scene, he commonly slumbers
in another ; and, if he pleases you in the first three acts,
he is frequently so tired with his labour, that he goes
heavily in the fourth, and sinks under his burden in
20 the fifth.

For Ben Johnson, the most judicious of poets, he
always writ properly, and as the character required ;
and I will not contest farther with my friends who call
that wit : it being very certain, that even folly itself, well
25 represented, is wit in a larger signification ; and that
there is fancy, as well as judgment, in it, though not so
much or noble : because all poetry being imitation, that
of folly is a lower exercise of fancy, though perhaps as
difficult as the other ; for 'tis a kind of looking down-
30 ward in the poet, and representing that part of mankind
which is below him.

In these low characters of vice and folly, lay the excellency of that inimitable writer ; who, when at any time
he aimed at wit in the stricter sense, that is, sharpness
35 of conceit, was forced either to borrow from the Ancients,

as to my knowledge he did very much from Plautus ; or, when he trusted himself alone, often fell into meanness of expression.   Nay, he was not free from the lowest and most grovelling kind of wit, which we call clenches, of which *Every Man in his Humour* is infinitely full ; and, 5 which is worse, the wittiest persons in the drama speak them.   His other comedies are not exempt from them. Will you give me leave to name some few ?   Asper, in which character he personates himself (and he neither was nor thought himself a fool), exclaiming against the 10 ignorant judges of the age, speaks thus :

> How monstrous and detested is't, to see
> A fellow, that has neither art nor brain,
> Sit like an *Aristarchus*, or *stark-ass*,
> Taking men's lines, with a *tobacco face*,   15
> In *snuff*, &c.

And presently after : *I mar'le whose wit 'twas to put a prologue in yond Sackbut's mouth.   They might well think he would be out of tune, and yet you'd play upon him too.—* Will you have another of the same stamp ?   *O, I cannot* 20 *abide these limbs of* sattin, *or rather* Satan.

But, it may be, you will object that this was Asper, Macilente, or Carlo Buffone : you shall, therefore, hear him speak in his own person, and that in the two last lines, or sting of an epigram.   'Tis inscribed to *Fine* 25 *Grand*, who, he says, was indebted to him for many things which he reckons there ; and concludes thus :

> Forty things more, dear *Grand*, which you know true,
> For which, or pay me quickly, or I'll pay you.

This was then the mode of wit, the vice of the age, 30 and not Ben Johnson's ; for you see, a little before him, that admirable wit, Sir Philip Sidney, perpetually playing with his words.   In his time, I believe, it ascended first into the pulpit, where (if you will give me leave to clench too) it yet finds the benefit of its clergy ; for they are 35

commonly the first corrupters of eloquence, and the last
reformed from vicious oratory ; as a famous Italian has
observed before me, in his *Treatise of the Corruption
of the Italian Tongue* ; which he principally ascribes to
5 priests and preaching friars.

But, to conclude with what brevity I can, I will only
add this, in defence of our present writers, that, if they
reach not some excellencies of Ben Johnson (which no
age, I am confident, ever shall), yet, at least, they are
10 above that meanness of thought which I have taxed, and
which is frequent in him.

That the wit of this age is much more courtly, may
easily be proved, by viewing the characters of gentlemen
which were written in the last.   First, for Johnson :—
15 Truewit, in the *Silent Woman*, was his masterpiece ; and
Truewit was a scholar-like kind of man, a gentleman
with an allay of pedantry, a man who seems mortified
to the world, by much reading.   The best of his discourse
is drawn, not from the knowledge of the town, but books ;
20 and, in short, he would be a fine gentleman in an univer-
sity.   Shakespeare showed the best of his skill in his
Mercutio ; and he said himself, that he was forced to kill
him in the third act, to prevent being killed by him.   But,
for my part, I cannot find he was so dangerous a person :
25 I see nothing in him but what was so exceeding harm-
less, that he might have lived to the end of the play, and
died in his bed, without offence to any man.

Fletcher's Don John is our only bugbear ; and yet
I may affirm, without suspicion of flattery, that he now
30 speaks better, and that his character is maintained with
much more vigour in the fourth and fifth acts, than it
was by Fletcher in the three former.   I have always
acknowledged the wit of our predecessors, with all the
veneration which becomes me ; but, I am sure, their wit
35 was not that of gentlemen ;   there was ever somewhat

that was ill-bred and clownish in it, and which confessed
the conversation of the authors.

And this leads me to the last and greatest advantage
of our writing, which proceeds from *conversation*. In
the age wherein those poets lived, there was less of
gallantry than in ours ; neither did they keep the best
company of theirs. Their fortune has been much like
that of Epicurus, in the retirement of his gardens ; to
live almost unknown, and to be celebrated after their
decease. I cannot find that any of them had been conversant in courts, except Ben Johnson ; and his genius
lay not so much that way, as to make an improvement
by it. Greatness was not then so easy of access, nor
conversation so free, as now it is. I cannot, therefore,
conceive it any insolence to affirm, that, by the knowledge and pattern of their wit who writ before us, and by
the advantage of our own conversation, the discourse
and raillery of our comedies excel what has been written
by them. And this will be denied by none, but some
few old fellows who value themselves on their acquaintance with the *Black Friars* ; who, because they saw their
plays, would pretend a right to judge ours. The memory
of these grave gentlemen is their only plea for being
wits. They can tell a story of Ben Johnson, and, perhaps, have had fancy enough to give a supper in the
Apollo, that they might be called his sons ; and, because
they were drawn in to be laughed at in those times, they
think themselves now sufficiently entitled to laugh at
ours. Learning I never saw in any of them ; and wit
no more than they could remember. In short, they were
unlucky to have been bred in an unpolished age, and
more unlucky to live to a refined one. They have lasted
beyond their own, and are cast behind ours ; and, not
contented to have known little at the age of twenty, they
boast of their ignorance at threescore.

Now, if they ask me, whence it is that our conversation is so much refined ? I must freely, and without flattery, ascribe it to the court ; and, in it, particularly to the King, whose example gives a law to it. His own mis-
5 fortunes, and the nation's, afforded him an opportunity, which is rarely allowed to sovereign princes, I mean of travelling, and being conversant in the most polished courts of Europe ; and, thereby, of cultivating a spirit which was formed by nature to receive the impressions
10 of a gallant and generous education. At his return, he found a nation lost as much in barbarism as in rebellion ; and, as the excellency of his nature forgave the one, so the excellency of his manners reformed the other. The desire of imitating so great a pattern first awakened the
15 dull and heavy spirits of the English from their natural reservedness ; loosened them from their stiff forms of conversation, and made them easy and pliant to each other in discourse. Thus, insensibly, our way of living became more free ; and the fire of the English wit, which
20 was before stifled under a constrained, melancholy way of breeding, began first to display its force, by mixing the solidity of our nation with the air and gaiety of our neighbours. This being granted to be true, it would be a wonder if the poets, whose work is imitation, should
25 be the only persons in three kingdoms who should not receive advantage by it ; or, if they should not more easily imitate the wit and conversation of the present age than of the past.

Let us therefore admire the beauties and the heights
30 of Shakespeare, without falling after him into a careless-ness, and, as I may call it, a lethargy of thought, for whole scenes together. Let us imitate, as we are able, the quickness and easiness of Fletcher, without proposing him as a pattern to us, either in the redundancy of his
35 matter, or the incorrectness of his language. Let us

admire his wit and sharpness of conceit ; but let us at
the same time acknowledge, that it was seldom so fixed,
and made proper to his character, as that the same
things might not be spoken by any person in the play.
Let us applaud his scenes of love ; but let us confess, 5
that he understood not either greatness or perfect honour
in the parts of any of his women.   In fine, let us allow,
that he had so much fancy, as when he pleased he could
write wit ; but that he wanted so much judgment, as
seldom to have written humour, or described a pleasant 10
folly.   Let us ascribe to Johnson, the height and accuracy
of judgment in the ordering of his plots, his choice of
characters, and maintaining what he had chosen to the
end.   But let us not think him a perfect pattern of imitation, except it be in humour ; for love, which is the 15
foundation of all comedies in other languages, is scarcely
mentioned in any of his plays ; and for humour itself,
the poets of this age will be more wary than to imitate
the meanness of his persons.   Gentlemen will now be
entertained with the follies of each other ; and, though 20
they allow Cobb and Tib to speak properly, yet they are
not much pleased with their tankard or with their rags.
And surely their conversation can be no jest to them on
the theatre, when they would avoid it in the street.

   To conclude all, let us render to our predecessors 25
what is their due, without confining ourselves to a servile
imitation of all they writ ; and, without assuming to
ourselves the title of better poets, let us ascribe to the
gallantry and civility of our age the advantage which
we have above them, and to our knowledge of the cus- 30
toms and manner of it the happiness we have to please
beyond them.

THE AUTHOR'S APOLOGY

FOR HEROIC POETRY AND POETIC LICENCE,
PREFIXED TO ' THE STATE OF INNOCENCE
AND FALL OF MAN,' AN OPERA, 1677

To satisfy the curiosity of those who will give themselves the trouble of reading the ensuing poem, I think
myself obliged to render them a reason why I publish
an opera which was never acted. In the first place,
5 I shall not be ashamed to own that my chiefest motive
was the ambition which I acknowledged in the Epistle.
I was desirous to lay at the feet of so beautiful and excellent a Princess a work, which, I confess, was unworthy
her, but which, I hope, she will have the goodness to
10 forgive. I was also induced to it in my own defence ;
many hundred copies of it being dispersed abroad
without my knowledge or consent : so that every one
gathering new faults, it became at length a libel against
me ; and I saw, with some disdain, more nonsense than
15 either I, or as bad a poet, could have crammed into
it, at a month's warning ; in which time 'twas wholly
written, and not since revised. After this, I cannot,
without injury to the deceased author of *Paradise Lost*,
but acknowledge, that this poem has received its entire
20 foundation, part of the design, and many of the ornaments, from him. What I have borrowed will be so
easily discerned from my mean productions, that I shall

not need to point the reader to the places : and truly
I should be sorry, for my own sake, that any one should
take the pains to compare them together ; the original
being undoubtedly one of the greatest, most noble, and
most sublime poems which either this age or nation has 5
produced. And though I could not refuse the partiality
of my friend, who is pleased to commend me in his
verses, I hope they will rather be esteemed the effect
of his love to me, than of his deliberate and sober
judgment. His genius is able to make beautiful what 10
he pleases : yet, as he has been too favourable to me,
I doubt not but he will hear of his kindness from many
of our contemporaries ; for we are fallen into an age
of illiterate, censorious, and detracting people, who, thus
qualified, set up for critics.   15

   In the first place, I must take leave to tell them, that
they wholly mistake the nature of criticism who think
its business is principally to find fault. Criticism, as it
was first instituted by Aristotle, was meant a standard
of judging well ; the chiefest part of which is, to observe 20
those excellencies which should delight a reasonable
reader. If the design, the conduct, the thoughts, and
the expressions of a poem, be generally such as proceed
from a true genius of Poetry, the critic ought to pass his
judgment in favour of the. author. 'Tis malicious and 25
unmanly to snarl at the little lapses of a pen, from which
Virgil himself stands not exempted. Horace acknowledges, that honest Homer nods sometimes : he is not
equally awake in every line ; but he leaves it also as
a standing measure for our judgments,   30

> . . . *Non, ubi plura nitent in carmine, paucis*
> *Offendi maculis, quas aut incuria fudit,*
> *Aut humana parum cavit natura.* . . .

And Longinus, who was undoubtedly, after Aristotle,
the greatest critic amongst the Greeks, in his twenty- 35

seventh chapter ΠΕΡΙ ῩΨΟΥΣ, has judiciously preferred
the sublime genius that sometimes errs, to the middling
or indifferent one, which makes few faults, but seldom
or never rises to any excellence. He compares the first
5 to a man of large possessions, who has not leisure to
consider of every slight expense, will not debase himself
to the management of every trifle : particular sums are
not laid out, or spared, to the greatest advantage in his
economy ; but are sometimes suffered to run to waste,
10 while he is only careful of the main. On the other side,
he likens the mediocrity of wit to one of a mean fortune,
who manages his store with extreme frugality, or rather
parsimony ; but who, with fear of running into profuse-
ness, never arrives to the magnificence of living. This
15 kind of genius writes indeed correctly. A wary man he
is in grammar, very nice as to solecism or barbarism,
judges to a hair of little decencies, knows better than
any man what is not to be written, and never hazards
himself so far as to fall, but plods on deliberately, and,
20 as a grave man ought, is sure to put his staff before
him ; in short, he sets his heart upon it, and with wonderful care makes his business sure ; that is, in plain
English, neither to be blamed nor praised.—I could,
says my author, find out some blemishes in Homer ;
25 and am perhaps as naturally inclined to be disgusted
at a fault as another man ; but, after all, to speak impartially, his failings are such, as are only marks of human
frailty : they are little mistakes, or rather negligences,
which have escaped his pen in the fervour of his writing ;
30 the sublimity of his spirit carries it with me against his
carelessness ; and though Apollonius his *Argonauts*, and
Theocritus his *Eidullia*, are more free from errors, there
is not any man of so false a judgment, who would
choose rather to have been Apollonius or Theocritus
35 than Homer.

'Tis worth our consideration a little, to examine how much these hypercritics of English poetry differ from the opinion of the Greek and Latin judges of antiquity ; from the Italians and French, who have succeeded them ; and, indeed, from the general taste and approbation of 5 all ages. Heroic Poetry, which they condemn, has ever been esteemed, and ever will be, the greatest work of human nature : in that rank has Aristotle placed it ; and Longinus is so full of the like expressions, that he abundantly confirms the other's testimony. Horace as plainly 10 delivers his opinion, and particularly praises Homer in these verses—

> *Trojani Belli scriptorem, maxime Lolli,*
> *Dum tu declamas Romæ, Praeneste relegi :*
> *Qui quid sit pulchrum, quid turpe, quid utile, quid non,* 15
> *Plenius ac melius Chrysippo et Crantore dicit.*

And in another place, modestly excluding himself from the number of poets, because he only writ odes and satires, he tells you a poet is such an one,

> *. . . cui mens divinior, atque os* 20
> *Magna sonaturum.*

Quotations are superfluous in an established truth ; otherwise I could reckon up, amongst the moderns, all the Italian commentators on Aristotle's book of poetry ; and, amongst the French, the greatest of this age, Boileau 25 and Rapin ; the latter of which is alone sufficient, were all other critics lost, to teach anew the rules of writing. Any man, who will seriously consider the nature of an Epic Poem, how it agrees with that of Poetry in general, which is to instruct and to delight, what actions it de- 30 scribes, and what persons they are chiefly whom it informs, will find it a work which indeed is full of difficulty in the attempt, but admirable when it is well performed. I write not this with the least intention to undervalue the other parts of poetry : for Comedy 35

is both excellently instructive, and extremely pleasant ; satire lashes vice into reformation, and humour represents folly so as to render it ridiculous. Many of our present writers are eminent in both these kinds ; and,
5 particularly, the author of the *Plain Dealer*, whom I am proud to call my friend, has obliged all honest and virtuous men, by one of the most bold, most general, and most useful satires, which has ever been presented on the English theatre. I do not dispute the preference
10 of Tragedy ; let every man enjoy his taste : but 'tis unjust, that they, who have not the least notion of heroic writing, should therefore condemn the pleasure which others receive from it, because they cannot comprehend it. Let them please their appetites in eating what they
15 like ; but let them not force their dish on all the table. They, who would combat general authority with particular opinion, must first establish themselves a reputation of understanding better than other men. Are all the flights of Heroic Poetry to be concluded bombast, unnatural, and
20 mere madness, because they are not affected with their excellencies ? It is just as reasonable as to conclude there is no day, because a blind man cannot distinguish of light and colours. Ought they not rather, in modesty, to doubt of their own judgments, when they think this
25 or that expression in Homer, Virgil, Tasso, or Milton's *Paradise*, to be too far strained, than positively to conclude that 'tis all fustian, and mere nonsense ? 'Tis true, there are limits to be set betwixt the boldness and rashness of a poet ; but he must understand those limits
30 who pretends to judge as well as he who undertakes to write : and he who has no liking to the whole, ought, in reason, to be excluded from censuring of the parts. He must be a lawyer before he mounts the tribunal ; and the judicature of one court, too, does not qualify a man
35 to preside in another. He may be an excellent pleader

in the Chancery, who is not fit to rule the Common
Pleas. But I will presume for once to tell them, that
the boldest strokes of poetry, when they are managed
artfully, are those which most delight the reader.

Virgil and Horace, the severest writers of the severest 5
age, have made frequent use of the hardest metaphors,
and of the strongest hyperboles ; and in this case the
best authority is the best argument ; for generally to
have pleased, and through all ages, must bear the force
of universal tradition. And if you would appeal from 10
thence to right reason, you will gain no more by it in
effect, than, first, to set up your reason against those
authors ; and, secondly, against all those who have
admired them. You must prove, why that ought not to
have pleased, which has pleased the most learned, and 15
the most judicious ; and, to be thought knowing, you
must first put the fool upon all mankind. If you can
enter more deeply, than they have done, into the causes
and resorts of that which moves pleasure in a reader,
the field is open, you may be heard : but those springs 20
of human nature are not so easily discovered by every
superficial judge : it requires Philosophy, as well as
Poetry, to sound the depth of all the passions ; what
they are in themselves, and how they are to be provoked : and in this science the best poets have excelled. 25
Aristotle raised the fabric of his *Poetry* from observation
of those things in which Euripides, Sophocles, and
Aeschylus pleased : he considered how they raised the
passions, and thence has drawn rules for our imitation.
From hence have sprung the tropes and figures, for 30
which they wanted a name, who first practised them,
and succeeded in them. Thus I grant you, that the
knowledge of Nature was the original rule ; and that all
poets ought to study her, as well as Aristotle and
Horace, her interpreters. But then this also undeniably 35

follows, that those things, which delight all ages, must have been an imitation of Nature ; which is all I contend. Therefore is Rhetoric made an art ; therefore the names of so many tropes and figures were invented ;
5 because it was observed they had such and such effect upon the audience. Therefore catachreses and hyperboles have found their place amongst them ; not that they were to be avoided, but to be used judiciously, and placed in poetry, as heightenings and shadows are in
10 painting, to make the figure bolder, and cause it to stand off to sight.

> *Nec retia cervis*
> *Ulla dolum meditantur*

says Virgil in his Eclogues : and speaking of Leander,
15 in his Georgics,

> *Nocte natat cæca serus freta, quem super ingens*
> *Porta tonat coeli, et scopulis illisa reclamant*
> *Æquora.*

In both of these, you see, he fears not to give voice and
20 thoughts to things inanimate.

Will you arraign your master, Horace, for his hardness of expression, when he describes the death of Cleopatra, and says she did *asperos tractare serpentes, ut atrum corpore combiberet venenum*, because the body, in
25 that action, performs what is proper to the mouth ?

As for hyperboles, I will neither quote Lucan, nor Statius, men of an unbounded imagination, but who often wanted the poise of judgment. The divine Virgil was not liable to that exception ; and yet he describes
30 Polyphemus thus—

> *. . . Graditurque per aequor*
> *Jam medium ; necdum fluctus latera ardua tinxit.*

In imitation of this place, our admirable Cowley thus paints Goliah—

35
> The valley, now, this monster seem'd to fill ;
> And we, methought, look'd up to him from our hill:

where the two words, *seemed* and *methought*, have molli-
fied the figure ; and yet if they had not been there, the
fright of the Israelites might have excused their belief
of the giant's stature.

In the eighth of the Æneids, Virgil paints the swift- 5
ness of Camilla thus :

> *Illa vel intactæ segetis per summa volaret*
> *Gramina, nec teneras cursu læsisset aristas ;*
> *Vel mare per medium, fluctu suspensa tumenti,*
> *Ferret iter, celeres nec tingeret æquore plantas.* 10

You are not obliged, as in History, to a literal belief
of what the poet says ; but you are pleased with the
image, without being cozened by the fiction.

Yet even in History, Longinus quotes Herodotus on
this occasion of hyperboles. The Lacedemonians, says 15
he, at the straits of Thermopylæ, defended themselves
to the last extremity ; and when their arms failed them,
fought it out with their nails and teeth ; till at length
(the Persians shooting continually upon them) they lay
buried under the arrows of their enemies. It is not 20
reasonable (continues the critic) to believe, that men
could defend themselves with their nails and teeth from
an armed multitude ; nor that they lay buried under
a pile of darts and arrows ; and yet there wants not
probability for the figure : because the hyperbole seems 25
not to have been made for the sake of the description,
but rather to have been produced from the occasion.

'Tis true, the boldness of the figures is to be hidden
sometimes by the address of the poet ; that they may
work their effect upon the mind, without discovering 30
the art which caused it. And therefore they are principally to be used in passion ; when we speak more
warmly, and with more precipitation than at other
times : for then, *si vis me flere, dolendum est primum
ipsi tibi ;* the poet must put on the passion he endeavours 35

to represent : a man in such an occasion is not cool
enough, either to reason rightly, or to talk calmly.
Aggravations are then in their proper places ; interro-
gations, exclamations, hyperbata, or a disordered con-
5 nexion of discourse, are graceful there, because they
are natural.   The sum of all depends on what before
I hinted, that this boldness of expression is not to be
blamed, if it be managed by the coolness and discretion
which is necessary to a poet.

10   Yet before I leave this subject, I cannot but take
notice how disingenuous our adversaries appear : all
that is dull, insipid, languishing, and without sinews, in
a poem, they call an imitation of Nature : they only
offend our most equitable judges, who think beyond
15 them ; and lively images and elocution are never to be
forgiven.

What fustian, as they call it, have I heard these
gentlemen find out in Mr. Cowley's *Odes* ! I acknowledge myself unworthy to defend so excellent an author,
20 neither have I room to do it here ; only in general I will
say, that nothing can appear more beautiful to me, than
the strength of those images which they condemn.

Imaging is, in itself, the very height and life of Poetry.
It is, as Longinus describes it, a discourse, which, by
25 a kind of enthusiasm, or extraordinary emotion of the
soul, makes it seem to us that we behold those things
which the poet paints, so as to be pleased with them,
and to admire them.

If poetry be imitation, that part of it must needs be
30 best which describes most lively our actions and passions ; our virtues and our vices ; our follies and our
humours : for neither is Comedy without its part of
imaging ; and they who do it best are certainly the most
excellent in their kind.   This is too plainly proved
35 to be denied.   But how are poetical fictions, how are

hippocentaurs and chimeras, or how are angels and immaterial substances to be imaged ; which, some of them, are things quite out of nature ; others, such whereof we can have no notion ? This is the last refuge of our adversaries ; and more than any of them 5 have yet had the wit to object against us. The answer is easy to the first part of it : the fiction of some beings which are not in nature (second notions, as the logicians call them) has been founded on the conjunction of two natures, which have a real separate being. So hippo- 10 centaurs were imaged, by joining the natures of a man and horse together ; as Lucretius tells us, who has used this word of *image* oftener than any of the poets—

> *Nam certe ex vivo centauri non fit imago,*
> *Nulla fuit quoniam talis natura animai :*   15
> *Verum ubi equi atque hominis, casu, convenit imago,*
> *Hærescit facile extemplo, &c.*

The same reason may also be alleged for chimeras and the rest. And poets may be allowed the like liberty for describing things which really exist not, if 20 they are founded on popular belief. Of this nature are fairies, pigmies, and the extraordinary effects of magic ; for 'tis still an imitation, though of other men's fancies : and thus are Shakespeare's *Tempest*, his *Midsummer Night's Dream*, and Ben Johnson's *Masque of Witches* 25 to be defended. For immaterial substances, we are authorized by Scripture in their description : and herein the text accommodates itself to vulgar apprehension, in giving angels the likeness of beautiful young men. Thus, after the pagan divinity, has Homer drawn his 30 gods with human faces : and thus we have notions of things above us, by describing them like other beings more within our knowledge.

I wish I could produce any one example of excellent imaging in all this poem. Perhaps I cannot ; but that 35

which comes nearest it, is in these four lines, which
have been sufficiently canvassed by my well-natured
censors—

> Seraph and cherub, careless of their charge,
> 5   And wanton, in full ease now live at large :
> Unguarded leave the passes of the sky,
> And all dissolved in hallelujahs lie.

I have heard (says one of them) of anchovies dissolved
in sauce ; but never of an angel in hallelujahs. A mighty
10 witticism ! (if you will pardon a new word,) but there is
some difference between a laugher and a critic. He
might have burlesqued Virgil too, from whom I took
the image : *Invadunt urbem, somno vinoque sepultam.*
A city's being buried, is just as proper on occasion, as
15 an angel's being dissolved in ease, and songs of triumph.
Mr. Cowley lies as open too in many places—

> Where their vast courts the mother waters keep, &c.

For if the mass of waters be the mothers, then their
daughters, the little streams, are bound, in all good
20 manners, to make courtesy to them, and ask them
blessing. How easy 'tis to turn into ridicule the best
descriptions, when once a man is in the humour of
laughing, till he wheezes at his own dull jest ! But an
image, which is strongly and beautifully set before the
25 eyes of the reader, will still be poetry when the merry
fit is over, and last when the other is forgotten.

I promised to say somewhat of Poetic Licence, but
have in part anticipated my discourse already. Poetic
Licence I take to be the liberty which poets have
30 assumed to themselves, in all ages, of speaking things in
verse, which are beyond the severity of prose. 'Tis
that particular character which distinguishes and sets
the bounds betwixt *oratio soluta* and poetry. This, as
to what regards the thought or imagination of a poet,

consists in fiction : but then those thoughts must be
expressed ; and here arise two other branches of it ; for
if this licence be included in a single word, it admits of
tropes ; if in a sentence or proposition, of figures ; both
which are of a much larger extent, and more forcibly to 5
be used in verse than prose. This is that birthright
which is derived to us from our great forefathers, even
from Homer down to Ben ; and they who would deny
it to us, have, in plain terms, the fox's quarrel to the
grapes—they cannot reach it.   10

How far these liberties are to be extended, I will not
presume to determine here, since Horace does not.
But it is certain that they are to be varied, according to
the language and age in which an author writes. That
which would be allowed to a Grecian poet, Martial tells 15
you, would not be suffered in a Roman. And 'tis
evident that the English does more nearly follow the
strictness of the latter than the freedoms of the former.
Connexion of epithets, or the conjunction of two words
in one, are frequent and elegant in the Greek, which yet 20
Sir Philip Sidney, and the translator of Du Bartas,
have unluckily attempted in the English ; though this,
I confess, is not so proper an instance of poetic licence,
as it is of variety of idiom in languages.

Horace a little explains himself on this subject of 25
Licentia Poetica, in these verses—

> . . . . *Pictoribus atque Poetis*
> *Quidlibet audendi semper fuit æqua potestas :*
> *Sed non, ut placidis coeant immitia, non ut*
> *Serpentes avibus geminentur, tigribus hædi.*   30

He would have a poem of a piece ; not to begin with
one thing, and end with another : he restrains it so far,
that thoughts of an unlike nature ought not to be joined
together. That were indeed to make a chaos. He
taxed not Homer, nor the divine Virgil, for interesting 35

their gods in the wars of Troy and Italy; neither, had he now lived, would he have taxed Milton, as our false critics have presumed to do, for his choice of a supernatural argument; but he would have blamed my author, 5 who was a Christian, had he introduced into his poem heathen deities, as Tasso is condemned by Rapin on the like occasion; and as Camoens, the author of the *Lusiads*, ought to be censured by all his readers, when he brings in Bacchus and Christ into the same adventure 10 of his fable.

From that which has been said, it may be collected, that the definition of Wit (which has been so often attempted, and ever unsuccessfully by many poets) is only this: that it is a propriety of thoughts and words; 15 or, in other terms, thoughts and words elegantly adapted to the subject. If our critics will join issue on this definition, that we may *convenire in aliquo tertio*; if they will take it as a granted principle, it will be easy to put an end to this dispute. No man will disagree from 20 another's judgment concerning the dignity of style in Heroic Poetry; but all reasonable men will conclude it necessary, that sublime subjects ought to be adorned with the sublimest, and consequently often with the most figurative expressions. In the meantime I will 25 not run into their fault of imposing my opinions on other men, any more than I would my writings on their taste: I have only laid down, and that superficially enough, my present thoughts; and shall be glad to be taught better by those who pretend to reform our 30 Poetry.

ALL FOR LOVE, OR THE WORLD
WELL LOST

(1678)

PREFACE

THE death of Antony and Cleopatra is a subject which
has been treated by the greatest wits of our nation, after
Shakespeare ; and by all so variously, that their example
has given me the confidence to try myself in this bow of
Ulysses amongst the crowd of suitors ; and, withal, to 5
take my own measures, in aiming at the mark. I doubt
not but the same motive has prevailed with all of us in
this attempt ; I mean the excellency of the moral : for
the chief persons represented were famous patterns of
unlawful love ; and their end accordingly was unfor- 10
tunate. All reasonable men have long since concluded,
that the hero of the poem ought not to be a character
of perfect virtue, for then he could not, without injustice,
be made unhappy ; nor yet altogether wicked, because
he could not then be pitied. I have therefore steered 15
the middle course ; and have drawn the character of
Antony as favourably as Plutarch, Appian, and Dion
Cassius would give me leave ; the like I have observed
in Cleopatra. That which is wanting to work up the
pity to a greater height, was not afforded me by the 20
story ; for the crimes of love, which they both committed,
were not occasioned by any necessity, or fatal ignorance,

but were wholly voluntary ; since our passions are, or ought to be, within our power. The fabric of the play is regular enough, as to the inferior parts of it ; and the Unities of Time, Place, and Action, more exactly
5 observed, than perhaps the English theatre requires. Particularly, the action is so much one, that it is the only of the kind without episode, or underplot ; every scene in the tragedy conducing to the main design, and every act concluding with a turn of it. The greatest
10 error in the contrivance seems to be in the person of Octavia ; for, though I might use the privilege of a poet, to introduce her into Alexandria, yet I had not enough considered, that the compassion she moved to herself and children was destructive to that which I reserved
15 for Antony and Cleopatra ; whose mutual love being founded upon vice, must lessen the favour of the audience to them, when virtue and innocence were oppressed by it. And, though I justified Antony in some measure, by making Octavia's departure to proceed wholly from
20 herself ; yet the force of the first machine still remained ; and the dividing of pity, like the cutting of a river into many channels, abated the strength of the natural stream. But this is an objection which none of my critics have urged against me ; and therefore I might have let it
25 pass, if I could have resolved to have been partial of myself. The faults my enemies have found are rather cavils concerning little and not essential decencies ; which a master of the ceremonies may decide betwixt us. The French poets, I confess, are strict observers
30 of these punctilios : they would not, for example, have suffered Cleopatra and Octavia to have met ; or, if they had met, there must have only passed betwixt them some cold civilities, but no eagerness of repartee, for fear of offending against the greatness of their characters,
35 and the modesty of their sex. This objection I foresaw

and at the same time contemned ; for I judged it both
natural and probable, that Octavia, proud of her new-
gained conquest, would search out Cleopatra to triumph
over her ; and that Cleopatra, thus attacked, was not of
a spirit to shun the encounter : and 'tis not unlikely, that 5
two exasperated rivals should use such satire as I have
put into their mouths ; for, after all, though the one were
a Roman, and the other a queen, they were both women.
'Tis true, some actions, though natural, are not fit to be
represented ; and broad obscenities in words ought in 10
good manners to be avoided : expressions therefore are
a modest clothing of our thoughts, as breeches and petti-
coats are of our bodies. If I have kept myself within
the bounds of modesty, all beyond it is but nicety and
affectation ; which is no more but modesty depraved into 15
a vice. They betray themselves who are too quick of
apprehension in such cases, and leave all reasonable
men to imagine worse of them, than of the poet.

Honest Montaigne goes yet further : *Nous ne sommes
que ceremonie ; la ceremonie nous emporte, et laissons la* 20
substance des choses. Nous nous tenons aux branches, et
abandonnons le tronc et le corps. Nous avons appris aux
dames de rougir, oyans seulement nommer ce qu' elles ne
craignent aucunement à faire : nous n' osons appeller à
droit nos membres, et ne craignons pas de les employer 25
à toute sorte de debauche. La ceremonie nous defend
d' exprimer par paroles les choses licites et naturelles, et
nous l' en croyons ; la raison nous defend de n' en faire
point d' illicites et mauvaises, et personne ne l' en croit.
My comfort is, that by this opinion my enemies are 30
but sucking critics, who would fain be nibbling ere their
teeth are come.

Yet in this nicety of manners does the excellency
of French poetry consist : their heroes are the most
civil people breathing ; but their good breeding seldom 35

extends to a word of sense ; all their wit is in their
ceremony ; they want the genius which animates our
stage ; and therefore 'tis but necessary, when they cannot please, that they should take care not to offend.
5 But as the civilest man in the company is commonly
the dullest, so these authors, while they are afraid to
make you laugh or cry, out of pure good manners
make you sleep. They are so careful not to exasperate
a critic, that they never leave him any work ; so busy
10 with the broom, and make so clean a riddance, that there
is little left either for censure or for praise : for no part
of a poem is worth our discommending, where the whole
is insipid ; as when we have once tasted of palled wine,
we stay not to examine it glass by glass. But while
15 they affect to shine in trifles, they are often careless in
essentials. Thus, their Hippolytus is so scrupulous
in point of decency, that he will rather expose himself
to death, than accuse his stepmother to his father ; and
my critics I am sure will commend him for it : but we of
20 grosser apprehensions are apt to think that this excess
of generosity is not practicable, but with fools and madmen. This was good manners with a vengeance ; and
the audience is like to be much concerned at the misfortunes of this admirable hero : but take Hippolytus out
25 of his poetic fit, and I suppose he would think it a wiser
part to set the saddle on the right horse, and choose
rather to live with the reputation of a plain-spoken,
honest man, than to die with the infamy of an incestuous
villain. In the meantime we may take notice, that
30 where the poet ought to have preserved the character
as it was delivered to us by antiquity, when he should
have given us the picture of a rough young man, of the
Amazonian strain, a jolly huntsman, and both by his
profession and his early rising a mortal enemy to love,
35 he has chosen to give him the turn of gallantry, sent him

to travel from Athens to Paris, taught him to make love, and transformed the Hippolytus of Euripides into Monsieur Hippolyte. I should not have troubled myself thus far with French poets, but that I find our *Chedreux* critics wholly form their judgments by them. But for 5 my part, I desire to be tried by the laws of my own country ; for it seems unjust to me, that the French should prescribe here, till they have conquered. Our little sonneteers, who follow them, have too narrow souls to judge of Poetry. Poets themselves are the 10 most proper, though I conclude not the only critics. But till some genius, as universal as Aristotle, shall arise, one who can penetrate into all arts and sciences, without the practice of them, I shall think it reasonable, that the judgment of an artificer in his own art should 15 be preferable to the opinion of another man ; at least where he is not bribed by interest, or prejudiced by malice. And this, I suppose, is manifest by plain induction : for, first, the crowd cannot be presumed to have more than a gross instinct, of what pleases or displeases 20 them : every man will grant me this ; but then, by a particular kindness to himself, he draws his own stake first, and will be distinguished from the multitude, of which other men may think him one. But, if I come closer to those who are allowed for witty men, either by the 25 advantage of their quality, or by common fame, and affirm that neither are they qualified to decide sovereignly concerning poetry, I shall yet have a strong party of my opinion ; for most of them severally will exclude the rest, either from the number of witty men, 30 or at least of able judges. But here again they are all indulgent to themselves ; and every one who believes himself a wit, that is, every man, will pretend at the same time to a right of judging. But to press it yet further,there are many witty men, but few poets ; neither 35

O 2

have all poets a taste of Tragedy. And this is the rock
on which they are daily splitting. Poetry, which is
a picture of Nature, must generally please ; but 'tis not
to be understood that all parts of it must please every
5 man ; therefore is not Tragedy to be judged by a witty
man, whose taste is only confined to Comedy. Nor is
every man, who loves Tragedy, a sufficient judge of it ;
he must understand the excellencies of it too, or he will
only prove a blind admirer, not a critic. From hence
10 it comes that so many satires on poets, and censures
of their writings, fly abroad. Men of pleasant conversation (at least esteemed so), and endued with a trifling
kind of fancy, perhaps helped out with some smattering
of Latin, are ambitious to distinguish themselves from
15 the herd of gentlemen, by their Poetry—

> *Rarus enim ferme sensus communis in illa*
> *Fortuna.*

And is not this a wretched affectation, not to be contented with what fortune has done for them, and sit down
20 quietly with their estates, but they must call their wits
in question, and needlessly expose their nakedness to
public view ? Not considering that they are not to
expect the same approbation from sober men, which
they have found from their flatterers after the third
25 bottle. If a little glittering in discourse has passed
them on us for witty men, where was the necessity
of undeceiving the world ? Would a man who has an
ill title to an estate, but yet is in possession of it ; would
he bring it of his own accord, to be tried at Westminster ?
30 We who write, if we want the talent, yet have the excuse
that we do it for a poor subsistence ; but what can be
urged in their defence, who, not having the vocation of
poverty to scribble, out of mere wantonness take pains
to make themselves ridiculous ? Horace was certainly

in the right, when he said *that no man is satisfied with his own condition.* A poet is not pleased, because he is not rich ; and the rich are discontented, because the poets will not admit them of their number. Thus the case is hard with writers : if they succeed not, they must 5 starve ; and if they do, some malicious satire is prepared to level them, for daring to please without their leave. But while they are so eager to destroy the fame of others, their ambition is manifest in their concernment ; some poem of their own is to be produced, and the slaves 10 are to be laid flat with their faces on the ground, that the monarch may appear in the greater majesty.

Dionysius and Nero had the same longings, but with all their power they could never bring their business well about. 'Tis true, they proclaimed themselves poets 15 by sound of trumpet ; and poets they were, upon pain of death to any man who durst call them otherwise. The audience had a fine time on 't, you may imagine ; they sat in a bodily fear, and looked as demurely as they could : for it was a hanging matter to laugh un- 20 seasonably ; and the tyrants were suspicious, as they had reason, that their subjects had 'em in the wind ; so, every man, in his own defence, set as good a face upon the business as he could. 'Twas known beforehand that the monarchs were to be crowned laureates ; but 25 when the show was over, and an honest man was suffered to depart quietly, he took out his laughter which he had stifled, with a firm resolution never more to see an Emperor's play, though he had been ten years a-making it. In the meantime the true poets were they who made 30 the best markets, for they had wit enough to yield the prize with a good grace, and not contend with him who had thirty legions. They were sure to be rewarded, if they confessed themselves bad writers, and that was somewhat better than to be martyrs for their reputation. 35

Lucan's example was enough to teach them manners ; and after he was put to death, for overcoming Nero, the Emperor carried it without dispute for the best poet in his dominions. No man was ambitious of that grinning 5 honour ; for if he heard the malicious trumpeter proclaiming his name before his betters, he knew there was but one way with him. Mæcenas took another course, and we know he was more than a great man, for he was witty too : but finding himself far gone in Poetry, which 10 Seneca assures us was not his talent, he thought it his best way to be well with Virgil and with Horace ; that at least he might be a poet at the second hand ; and we see how happily it has succeeded with him ; for his own bad poetry is forgotten, and their panegyrics of him still 15 remain. But they who should be our patrons are for no such expensive ways to fame ; they have much of the poetry of Mæcenas, but little of his liberality. They are for persecuting Horace and Virgil, in the persons of their successors ; for such is every man who has any 20 part of their soul and fire, though in a less degree. Some of their little zanies yet go further ; for they are persecutors even of Horace himself, as far as they are able, by their ignorant and vile imitations of him ; by making an unjust use of his authority, and turning 25 his artillery against his friends. But how would he disdain to be copied by such hands ! I dare answer for him, he would be more uneasy in their company, than he was with Crispinus, their forefather, in the Holy Way ; and would no more have allowed them a place amongst 30 the critics, than he would Demetrius the mimic, and Tigellius the buffoon ;

> . . . . *Demetri, teque, Tigelli,*
> *Discipulorum inter jubeo plorare cathedras.*

With what scorn would he look down on such miserable

translators, who make doggerel of his Latin, mistake his
meaning, misapply his censures, and often contradict
their own ? He is fixed as a landmark to set out the
bounds of poetry—

> . . . . *Saxum antiquum, ingens,—*   5
> *Limes agro positus, litem ut discerneret arvis.*

But other arms than theirs, and other sinews are
required, to raise the weight of such an author ; and
when they would toss him against enemies—

> *Genua labant, gelidus concrevit frigore sanguis.*   10
> *Tum lapis ipse, viri vacuum per inane volutus,*
> *Nec spatium evasit totum, nec pertulit ictum.*

For my part, I would wish no other revenge, either
for myself, or the rest of the poets, from this rhyming
judge of the twelvepenny gallery, this legitimate son of 15
Sternhold, than that he would subscribe his name to his
censure, or (not to tax him beyond his learning) set his
mark : for, should he own himself publicly, and come
from behind the lion's skin, they whom he condemns
would be thankful to him, they whom he praises would 20
choose to be condemned ; and the magistrates, whom
he has elected, would modestly withdraw from their
employment, to avoid the scandal of his nomination.
The sharpness of his satire, next to himself, falls most
heavily on his friends, and they ought never to forgive 25
him for commending them perpetually the wrong way,
and sometimes by contraries. If he have a friend, whose
hastiness in writing is his greatest fault, Horace would
have taught him to have minced the matter, and to have
called it readiness of thought, and a flowing fancy ; for 30
friendship will allow a man to christen an imperfection
by the name of some neighbour's virtue—

> *Vellem in amicitia sic erraremus ; et isti*
> *Errori nomen virtus posuisset honestum.*

But he would never have allowed him to have called
a slow man hasty, or a hasty writer a slow drudge,
as Juvenal explains it—

> . . . . *Canibus pigris, scabieque vetusta*
> 5 *Laevibus, et siccae lambentibus ora lucernae,*
> *Nomen erit, Pardus, Tigris, Leo ; si quid adhuc est*
> *Quod fremit in terris violentius.*

Yet Lucretius laughs at a foolish lover, even for excus-
ing the imperfections of his mistress—

> 10 *Nigra μελίχροος est, immunda et foetida ἄκοσμος.*
> *Balba loqui, non quit, τραυλίζει ; muta pudens est, &c.*

But to drive it *ad Æthiopem cygnum* is not to be
endured. I leave him to interpret this by the benefit
of his French version on the other side, and without
15 further considering him, than I have the rest of my
illiterate censors, whom I have disdained to answer,
because they are not qualified for judges. It remains
that I acquaint the reader, that I have endeavoured in
this play to follow the practice of the Ancients, who, as
20 Mr. Rymer has judiciously observed, are and ought to
be our masters. Horace likewise gives it for a rule in
his art of poetry—

> . . . *Vos exemplaria Græca*
> *Nocturna versate manu, versate diurna.*

25　Yet, though their models are regular, they are too
little for English tragedy ; which requires to be built
in a larger compass. I could give an instance in the
Œdipus Tyrannus, which was the masterpiece of Sophocles ; but I reserve it for a more fit occasion, which
30 I hope to have hereafter. In my style, I have professed
to imitate the divine Shakespeare ; which that I might
perform more freely, I have disencumbered myself from
rhyme. Not that I condemn my former way, but that
this is more proper to my present purpose. I hope

I need not to explain myself, that I have not copied my author servilely : words and phrases must of necessity receive a change in succeeding ages ; but it is almost a miracle that much of his language remains so pure ; and that he who began Dramatic Poetry amongst us, 5 untaught by any, and as Ben Johnson tells us, without learning, should by the force of his own genius perform so much, that in a manner he has left no praise for any who come after him. The occasion is fair, and the subject would be pleasant to handle the difference of 10 styles betwixt him and Fletcher, and wherein, and how far they are both to be imitated. But since I must not be over-confident of my own performance after him, it will be prudence in me to be silent. Yet, I hope, I may affirm, and without vanity, that, by imitating him, I have 15 excelled myself throughout the play ; and particularly, that I prefer the scene betwixt Antony and Ventidius in the first act, to anything which I have written in this kind.

TROILUS AND CRESSIDA

(1679)

PREFACE

CONTAINING THE GROUNDS OF CRITICISM
IN TRAGEDY

THE poet Æschylus was held in the same veneration
by the Athenians of after ages as Shakespeare is by
us ; and Longinus has judged, in favour of him, that
he had a noble boldness of expression, and that his
5 imaginations were lofty and heroic ; but, on the other
side, Quintilian affirms that he was daring to extravagance. 'Tis certain that he affected pompous words,
and that his sense too often was obscured by figures ;
notwithstanding these imperfections, the value of his
10 writings after his decease was such, that his countrymen
ordained an equal reward to those poets who could
alter his plays to be acted on the theatre, with those
whose productions were wholly new, and of their own.
The case is not the same in England ; though the
15 difficulties of altering are greater, and our reverence
for Shakespeare much more just, than that of the
Grecians for Æschylus. In the age of that poet, the
Greek tongue was arrived to its full perfection ; they
had then amongst them an exact standard of writing
20 and of speaking : the English language is not capable

of such a certainty ; and we are at present so far from
it, that we are wanting in the very foundation of it,
a perfect grammar. Yet it must be allowed to the
present age, that the tongue in general is so much
refined since Shakespeare's time, that many of his 5
words, and more of his phrases, are scarce intelligible.
And of those which we understand, some are ungram-
matical, others coarse ; and his whole style is so
pestered with figurative expressions, that it is as
affected as it is obscure. 'Tis true, that in his latter 10
plays he had worn off somewhat of the rust ; but the
tragedy which I have undertaken to correct was in all
probability one of his first endeavours on the stage.

The original story was written by one Lollius,
a Lombard, in Latin verse, and translated by Chaucer 15
into English ; intended, I suppose, a satire on the
inconstancy of women : I find nothing of it among
the Ancients ; not so much as the name Cressida
once mentioned. Shakespeare (as I hinted), in the
apprenticeship of his writing, modelled it into that 20
play, which is now called by the name of *Troilus and
Cressida*, but so lamely is it left to us, that it is not
divided into acts ; which fault I ascribe to the actors
who printed it after Shakespeare's death ; and that
too so carelessly, that a more uncorrect copy I never 25
saw. For the play itself, the author seems to have
begun it with some fire ; the characters of Pandarus
and Thersites are promising enough ; but as if he grew
weary of his task, after an entrance or two, he lets
them fall : and the latter part of the tragedy is nothing 30
but a confusion of drums and trumpets, excursions and
alarms. The chief persons, who give name to the
tragedy, are left alive ; Cressida is false, and is not
punished. Yet, after all, because the play was Shakespeare's, and that there appeared in some places of it 35

the admirable genius of the author, I undertook to
remove that heap of rubbish under which many excellent thoughts lay wholly buried. Accordingly, I new-
modelled the plot, threw out many unnecessary persons,
5 improved those characters which were begun and left
unfinished, as Hector, Troilus, Pandarus, and Thersites,
and added that of Andromache. After this, I made,
with no small trouble, an order and connexion of all
the scenes ; removing them from the places where they
10 were inartificially set ; and, though it was impossible
to keep them all unbroken, because the scene must be
sometimes in the city and sometimes in the camp, yet
I have so ordered them, that there is a coherence of
them with one another, and a dependence on the main
15 design ; no leaping from Troy to the Grecian tents,
and thence back again, in the same. act, but a due
proportion of time allowed for every motion. I need
not say that I have refined his language, which before
was obsolete ; but I am willing to acknowledge, that
20 as I have often drawn his English nearer to our times,
so I have sometimes conformed my own to his ; and
consequently, the language is not altogether so pure
as it is significant. The scenes of Pandarus and Cressida, of Troilus and Pandarus, of Andromache with
25 Hector and the Trojans, in the second act, are wholly
new ; together with that of Nestor and Ulysses with
Thersites, and that of Thersites with Ajax and Achilles.
I will not wear my reader with the scenes which are
added of Pandarus and the lovers, in the third, and
30 those of Thersites, which are wholly altered ; but I
cannot omit the last scene in it, which is almost half
the act, betwixt Troilus and Hector. The occasion of
raising it was hinted to me by Mr. Betterton ; the
contrivance and working of it was my own. They
35 who think to do me an injury by saying that it is an

imitation of the scene betwixt Brutus and Cassius, do
me an honour by supposing I could imitate the incomparable Shakespeare ; but let me add, that if Shakespeare's scene, or the faulty copy of it in Amintor and
Melantius, had never been, yet Euripides had furnished 5
me with an excellent example in his *Iphigenia*, between
Agamemnon and Menelaus ; and from thence, indeed,
the last turn of it is borrowed. The occasion which
Shakespeare, Euripides, and Fletcher, have all taken,
is the same, grounded upon friendship ; and the quarrel 10
of two virtuous men, raised by natural degrees to the
extremity of passion, is conducted in all three, to
the declination of the same passion, and concludes
with a warm renewing of their friendship. But the
particular groundwork which Shakespeare has taken 15
is incomparably the best ; because he has not only
chosen two of the greatest heroes of their age, but
has likewise interested the liberty of Rome, and their
own honours, who were the redeemers of it, in this
debate. And if he has made Brutus, who was naturally 20
a patient man, to fly into excess at first, let it be
remembered in his defence, that, just before, he has
received the news of Portia's death ; whom the poet,
on purpose neglecting a little chronology, supposes to
have died before Brutus, only to give him an occasion 25
of being more easily exasperated. Add to this, that
the injury he had received from Cassius had long
been brooding in his mind ; and that a melancholy
man, upon consideration of an affront, especially from
a friend, would be more eager in his passion than he 30
who had given it, though naturally more choleric.
Euripides, whom I have followed, has raised the quarrel
betwixt two brothers, who were friends. The foundation of the scene was this : the Grecians were wind-
bound at the port of Aulis, and the oracle had said 35

that they could not sail, unless Agamemnon delivered
up his daughter to be sacrificed : he refuses ; his brother
Menelaus urges the public safety ; the father defends
himself by arguments of natural affection, and hereupon
5 they quarrel. Agamemnon is at last convinced, and
promises to deliver up Iphigenia, but so passionately
laments his loss, that Menelaus is grieved to have
been the occasion of it, and, by a return of kindness,
offers to intercede for him with the Grecians, that his
10 daughter might not be sacrificed. But my friend
Mr. Rymer has so largely, and with so much judgment,
described this scene, in comparing it with that of
Melantius and Amintor, that it is superfluous to say
more of it ; I only named the heads of it, that any
15 reasonable man might judge it was from thence
I modelled my scene betwixt Troilus and Hector.
I will conclude my reflections on it, with a passage
of Longinus, concerning Plato's imitation of Homer :
' We ought not to regard a good imitation as a theft,
20 but as a beautiful idea of him who undertakes to
imitate, by forming himself on the invention and the
work of another man ; for he enters into the lists like
a new wrestler, to dispute the prize with the former
champion. This sort of emulation, says Hesiod, is
25 honourable, Ἀγαθὴ δ᾽ ἔρις ἐστὶ βρότοισιν—when we combat
for victory with a hero, and are not without glory even
in our overthrow. Those great men, whom we propose
to ourselves as patterns of our imitation, serve us as
a torch, which is lifted up before us, to enlighten our
30 passage, and often elevate our thoughts as high as the
conception we have of our author's genius.'
I have been so tedious in three acts, that I shall
contract myself in the two last. The beginning scenes
of the fourth act are either added or changed wholly
35 by me ; the middle of it is Shakespeare altered, and

mingled with my own ; three or four of the last scenes
are altogether new. And the whole fifth act, both the
plot and the writing, are my own additions.

But having written so much for imitation of what is
excellent, in that part of the Preface which related only 5
to myself, methinks it would neither be unprofitable
nor unpleasant to inquire how far we ought to imitate
our own poets, Shakespeare and Fletcher, in their
tragedies ; and this will occasion another inquiry, how
those two writers differ between themselves : but since 10
neither of these questions can be solved, unless some
measures be first taken by which we may be enabled
to judge truly of their writings, I shall endeavour, as
briefly as I can, to discover the grounds and reason
of all criticism, applying them in this place only to 15
Tragedy. Aristotle with his interpreters, and Horace,
and Longinus, are the authors to whom I owe my
lights ; and what part soever of my own plays, or of
this, which no mending could make regular, shall fall
under the condemnation of such judges, it would be 20
impudence in me to defend. I think it no shame to
retract my errors, and am well pleased to suffer in the
cause, if the art may be improved at my expense :
I therefore proceed to

THE GROUNDS OF CRITICISM IN TRAGEDY. 25

Tragedy is thus defined by Aristotle (omitting what
I thought unnecessary in his definition). It is an
imitation of one entire, great, and probable action ; not
told, but represented ; which, by moving in us fear and
pity, is conducive to the purging of those two passions 30
in our minds. More largely thus : Tragedy describes
or paints an action, which action must have all the
proprieties above named. First, it must be one or
single ; that is, it must not be a history of one man's

life, suppose of Alexander the Great, or Julius Caesar, but one single action of theirs. This condemns all Shakespeare's historical plays, which are rather chronicles represented, than tragedies ; and all double
5 action of plays. As, to avoid a satire upon others, I will make bold with my own *Marriage à la Mode*, where there are manifestly two actions, not depending on one another ; but in *Œdipus* there cannot properly be said to be two actions, because the love of Adrastus
10 and Eurydice has a necessary dependence on the principal design into which it is woven. The natural reason of this rule is plain ; for two different independent actions distract the attention and concernment of the audience, and consequently destroy the intention
15 of the poet ; if his business be to move terror and pity, and one of his actions be comical, the other tragical, the former will divert the people, and utterly make void his greater purpose. Therefore, as in perspective, so in Tragedy, there must be a point of sight in which
20 all the lines terminate ; otherwise the eye wanders, and the work is false. This was the practice of the Grecian stage. But Terence made an innovation in the Roman : all his plays have double actions ; for it was his custom to translate two Greek comedies, and to weave them
25 into one of his, yet so, that both their actions were comical, and one was principal, the other but secondary or subservient. And this has obtained on the English stage, to give us the pleasure of variety.

As the action ought to be one, it ought, as such, to
30 have order in it ; that is, to have a natural beginning, a middle, and an end. A natural beginning, says Aristotle, is that which could not necessarily have been placed after another thing ; and so of the rest. This consideration will arraign all plays after the new
35 model of Spanish plots, where accident is heaped upon

accident, and that which is first might as reasonably
be last ; an inconvenience not to be remedied, but by
making one accident naturally produce another, otherwise it is a farce and not a play. Of this nature is the
Slighted Maid ; where there is no scene in the first act, 5
which might not by as good reason be in the fifth.
And if the action ought to be one, the tragedy ought
likewise to conclude with the action of it. Thus in
Mustapha, the play should naturally have ended with
the death of Zanger, and not have given us the grace- 10
cup after dinner, of Solyman's divorce from Roxolana.

The following properties of the action are so easy,
that they need not my explaining. It ought to be
great, and to consist of great persons, to distinguish
it from Comedy, where the action is trivial, and the 15
persons of inferior rank. The last quality of the action
is, that it ought to be probable, as well as admirable
and great. 'Tis not necessary that there should be
historical truth in it ; but always necessary that there
should be a likeness of truth, something that is more 20
than barely possible ; *probable* being that which succeeds,
or happens, oftener than it misses. To invent therefore a probability, and to make it wonderful, is the
most difficult undertaking in the art of Poetry ; for that
which is not wonderful is not great ; and that which 25
is not probable will not delight a reasonable audience.
This action, thus described, must be represented and
not told, to distinguish Dramatic Poetry from Epic : but
I hasten to the end or scope of Tragedy, which is, to
rectify or purge our passions, fear and pity. 30

To instruct delightfully is the general end of all
poetry. Philosophy instructs, but it performs its work
by precept ; which is not delightful, or not so delightful
as example. To purge the passions by example, is
therefore the particular instruction which belongs to 35

Tragedy. Rapin, a judicious critic, has observed from Aristotle, that pride and want of commiseration are the most predominant vices in mankind; therefore, to cure us of these two, the inventors of Tragedy have
5 chosen to work upon two other passions, which are fear and pity. We are wrought to fear by their setting before our eyes some terrible example of misfortune, which happened to persons of the highest quality; for such an action demonstrates to us that no condition is
10 privileged from the turns of fortune; this must of necessity cause terror in us, and consequently abate our pride. But when we see that the most virtuous, as well as the greatest, are not exempt from such misfortunes, that consideration moves pity in us, and
15 insensibly works us to be helpful to, and tender over, the distressed; which is the noblest and most god-like of moral virtues. Here it is observable, that it is absolutely necessary to make a man virtuous, if we desire he should be pitied: we lament not, but detest,
20 a wicked man; we are glad when we behold his crimes are punished, and that poetical justice is done upon him. Euripides was censured by the critics of his time for making his chief characters too wicked; for example, Phædra, though she loved her son-in-law with
25 reluctancy, and that it was a curse upon her family for offending Venus, yet was thought too ill a pattern for the stage. Shall we therefore banish all characters of villany? I confess I am not of that opinion; but it is necessary that the hero of the play be not a villain;
30 that is, the characters, which should move our pity, ought to have virtuous inclinations, and degrees of moral goodness in them. As for a perfect character of virtue, it never was in Nature, and therefore there can be no imitation of it; but there are alloys of frailty
35 to be allowed for the chief persons, yet so that the

good which is in them shall outweigh the bad, and consequently leave room for punishment on the one side, and pity on the other.

After all, if any one will ask me, whether a tragedy cannot be made upon any other grounds than those 5 of exciting pity and terror in us ;—Bossu, the best of modern critics, answers thus in general : That all excellent arts, and particularly that of poetry, have been invented and brought to perfection by men of a transcendent genius ; and that, therefore, they, who practise 10 afterwards the same arts, are obliged to tread in their footsteps, and to search in their writings the foundation of them ; for it is not just that new rules should destroy the authority of the old. But Rapin writes more particularly thus, that no passions in a story are so proper 15 to move our concernment as fear and pity ; and that it is from our concernment we receive our pleasure, is undoubted ; when the soul becomes agitated with fear for one character, or hope for another, then it is that we are pleased in Tragedy, by the interest which we 20 take in their adventures.

Here, therefore, the general answer may be given to the first question, how far we ought to imitate Shakespeare and Fletcher in their plots ; namely, that we ought to follow them so far only as they have copied 25 the excellencies of those who invented and brought to perfection Dramatic Poetry ; those things only excepted, which religion, custom of countries, idioms of languages, etc., have altered in the superstructures, but not in the foundation of the design. 30

How defective Shakespeare and Fletcher have been in all their plots, Mr. Rymer has discovered in his criticisms : neither can we, who follow them, be excused from the same, or greater errors ; which are the more unpardonable in us, because we want their beauties to 35

countervail our faults. The best of their designs, the
most approaching to antiquity, and the most conducing
to move pity, is the *King and no King ;* which, if the
farce of Bessus were thrown away, is of that inferior
5 sort of tragedies, which end with a prosperous event.
It is probably derived from the story of Œdipus, with
the character of Alexander the Great, in his extravagances, given to Arbaces. The taking of this play,
amongst many others, I cannot wholly ascribe to the
10 excellency of the action ; for I find it moving when it
is read : 'tis true, the faults of the plot are so evidently
proved, that they can no longer be denied. The
beauties of it must therefore lie either in the lively
touches of the passion ; or we must conclude, as I think
15 we may, that even in imperfect plots there are less
degrees of Nature, by which some faint emotions of
pity and terror are raised in us : as a less engine will
raise a less proportion of weight, though not so much
as one of Archimedes' making ; for nothing can move
20 our nature, but by some natural reason, which works
upon passions   And, since we acknowledge the effect,
there must be something in the cause.

The difference between Shakespeare and Fletcher
in their plotting seems to be this ; that Shakespeare
25 generally moves more terror, and Fletcher more compassion : for the first had a more masculine, a bolder
and more fiery genius ; the second, a more soft and
womanish. In the mechanic beauties of the plot, which
are the observation of the three Unities, Time, Place,
30 and Action, they are both deficient ; but Shakespeare
most. Ben Johnson reformed those errors in his
comedies, yet one of Shakespeare's was regular before
him ; which is, *The Merry Wives of Windsor.* For
what remains concerning the design, you are to be
35 referred to our English critic. That method which he

has prescribed to raise it, from mistake, or ignorance of the crime, is certainly the best, though it is not the only ; for amongst all the tragedies of Sophocles, there is but one, *Œdipus*, which is wholly built after that model.   5

After the plot, which is the foundation of the play, the next thing to which we ought to apply our judgment, is the manners ; for now the poet comes to work above ground. The groundwork, indeed, is that which is most necessary, as that upon which depends the 10 firmness of the whole fabric ; yet it strikes not the eye so much, as the beauties or imperfections of the manners, the thoughts, and the expressions.

The first rule which Bossu prescribes to the writer of an Heroic Poem, and which holds too by the same 15 reason in all Dramatic Poetry, is to make the moral of the work ; that is, to lay down to yourself what that precept of morality shall be, which you would insinuate into the people ; as, namely, Homer's (which I have copied in my *Conquest of Granada*), was, that union 20 preserves a commonwealth, and discord destroys it ; Sophocles, in his *Œdipus*, that no man is to be accounted happy before his death. 'Tis the moral that directs the whole action of the play to one centre ; and that action or fable is the example built upon the moral, 25 which confirms the truth of it to our experience : when the fable is designed, then, and not before, the persons are to be introduced, with their manners, characters, and passions.

The manners, in a poem, are understood to be those 30 inclinations, whether natural or acquired, which move and carry us to actions, good, bad, or indifferent, in a play ; or which incline the persons to such or such actions. I have anticipated part of this discourse already, in declaring that a poet ought not to make the manners 35

perfectly good in his best persons ; but neither are they to be more wicked in any of his characters than necessity requires. To produce a villain, without other reason than a natural inclination to villany, is, in Poetry,
5 to produce an effect without a cause ; and to make him more a villain than he has just reason to be, is to make an effect which is stronger than the cause.

The manners arise from many causes ; and are either distinguished by complexion, as choleric and phlegmatic,
10 or by the differences of age or sex, of climates, or quality of the persons, or their present condition. They are likewise to be gathered from the several virtues, vices, or passions, and many other commonplaces, which a poet must be supposed to have learned from natural
15 Philosophy, Ethics, and History ; of all which, whosoever is ignorant, does not deserve the name of poet.

But as the manners are useful in this art, they may be all comprised under these general heads : first, they must be apparent ; that is, in every character of the
20 play, some inclinations of the person must appear ; and these are shown in the actions and discourse. Secondly, the manners must be suitable, or agreeing to the persons ; that is, to the age, sex, dignity, and the other general heads of manners : thus, when a poet has given
25 the dignity of a king to one of his persons, in all his actions and speeches, that person must discover majesty, magnanimity, and jealousy of power, because these are suitable to the general manners of a king. The third property of manners is resemblance ; and this is founded
30 upon the particular characters of men, as we have them delivered to us by relation or history ; that is, when a poet has the known character of this or that man before him, he is bound to represent him such, at least not contrary to that which fame has reported him to
35 have been. Thus, it is not a poet's choice to make

Ulysses choleric, or Achilles patient, because Homer has described 'em quite otherwise. Yet this is a rock on which ignorant writers daily split ; and the absurdity is as monstrous as if a painter should draw a coward running from a battle, and tell us it was the picture of 5 Alexander the Great.

The last property of manners is, that they be constant and equal, that is, maintained the same through the whole design : thus, when Virgil had once given the name of *pious* to Æneas, he was bound to show him 10 such, in all his words and actions, through the whole poem. All these properties Horace has hinted to a judicious observer : 1. *Notandi sunt tibi mores ; 2. Aut famam sequere ; 3. Aut sibi convenientia finge ; 4. Servetur ad imum, qualis ab incepto processerit, et sibi constet.* 15

From the manners, the characters of persons are derived ; for, indeed, the characters are no other than the inclinations, as they appear in the several persons of the poem ; a character being thus defined,—that which distinguishes one man from another. Not to 20 repeat the same things over again, which have been said of the manners, I will only add what is necessary here. A character, or that which distinguishes one man from all others, cannot be supposed to consist of one particular virtue, or vice, or passion only ; but 't is 25 a composition of qualities which are not contrary to one another in the same person ; thus, the same man may be liberal and valiant, but not liberal and covetous ; so in a comical character, or humour (which is an inclination to this or that particular folly), Falstaff is a liar, 30 and a coward, a glutton, and a buffoon, because all these qualities may agree in the same man ; yet it is still to be observed, that one virtue, vice, and passion, ought to be shown in every man, as predominant over all the rest ; as covetousness in Crassus, love of his country 35 in Brutus ; and the same in characters which are feigned.

The chief character or hero in a tragedy, as I have already shown, ought in prudence to be such a man
5 who has so much more of virtue in him than of vice, that he may be left amiable to the audience, which otherwise cannot have any concernment for his sufferings ; and it is on this one character, that the pity and terror must be principally, if not wholly, founded : a rule
10 which is extremely necessary, and which none of the critics, that I know, have fully enough discovered to us. For terror and compassion work but weakly when they are divided into many persons. If Creon had been the chief character in *Œdipus*, there had neither been terror
15 nor compassion moved ; but only detestation of the man, and joy for his punishment ; if Adrastus and Eurydice had been made more appearing characters, then the pity had been divided, and lessened on the part of Œdipus : but making Œdipus the best and
20 bravest person, and even Jocasta but an underpart to him, his virtues, and the punishment of his fatal crime, drew both the pity and the terror to himself.

By what has been said of the manners, it will be easy for a reasonable man to judge whether the characters
25 be truly or falsely drawn in a tragedy ; for if there be no manners appearing in the characters, no concernment for the persons can be raised ; no pity or horror can be moved, but by vice or virtue ; therefore, without them, no person can have any business in the play. If the
30 inclinations be obscure, it is a sign the poet is in the dark, and knows not what manner of man he presents to you ; and consequently you can have no idea, or very imperfect, of that man ; nor can judge what resolutions he ought to take ; or what words or actions are
35 proper for him. Most comedies made up of accidents

or adventures are liable to fall into this error ; and
tragedies with many turns are subject to it ; for the
manners can never be evident, where the surprises of
fortune take up all the business of the stage ; and where
the poet is more in pain to tell you what happened to 5
such a man, than what he was. 'Tis one of the excellencies of Shakespeare, that the manners of his persons
are generally apparent, and you see their bent and
inclinations. Fletcher comes far short of him in this,
as indeed he does almost in everything : there are but 10
glimmerings of manners in most of his comedies, which
run upon adventures ; and in his tragedies, Rollo, Otto
the King and no King, Melantius, and many others of
his best, are but pictures shown you in the twilight ;
you know not whether they resemble vice or virtue, and 15
they are either good, bad, or indifferent, as the present
scene requires it. But of all poets, this commendation
is to be given to Ben Johnson, that the manners, even
of the most inconsiderable persons in his plays, are
everywhere apparent. 20

By considering the second quality of manners, which
is, that they be suitable to the age, quality, country,
dignity, etc., of the character, we may likewise judge
whether a poet has followed Nature. In this kind,
Sophocles and Euripides have more excelled among 25
the Greeks than Æschylus ; and Terence more than
Plautus, among the Romans. Thus, Sophocles gives
to Œdipus the true qualities of a king, in both those
plays which bear his name ; but in the latter, which is
the *Œdipus Colonæus*, he lets fall on purpose his tragic 30
style ; his hero speaks not in the arbitrary tone ; but
remembers, in the softness of his complaints, that he is
an unfortunate blind old man ; that he is banished from
his country, and persecuted by his next relations. The
present French poets are generally accused, that where- 35

soever they lay the scene, or in whatsoever age, the manners of their heroes are wholly French. Racine's Bajazet is bred at Constantinople ; but his civilities are conveyed to him, by some secret passage, from Ver-
5 sailles into the Seraglio. But our Shakespeare, having ascribed to Henry the Fourth the character of a king and of a father, gives him the perfect manners of each relation, when either he transacts with his son or with his subjects. Fletcher, on the other side, gives neither
10 to Arbaces, nor to his king, in the *Maid's Tragedy*, the qualities which are suitable to a monarch ; though he may be excused a little in the latter, for the king there is not uppermost in the character ; 'tis the lover of Evadne, who is king only in a second consideration ;
15 and though he be unjust, and has other faults which shall be nameless, yet he is not the hero of the play. 'Tis true, we find him a lawful prince (though I never heard of any king that was in Rhodes), and therefore Mr. Rymer's criticism stands good ; that he should not
20 be shown in so vicious a character. Sophocles has been more judicious in his *Antigona* ; for, though he represents in Creon a bloody prince, yet he makes him not a lawful king, but an usurper, and Antigona herself is the heroine of the tragedy : but when Philaster
25 wounds Arethusa and the boy ; and Perigot his mistress, in the *Faithful Shepherdess*, both these are contrary to the character of manhood. Nor is *Valentinian* managed much better ; for, though Fletcher has taken his picture truly, and shown him as he was, an effeminate, volup-
30 tuous man, yet he has forgotten that he was an emperor, and has given him none of those royal marks which ought to appear in a lawful successor of the throne. If it be inquired, what Fletcher should have done on this occasion ; ought he not to have represented Valentinian
35 as he was ;—Bossu shall answer this question for me, by

an instance of the like nature : Mauritius, the Greek
emperor, was a prince far surpassing Valentinian, for he
was endued with many kingly virtues ; he was religious,
merciful, and valiant, but withal he was noted of extreme
covetousness, a vice which is contrary to the character 5
of a hero, or a prince : therefore, says the critic, that
emperor was no fit person to be represented in a tragedy,
unless his good qualities were only to be shown, and
his covetousness (which sullied them all) were slurred
over by the artifice of the poet. To return once more 10
to Shakespeare ; no man ever drew so many characters,
or generally distinguished 'em better from one another,
excepting only Johnson. I will instance but in one, to
show the copiousness of his intention ; it is that of
Caliban, or the monster, in the *Tempest*. He seems 15
there to have created a person which was not in Nature,
a boldness which, at first sight, would appear intoler-
able ; for he makes him a species of himself, begotten
by an incubus on a witch ; but this, as I have elsewhere
proved, is not wholly beyond the bounds of credibility, 20
at least the vulgar still believe it. We have the separated notions of a spirit, and of a witch (and spirits,
according to Plato, are vested with a subtle body ;
according to some of his followers, have different
sexes) ; therefore, as from the distinct apprehensions of 25
a horse, and of a man, imagination has formed a
centaur ; so, from those of an incubus and a sorceress,
Shakespeare has produced his monster. Whether or
no his generation can be defended, I leave to philosophy ; but of this I am certain, that the poet has most 30
judiciously furnished him with a person, a language,
and a character, which will suit him, both by father's
and mother's side : he has all the discontents and malice
of a witch, and of a devil, besides a convenient proportion of the deadly sins ; gluttony, sloth, and lust, are 35

manifest ; the dejectedness of a slave is likewise given
him, and the ignorance of one bred up in a desert
island. His person is monstrous, and he is the product
of unnatural lust ; and his language is as hobgoblin as
5 his person ; in all things he is distinguished from other
mortals. The characters of Fletcher are poor and
narrow, in comparison of Shakespeare's ; I remember
not one which is not borrowed from him ; unless you
will accept that strange mixture of a man in the *King*
10 *and no King ;* so that in this part Shakespeare is
generally worth our imitation ; and to imitate Fletcher
is but to copy after him who was a copyer.

Under this general head of manners, the passions
are naturally included as belonging to the characters.
15 I speak not of pity and of terror, which are to be moved
in the audience by the plot ; but of anger, hatred, love,
ambition, jealousy, revenge, etc., as they are shown in
this or that person of the play. To describe these
naturally, and to move them artfully, is one of the
20 greatest commendations which can be given to a poet :
to write pathetically, says Longinus, cannot proceed
but from a lofty genius. A poet must be born with this
quality : yet, unless he help himself by an acquired
knowledge of the passions, what they are in their own
25 nature, and by what springs they are to be moved, he
will be subject either to raise them where they ought
not to be raised, or not to raise them by the just degrees
of nature, or to amplify them beyond the natural bounds,
or not to observe the crisis and turns of them, in their
30 cooling and decay ; all which errors proceed from want
of judgment in the poet, and from being unskilled in the
principles of Moral Philosophy. Nothing is more
frequent in a fanciful writer, than to foil himself by not
managing his strength ; therefore, as in a wrestler,
35 there is first required some measure of force, a well-knit

body and active limbs, without which all instruction
would be vain ; yet, these being granted, if he want the
skill which is necessary to a wrestler, he shall make but
small advantage of his natural robustuousness : so, in
a poet, his inborn vehemence and force of spirit will 5
only run him out of breath the sooner, if it be not
supported by the help of Art. The roar of passion,
indeed, may please an audience, three parts of which
are ignorant enough to think all is moving which is
noise, and it may stretch the lungs of an ambitious 10
actor, who will die upon the spot for a thundering clap ;
but it will move no other passion than indignation and
contempt from judicious men. Longinus, whom I have
hitherto followed, continues thus : *If the passions be*
artfully employed, the discourse becomes vehement and 15
lofty : if otherwise, there is nothing more ridiculous
than a great passion out of season : and to this purpose
he animadverts severely upon Æschylus, who writ
nothing in cold blood, but was always in a rapture, and
in fury with his audience : the inspiration was still upon 20
him, he was ever tearing it upon the tripos ; or (to run
off as madly as he does, from one similitude to another)
he was always at high-flood of passion, even in the dead
ebb and lowest water-mark of the scene. He who
would raise the passion of a judicious audience, says 25
a learned critic, must be sure to take his hearers along
with him ; if they be in a calm, 'tis in vain for him to be
in a huff ; he must move them by degrees, and kindle
with 'em ; otherwise he will be in danger of setting his
own heap of stubble on fire, and of burning out by 30
himself, without warming the company that stand about
him. They who would justify the madness of Poetry
from the authority of Aristotle, have mistaken the text,
and consequently the interpretation : I imagine it to be
false read, where he says of Poetry, that it is Εὐφυοῦς ἤ 35

μανικοῦ, that it had always somewhat in it either of a genius, or of a madman. 'Tis more probable that the original ran thus, that Poetry was Εὐφυοῦς οὐ μανικοῦ, that it belongs to a witty man, but not to a madman. 5 Thus then the passions, as they are considered simply and in themselves, suffer violence when they are perpetually maintained at the same height ; for what melody can be made on that instrument, all whose strings are screwed up at first to their utmost stretch, and to the 10 same sound ? But this is not the worst : for the characters likewise bear a part in the general calamity, if you consider the passions as embodied in them ; for it follows of necessity, that no man can be distinguished from another by his discourse, when every man is 15 ranting, swaggering, and exclaiming with the same excess : as if it were the only business of all the characters to contend with each other for the prize at Billingsgate ; or that the scene of the tragedy lay in Bet'lem. Suppose the poet should intend this man to 20 be choleric, and that man to be patient ; yet when they are confounded in the writing, you cannot distinguish them from one another : for the man who was called patient and tame is only so before he speaks ; but let his clack be set agoing, and he shall tongue it as 25 impetuously, and as loudly, as the errantest hero in the play. By this means, the characters are only distinct in name ; but, in reality, all the men and women in the play are the same person. No man should pretend to write, who cannot temper his fancy with his judgment : 30 nothing is more dangerous to a raw horseman, than a hot-mouthed jade without a curb.

It is necessary therefore for a poet, who would concern an audience by describing of a passion, first to prepare it, and not to rush upon it all at once. Ovid has 35 judiciously shown the difference of these two ways, in

the speeches of Ajax and Ulysses : Ajax, from the very
beginning, breaks out into his exclamations, and is
swearing by his Maker,——*Agimus, proh Jupiter, inquit.*
Ulysses, on the contrary, prepares his audience with all
the submissiveness he can practise, and all the calmness 5
of a reasonable man ; he found his judges in a tranquil-
lity of spirit, and therefore set out leisurely and softly
with 'em, till he had warmed 'em by degrees ; and then
he began to mend his pace, and to draw them along
with his own impetuousness : yet so managing his 10
breath, that it might not fail him at his need, and
reserving his utmost proofs of ability even to the last.
The success, you see, was answerable ; for the crowd
only applauded the speech of Ajax—

> . . . *Vulgique secutum*   15
> *Ultima murmur erat :*

but the judges awarded the prize, for which they contended, to Ulysses—

> *Mota manus procerum est ; et quid facundia posset*
> *Tum patuit, fortisque viri tulit arma disertus.*   20

The next necessary rule is, to put nothing into the
discourse which may hinder your moving of the passions.
Too many accidents, as I have said, encumber the poet,
as much as the arms of Saul did David ; for the variety
of passions which they produce are ever crossing and 25
justling each other out of the way. He who treats of
joy and grief together is in a fair way of causing neither
of those effects. There is yet another obstacle to be
removed, which is pointed wit, and sentences affected
out of season ; these are nothing of kin to the violence 30
of passion : no man is at leisure to make sentences and
similes, when his soul is in an agony. I the rather
name this fault, that it may serve to mind me of my
former errors ; neither will I spare myself, but give an

example of this kind from my *Indian Emperor*. Monte-
zuma, pursued by his enemies, and seeking sanctuary,
stands parleying without the fort, and describing his
danger to Cydaria, in a simile of six lines—

5   As on the sands the frighted traveller
          Sees the high seas come rolling from afar, &c.

My Indian potentate was well skilled in the sea for
an inland prince, and well improved since the first act,
when he sent his son to discover it. The image had
10 not been amiss from another man, at another time : *sed
nunc non erat hisce locus :* he destroyed the concernment
which the audience might otherwise have had for him ;
for they could not think the danger near when he had
the leisure to invent a simile.

15   If Shakespeare be allowed, as I think he must, to have
made his characters distinct, it will easily be inferred
that he understood the nature of the passions : because it
has been proved already that confused passions make
undistinguishable characters : yet I cannot deny that he
20 has his failings ; but they are not so much in the
passions themselves, as in his manner of expression :
he often obscures his meaning by his words, and sometimes makes it unintelligible. I will not say of so great
a poet, that he distinguished not the blown puffy style
25 from true sublimity ; but I may venture to maintain,
that the fury of his fancy often transported him beyond
the bounds of judgment, either in coining of new words
and phrases, or racking words which were in use, into
the violence of a catachresis. It is not that I would
30 explode the use of metaphors from passion, for Longinus
thinks 'em necessary to raise it : but to use 'em at
every word, to say nothing without a metaphor, a simile,
an image, or description, is, I doubt, to smell a little too
strongly of the buskin. I must be forced to give an

example of expressing passion figuratively ; but that
I may do it with respect to Shakespeare, it shall not be
taken from anything of his : 'tis an exclamation against
Fortune, quoted in his *Hamlet* but written by some
other poet—   5

> Out, out, thou strumpet, Fortune ! all you gods,
> In general synod, take away her power ;
> Break all the spokes and felleys from her wheel,
> And bowl the round nave down the hill of Heav'n,
> As low as to the fiends.   10

And immediately after, speaking of Hecuba, when
Priam was killed before her eyes—

> The mobbled queen
> Threatning the flame, ran up and down
> With bisson rheum ; a clout about that head   15
> Where late the diadem stood ; and for a robe,
> About her lank and all o'er-teemed loins,
> A blanket in th' alarm of fear caught up.
> Who this had seen, with tongue in venom steep'd
> 'Gainst Fortune's state would treason have pronounced ;   20
> But if the gods themselves did see her then,
> When she saw Pyrrhus make malicious sport
> In mincing with his sword her husband's limbs,
> The instant burst of clamour that she made
> (Unless things mortal move them not at all)   25
> Would have made milch the burning eyes of heaven,
> And passion in the gods.

What a pudder is here kept in raising the expression
of trifling thoughts ! Would not a man have thought
that the poet had been bound prentice to a wheelwright, 30
for his first rant ? and had followed a ragman, for the
clout and blanket in the second ? Fortune is painted
on a wheel, and therefore the writer, in a rage, will have
poetical justice done upon every member of that engine :
after this execution, he bowls the nave down-hill, from 35
Heaven, to the fiends (an unreasonable long mark,
a man would think) ; 'tis well there are no solid orbs to
stop it in the way, or no element of fire to consume it :

but when it came to the earth, it must be monstrous heavy, to break ground as low as the centre. His making milch the burning eyes of heaven was a pretty tolerable flight too : and I think no man ever drew milk
5 out of eyes before him : yet, to make the wonder greater, these eyes were burning. Such a sight indeed were enough to have raised passion in the gods ; but to excuse the effects of it, he tells you, perhaps they did not see it. Wise men would be glad to find a little
10 sense couched under all these pompous words ; for bombast is commonly the delight of that audience which loves Poetry, but understands it not : and as commonly has been the practice of those writers, who, not being able to infuse a natural passion into the mind,
15 have made it their business to ply the ears, and to stun their judges by the noise. But Shakespeare does not often thus ; for the passions in his scene between Brutus and Cassius are extremely natural, the thoughts are such as arise from the matter, the expression of 'em
20 not viciously figurative. I cannot leave this subject, before I do justice to that divine poet, by giving you one of his passionate descriptions : 'tis of Richard the Second when he was deposed, and led in triumph through the streets of London by Henry of Bulling-
25 brook : the painting of it is so lively, and the words so moving, that I have scarce read anything comparable to it in any other language. Suppose you have seen already the fortunate usurper passing through the crowd, and followed by the shouts and acclamations of
30 the people ; and now behold King Richard entering upon the scene : consider the wretchedness of his condition, and his carriage in it ; and refrain from pity, if you can—

　　　As in a theatre, the eyes of men,
35　　After a well-graced actor leaves the stage,

Are idly bent on him that enters next,
Thinking his prattle to be tedious:
Even so, or with much more contempt, men's eyes
Did scowl on Richard: no man cried, God save him
No joyful tongue gave him his welcome home,   5
But dust was thrown upon his sacred head,
Which with such gentle sorrow he shook off,
His face still combating with tears and smiles
(The badges of his grief and patience),
That had not God (for some strong purpose) steel'd   10
The hearts of men, they must perforce have melted,
And barbarism itself have pitied him.

To speak justly of this whole matter : 'tis neither
height of thought that is discommended, nor pathetic
vehemence, nor any nobleness of expression in its
proper place ; but 'tis a false measure of all these,
something which is like them, and is not them ; 'tis the
Bristol-stone, which appears like a diamond ; 'tis an
extravagant thought, instead of a sublime one ; 'tis
roaring madness, instead of vehemence ; and a sound
of words, instead of sense. If Shakespeare were
stripped of all the bombasts in his passions, and dressed
in the most vulgar words, we should find the beauties
of his thoughts remaining ; if his embroideries were
burnt down, there would still be silver at the bottom of
the melting-pot : but I fear (at least let me fear it for
myself) that we, who ape his sounding words, have
nothing of his thought, but are all outside ; there is not
so much as a dwarf within our giant's clothes. Therefore, let not Shakespeare suffer for our sakes ; 'tis our
fault, who succeed him in an age which is more refined,
if we imitate him so ill, that we copy his failings only,
and make a virtue of that in our writings which in his
was an imperfection.

For what remains, the excellency of that poet was, as
I have said, in the more manly passions ; Fletcher's in
the softer : Shakespeare writ better betwixt man and

man ; Fletcher, betwixt man and woman : consequently, the one described friendship better ; the other love : yet Shakespeare taught Fletcher to write love : and Juliet and Desdemona are originals. 'Tis true, the 5 scholar had the softer soul ; but the master had the kinder. Friendship is both a virtue and a passion essentially ; love is a passion only in its nature, and is not a virtue but by accident : good nature makes friendship ; but effeminacy love. Shakespeare had an 10 universal mind, which comprehended all characters and passions ; Fletcher a more confined and limited : for though he treated love in perfection, yet honour, ambition, revenge, and generally all the stronger passions, he either touched not, or not masterly. To conclude 15 all, he was a limb of Shakespeare.

I had intended to have proceeded to the last property of manners, which is, that they must be constant, and the characters maintained the same from the beginning to the end ; and from thence to have proceeded to the 20 thoughts and expressions suitable to a tragedy : but I will first see how this will relish with the age. It is, I confess, but cursorily written ; yet the judgment, which is given here, is generally founded upon experience : but because many men are shocked at the 25 name of rules, as if they were a kind of magisterial prescription upon poets, I will conclude with the words of Rapin, in his *Reflections* on Aristotle's work *of Poetry :* ' If the rules be well considered, we shall find them to be made only to reduce Nature into method, to 30 trace her step by step, and not to suffer the least mark of her to escape us : 'tis only by these, that probability in fiction is maintained, which is the soul of poetry. They are founded upon good sense, and sound reason, rather than on authority ; for though Aristotle and 35 Horace are produced, yet no man must argue, that

what they write is true, because they writ it ; but 'tis
evident, by the ridiculous mistakes and gross absurdities which have been made by those poets who have
taken their fancy only for their guide, that if this fancy
be not regulated, it is a mere caprice, and utterly in- 5
capable to produce a reasonable and judicious poem.'

PREFACE

TO THE

TRANSLATION OF OVID'S EPISTLES

[1680]

THE Life of Ovid being already written in our
language, before the translation of his *Metamorphoses*,
I will not presume so far upon myself, to think I can
add any thing to Mr. Sandys his undertaking. The
5 English reader may there be satisfied, that he flourished
in the reign of Augustus Cæsar ; that he was extracted
from an ancient family of Roman knights ; that he was
born to the inheritance of a splendid fortune ; that he
was designed to the study of the Law, and had made
10 considerable progress in it, before he quitted that
profession, for this of Poetry, to which he was more
naturally formed. The cause of his banishment is
unknown ; because he was himself unwilling further to
provoke the Emperor, by ascribing it to any other
15 reason than what was pretended by Augustus, which
was, the lasciviousness of his *Elegies*, and his *Art of
Love*. 'Tis true, they are not to be excused in the
severity of manners, as being able to corrupt a larger
Empire, if there were any, than that of Rome ; yet this
20 may be said in behalf of Ovid, that no man has ever
treated the passion of love with so much delicacy of

thought, and of expression, or searched into the nature of it more philosophically than he. And the Emperor who condemned him had as little reason as another man to punish that fault with so much severity, if at least he were the author of a certain epigram, which is 5 ascribed to him, relating to the cause of the first civil war betwixt himself and Mark Anthony the Triumvir, which is more fulsome than any passage I have met with in our poet. To pass by the naked familiarity of his expressions to Horace, which are cited in that 10 author's life, I need only mention one notorious act of his, in taking Livia to his bed, when she was not only married, but with child by her husband then living. But deeds, it seems, may be justified by arbitrary power, when words are questioned in a poet. There 15 is another guess of the grammarians, as far from truth as the first from reason ; they will have him banished for some favours, which they say he received from Julia, the daughter of Augustus, whom they think he celebrates under the name of Corinna in his *Elegies.* 20 But he who will observe the verses which are made to that mistress, may gather from the whole contexture of them, that Corinna was not a woman of the highest quality. If Julia were then married to Agrippa, why should our poet make his petition to Isis for her safe 25 delivery, and afterwards condole her miscarriage ; which for aught he knew, might be by her own husband ? Or indeed how durst he be so bold to make the least discovery of such a crime, which was no less than capital, especially committed against a person of Agrippa's 30 rank ? Or if it were before her marriage, he would surely have been more discreet, than to have published an accident which must have been fatal to them both. But what most confirms me against this opinion is, that Ovid himself complains that the true person of Corinna 35

was found out by the fame of his verses to her ; which
if it had been Julia, he durst not have owned ; and
besides, an immediate punishment must have followed.
He seems himself more truly to have touched at the
5 cause of his exile in those obscure verses :—

> *Cur aliquid vidi ?   cur noxia lumina feci ?*
> *Cur imprudenti cognita culpa mihi est ?*
> *Inscius Actæon vidit sine veste Dianam,*
> *Præda fuit canibus non minus ille suis.*

10 Namely, that he had either seen, or was conscious to
somewhat, which had procured him his disgrace.   But
neither am I satisfied, that this was the incest of the
Emperor with his own daughter : for Augustus was of
a nature too vindicative to have contented himself with
15 so small a revenge, or so unsafe to himself, as that of
simple banishment, and would certainly have secured
his crimes from public notice, by the death of him who
was witness to them.   Neither have historians given us
any sight into such an action of this Emperor : nor
20 would he (the greatest politician of his time), in all
probability, have managed his crimes with so little
secrecy, as not to shun the observation of any man.
It seems more probable, that Ovid was either the con-
fidant of some other passion, or that he had stumbled,
25 by some inadvertency, upon the privacies of Livia, and
seen her in a bath : for the words *sine veste Dianam,*
agree better with Livia, who had the fame of chastity,
than with either of the Julias, who were both noted of
incontinency.   The first verses which were made by
30 him in his youth, and recited publicly, according to the
custom, were, as he himself assures us, to Corinna :
his banishment happened not till the age of fifty ; from
which it may be deduced, with probability enough, that
the love of Corinna did not occasion it : nay, he tells us
35 plainly, that his offence was that of error only, not of

wickedness ; and in the same paper of verses also, that the cause was notoriously known at Rome, though it be left so obscure to after ages.

But to leave conjectures on a subject so uncertain, and to write somewhat more authentic of this poet. That he frequented the court of Augustus, and was well received in it, is most undoubted : all his poems bear the character of a court, and appear to be written, as the French call it, *cavalièrement :* add to this, that the titles of many of his *Elegies,* and more of his *Letters* in his banishment, are addressed to persons well known to us, even at this distance, to have been considerable in that court.

Nor was his acquaintance less with the famous poets of his age, than with the noblemen and ladies. He tells you himself, in a particular account of his own life, that Macer, Horace, Tibullus, Propertius, and many others of them, were his familiar friends, and that some of them communicated their writings to him ; but that he had only seen Virgil.

If the imitation of Nature be the business of a poet, I know no author, who can justly be compared with ours, especially in the description of the passions. And to prove this, I shall need no other judges than the generality of his readers : for, all passions being inborn with us, we are almost equally judges when we are concerned in the representation of them. Now I will appeal to any man, who has read this poet, whether he finds not the natural emotion of the same passion in himself, which the poet describes in his feigned persons ? His thoughts, which are the pictures and results of those passions, are generally such as naturally arise from those disorderly motions of our spirits. Yet, not to speak too partially in his behalf, I will confess, that the copiousness of his wit was such, that he often writ

too pointedly for his subject, and made his persons speak
more eloquently than the violence of their passion would
admit : so that he is frequently witty out of season ;
leaving the imitation of Nature, and the cooler dictates
5 of his judgment, for the false applause of Fancy. Yet
he seems to have found out this imperfection in his
riper age ; for why else should he complain that his
Metamorphosis was left unfinished ? Nothing sure can
be added to the wit of that poem, or of the rest ; but
10 many things ought to have been retrenched, which
I suppose would have been the business of his age,
if his misfortunes had not come too fast upon him.
But take him uncorrected, as he is transmitted to us,
and it must be acknowledged, in spite of his Dutch
15 friends, the commentators, even of Julius Scaliger himself, that Seneca's censure will stand good against him ;
Nescivit quod bene cessit relinquere : he never knew how
to give over, when he had done well ; but, continually
varying the same sense an hundred ways, and taking up
20 in another place what he had more than enough in-
culcated before, he sometimes cloys his readers, instead
of satisfying them ; and gives occasion to his translators,
who dare not cover him, to blush at the nakedness of
their father. This, then, is the allay of Ovid's writings,
25 which is sufficiently recompensed by his other excel-
lences : nay, this very fault is not without its beauties ;
for the most severe censor cannot but be pleased with
the prodigality of his wit, though at the same time he
could have wished that the master of it had been
30 a better manager. Every thing which he does becomes
him, and if sometimes he appears too gay, yet there is
a secret gracefulness of youth which accompanies his
writings, though the staidness and sobriety of age be
wanting. In the most material part, which is the con-
35 duct, 'tis certain, that he seldom has miscarried ; for if

his *Elegies* be compared with those of Tibullus and Propertius, his contemporaries, it will be found that those poets seldom designed before they writ ; and though the language of Tibullus be more polished, and the learning of Propertius, especially in his Fourth Book, 5 more set out to ostentation ; yet their common practice was to look no further before them than the next line ; whence it will inevitably follow, that they can drive to no certain point, but ramble from one subject to another, and conclude with somewhat, which is not of a piece 10 with their beginning :—

> *Purpureus late qui splendeat, unus et alter*
> *Assuitur pannus . . .*

as Horace says ; though the verses are golden, they are but patched into the garment. But our Poet has always 15 the goal in his eye, which directs him in his race ; some beautiful design, which he first establishes, and then contrives the means, which will naturally conduct it to his end. This will be evident to judicious readers in this work of his *Epistles*, of which somewhat, at least in 20 general, will be expected.

The title of them in our late editions is *Epistolæ Heroidum*, the Letters of the *Heroines*. But Heinsius has judged more truly, that the inscription of our author was barely *Epistles ;* which he concludes from his cited 25 verses, where Ovid asserts this work as his own invention, and not borrowed from the Greeks, whom (as the masters of their learning) the Romans usually did imitate. But it appears not from their writings, that any of the Grecians ever touched upon this way, which 30 our poet therefore justly has vindicated to himself. I quarrel not at the word *Heroidum*, because it is used by Ovid in his *Art of Love*—

> *Jupiter ad veteres supplex Heroidas ibat.*

But sure he could not be guilty of such an oversight, to call his work by the name of *Heroines*, when there are divers men, or heroes, as namely Paris, Leander, and Acontius, joined in it. Except Sabinus, who writ some
5 answers to Ovid's *Letters*,

(Quam celer e toto rediit meus orbe Sabinus,)

I remember not any of the Romans who have treated this subject, save only Propertius, and that but once, in his Epistle of *Arethusa to Lycotas*, which is written so
10 near the style of Ovid, that it seems to be but an imitation ; and therefore ought not to defraud our poet of the glory of his invention.

Concerning this work of the *Epistles*, I shall content myself to observe these few particulars : first, that they
15 are generally granted to be the most perfect pieces of Ovid, and that the style of them is tenderly passionate and courtly ; two properties well agreeing with the persons, which were heroines, and lovers. Yet where the characters were lower, as in Œnone and Hero, he
20 has kept close to Nature, in drawing his images after a country life, though perhaps he has Romanized his Grecian dames too much, and made them speak, sometimes, as if they had been born in the city of Rome, and under the Empire of Augustus. There seems to
25 be no great variety in the particular subjects which he has chosen ; most of the *Epistles* being written from ladies, who were forsaken by their lovers : which is the reason that many of the same thoughts come back upon us in divers letters : but of the general character of
30 women, which is modesty, he has taken a most becoming care ; for his amorous expressions go no further than virtue may allow, and therefore may be read, as he intended them, by matrons without a blush.

Thus much concerning the Poet, whom you find

translated by divers hands, that you may at least have that variety in the English which the subject denied to the author of the Latin : it remains that I should say somewhat of Poetical Translations in general, and give my opinion (with submission to better judgments), which 5 way of version seems to be the most proper.

All translation, I suppose, may be reduced to these three heads.

First, that of metaphrase, or turning an author word by word, and line by line, from one language into 10 another. Thus, or near this manner, was Horace his *Art of Poetry* translated by Ben Johnson. The second way is that of paraphrase, or translation with latitude, where the author is kept in view by the translator, so as never to be lost, but his words are not so strictly 15 followed as his sense ; and that too is admitted to be amplified, but not altered. Such is Mr. Waller's translation of Virgil's Fourth *Æneid*. The third way is that of imitation, where the translator (if now he has not lost that name) assumes the liberty, not only to 20 vary from the words and sense, but to forsake them both as he sees occasion ; and taking only some general hints from the original, to run division on the ground-work, as he pleases. Such is Mr. Cowley's practice in turning two Odes of Pindar, and one of Horace, into 25 English.

Concerning the first of these methods, our master Horace has given us this caution :

> *Nec verbum verbo curabis reddere, fidus*
> *Interpres . . .*   30
>
> Nor word for word too faithfully translate ;

as the Earl of Roscommon has excellently rendered it. Too faithfully is, indeed, pedantically : 'tis a faith like that which proceeds from superstition, blind and zealous.

Take it in the expression of Sir John Denham to
Sir Richard Fanshaw, on his version of the *Pastor
Fido* :—

5

> That servile path thou nobly dost decline,
> Of tracing word by word, and line by line :
> A new and nobler way thou dost pursue,
> To make translations and translators too :
> They but preserve the ashes, thou the flame,
> True to his sense, but truer to his fame.

10 'Tis almost impossible to translate verbally, and well,
at the same time ; for the Latin (a most severe and
compendious language) often expresses that in one
word, which either the barbarity or the narrowness of
modern tongues cannot supply in more. 'Tis frequent,
15 also, that the conceit is couched in some expression,
which will be lost in English :—

> *Atque iidem venti vela fidemque ferent.*

What poet of our nation is so happy as to express this
thought literally in English, and to strike wit, or almost
20 sense, out of it ?

In short, the verbal copier is encumbered with so
many difficulties at once, that he can never disentangle
himself from all. He is to consider, at the same time,
the thought of his author, and his words, and to find
25 out the counterpart to each in another language ; and,
besides this, he is to confine himself to the compass of
numbers, and the slavery of rhyme. 'Tis much like
dancing on ropes with fettered legs : a man may shun
a fall by using caution ; but the gracefulness of motion
30 is not to be expected : and when we have said the best
of it, 'tis but a foolish task ; for no sober man would
put himself into a danger for the applause of escaping
without breaking his neck. We see Ben Johnson could
not avoid obscurity in his literal translation of Horace,

attempted in the same compass of lines : nay, Horace
himself could scarce have done it to a Greek poet :—

Brevis esse laboro, obscurus fio :

either perspicuity or gracefulness will frequently be
wanting. Horace has indeed avoided both these rocks 5
in his translation of the three first lines of Homer's
Odysseis, which he has contracted into two :—

Dic mihi musa virum captæ post tempora Trojæ,
Qui mores hominum multorum vidit, et urbes.

Muse, speak the man, who, since the siege of Troy, 10
So many towns, such change of manners saw.
EARL OF ROSCOMMON.

But then the sufferings of Ulysses, which are a considerable part of that sentence, are omitted :—

῝Ος μάλα πολλὰ πλάγχθη. 15

The consideration of these difficulties, in a servile,
literal translation, not long since made two of our
famous wits, Sir John Denham and Mr. Cowley, to
contrive another way of turning authors into our tongue,
called, by the latter of them, imitation. As they were 20
friends, I suppose they communicated their thoughts
on this subject to each other ; and therefore their
reasons for it are little different, though the practice of
one is much more moderate. I take imitation of an
author, in their sense, to be an endeavour of a later 25
poet to write like one who has written before him, on
the same subject ; that is, not to translate his words, or
to be confined to his sense, but only to set him as
a pattern, and to write, as he supposes that author
would have done, had he lived in our age, and in our 30
country. Yet I dare not say, that either of them have
carried this libertine way of rendering authors (as
Mr. Cowley calls it) so far as my definition reaches ;
for in the *Pindaric Odes*, the customs and ceremonies

of ancient Greece are still preserved. But I know not
what mischief may arise hereafter from the example of
such an innovation, when writers of unequal parts to
him shall imitate so bold an undertaking. To add and
5 to diminish what we please, which is the way avowed
by him, ought only to be granted to Mr. Cowley, and
that too only in his translation of Pindar ; because he
alone was able to make him amends, by giving him
better of his own, whenever he refused his author's
10 thoughts. Pindar is generally known to be a dark
writer, to want connection, (I mean as to our understanding,) to soar out of sight, and leave his reader at
a gaze. So wild and ungovernable a poet cannot be
translated literally ; his genius is too strong to bear
15 a chain, and Samson-like he shakes it off. A genius
so elevated and unconfined as Mr. Cowley's, was but
necessary to make Pindar speak English, and that was
to be performed by no other way than imitation. But
if Virgil, or Ovid, or any regular intelligible authors, be
20 thus used, 'tis no longer to be called their work, when
neither the thoughts nor words are drawn from the
original ; but instead of them there is something new
produced, which is almost the creation of another hand.
By this way, 'tis true, somewhat that is excellent may
25 be invented, perhaps more excellent than the first
design ; though Virgil must be still excepted, when
that *perhaps* takes place. Yet he who is inquisitive to
know an author's thoughts will be disappointed in his
expectation ; and 'tis not always that a man will be
30 contented to have a present made him, when he expects
the payment of a debt. To state it fairly ; imitation of
an author is the most advantageous way for a translator
to show himself, but the greatest wrong which can be
done to the memory and reputation of the dead. Sir
35 John Denham (who advised more liberty than he took

himself) gives his reason for his innovation, in his admirable Preface before the translation of the Second *Æneid : Poetry is of so subtile a spirit, that, in pouring out of one language into another, it will all evaporate ; and, if a new spirit be not added in the transfusion,* 5 *there will remain nothing but a* caput mortuum. I confess this argument holds good against a literal translation ; but who defends it ? Imitation and verbal version are, in my opinion, the two extremes which ought to be avoided ; and therefore, when I have 10 proposed the mean betwixt them, it will be seen how far his argument will reach.

No man is capable of translating poetry, who, besides a genius to that art, is not a master both of his author's language, and of his own ; nor must we understand the 15 language only of the poet, but his particular turn of thoughts and expression, which are the characters that distinguish, and as it were individuate him from all other writers. When we are come thus far, 'tis time to look into ourselves, to conform our genius to his, 20 to give his thought either the same turn, if our tongue will bear it, or, if not, to vary but the dress, not to alter or destroy the substance. The like care must be taken of the more outward ornaments, the words. When they appear (which is but seldom) literally graceful, it 25 were an injury to the author that they should be changed. But since every language is so full of its own proprieties, that what is beautiful in one, is often barbarous, nay sometimes nonsense, in another, it would be unreasonable to limit a translator to the 30 narrow compass of his author's words : 'tis enough if he choose out some expression which does not vitiate the sense. I suppose he may stretch his chain to such a latitude ; but by innovation of thoughts, methinks he breaks it. By this means the spirit of an author may 35

be transfused, and yet not lost : and thus 'tis plain,
that the reason alleged by Sir John Denham has no
farther force than to expression ; for thought, if it be
translated truly, cannot be lost in another language ;
5 but the words that convey it to our apprehension
(which are the image and ornament of that thought,)
may be so ill chosen, as to make it appear in an
unhandsome dress, and rob it of its native lustre.
There is, therefore, a liberty to be allowed for the
10 expression ; neither is it necessary that words and
lines should be confined to the measure of their original.
The sense of an author, generally speaking, is to be
sacred and inviolable. If the fancy of Ovid be luxuriant,
'tis his character to be so ; and if I retrench it, he is
15 no longer Ovid. It will be replied, that he receives
advantage by this lopping of his superfluous branches ;
but I rejoin, that a translator has no such right. When
a painter copies from the life, I suppose he has no
privilege to alter features and lineaments, under pre-
20 tence that his picture will look better : perhaps the
face which he has drawn would be more exact, if the
eyes or nose were altered ; but 'tis his business to
make it resemble the original. In two cases only there
may a seeming difficulty arise ; that is, if the thought
25 be notoriously trivial or dishonest ; but the same answer
will serve for both, that then they ought not to be
translated :—

> . . . *Et quæ*
> *Desperes tractata nitescere posse, relinquas.*

30 Thus I have ventured to give my opinion on this
subject against the authority of two great men, but
I hope without offence to either of their memories ; for
I both loved them living, and reverence them now they
are dead. But if, after what I have urged, it be thought
35 by better judges that the praise of a translation consists

in adding new beauties to the piece, thereby to recompense the loss which it sustains by change of language, I shall be willing to be taught better, and to recant. In the meantime it seems to me that the true reason why we have so few versions which are tolerable, is not 5 from the too close pursuing of the author's sense, but because there are so few who have all the talents which are requisite for translation, and that there is so little praise and so small encouragement for so considerable a part of learning.   10

To apply, in short, what has been said to this present work, the reader will here find most of the Translations with some little latitude or variation from the author's sense. That of *Œnone to Paris* is in Mr. Cowley's way of imitation only. I was desired to say that the author, 15 who is of the fair sex, understood not Latin. But if she does not, I am afraid she has given us occasion to be ashamed who do.

For my own part, I am ready to acknowledge that I have transgressed the rules which I have given ; and 20 taken more liberty than a just translation will allow. But so many gentlemen whose wit and learning are well known being joined in it, I doubt not but that their excellencies will make you ample satisfaction for my errors.   25

DEDICATION

OF THE SPANISH FRIAR,

OR THE DOUBLE DISCOVERY

[1681]

TO THE RIGHT HONOURABLE

JOHN, LORD HAUGHTON

MY LORD,

WHEN I first designed this play, I found, or thought I found, somewhat so moving in the serious part of it, and so pleasant in the comic, as might deserve
5 a more than ordinary care in both ; accordingly, I used the best of my endeavour, in the management of two plots, so very different from each other, that it was not perhaps the talent of every writer to have made them of a piece. Neither have I attempted other plays of
10 the same nature, in my opinion, with the same judgment, though with like success. And though many poets may suspect themselves for the fondness and partiality of parents to their youngest children, yet I hope I may stand exempted from this rule, because
15 I know myself too well to be ever satisfied with my own conceptions, which have seldom reached to those ideas that I had within me ; and consequently, I presume

I may have liberty to judge when I write more or less pardonably, as an ordinary marksman may know certainly when he shoots less wide at what he aims. Besides, the care and pains I have bestowed on this, beyond my other tragi-comedies, may reasonably make 5 the world conclude, that either I can do nothing tolerably, or that this poem is not much amiss. Few good pictures have been finished at one sitting ; neither can a true just play, which is to bear the test of ages, be produced at a heat, or by the force of fancy, 10 without the maturity of judgment. For my own part, I have both so just a diffidence of myself, and so great a reverence for my audience, that I dare venture nothing without a strict examination ; and am as much ashamed to put a loose indigested play upon the public, as I should 15 be to offer brass money in a payment ; for though it should be taken (as it is too often on the stage), yet it will be found in the second telling ; and a judicious reader will discover, in his closet, that trashy stuff, whose glittering deceived him in the action. I have 20 often heard the stationer sighing in his shop, and wishing for those hands to take off his melancholy bargain which clapped its performance on the stage. In a play-house, everything contributes to impose upon the judgment ; the lights, the scenes, the habits, and, 25 above all, the grace of action, which is commonly the best where there is the most need of it, surprise the audience, and cast a mist upon their understandings ; not unlike the cunning of a juggler, who is always staring us in the face, and overwhelming us with 30 gibberish, only that he may gain the opportunity of making the cleaner conveyance of his trick. But these false beauties of the stage are no more lasting than a rainbow ; when the actor ceases to shine upon them, when he gilds them no longer with his reflection, they 35

vanish in a twinkling. I have sometimes wondered, in
the reading, what was become of those glaring colours
which amazed me in *Bussy D'Amboys* upon the theatre ;
but when I had taken up what I supposed a fallen star,
5 I found I had been cozened with a jelly ; nothing but
a cold, dull mass, which glittered no longer than it was
shooting ; a dwarfish thought, dressed up in gigantic
words, repetition in abundance, looseness of expression,
and gross hyperboles ; the sense of one line expanded
10 prodigiously into ten ; and, to sum up all, uncorrect
English, and a hideous mingle of false poetry, and true
nonsense ; or, at best, a scantling of wit, which lay
gasping for life, and groaning beneath a heap of
rubbish.   A famous modern poet used to sacrifice
15 every year a Statius to Virgil's *Manes* ; and I have
indignation enough to burn a *D'Amboys* annually, to
the memory of Johnson. But now, My Lord, I am
sensible, perhaps too late, that I have gone too far :
for, I remember some verses of my own *Maximin* and
20 *Almanzor*, which cry vengeance upon me for their
extravagance, and which I wish heartily in the same fire
with Statius and Chapman. All I can say for those
passages, which are, I hope, not many, is, that I knew
they were bad enough to please, even when I writ them ;
25 but I repent of them amongst my sins ; and if any of
their fellows intrude by chance into my present writings,
I draw a stroke over all those Delilahs of the theatre ;
and am resolved I will settle myself no reputation by
the applause of fools. 'Tis not that I am mortified to
30 all ambition, but I scorn as much to take it from half-
witted judges, as I should to raise an estate by cheating
of bubbles.   Neither do I discommend the lofty style
in Tragedy, which is naturally pompous and magnificent ;
but nothing is truly sublime that is not just and proper.
35 If the Ancients had judged by the same measures which

a common reader takes, they had concluded Statius to
have written higher than Virgil, for,

Quæ superimposito moles geminata Colosso

carries a more thundering kind of sound than

Tityre tu patulæ recubans sub tegmine fagi : 5

yet Virgil had all the majesty of a lawful prince, and
Statius only the blustering of a tyrant. But when men
affect a virtue which they cannot easily reach, they fall
into a vice which bears the nearest resemblance to it.
Thus an injudicious poet who aims at loftiness runs 10
easily into the swelling puffy style, because it looks like
greatness. I remember, when I was a boy, I thought
inimitable Spenser a mean poet, in comparison of
Sylvester's *Dubartas*, and was rapt into an ecstasy when
I read these lines :— 15

> *Now, when the Winter's keener breath began*
> *To chrystallize the Baltick Ocean ;*
> *To glaze the Lakes, to bridle up the Floods,*
> *And periwig with Snow the bald-pate Woods.*

I am much deceived if this be not abominable fustian, 20
that is, thoughts and words ill-sorted, and without the
least relation to each other ; yet I dare not answer for
an audience, that they would not clap it on the stage :
so little value there is to be given to the common cry,
that nothing but madness can please madmen, and 25
a poet must be of a piece with the spectators, to gain
a reputation with them. But as in a room contrived
for state, the height of the roof should bear a proportion
to the area ; so, in the heightenings of Poetry, the
strength and vehemence of figures should be suited to 30
the occasion, the subject, and the persons. All beyond
this is monstrous : 'tis out of Nature, 'tis an excrescence,
and not a living part of Poetry. I had not said thus
much, if some young gallants, who pretend to criticism,

had not told me that this tragi-comedy wanted the dignity of style ; but as a man who is charged with a crime of which he thinks himself innocent, is apt to be too eager in his own defence, so perhaps I have vindi-
5 cated my play with more partiality than I ought, or than such a trifle can deserve. Yet, whatever beauties it may want, 'tis free at least from the grossness of those faults I mentioned : what credit it has gained upon the stage, I value no further than in reference to
10 my profit, and the satisfaction I had in seeing it repre-sented with all the justness and gracefulness of action. But, as 'tis my interest to please my audience, so 'tis my ambition to be read : that I am sure is the more lasting and the nobler design : for the propriety of thoughts
15 and words, which are the hidden beauties of a play, are but confusedly judged in the vehemence of action : all things are there beheld as in a hasty motion, where the objects only glide before the eye and disappear. The most discerning critic can judge no more of these
20 silent graces in the action than he who rides post through an unknown country can distinguish the situation of places, and the nature of the soil. The purity of phrase, the clearness of conception and expression, the boldness maintained to majesty, the
25 significancy and sound of words, not strained into bom-bast, but justly elevated ; in short, those very words and thoughts, which cannot be changed, but for the worse, must of necessity escape our transient view upon the theatre ; and yet without all these a play may take.
30 For if either the story move us, or the actor help the lameness of it with his performance, or now and then a glittering beam of wit or passion strike through the obscurity of the poem, any of these are sufficient to effect a present liking, but not to fix a lasting admira-
35 tion ; for nothing but truth can long continue ; and

time is the surest judge of truth. I am not vain enough
to think I have left no faults in this, which that touch-
stone will not discover ; neither indeed is it possible to
avoid them in a play of this nature. There are evidently
two actions in it ; but it will be clear to any judicious 5
man, that with half the pains I could have raised a play
from either of them ; for this time I satisfied my own
humour, which was to tack two plays together ; and to
break a rule for the pleasure of variety. The truth is,
the audience are grown weary of continued melancholy 10
scenes ; and I dare venture to prophesy, that few
tragedies except those in verse shall succeed in this
age, if they are not lightened with a course of mirth.
For the feast is too dull and solemn without the fiddles.
But how difficult a task this is, will soon be tried ; for 15
a several genius is required to either way ; and, without
both of 'em, a man, in my opinion, is but half a poet for
the stage. Neither is it so trivial an undertaking, to
make a tragedy end happily ; for 'tis more difficult to
save than 'tis to kill. The dagger and the cup of poison 20
are always in a readiness ; but to bring the action to
the last extremity, and then by probable means to recover
all, will require the art and judgment of a writer, and
cost him many a pang in the performance.

And now, My Lord, I must confess, that what I have 25
written looks more like a Preface, than a Dedication ;
and truly it was thus far my design, that I might entertain you with somewhat in my own art which might be
more worthy of a noble mind, than the stale exploded
trick of fulsome panegyrics. 'Tis difficult to write justly 30
on anything, but almost impossible in praise. I shall
therefore waive so nice a subject ; and only tell you,
that, in recommending a Protestant play to a Protestant
patron, as I do myself an honour, so I do your noble
family a right, who have been always eminent in the 35

support and favour of our religion and liberties. And if the promises of your youth, your education at home, and your experience abroad, deceive me not, the principles you have embraced are such, as will no way degenerate from your ancestors, but refresh their memory in the minds of all true Englishmen, and renew their lustre in your person ; which, My Lord, is not more the wish, than it is the constant expectation, of your Lordship's

Most obedient,
faithful Servant,
JOHN DRYDEN.

SYLVÆ :

OR, THE SECOND PART OF POETICAL
MISCELLANIES

[1685]

PREFACE

FOR this last half year I have been troubled with the
disease (as I may call it) of translation ; the cold prose
fits of it, which are always the most tedious with me,
were spent in the *History of the League :* the hot, which
succeeded them, in this volume of Verse Miscellanies. 5
The truth is, I fancied to myself a kind of ease in the
change of the paroxysm ; never suspecting but that
the humour would have wasted itself in two or three
Pastorals of Theocritus, and as many *Odes* of Horace.
But finding, or at least thinking I found, something that 10
was more pleasing in them than my ordinary productions, I encouraged myself to renew my old acquaintance
with Lucretius and Virgil ; and immediately fixed upon
some parts of them, which had most affected me in
the reading.   These were my natural impulses for the 15
undertaking.   But there was an accidental motive which
was full as forcible, and God forgive him who was the
occasion of it.   It was my Lord Roscommon's *Essay
on Translated Verse,* which made me uneasy till I tried
whether or no I was capable of following his rules, and 20

of reducing the speculation into practice. For many
a fair precept in poetry is, like a seeming demonstration
in the mathematics, very specious in the diagram, but
failing in the mechanic operation.   I think I have
5 generally observed his instructions ; I am sure my
reason is sufficiently convinced both of their truth and
usefulness ; which, in other words, is to confess no less
a vanity, than to pretend that I have at least in some
places made examples to his rules. Yet withal, I must
10 acknowledge, that I have many times exceeded my
commission ; for I have both added and omitted, and
even sometimes very boldly made such expositions of
my authors, as no Dutch commentator will forgive me.
Perhaps, in such particular passages, I have thought
15 that I discovered some beauty yet undiscovered by
those pedants, which none but a poet could have found.
Where I have taken away some of their expressions,
and cut them shorter, it may possibly be on this consideration, that what was beautiful in the Greek or
20 Latin, would not appear so shining in the English : and
where I have enlarged them, I desire the false critics
would not always think, that those thoughts are wholly
mine, but that either they are secretly in the poet, or
may be fairly deduced from him ; or at least, if both
25 those considerations should fail, that my own is of
a piece with his, and that if he were living, and an
Englishman, they are such as he would probably have
written.

For, after all, a translator is to make his author appear
30 as charming as possibly he can, provided he maintains
his character, and makes him not unlike himself.
Translation is a kind of drawing after the life ; where
every one will acknowledge there is a double sort of
likeness, a good one and a bad.   'Tis one thing to
35 draw the outlines true, the features like, the proportions

exact, the colouring itself perhaps tolerable ; and another thing to make all these graceful, by the posture, the shadowings, and, chiefly, by the spirit which animates the whole. I cannot, without some indignation, look on an ill copy of an excellent original ; much less can 5 I behold with patience Virgil, Homer, and some others, whose beauties I have been endeavouring all my life to imitate, so abused, as I may say, to their faces, by a botching interpreter. What English readers, unacquainted with Greek or Latin, will believe me, or any 10 other man, when we commend those authors, and confess we derive all that is pardonable in us from their fountains, if they take those to be the same poets whom our Oglebys have translated ? But I dare assure them, that a good poet is no more like himself in a dull 15 translation, than his carcass would be to his living body. There are many who understand Greek and Latin, and yet are ignorant of their mother-tongue. The proprieties and delicacies of the English are known to few ; 'tis impossible even for a good wit to understand and 20 practise them, without the help of a liberal education, long reading, and digesting of those few good authors we have amongst us, the knowledge of men and manners, the freedom of habitudes and conversation with the best company of both sexes ; and, in short, without 25 wearing off the rust which he contracted while he was laying in a stock of learning. Thus difficult it is to understand the purity of English, and critically to discern not only good writers from bad, and a proper style from a corrupt, but also to distinguish that which is 30 pure in a good author, from that which is vicious and corrupt in him. And for want of all these requisites, or the greatest part of them, most of our ingenious young men take up some cried-up English poet for their model, adore him, and imitate him, as they think, without 35

knowing wherein he is defective, where he is boyish
and trifling, wherein either his thoughts are improper to
his subject, or his expressions unworthy of his thoughts,
or the turn of both is unharmonious. Thus it appears
5 necessary, that a man should be a nice critic in his
mother-tongue before he attempts to translate a foreign
language. Neither is it sufficient, that he be able to
judge of words and style ; but he must be a master of
them too ; he must perfectly understand his author's
10 tongue, and absolutely command his own. So that to
be a thorough translator, he must be a thorough poet.
Neither is it enough to give his author's sense in good
English, in poetical expressions, and in musical numbers ; for though all these are exceeding difficult to
15 perform, there yet remains an harder task ; and 'tis a
secret of which few translators have sufficiently thought.
I have already hinted a word or two concerning it ; that
is, the maintaining the character of an author, which
distinguishes him from all others, and makes him appear
20 that individual poet whom you would interpret. For
example, not only the thoughts, but the style and versification of Virgil and Ovid are very different : yet
I see, even in our best poets, who have translated some
parts of them, that they have confounded their several
25 talents ; and, by endeavouring only at the sweetness and
harmony of numbers, have made them both so much
alike, that, if I did not know the originals, I should
never be able to judge by the copies which was Virgil,
and which was Ovid. It was objected against a late
30 noble painter, that he drew many graceful pictures, but
few of them were like. And this happened to him,
because he always studied himself more than those who
sat to him. In such translators I can easily distinguish
the hand which performed the work, but I cannot dis-
35 tinguish their poet from another. Suppose two authors

are equally sweet, yet there is a great distinction to
be made in sweetness, as in that of sugar and that of
honey. I can make the difference more plain, by giving
you (if it be worth knowing) my own method of proceeding, in my translations out of four several poets in 5
this volume ; Virgil, Theocritus, Lucretius, and Horace.
In each of these, before I undertook them, I considered
the genius and distinguishing character of my author.
I looked on Virgil as a succinct and grave majestic
writer ; one who weighed not only every thought, but 10
every word and syllable ; who was still aiming to crowd
his sense into as narrow a compass as possibly he
could ; for which reason he is so very figurative, that he
requires (I may almost say) a grammar apart to construe
him. His verse is everywhere sounding the very thing 15
in your ears, whose sense it bears ; yet the numbers
are perpetually varied, to increase the delight of the
reader ; so that the same sounds are never repeated
twice together. On the contrary, Ovid and Claudian,
though they write in styles differing from each other, 20
yet have each of them but one sort of music in their
verses. All the versification and little variety of
Claudian is included within the compass of four or five
lines, and then he begins again in the same tenor ;
perpetually closing his sense at the end of a verse, and 25
that verse commonly which they call golden, or two
substantives and two adjectives, with a verb betwixt them
to keep the peace. Ovid, with all his sweetness, has as
little variety of numbers and sound as he : he is always,
as it were, upon the hand-gallop, and his verse runs 30
upon carpet-ground. He avoids, like the other, all
synalœphas, or cutting off one vowel when it comes
before another in the following word ; so that, minding
only smoothness, he wants both variety and majesty.
But to return to Virgil : though he is smooth where 35

smoothness is required, yet he is so far from affecting
it, that he seems rather to disdain it ; frequently makes
use of synalœphas, and concludes his sense in the
middle of his verse. He is everywhere above conceits
5 of epigrammatic wit, and gross hyperboles ; he maintains majesty in the midst of plainness ; he shines, but
glares not ; and is stately without ambition, which is
the vice of Lucan. I drew my definition of poetical wit
from my particular consideration of him : for propriety
10 of thoughts and words are only to be found in him ; and
where they are proper they will be delightful. Pleasure
follows of necessity, as the effect does the cause ; and
therefore is not to be put into the definition. This
exact propriety of Virgil I particularly regarded as a
15 great part of his character ; but must confess, to my
shame, that I have not been able to translate any part
of him so well, as to make him appear wholly like
himself. For where the original is close, no version
can reach it in the same compass. Hannibal Caro's,
20 in the Italian, is the nearest, the most poetical, and the
most sonorous of any translation of the *Æneids ;* yet,
though he takes the advantage of blank verse, he commonly allows two lines for one of Virgil, and does not
always hit his sense. Tasso tells us, in his letters, that
25 Sperone Speroni, a great Italian wit, who was his contemporary, observed of Virgil and Tully, that the Latin
orator endeavoured to imitate the copiousness of Homer,
the Greek poet ; and that the Latin poet made it his
business to reach the conciseness of Demosthenes, the
30 Greek orator. Virgil therefore, being so very sparing
of his words, and leaving so much to be imagined by
the reader, can never be translated as he ought, in
any modern tongue. To make him copious, is to alter
his character ; and to translate him line for line, is im-
35 possible ; because the Latin is naturally a more succinct

language than either the Italian, Spanish, French, or
even than the English, which, by reason of its monosyllables, is far the most compendious of them. Virgil
is much the closest of any Roman poet, and the Latin
hexameter has more feet than the English heroic.   5
Besides all this, an author has the choice of his own
thoughts and words, which a translator has not ; he is
confined by the sense of the inventor to those expressions which are the nearest to it : so that Virgil, studying
brevity, and having the command of his own language, 10
could bring those words into a narrow compass, which
a translator cannot render without circumlocutions.
In short, they, who have called him the torture of
grammarians, might also have called him the plague
of translators ; for he seems to have studied not to be 15
translated. I own that, endeavouring to turn his *Nisus
and Euryalus* as close as I was able, I have performed
that episode too literally ; that, giving more scope to
Mezentius and Lausus, that version, which has more of
the majesty of Virgil, has less of his conciseness ; and 20
all that I can promise for myself, is only that I have
done both better than Ogleby, and perhaps as well as
Caro ; so that, methinks, I come like a malefactor, to
make a speech upon the gallows, and to warn all other
poets, by my sad example, from the sacrilege of trans- 25
lating Virgil. Yet, by considering him so carefully as
I did before my attempt, I have made some faint
resemblance of him ; and had I taken more time, might
possibly have succeeded better ; but never so well as to
have satisfied myself.   30
He who excels all other poets in his own language,
were it possible to do him right, must appear above
them in our tongue, which, as my Lord Roscommon
justly observes, approaches nearest to the Roman in
its majesty ; nearest indeed, but with a vast interval 35

betwixt them.   There is an inimitable grace in Virgil's
words, and in them principally consists that beauty,
which gives so unexpressible a pleasure to him who
best understands their force.   This diction of his,
5 I must once again say, is never to be copied ; and, since
it cannot, he will appear but lame in the best translation.
The turns of his verse, his breakings, his propriety,
his numbers, and his gravity, I have as far imitated, as
the poverty of our language, and the hastiness of my
10 performance, would allow.   I may seem sometimes to
have varied from his sense ; but I think the greatest
variations may be fairly deduced from him ; and where
I leave his commentators, it may be I understand him
better : at least I writ without consulting them in many
15 places.   But two particular lines in *Mezentius and
Lausus*, I cannot so easily excuse.   They are indeed
remotely allied to Virgil's sense ; but they are too like
the trifling tenderness of Ovid, and were printed before
I had considered them enough to alter them.   The first
20 of them I have forgotten, and cannot easily retrieve,
because the copy is at the press.   The second is this :

> When Lausus died, I was already slain.

This appears pretty enough at first sight ; but I am
convinced, for many reasons, that the expression is too
25 bold ; that Virgil would not have said it, though Ovid
would.   The reader may pardon it, if he please, for the
freeness of the confession ; and instead of that, and the
former, admit these two lines, which are more according
to the author—

30
> Nor ask I life, nor fought with that design ;
> As I had used my fortune, use thou thine.

Having with much ado got clear of Virgil, I have, in
the next place, to consider the genius of Lucretius,
whom I have translated more happily in those parts of

him which I undertook. If he was not of the best age
of Roman poetry, he was at least of that which preceded it ; and he himself refined it to that degree of
perfection, both in the language and the thoughts, that
he left an easy task to Virgil ; who, as he succeeded 5
him in time, so he copied his excellencies ; for the
method of the *Georgics* is plainly derived from him.
Lucretius had chosen a subject naturally crabbed ; he
therefore adorned it with poetical descriptions, and
precepts of morality, in the beginning and ending of 10
his books ; which you see Virgil has imitated with great
success in those four books, which, in my opinion, are
more perfect in their kind than even his divine *Æneids*.
The turn of his verse he has likewise followed in those
places which Lucretius has most laboured, and some of 15
his very lines he has transplanted into his own works,
without much variation. If I am not mistaken, the
distinguishing character of Lucretius (I mean of his
soul and genius) is a certain kind of noble pride, and
positive assertion of his opinions. He is everywhere 20
confident of his own reason, and assuming an absolute
command, not only over his vulgar reader, but even
his patron Memmius. For he is always bidding him
attend, as if he had the rod over him ; and using a
magisterial authority, while he instructs him. From his 25
time to ours, I know none so like him, as our poet and
philosopher of Malmesbury. This is that perpetual
dictatorship, which is exercised by Lucretius ; who,
though often in the wrong, yet seems to deal *bonâ fide*
with his reader, and tells him nothing but what he 30
thinks ; in which plain sincerity, I believe, he differs
from our Hobbes, who could not but be convinced, or
at least doubt, of some eternal truths, which he had
opposed. But for Lucretius, he seems to disdain all
manner of replies and is so confident of his cause, that 35

he is beforehand with his antagonists ; urging for them whatever he imagined they could say, and leaving them, as he supposes, without an objection for the future. All this, too, with so much scorn and indignation, as if he 5 were assured of the triumph, before he entered into the lists. From this sublime and daring genius of his, it must of necessity come to pass, that his thoughts must be masculine, full of argumentation, and that sufficiently warm. From the same fiery temper proceeds the 10 loftiness of his expressions, and the perpetual torrent of his verse, where the barrenness of his subject does not too much constrain the quickness of his fancy. For there is no doubt to be made, but that he could have been everywhere as poetical, as he is in his descriptions, 15 and in the moral part of his philosophy, if he had not aimed more to instruct, in his System of Nature, than to delight. But he was bent upon making Memmius a materialist, and teaching him to defy an invisible power : in short, he was so much an atheist, that he 20 forgot sometimes to be a poet. These are the considerations, which I had of that author, before I attempted to translate some parts of him. And accordingly I laid by my natural diffidence and scepticism for a while, to take up that dogmatical way of his, which, 25 as I said, is so much his character, as to make him that individual poet. As for his opinions concerning the mortality of the soul, they are so absurd, that I cannot, if I would, believe them. I think a future state demonstrable even by natural arguments ; at least to take 30 away rewards and punishments is only a pleasing prospect to a man, who resolves beforehand not to live morally. But on the other side, the thought of being nothing after death is a burden unsupportable to a virtuous man, even though a heathen. We naturally 35 aim at happiness, and cannot bear to have it confined

to the shortness of our present being ; especially when
we consider, that virtue is generally unhappy in this
world, and vice fortunate. So that 'tis hope of futurity
alone, that makes this life tolerable, in expectation of
a better. Who would not commit all the excesses, to 5
which he is prompted by his natural inclinations, if he
may do them with security while he is alive, and be
uncapable of punishment after he is dead ? If he
be cunning and secret enough to avoid the laws, there
is no band of morality to restrain him : for fame and 10
reputation are weak ties ; many men have not the least
sense of them ; powerful men are only awed by them, as
they conduce to their interest, and that not always, when
a passion is predominant ; and no man will be contained within the bounds of duty, when he may safely 15
transgress them. These are my thoughts abstractedly,
and without entering into the notions of our Christian
faith, which is the proper business of divines.

But there are other arguments in this poem (which
I have turned into English) not belonging to the mortality 20
of the soul, which are strong enough to a reasonable
man, to make him less in love with life, and consequently in less apprehensions of death. Such as
are the natural satiety proceeding from a perpetual
enjoyment of the same things ; the inconveniencies of old 25
age, which make him incapable of corporeal pleasures ;
the decay of understanding and memory, which render
him contemptible, and useless to others. These, and
many other reasons, so pathetically urged, so beautifully
expressed, so adorned with examples, and so admirably 30
raised by the *prosopopœia* of Nature, who is brought in
speaking to her children with so much authority and
vigour, deserve the pains I have taken with them, which
I hope have not been unsuccessful, or unworthy of my
author : at least I must take the liberty to own that 35

I was pleased with my own endeavours, which but rarely happens to me ; and that I am not dissatisfied upon the review of anything I have done in this author.

5 It is true, there is something, and that of some moment, to be objected against my Englishing the *Nature of Love,* from the fourth book of Lucretius ; and I can less easily answer why I translated it, than why I thus translated it. The objection arises from 10 the obscenity of the subject ; which is aggravated by the too lively and alluring delicacy of the verses. In the first place, without the least formality of an excuse, I own it pleased me ; and let my enemies make the worst they can of this confession. I am not yet so 15 secure from that passion, but that I want my author's antidotes against it. He has given the truest and most philosophical account, both of the disease and remedy, which I ever found in any author ; for which reasons I translated him. But it will be asked, why 20 I turned him into this luscious English, for I will not give it a worse word. Instead of an answer, I would ask again of my supercilious adversaries, whether I am not bound, when I translate an author, to do him all the right I can, and to translate him to the best advan- 25 tage ? If, to mince his meaning, which I am satisfied was honest and instructive, I had either omitted some part of what he said, or taken from the strength of his expression, I certainly had wronged him ; and that freeness of thought and words being thus cashiered 30 in my hands, he had no longer been Lucretius. If nothing of this kind be to be read, physicians must not study nature, anatomies must not be seen, and some- what I could say of particular passages in books which, to avoid profaneness, I do not name. But the 35 intention qualifies the act ; and both mine and my

author's were to instruct, as well as please. 'Tis most
certain, that barefaced bawdry is the poorest pretence
to wit imaginable. If I should say otherwise, I should
have two great authorities against me : the one is the
Essay on Poetry, which I publicly valued before I knew 5
the author of it, and with the commendation of which
my Lord Roscommon so happily begins his *Essay on
Translated Verse ;* the other is no less than our admired
Cowley, who says the same thing in other words ; for,
in his *Ode concerning Wit*, he writes thus of it :—   10

> Much less can that have any place,
> At which a virgin hides her face ;
> Such dross the fire must purge away ; 'tis just
> The author blush, there where the reader must.

Here indeed Mr. Cowley goes further than the 15
Essay : for he asserts plainly, that obscenity has no
place in wit ; the other only says, 'tis a poor pretence
to it, or an ill sort of wit, which has nothing more
to support it than barefaced ribaldry ; which is both
unmannerly in itself, and fulsome to the reader. But 20
neither of these will reach my case : for, in the first
place, I am only the translator, not the inventor ; so that
the heaviest part of the censure falls upon Lucretius,
before it reaches me : in the next place, neither he nor
I have used the grossest words, but the cleanliest meta- 25
phors we could find, to palliate the broadness of the
meaning ; and, to conclude, have carried the poetical
part no further, than the philosophical exacted.

There is one mistake of mine, which I will not lay to
the printer's charge, who has enough to answer for in 30
false pointings ; it is in the word *viper ;* I would have
the verse run thus—

> The scorpion, love, must on the wound be bruised.

There are a sort of blundering, half-witted people
who make a great deal of noise about a verbal slip ; 35

though Horace would instruct them better in true
criticism—

>   . . . *non ego paucis*
> *Offendar maculis, quas aut incuria fudit,*
> 5   *Aut humana parum cavit natura.*

True judgment in Poetry, like that in Painting, takes
a view of the whole together, whether it be good or
not ; and where the beauties are more than the faults,
concludes for the poet against the little judge ; 'tis
10 a sign that malice is hard driven, when 'tis forced to lay
hold on a word or syllable ; to arraign a man is one
thing, and to cavil at him is another. In the midst of
an ill-natured generation of scribblers, there is always
justice enough left in mankind to protect good writers :
15 and they too are obliged, both by humanity and interest,
to espouse each other's cause against false critics, who
are the common enemies. This last consideration puts
me in mind of what I owe to the ingenious and learned
translator of Lucretius. I have not here designed to
20 rob him of any part of that commendation which he has
so justly acquired by the whole author, whose fragments only fall to my portion. What I have now performed is no more than I intended above twenty years
ago. The ways of our translation are very different.
25 He follows him more closely than I have done, which
became an interpreter of the whole poem : I take more
liberty, because it best suited with my design, which
was, to make him as pleasing as I could. He had
been too voluminous, had he used my method in so long
30 a work ; and I had certainly taken his, had I made it
my business to translate the whole. The preference,
then, is justly his ; and I join with Mr. Evelyn in the
confession of it, with this additional advantage to him,
that his reputation is already established in this poet ;
35 mine is to make its fortune in the world. If I have

been anywhere obscure, in following our common author, or if Lucretius himself is to be condemned, I refer myself to his excellent annotations, which I have often read, and always with some new pleasure.

My Preface begins already to swell upon me, and 5 looks as if I were afraid of my reader, by so tedious a bespeaking of him ; and yet I have Horace and Theocritus upon my hands ; but the Greek gentleman shall quickly be dispatched, because I have more business with the Roman. 10

That which distinguishes Theocritus from all other poets, both Greek and Latin, and which raises him even above Virgil in his *Eclogues*, is the inimitable tenderness of his passions, and the natural expression of them in words so becoming of a pastoral. A simplicity 15 shines through all he writes : he shows his art and learning, by disguising both. His shepherds never rise above their country education in their complaints of love : there is the same difference betwixt him and Virgil, as there is betwixt Tasso's *Aminta* and the 20 *Pastor Fido* of Guarini. Virgil's shepherds are too well read in the philosophy of Epicurus and of Plato, and Guarini's seem to have been bred in courts ; but Theocritus and Tasso have taken theirs from cottages and plains. It was said of Tasso, in relation to his 25 similitudes, *mai esce del bosco :* that he never departed from the woods ; that is, all his comparisons were taken from the country. The same may be said of our Theocritus : he is softer than Ovid ; he touches the passions more delicately, and performs all this out of his 30 own fond, without diving into the arts and sciences for a supply. Even his Doric dialect has an incomparable sweetness in its clownishness, like a fair shepherdess in her country russet, talking in a Yorkshire tone. This was impossible for Virgil to imitate ; because the 35

severity of the Roman language denied him that advantage. Spenser has endeavoured it in his *Shepherd's Calendar ;* but neither will it succeed in English ; for which reason I forbore to attempt it. For Theocritus
5 writ to Sicilians, who spoke that dialect ; and I direct this part of my translations to our ladies, who neither understand, nor will take pleasure in such homely expressions. I proceed to Horace.

Take him in parts, and he is chiefly to be considered
10 in his three different talents, as he was a critic, a satirist, and a writer of odes. His morals are uniform, and run through all of them ; for let his Dutch commentators say what they will, his philosophy was Epicurean ; and he made use of Gods and Providence
15 only to serve a turn in Poetry. But since neither his Criticisms, which are the most instructive of any that are written in this art, nor his Satires, which are incomparably beyond Juvenal's, (if to laugh and rally is to be preferred to railing and declaiming,) are no part
20 of my present undertaking, I confine myself wholly to his Odes. These are also of several sorts : some of them are panegyrical, others moral, the rest jovial, or (if I may so call them) Bacchanalian. As difficult as he makes it, and as indeed it is, to imitate Pindar, yet, in
25 his most elevated flights, and in the sudden changes of his subject with almost imperceptible connexions, that Theban poet is his master. But Horace is of the more bounded fancy, and confines himself strictly to one sort of verse, or stanza, in every Ode. That which
30 will distinguish his style from all other poets, is the elegance of his words, and the numerousness of his verse ; there is nothing so delicately turned in all the Roman language. There appears in every part of his diction, or (to speak English) in all his expressions,
35 a kind of noble and bold purity. His words are chosen

with as much exactness as Virgil's ; but there seems to
be a greater spirit in them. There is a secret happiness attends his choice, which in Petronius is called
curiosa felicitas, and which I suppose he had from the
feliciter audere of Horace himself. But the most distin- 5
guishing part of all his character seems to me to be his
briskness, his jollity, and his good humour ; and those
I have chiefly endeavoured to copy ; his other excellencies, I confess, are above my imitation. One Ode,
which infinitely pleased me in the reading, I have 10
attempted to translate in Pindaric verse : 'tis that
which is inscribed to the present Earl of Rochester,
to whom I have particular obligations which this small
testimony of my gratitude can never pay. 'Tis his
darling in the Latin, and I have taken some pains to 15
make it my master-piece in English : for which reason
I took this kind of verse, which allows more latitude
than any other. Every one knows it was introduced
into our language, in this age, by the happy genius
of Mr. Cowley. The seeming easiness of it has made it 20
spread ; but it has not been considered enough, to be
so well cultivated. It languishes in almost every hand
but his, and some very few, whom (to keep the rest in
countenance) I do not name. He, indeed, has brought
it as near perfection as was possible in so short a time. 25
But if I may be allowed to speak my mind modestly,
and without injury to his sacred ashes, somewhat of the
purity of English, somewhat of more equal thoughts,
somewhat of sweetness in the numbers, in one word,
somewhat of a finer turn and more lyrical verse, is yet 30
wanting. As for the soul of it, which consists in the
warmth and vigour of fancy, the masterly figures, and
the copiousness of imagination, he has excelled all
others in this kind. Yet if the kind itself be capable of
more perfection, though rather in the ornamental parts 35

of it than the essential, what rules of morality or respect
have I broken, in naming the defects, that they may
hereafter be amended ?   Imitation is a nice point, and
there are few poets who deserve to be models in all
5 they write.   Milton's *Paradise Lost* is admirable ; but
am I therefore bound to maintain, that there are no
flats amongst his elevations, when 'tis evident he creeps
along sometimes for above an hundred lines together ?
Cannot I admire the height of his invention, and the
10 strength of his expression, without defending his antiquated words, and the perpetual harshness of their
sound ?   It is as much commendation as a man can
bear, to own him excellent ; all beyond it is idolatry.
Since Pindar was the prince of lyric poets, let me have
15 leave to say, that, in imitating him, our numbers should,
for the most part, be lyrical : for variety, or rather where
the majesty of thought requires it, they may be stretched
to the English heroic of five feet, and to the French
Alexandrine of six.   But the ear must preside, and
20 direct the judgment to the choice of numbers : without
the nicety of this, the harmony of Pindaric verse can
never be complete ; the cadency of one line must be
a rule to that of the next ; and the sound of the former
must slide gently into that which follows, without leap-
25 ing from one extreme into another.   It must be done like
the shadowings of a picture, which fall by degrees into
a darker colour.   I shall be glad, if I have so explained
myself as to be understood ; but if I have not, *quod
nequeo dicere, et sentio tantum*, must be my excuse.
30   There remains much more to be said on this subject ;
but, to avoid envy, I will be silent.   What I have
said is the general opinion of the best judges, and in a
manner has been forced from me, by seeing a noble sort
of poetry so happily restored by one man, and so
35 grossly copied by almost all the rest.   A musical ear,

and a great genius, if another Mr. Cowley could
arise in another age, may bring it to perfection. In
the meantime,

> *. . . fungar vice cotis, acutum*
> *Reddere quæ ferrum valet, expers ipsa secandi.* 5

I hope it will not be expected from me, that I should
say anything of my fellow undertakers in this Miscellany. Some of them are too nearly related to me, to
be commended without suspicion of partiality ; others
I am sure need it not ; and the rest I have not perused. 10

To conclude, I am sensible that I have written this
too hastily and too loosely ; I fear I have been tedious,
and, which is worse, it comes out from the first draught,
and uncorrected. This I grant is no excuse ; for it
may be reasonably urged, why did he not write with 15
more leisure, or if he had it not, (which was certainly
my case,) why did he attempt to write on so nice a
subject ? The objection is unanswerable ; but, in part
of recompense, let me assure the reader, that, in hasty
productions, he is sure to meet with an author's present 20
sense, which cooler thoughts would possibly have dis-
guised. There is undoubtedly more of spirit, though
not of judgment, in these uncorrect essays ; and consequently, though my hazard be the greater, yet the
reader's pleasure is not the less. 25

JOHN DRYDEN.

ALBION AND ALBANIUS,
AN OPERA

[1685]

THE PREFACE

IF Wit has truly been defined, 'a propriety of thoughts
and words,' then that definition will extend to all sorts
of Poetry : and, among the rest, to this present entertainment of an opera. Propriety of thought is that fancy
5 which arises naturally from the subject, or which the
poet adapts to it. Propriety of words is the clothing
of those thoughts with such expressions as are naturally
proper to them ; and from both these, if they are judiciously performed, the delight of poetry results. An opera
10 is a poetical tale, or fiction, represented by vocal and
instrumental music, adorned with scenes, machines, and
dancing. The supposed persons of this musical drama
are generally supernatural, as gods, and goddesses, and
heroes, which at least are descended from them, and
15 are in due time to be adopted into their number. The
subject, therefore, being extended beyond the limits of
human nature, admits of that sort of marvellous and
surprising conduct, which is rejected in other plays.
Human impossibilities are to be received as they are
20 in faith ; because, where gods are introduced, a supreme
power is to be understood, and second causes are out
of doors. Yet propriety is to be observed even here.

The gods are all to manage their peculiar provinces ;
and what was attributed by the heathens to one power
ought not to be performed by any other. Phœbus must
foretell, Mercury must charm with his caduceus, and
Juno must reconcile the quarrels of the marriage-bed. 5
To conclude, they must all act according to their distinct
and peculiar characters. If the persons represented
were to speak upon the stage, it would follow, of necessity, that the expressions should be lofty, figurative, and
majestical : but the nature of an opera denies the fre- 10
quent use of these poetical ornaments ; for vocal music,
though it often admits a loftiness of sound, yet always
exacts an harmonious sweetness ; or, to distinguish yet
more justly, the recitative part of the opera requires
a more masculine beauty of expression and sound ; the 15
other, which, for want of a proper English word, I must
call the *songish part*, must abound in the softness and
variety of numbers ; its principal intention being to
please hearing rather than to gratify the understanding.
It appears, indeed, preposterous at first sight, that 20
rhyme, on any consideration, should take place of
reason ; but, in order to resolve the problem, this
fundamental proposition must be settled, that the first
inventors of any art or science, provided they have
brought it to perfection, are, in reason, to give laws to 25
it ; and, according to their model, all after-undertakers
are to build. Thus, in Epic Poetry, no man ought to
dispute the authority of Homer, who gave the first
being to that masterpiece of art, and endued it with
that form of perfection in all its parts that nothing was 30
wanting to its excellency. Virgil therefore, and those
very few who have succeeded him, endeavoured not to
introduce, or innovate, anything in a design already
perfected, but imitated the plan of the inventor ; and
are only so far true heroic poets as they have built on 35

the foundations of Homer. Thus, Pindar, the author
of those Odes, which are so admirably restored by
Mr. Cowley in our language, ought for ever to be the
standard of them ; and we are bound, according to
5 the practice of Horace and Mr. Cowley, to copy him.
Now, to apply this axiom to our present purpose, whosoever undertakes the writing of an opera (which is
a modern invention, though built indeed on the foundation of ethnic worship), is obliged to imitate the design
10 of the Italians, who have not yet invented, but brought
to perfection, this sort of dramatic musical entertainment. I have not been able, by any search, to get any
light, either of the time when it began, or of the first
author. But I have probable reasons, which induce
15 me to believe, that some Italians, having curiously
observed the gallantries of the Spanish Moors, at their
zambras, or royal feasts, where music, songs, and
dancing were in perfection, together with their machines,
which are usual at their *sortijas*, or running at the ring,
20 and other solemnities, may possibly have refined upon
those Moresque divertisements, and produced this
delightful entertainment, by leaving out the warlike
part of the carousels, and forming a poetical design for
the use of the machines, the songs, and dances. But
25 however it began (for this is only conjectural), we
know that, for some centuries, the knowledge of Music
has flourished principally in Italy, the mother of learning and of arts ; that Poetry and Painting have been
there restored and so cultivated by Italian masters, that
30 all Europe has been enriched out of their treasury ;
and the other parts of it, in relation to those delightful
arts, are still as much provincial to Italy, as they were
in the time of the Roman empire. Their first operas
seem to have been intended for the celebration of the
35 marriages of their princes, or for the magnificence of

some general time of joy; accordingly, the expenses
of them were from the purse of the sovereign, or of the
republic, as they are still practised at Venice, Rome,
and at other places, at their carnivals. Savoy and
Florence have often used them in their courts, at the 5
weddings of their dukes; and at Turin particularly,
was performed the *Pastor Fido*, written by the famous
Guarini, which is a pastoral opera made to solemnize
the marriage of a Duke of Savoy. The prologue of it
has given the design to all the French; which is a com- 10
pliment to the sovereign power by some god or god-
dess; so that it looks no less than a kind of embassy
from heaven to earth. I said in the beginning of this
preface, that the persons represented in operas are
generally gods, goddesses, and heroes descended from 15
them, who are supposed to be their peculiar care;
which hinders not, but that meaner persons may sometimes gracefully be introduced, especially if they have
relation to those first times, which poets call the Golden
Age; wherein, by reason of their innocence, those 20
happy mortals were supposed to have had a more
familiar intercourse with superior beings; and therefore shepherds might reasonably be admitted, as of all
callings the most innocent, the most happy, and who,
by reason of the spare time they had, in their almost 25
idle employment, had most leisure to make verses, and
to be in love; without somewhat of which passion, no
opera can possibly subsist.

It is almost needless to speak anything of that noble
language, in which this musical drama was first invented 30
and performed. All who are conversant in the Italian
cannot but observe that it is the softest, the sweetest,
the most harmonious, not only of any modern tongue,
but even beyond any of the learned. It seems indeed
to have been invented for the sake of Poetry and Music; 35

the vowels are so abounding in all words, especially in
terminations of them, that, excepting some few monosyllables, the whole language ends in them. Then the
pronunciation is so manly, and so sonorous, that their
5 very speaking has more of music in it than Dutch
poetry and song. It has withal derived so much
copiousness and eloquence from the Greek and Latin,
in the composition of words, and the formation of them,
that if, after all, we must call it barbarous, 'tis the most
10 beautiful and most learned of any barbarism in modern
tongues ; and we may at least as justly praise it, as
Pyrrhus did the Roman discipline and martial order,
that it was of barbarians (for so the Greeks called all
other nations), but had nothing in it of barbarity. This
15 language has in a manner been refined and purified
from the Gothic ever since the time of Dante, which is
above four hundred years ago ; and the French, who
now cast a longing eye to their country, are not less
ambitious to possess their elegance in Poetry and Music ;
20 in both which they labour at impossibilities. 'Tis true,
indeed, they have reformed their tongue, and brought
both their prose and poetry to a standard ; the sweetness, as well as the purity, is much improved, by throwing off the unnecessary consonants, which made their
25 spelling tedious, and their pronunciation harsh : but,
after all, as nothing can be improved beyond its own
species, or farther than its original nature will allow ; as
an ill voice, though ever so thoroughly instructed in the
rules of music, can never be brought to sing harmoni-
30 ously, nor many an honest critic ever arrive to be
a good poet ; so neither can the natural harshness of
the French, or their perpetual ill accent, be ever refined
into perfect harmony like the Italian. The English has
yet more natural disadvantages than the French ; our
35 original Teutonic, consisting most in monosyllables, and

those encumbered with consonants, cannot possibly be
freed from those inconveniences. The rest of our words,
which are derived from the Latin chiefly, and the French,
with some small sprinklings of Greek, Italian, and
Spanish, are some relief in Poetry, and help us to 5
soften our uncouth numbers ; which, together with our
English genius, incomparably beyond the trifling of
the French, in all the nobler parts of verse, will
justly give us the pre-eminence. But, on the other
hand, the effeminacy of our pronunciation (a defect 10
common to us and to the Danes), and our scarcity of
female rhymes, have left the advantage of musical composition for songs, though not for recitative, to our
neighbours.

Through these difficulties I have made a shift to 15
struggle in my part of the performance of this opera ;
which, as mean as it is, deserves at least a pardon,
because it has attempted a discovery beyond any former
undertaker of our nation ; only remember, that if there
be no North-East Passage to be found, the fault is in 20
Nature, and not in me ; or, as Ben Johnson tells us in
The Alchymist, when projection had failed, and the
glasses were all broken, there was enough, however,
in the bottoms of them, to cure the itch ; so I may thus
far be positive, that if I have not succeeded as I desire, 25
yet there is somewhat still remaining to satisfy the
curiosity, or itch of sight and hearing. Yet I have no
great reason to despair ; for I may, without vanity,
own some advantages, which are not common to every
writer ; such as are the knowledge of the Italian and 30
French language, and the being conversant with some
of their best performances in this kind ; which have
furnished me with such variety of measures, as have
given the composer, Monsieur Grabut, what occasions
he could wish, to show his extraordinary talent in 35

diversifying the recitative, the lyrical part, and the chorus ; in all which, not to attribute anything to my own opinion, the best judges, and those too of the best quality, who have honoured his rehearsals with their
5 presence, have no less commended the happiness of his genius than his skill. And let me have the liberty to add one thing, that he has so exactly expressed my sense in all places where I intended to move the passions, that he seems to have entered into my thoughts,
10 and to have been the poet as well as the composer. This I say, not to flatter him, but to do him right ; because amongst some English musicians, and their scholars, who are sure to judge after them, the imputation of being a Frenchman is enough to make a party,
15 who maliciously endeavour to decry him. But the knowledge of Latin and Italian poets, both which he possesses, besides his skill in music, and his being acquainted with all the performances of the French operas, adding to these the good sense to which he is
20 born, have raised him to a degree above any man who shall pretend to be his rival upon our stage. When any of our countrymen excel him, I shall be glad, for the sake of old England, to be shown my error ; in the meantime, let virtue be commended, though in the
25 person of a stranger.

If I thought it convenient, I could here discover some rules which I have given to myself in the writing of an opera in general, and of this opera in particular ; but I consider that the effect would only be to have my
30 own performance measured by the laws I gave ; and, consequently, to set up some little judges, who, not understanding throughly, would be sure to fall upon the faults, and not to acknowledge any of the beauties ; an hard measure, which I have often found from false
35 critics. Here, therefore, if they will criticize, they shall

do it out of their own fond ; but let them first be assured
that their ears are nice ; for there is neither writing
nor judgment on this subject without that good quality.
'Tis no easy matter, in our language, to make words so
smooth, and numbers so harmonious, that they shall 5
almost set themselves. And yet there are rules for
this in Nature, and as great a certainty of quantity in
our syllables, as either in the Greek or Latin : but let
poets and judges understand those first, and then let
them begin to study English. When they have chawed 10
a while upon these preliminaries, it may be they will
scarce adventure to tax me with want of thought and
elevation of fancy in this work ; for they will soon be
satisfied, that those are not of the nature of this sort of
writing. The necessity of double rhymes, and order- 15
ing of the words and numbers for the sweetness of the
voice, are the main hinges on which an opera must
move ; and both of these are without the compass of
any art to teach another to perform, unless Nature, in
the first place, has done her part, by enduing the poet 20
with that nicety of hearing, that the discord of sounds
in words shall as much offend him as a seventh in
music would a good composer. I have therefore no
need to make excuses for meanness of thought in many
places : the Italians, with all the advantages of their 25
language, are continually forced upon it, or, rather,
affect it. The chief secret is the choice of words ; and,
by this choice, I do not here mean elegancy of expression, but propriety of sound, to be varied according to
the nature of the subject. Perhaps a time may come 30
when I may treat of this more largely, out of some
observations which I have made from Homer and
Virgil, who, amongst all the poets, only understood
the art of numbers, and of that which was properly
called *rhythmus* by the ancients. 35

The same reasons which depress thought in an opera have a stronger effect upon the words, especially in our language ; for there is no maintaining the purity of English in short measures, where the rhyme returns
5 so quick, and is so often female, or double rhyme, which is not natural to our tongue, because it consists too much of monosyllables, and those, too, most commonly clogged with consonants ; for which reason I am often forced to coin new words, revive some that are anti-
10 quated, and botch others ; as if I had not served out my time in poetry, but was bound apprentice to some doggrel rhymer, who makes songs to tunes, and sings them for a livelihood. It is true, I have not been often put to this drudgery ; but where I have, the words will
15 sufficiently show that I was then a slave to the composition, which I will never be again : it is my part to invent, and the musician's to humour that invention. I may be counselled, and will always follow my friend's advice where I find it reasonable, but will never part
20 with the power of the militia.

I am now to acquaint my reader with somewhat more particular concerning this opera, after having begged his pardon for so long a preface to so short a work. It was originally intended only for a prologue to a play of
25 the nature of *the Tempest* ; which is a tragedy mixed with opera, or a drama, written in blank verse, adorned with scenes, machines, songs, and dances, so that the fable of it is all spoken and acted by the best of the comedians ; the other part of the entertainment to be
30 performed by the same singers and dancers who were introduced in this present opera. It cannot properly be called a play, because the action of it is supposed to be conducted sometimes by supernatural means, or magic ; nor an opera, because the story of it is not
35 sung. But more of this at its proper time. But some

intervening accidents have hitherto deferred the performance of the main design, I proposed to the actors
to turn the intended prologue into an entertainment by
itself, as you now see it, by adding two acts more to
what I had already written. The subject of it is wholly 5
allegorical ; and the allegory itself so very obvious, that
it will no sooner be read than understood. It is divided,
according to the plain and natural method of every
action, into three parts. For even Aristotle himself
is contented to say simply, that in all actions there is 10
a beginning, a middle, and an end ; after which model
all the Spanish plays are built.

The descriptions of the scenes and other decorations
of the stage I had from Mr. Betterton, who has spared
neither for industry, nor cost, to make this entertain- 15
ment perfect, nor for invention of the ornaments to
beautify it.

To conclude, though the enemies of the composer are
not few, and that there is a party formed against him
of his own profession, I hope, and am persuaded, that 20
this prejudice will turn in the end to his advantage.
For the greatest part of an audience is always un-
interested, though seldom knowing ; and if the music
be well composed, and well performed, they who find
themselves pleased will be so wise as not to be imposed 25
upon, and fooled out of their satisfaction. The newness
of the undertaking is all the hazard. When operas
were first set up in France they were not followed over
eagerly ; but they gained daily upon their hearers, till
they grew to that height of reputation which they now 30
enjoy. The English, I confess, are not altogether so
musical as the French ; and yet they have been pleased
already with *the Tempest*, and some pieces that followed,
which were neither much better written nor so well
composed as this. If it finds encouragement, I dare 35

promise myself to mend my hand, by making a more
pleasing fable. In the meantime, every loyal Englishman cannot but be satisfied with the moral of this,
which so plainly represents the double restoration of
5 his Sacred Majesty.

POSTSCRIPT.

This Preface being wholly written before the death
of my late Royal Master (*quem semper acerbum, semper
honoratum, sic di voluistis habebo*) I have now lately
10 reviewed it, as supposing I should find many notions
in it that would require correction on cooler thoughts.
After four months lying by me, I looked on it as no
longer mine, because I had wholly forgotten it ; but
I confess with some satisfaction, and perhaps a little
15 vanity, that I found myself entertained by it ; my own
judgment was new to me, and pleased me when I looked
on it as another man's. I see no opinion that I would
retract or alter, unless it be, that possibly the Italians
went not so far as Spain for the invention of their
20 operas. They might have it in their own country ; and
that by gathering up the shipwrecks of the Athenian
and Roman theatres, which we know were adorned with
scenes, music, dances, and machines, especially the
Grecian. But of this the learned Monsieur Vossius,
25 who has made our nation his second country, is the
best, and perhaps the only judge now living. As for
the opera itself, it was all composed, and was just ready
to have been performed, when he, in honour of whom
it was principally made, was taken from us.
30 He had been pleased twice or thrice to command
that it should be practised before him, especially the
first and third acts of it ; and publicly declared, more
than once, that the composition and choruses were
more just and more beautiful than any he had heard

in England. How nice an ear he had in music is
sufficiently known ; his praise therefore has established
the reputation of it above censure, and made it in
manner sacred. 'Tis therefore humbly and religiously
dedicated to his memory.   5

It might reasonably have been expected that his death
must have changed the whole fabric of the opera, or at
least a great part of it. But the design of it originally
was so happy, that it needed no alteration, properly so
called ; for the addition of twenty or thirty lines in the 10
apotheosis of Albion has made it entirely of a piece.
This was the only way which could have been invented
to save it from botched ending ; and it fell luckily into
my imagination ; as if there were a kind of fatality
even in the most trivial things concerning the succes- 15
sion : a change was made, and not for the worse,
without the least confusion or disturbance ; and those
very causes, which seemed to threaten us with troubles,
conspired to produce our lasting happiness.

NOTES

EPISTLE DEDICATORY OF 'THE RIVAL LADIES'
(1664).

ROGER BOYLE, Earl of Orrery (1621–1679), author of *Parthenissa that most Fam'd Romance*, 1654 (an imitation of the manner of the *Grand Cyrus*), and of several plays. *Henry the Fifth* was acted in this year, 1664 ; *Mustapha,* the most successful of Lord Orrery's heroic plays, in 1665 (Pepys, Apr. 3, 1665, ' at the Duke's ' ; Betterton acted Solyman the Magnificent) ; the *Black Prince,* in 1667 ; *Tryphon,* a tragedy in rhyme, in 1668 (Pepys, Dec. 8, 1668) : these were published in 1669, fol. *Guzman,* a comedy in prose, acted in 1669, was published in 1693. *Herod the Great* was printed in 1694, but never acted.

Page 3, line 8. *a romance* : Cyropaedia.

l. 9. *a tragedy* : Ajax. (Suetonius, *Aug.* 85) ' Nam tragoediam magno impetu exorsus, non succedenti stilo, abolevit, quaerentibusque amicis quidnam Aiax ageret, respondit, Aiacem suum in spongiam incubuisse.'

P. 4, l. 20. *invisible* : Congreve's emendation. The old copies (including the Folio 1701) have *invincible,* which reading is retained by Malone. Malone probably remembered ' his dimensions to any thick sight were invincible,' 2 Hen. IV, i. 2, which in his commentary he interprets ' not to be mastered.' But neither this uncommon usage of the word, nor the ordinary meaning of *invincible,* agrees with Dryden's context, or his general manner of expressing himself. Either meaning of *invincible* would be puzzling, and Dryden does not make difficulties for his readers in the subordinate parts of his sentences. It is true that it was never corrected in the editions published in Dryden's lifetime ; but Dryden was not fond of revising.

P. 5, l. 26. *leave to borrow words from other nations.* See *Introduction,* p. xxx.

l. 35. *Queen* Gorboduc. The commentator is obliged to repeat that Gorboduc was a king of Britain, and that his tragedy was written in blank verse, except the choruses.

P. 6, l. 1. *Lord Buckhurst, afterwards Earl of Dorset.* Thomas Sackville (1536–1608), Lord Buckhurst 1567, Lord Treasurer 1599, Earl of Dorset 1604, author of *Gorboduc* and of the *Induction* to the *Mirror for Magistrates,* with the *Tragedy of Henry Duke of Buckingham* in the same work, was great-grandfather of Charles, Lord Buckhurst (*Eugenius* in the *Essay of Dramatic Poesy*) ; see below, p. 289.

l. 10. *Barclay.* Jean Barclay, whose father came from Aberdeen to France, was born at Pont à Mousson in 1582 ; died in 1621. His best known work is *Argenis,* a Latin romance requiring a key to explain its allegory of contemporary history. Cowper recommended it as ' the most amusing romance that ever was written. It is the only one indeed of an old date that I ever had the patience to go through with. It is interesting in a high degree ; richer in incident than can be imagined, full of surprises, which the reader never forestalls, and yet free from all entanglement and confusion. The style too appears to me to be such as would not dishonour Tacitus himself ' (to Mr. Rose, Aug. 27, 1787). Dryden's quotation is from the *Icon Animarum,* c. iv, the fourth part of the *Satyricon* of *Euphormio,* Barclay's ' Varronian Satire ' (cf. the *Preface to Juvenal,* vol. ii. p. 67).

Malone, in his *Additions and Emendations,* has given the passage : ' Anglis ut plurimum gravis animus . . . seipsos et suae gentis mores ingenia animos eximie mirantur,' &c.

P. 7, l. 14. *Mr. Waller.* This is Dryden's first acknowledgement of the authority of Waller, with whom is associated Sir John Denham, in the reformation of English verse. From this time onward the reference becomes a commonplace among historians of literature, like the recognition of Wyatt and Surrey as the founders of the Elizabethan school. See Preface to *Fables,* vol. ii. p. 259. Compare Dryden's Preface to Walsh's *Dialogue concerning Women,* 1691 : ' Mr. Waller, the father of our English numbers. . . . I hope the reader need not be told that Mr. Waller is only mentioned for honour's sake ; that I am desirous of laying hold on his memory on all occasions, and thereby acknowledging to the world that unless he had written, none of us could write.'

l. 25. *The Siege of Rhodes,* by Sir William Davenant, first acted and printed in 1656 ; acted, with a second part, in 1662 ; printed 1663, 4º. Also in Davenant's Works, 1673, fol. ' The First and Second Part as they were lately represented at His Highness the Duke of York's Theatre in Lincoln's Inn Fields. The First Part being lately Enlarg'd.'

l. 30. *Sir Philip Sidney, in his* Defence of Poesy. ' Now that Verse farre exceedeth Prose in the knitting up of the memory, the reason is Manifest,' &c. (ed. Arber, p. 50). But Sidney is not comparing rhyme and blank verse : ' one word so as it were begetting another as be it in ryme or measured verse, by the former a man shall have a neere gesse to the follower.'

P. 8, l. 8. *that like an high-ranging spaniel, it must have clogs tied to it.* Cf. Shakespeare, *Tempest*, i. 2. 81 :
' To trash for overtopping,'
and note in Madden, *Diary of Master William Silence*, 1897, p. 39.

P. 9, l. 2. *as Scaliger says of Claudian.* ' Maximus poeta Claudianus, solo argumento ignobiliore depressus, addit de ingenio quantum deest materiae ' (Scaligeri *Poetices* vi. *qui et Hypercriticus*, cap. 5).

ANNUS MIRABILIS : PREFACE
(1667).

P. 10, l. 18. *Admiral,* the Duke of York ; *Generals, ' Prince Rupert and Duke* Albemarl sent to sea ' is Dryden's note to stanza 47 in the Poem. Compare stanza 191 :
' Each several Ship a victory did gain,
As *Rupert* or as *Albemarl* were there.'

P. 11, l. 28. *those who rank Lucan rather among historians in verse, than epic poets.* Petronius, *Satyr.* c. 118, in the stock quotation, ' Non enim res gestae versibus comprehendendae sunt, quod longe melius historici faciunt,' &c., which is followed by the long specimen of a historical poem, declaimed by Eumolpus *ingenti bile.* Compare also Quintilian X. i. 90 : ' Lucanus ardens et concitatus et sententiis clarissimus et ut dicam quod sentio magis oratoribus quam poetis imitandus.' Dryden, like all the men of his time, was familiar with the sentence of Petronius, but here he is probably thinking mainly of a passage in Davenant's preface to *Gondibert*, which he had just been reading :—' Lucan, who chose to write the greatest actions that ever were allowed to be true (which for fear of contemporary witnesses, oblig'd him to a very close attendance upon Fame) did not observe that such an enterprize rather beseem'd an Historian than a Poet : For wise Poets think it more worthy to seek out truth in the Passions, than to record the truth of Actions ; and practise to describe Mankind just as we are perswaded or guided by instinct, not particular persons, as they are lifted or levell'd by the force of Fate, it being nobler to contemplate the general History of Nature, than a selected Diary of Fortune : And Painters are no more than Historians, when they draw eminent persons (though they term that drawing to the life) but when by assembling divers figures in a larger Volume they draw Passions (although they term it but Story) then they increase in dignity and become Poets.'

P. 11, l. 32. *quatrains.* Used by Surrey, Spenser (*Colin Clout's come Home again, &c.*), Sir John Davies (*Nosce Teipsum*), Davenant (*Gondibert*). Heroic couplets were not yet established as the noblest form of verse, though used by Cowley in his heroic poem *Davideis.*

P. 12, l. 22. *female rimes* : disyllabic rhymes, with the stress on the penultimate ; e. g. *sliding, dividing ; thrilling, fulfilling ; wonder, thunder.* Cf. Sidney, *Apologie for Poetrie,* ed. Arber, p. 71 : ' Lastly even the very ryme it selfe, the Italian cannot put in the last silable, by the French named the Masculine ryme, but still in the next to the last, which the French call the Female ; or the next before that, which the Italians terme *Sdrucciola.*' And above, p. 278, l. 5.

l. 26. *Alaric,* by George de Scudery ; *Pucelle,* by Jean Chapelain. See Preface to Juvenal, vol. ii. p. 28, and *Dedication of Æneis,* vol. ii. p. 165, l. 6, and note.

l. 30. Dryden has misnamed the verse of Chapman's *Iliads* ; not Alexandrine but Septenarian, fourteen syllables, ' common metre,' 8 s and 6 s.

l. 35. *Preface to* Gondibert. ' I shall say a little why I have chosen my interwoven *Stanza* of four, though I am not oblig'd to excuse the choice, for numbers in Verse must, like distinct kind of Musick, be exposed to the uncertain and different taste of several Ears. Yet I may declare, that I believ'd it would be more pleasant to the Reader in a Work of length, to give this respite or pause, between every *Stanza* (having endeavored that each should contain a period) than to run him out of breath with continued *Couplets.*'

P. 13, l. 5. *Lucan in the third of his* Pharsalia. l. 509 sqq. :
' Spes victis telluris abit, placuitque profundo
Fortunam tentare mari,' &c.

l. 12. *general terms.* Dryden changed his mind about *terms of art,* and in the *Dedication of the Æneis* has given the opposite view. The *Annus Mirabilis* is an Elizabethan poem reckless in the use of minute particulars. The admiration of technical terms in poetry is shared with Ronsard, who advised poets to learn the special dictionaries of trades. Thirty years later Dryden is in the position of Buffon, recommending the use of general terms where the style is to be dignified.

l. 15. *Descriptas servare,* &c. Hor. *A. P.* 86.

P. 14, l. 2. *Omnia sponte sua,* &c., a perversion of Virgil, *Georg.* ii. 460, ' fundit humo facilem victum iustissima tellus.'

ll. 22, 29. *Wit writing : Wit written.* The *school-distinction* which Dryden has in his mind is that of *Natura naturans* and *Natura naturata.* So in the case of Wit he distinguishes between Wit the faculty and Wit the product. Wit is of course used in the general meaning ; it is the intelligence of the poet. Dryden here again is following Davenant : ' Having describ'd the outward frame, the large rooms within, the lesser conveyances, and now the furniture ; it were orderly to let you examine the matter of which that furniture is made : But though every Owner who hath the vanity to show his ornaments or hangings must endure the curiosity and censure of him that beholds them ; yet I shall not give you the trouble of inquiring what is, but tell you of what I design'd their substance, which is, *Wit* : And *Wit* is the labourious and the lucky resultances of thought, having towards its excellence (as we say of the strokes of Painting) as well a happinesse, as care. Wit is not onely the luck and labor, but also the dexterity of thought, rounding the world, like the Sun, with unimaginable motion, and bringing swiftly home to the memory universal surveys.'—The Preface to *Gondibert.*

l. 24. *'Tis not the jerk or sting of an epigram,* &c. Compare *Dramatic Poesy,* p. 31, and *Of Heroic Plays,* p. 152, l. 19 ; *Defence of the Epilogue,* p. 173, l. 25.

P. 15, l. 9. This is one of the most systematic passages in Dryden : the functions of the poetic *Imagination* (called also *Wit*) are distinguished as *Invention, Fancy,* and *Elocution* ; the proper virtues of the Imagination, corresponding to its three modes, are Quickness, Fertility, and Accuracy. The use of the term *Imagination* in a comprehensive sense, with *Fancy* as one of its special applications, is to be noted.

P. 16, l. 19. *Totamque infusa,* &c. Virgil, *Aen.* vi. 726.

l. 23. *lumenque juventae. Aen.* i. 590.

P. 17, l. 1. *Materiam superabat opus.* Ovid, *Metam.* ii. 5 (of the Palace of the Sun).

l. 9. *Dixeris egregie,* &c. Hor. *A. P.* 47.

l. 32. *Et nova fictaque nuper,* &c. Hor. *A. P.* 52.

P. 18, l. 18. *Lazar,* i. e. leper, a term used more than once by Dryden, and always with reference to painting. Compare the Preface to *Tyrannic Love* : ' If with much pains and some success I have drawn a deformed piece, there is as much of art and as near an imitation of Nature in a Lazar, as in a Venus.'

l. 25. *stantes in curribus.* Juvenal, *Sat.* 8, at the beginning ⁚
' Stemmata quid faciunt ? quid prodest, Pontice, longo
Sanguine censeri, pictos ostendere vultus
Maiorum et stantis in curribus Aemilianos,' &c.

P. 18, l. 27. *spirantia,* &c. Virgil, *Aen.* vi. 847.

l. 33. *humi serpere.* Hor. *A. P.* 28 :

'Serpit humi tutus nimium timidusque procellae.'

P. 19, l. 1. *nunc non erat his locus.* Hor. *A. P.* 19.

l. 15. *I wrong the public to detain you longer.* Mr. Christie compares Horace, *Ep.* ii. 1. 3 :

'. . . in publica commoda peccem,
Si longo sermone morer tua tempora, Caesar.'

l. 20. *the younger Pliny.* Epist. vii. 28 : 'Igitur ad alios hanc sinistram diligentiam conferant, nec sunt parum multi, qui carpere amicos suos iudicium vocant : mihi numquam persuadebunt ut meos amari a me nimium putem.'

ESSAY OF DRAMATIC POESY
(1668).

P. 21. (Title-page of Essay.) The motto is from *A. P.* 304.

P. 24, l. 8. *Pompey.* Corneille's tragedy *La Mort de Pompée* (Paris, 1644) was twice translated into English ; by Mrs. Katherine Philips (Orinda), 1663 ; and in 1664, under the title of *Pompey the Great, a Tragedy,* by 'Certain Persons of Honour,' viz. Mr. Waller, Sir Charles Sedley, Lord Buckhurst. Corneille was informed of the English admiration for his works in a letter of Saint-Évremond in 1668 : 'M. Waller, un des plus beaux esprits du siècle, attend toujours vos pièces nouvelles, et ne manque pas d'en traduire un acte ou deux en vers anglais, pour sa satisfaction particulière.'

l. 18. *Spurina* : Valerius Maximus, iv. 5 (externa) : Dryden may have taken the example from Montaigne, ii. 23. *pars indocili,* &c. Hor. *Epod.* 16. 37.

P. 25, l. 5. *the French poet.* Not yet identified.

l. 24. *an excellent poem to the King* by Davenant, 1663, 4° ; in his works in folio, 1673 *(to the Kings most Sacred Majesty),* pp. 260–271 ; the lines quoted are on p. 268 (Malone).

P. 26, l. 20. *Even Tully,* &c. Cf. *De Finibus,* v. 1 'Tum Pomponius : At ego quem vos ut deditum Epicuro insectari soletis,' &c.

l. 27. *Caesar.* In his *Anticato* ; cf. Suetonius, *Jul.* 56 ; Plutarch, *Caesar,* at the beginning ; Juvenal, *Sat.* vi. 38.

P. 27, l. 7. *Tacitus. Annal.* i. 1 'Sine ira et studio quorum causas procul habeo.'

P. 28, l. 1. *That memorable day.* June 3, 1665.

l. 6. *While these vast floating bodies,* &c. The punctuation here is that of all the old editions, including the Folio and Congreve's. Modern editors (except Mr. W. H. Low) punctuate *universe : while.* Compare the opening of Cowley's *Discourse, by way of Vision, concerning the Government of Oliver Cromwell* : ' It was the Funeral Day of the late Man who made himself to be call'd *Protector*.   And though I bore but little affection either to the Memory of him, or to the Trouble and Folly of all publick Pageantry, yet I was forc'd by the Importunity of my Company to go along with them,' &c.

l. 19. *Eugenius.*   Charles Sackville, son of Richard 5th Earl of Dorset ; born Jan. 24, 1638 ; Lord Buckhurst in 1652 on his father's succession to the earldom ; created Earl of Middlesex, 1675 ; succeeded as 6th Earl of Dorset, 1677 ; F.R.S., 1699 ; died Jan. 29, 1707.   He served as a volunteer in the fleet in 1665, when he composed his song ' To all you ladies now at land.'   See the Preface to Juvenal, vol. ii. p. 15.

l. 20. *Crites.*   Sir Robert Howard (1626–1698), Dryden's brother-in-law.   His *Poems* were published in 1660, with verses from Dryden prefixed.   In 1665 *Foure New Plays* of Howard were published in folio ; viz. *Surprisal* and *Committee* (comedies), and *Vestal Virgin* and *Indian Queen* (tragedies).   The Preface of this volume led to Dryden's *Essay* (see p. 133).   *The Great Favourite, or the Duke of Lerma : a Tragedy,* was published in 1668, with Howard's answer.   Howard's *Five Plays* were published together in 1692.   He was represented as *Sir Positive At all* in Shadwell's comedy of *The Sullen Lovers*, 1668 ; see p. 111, l. 22, note.

l. 20. *Lisideius.*   Sir Charles Sedley, or Sidley (*c.* 1639–1701), was about the same age as Dryden, who dedicated *The Assignation* to him (1673), calling him the Tibullus of his age.   His plays are *Antony and Cleopatra* (1677), a rhyming tragedy ; *The Tyrant King of Crete* ; *The Mulberry Garden* (1668), founded on Molière's *École des Maris* ; *Bellamira, or, the Mistress* (1687), taken from the *Eunuchus* of Terence ; *The Grumbler.*

l. 20. *Neander.*   Dryden.

P. 30, l. 28. *says Tully. Pro Archia,* 10. 25.

P. 31, l. 9. *one of them.*   Robert Wild ; his ' famous poem ' came out in 1660. ' Iter Boreale.   Attempting something upon the Successful and Matchless March of the Lord General George Monck, from Scotland to London, The Last Winter, &c.   *Veni, Vidi, Vici.*   By a Rural Pen.   London, Printed on St. George's Day, Being the 23ᵈ of April, 1660.'   It opens with the following lines :

> ' The day is broke ! *Melpomene,* be gone ;
> Hag of my fancy, let me now alone :
> Night-mare my soul no more ; Go take thy flight
> Where Traytors Ghosts keep an eternal night ;

Flee to Mount *Caucasus*, and bear thy part
With the black Fowl that tears *Prometheus'* heart
For his bold Sacriledge : Go fetch the groans
Of defunct Tyrants, with them croke thy Tones ;
Go in Alecto with her flaming whip,
How she firks *Nol*, and makes old *Bradshaw* skip :
Go make thyself away. Thou shalt no more
Choke up my Standish with the blood and gore
Of English Tragedies : I now will chose
The merriest of the Nine to be my Muse.
And (come what will) I'll scribble once again ' : &c.

P. 31, l. 10. *clenches upon words.* Clench= paronomasia, play
upon words : cf. supra, and Prologue to *Troilus and Cressida* :
' The fulsome clench that nauseates the Town.' Compare also
Butler on Benlowes (*A Small Poet*) : ' There is no feat of activity
or gambol of wit that ever was performed by man, from him that
vaults on Pegasus to him that tumbles through the hoop of an
anagram, but Benlowes has got the mastery in it, whether it be
high-rope wit or low-rope wit. He has all sorts of echoes, rebuses,
chronograms, &c., besides carwitchets, clenches, and quibbles.'
Cf. also Cowley, *An Answer to a Copy of Verses sent me to Jersey* :
' The land is undefil'd with Clinches yet.'

l. 12. *Catachresis*. ' κατάχρησις, quam recte dicimus abu-
sionem, quae non habentibus nomen suum accommodat quod in
proximo est : sic *Equum Palladis arte Aedificant*, &c.' (Quintilian) :
' It is an improper kind of speech, somewhat more desperate than
a Metaphor, and is the expressing of one matter by the name of
another, which is incompatible with, and sometimes clean contrary to it,' &c. (*The Mysterie of Rhetorick Unveil'd*, by John
Smith, Gent., 1673).

l. 12. *Clevelandism*. John Cleveland (1613–1658), the
strongest of the Cavalier satirical poets, and one of the most
reckless followers of the ' metaphysical ' fashion in poetry. What
Dryden means by Clevelandism may be understood by a reference
to Cleveland's verses in memory of Mr. Edward King, in the little
volume published at Cambridge in 1638 :

' But can his spacious vertue find a grave
Within th' impostum'd bubble of a wave ?
Whose learning if we sound, we must confesse
The sea but shallow, and him bottomlesse.
Could not the winds to countermand thy death
With their whole card of lungs redeem thy breath
Or some new Iland in thy rescue peep,
To heave thy resurrection from the deep ?

That so the world might see thy safety wrought
With no less miracle then thy self was thought.
The famous Stagirite (who in his life
Had nature as familiar as his wife)
Bequeath'd his widow to survive with thee
Queen Dowager of all Philosophie.
An ominous legacie, that did portend
Thy fate, and Predecessour's second end !
Some have affirm'd that what on earth we find
The sea can parallel for shape and kind :
Books, arts and tongues were wanting, but in thee
Neptune hath got an Universitie.
  *   *   *   *   *   *   *   *   *
When we have fill'd the rundlets of our eyes
We'll issue't forth, and vent such elegies,
As that our tears shall seem the Irish Seas,
We floating Ilands, living Hebrides.'

l. 23. The ' other extremity of poetry ' is not as easily
identified as the first extreme ; possibly Flecknoe, as Malone
suggests.

l. 32. *ten little words.*
    ' While expletives their feeble aid do join,
    And ten low words oft creep in one dull line ' :
                           (Pope, *Essay on Criticism*, ll. 346–7).

P. 32, l. 5. *Martial*, viii. 19.

l. 32. *by the candles' ends.* Bids are accepted as long as the
candle-end is burning. Compare Dryden's *Life of Lucian*, referring to Lucian's *Auction of Philosophers* : ' those who accused
him for exposing Socrates, Plato, Diogenes, and other great
philosophers, to the laughter of the people, when Jupiter sold
them by an inch of candle.'

l. 33. *the great Ones.* Ones, the plural, was noted by Dryden
not long after as bad grammar. See *Defence of the Epilogue to the
Conquest of Granada*, p. 168, l. 27.

P. 33, l. 6. *Qui Bavium.* Virgil, *Ecl.* 3. 90.

l. 16. *Petronius. Satyr.* 2.

l. 20. Eugenius here opens up the question between Ancients
and Moderns. See *Introduction*, p. xxii.

l. 32. Hor. *Ep.* ii. 1. 76.

P. 34, l. 2. *Ibid.* 34.

P. 35, l. 8. *that the Drama is wholly ours.* Imitated from the
phrase of Quintilian x : ' Satira quidem tota nostra est.'

l. 9. *Eugenius his opinion.* Not as sometimes explained,
a corruption of the true genitive by false etymology, but an old

and common use of the pronoun to give the inflexion of the noun. Cf. below, p. 38, l. 24, *Horace his Art of Poetry,* and p. 55, l. 32.

P. 35, l. 17. On the influence of rhyme compare, besides the well-known couplet in *Hudibras,* Butler's remarks in prose on *A Small Poet* : ' When he writes he commonly steers the sense of his lines by the rhyme that is at the end of them, as butchers do calves by the tail.'

l. 22. *a standing measure,* i.e. a standard, some definite position agreed on by both parties. The dialogue has reached the point of the favourite opening of Socrates : ' define what you are talking about.'

P. 36, l. 1. *rather a description than a definition.* This anticipates the objection raised by Crites (l. 10), ' that it was only *a genere et fine.*' It is not a definition, because it does not give the specific difference ; it gives the *general class* to which a play belongs, and the end which it serves. The description might be used of a narrative poem, or of a novel, as well as of a play. Dryden thought that the specific difference between drama and narrative was not likely to be mistaken, and was therefore of less importance than the points here described.

l. 6. *humours,* in the old sense of the word, as in Ben Jonson ; peculiarities of disposition.

l. 7. *for the delight and instruction of mankind.* This clause was almost obligatory in every definition of any kind of poetry ; though Corneille had dared to leave out *instruction* in his essay on Drama, eight years before this.

l. 27. *every age has a kind of universal genius.* The Spirit of the Age was less familiar in Dryden's time than later, and remarks of this sort, implying cycles of progress in art, are not common. The work of Father Bouhours, *Entretiens d'Ariste et d'Eugène,* in which the progress of literature is appreciated, was not published till 1671.

l. 33. *the study of philosophy* : used in the ordinary English sense of the word for any kind of science ; as in ' philosophical instrument maker.' See Hegel, *Encyklopädie,* § 7, who quotes an advertisement from an English newspaper, ' The Art of Preserving the Hair, on Philosophical Principles.'

P. 37, l. 5. *from Aristotle to us.* The limits of the Dark Ages, or the Middle Ages, are here decided.

l. 23. *Paterculus. Hist. Rom.* i. 17.

l. 26. *that Second Book of his.* Aristotle in the *Poetics* undertook to speak about Comedy (c. 6, 1449 b 21 περὶ κωμῳδίας ὕστερον ἐροῦμεν), but this part of his dissertation is not extant.

P. 38, 1. 30. *Three Unities.* See *Introduction.*

P. 40, 1. 6. *the variation of painted scenes.* Scenery of a sort had been used in the mediaeval drama, and the Masques required elaborate changes of scene ; but there was little attempt at scenery on the regular stage till Davenant's *Siege of Rhodes*, in which elaborate scenes are described, as e.g. *The Scene before the First Entry* : ' The Curtain being drawn up, a lightsom Skie appear'd, discov'ring a Maritime Coast, full of craggy Rocks, and high Cliffs, with several Verdures naturally growing upon such situations ; and afar off, the true Prospect of the City of RHODES when it was in prosperous estate ; with so much view of the Gardens and Hills about it, as the narrowness of the Room could allow the Scene. In that part of the Horizon, terminated by the Sea, was represented the Turkish Fleet, making towards a Promontory, some few miles distant from the Town.' Settle's *Empress of Morocco*, 1673, was published with engravings of the scenery, and cost 2s. instead of 1s., the ordinary price of plays in quarto, stitcht.

1. 27. *liaison des scenes*—(N.B. *scenes* not *scènes* in Dryden's spelling, which is that of Corneille, and of the seventeenth century). This is explained by Corneille in his *Third Discourse* (1660), and in the *Examen* (1660) of his early comedy *La Suivante* (1637). In the *Discourse* he speaks of it as *ce nouvel usage qui passe en précepte.* ' Not to leave the stage empty ' is the practical rule, which has come to have more authority with dramatists than the Three Unities. Compare Prologue to *Maiden Queen*, p. 109, ' the scenes unbroken.'

P. 41, 1. 10. *Ben Johnson : Discoveries*, fourth section from the end. ' Now that it should be one and entire : One is considerable two ways ; either as it is only separate, and by itself ; or as being composed of many parts, it begins to be one as those parts grow or are wrought together. That it should be one the first way alone, and by itself, no man that hath tasted letters ever would say, especially having required before a just magnitude, and equal proportion of the parts in themselves. Neither of which can possibly be if the action be single and separate, not composed of parts, which laid together in themselves, with an equal and fitting proportion, tend to the same end ; which thing out of antiquity itself hath deceived many, and more this day it doth deceive.'

1. 18. *Corneille. Troisième Discours* : ' Il n'y doit avoir qu'une action complète qui laisse l'esprit de l'auditeur dans le calme ; mais elle ne peut le devenir que par plusieurs autres imparfaites, qui lui servent d'acheminement, et tiennent cet auditeur dans une agréable suspension.'

P. **42,** l. 3. *Caecilius.* Cf. Aulus Gellius, ii. 23, quoting Vulcatius (' in libro quem scripsit de poetis ') :
> ' Caecilio palmam Statio do comico,
> Plautus secundus facile exsuperat ceteros.'

Horace, *Ep.* ii. 1. 59 :
> ' Vincere Caecilius gravitate, Terentius arte.'

Dryden took his reference from the chapter of Velleius Paterculus, *Hist. Rom.* i. 17, which he elsewhere quotes : ' dulcesque Latini leporis facetiae per Caecilium Terentiumque et Afranium suppari aetate nituerunt.'

l. 7. *the half-Menander.* Suetonius, *Vit. Terent.* :
> ' Tu quoque, tu in summis, o dimidiate Menander,
> Poneris, et merito puri sermonis amator.'

l. 8. *Horace : Od.* i. 6. (' Scriberis Vario,' &c.) *Sat.* i. 9. 23 ; *ibid.* 10. 44 ; *A. P.* 55.

l. 8. *Martial,* viii. 18, ll. 5–8 :
> ' Sic Maro nec Calabri tentavit carmina Flacci
> Pindaricos posset cum superare modos,
> Et Vario cessit Romani laude cothurni
> Cum posset tragico fortius ore loqui.'

l. 8. *Velleius Paterculus* does not mention Varius.

l. 23. *Macrobius* in his *Saturnalia, passim.*

P. **44,** l. 1. *Nature.* See *Introduction*, p. xxiv, for the view of Nature in seventeenth-century criticism.

l. 20. *Velleius. Hist. Rom.* ii. 92 (for *admiratione* l. *veneratione*).

l. 35. *Aristotle.* The division is from Scaliger, *Poet,* i. 9 ' *Protasis* est in qua proponitur et narratur summa rei sine declaratione exitus . . . *Epitasis* in qua turbae aut excitantur aut intenduntur. *Catastasis* est vigor ac status fabulae, in qua res miscetur in ea fortunae tempestate in quam subducta est. *Catastrophe*, conversio negotii exagitati in tranquillitatem non expectatam.'

P. **45,** l. 8. *Counterturn.* Cf. Davenant, *Siege of Rhodes* (1663). *To the Reader* :—' our Scenes . . . confin'd to eleven foot in height and about fifteen in depth. . . . Therefore you cannot expect the chief ornaments belonging to a History dramatically digested into Turns and Counter-turns, to double Walks, and interweavings of design.'

l. 28. *Neve minor neu sit quinto productior actu. A. P.* 189.

P. **46,** l. 4. *Jornadas.* The Spanish poets borrowed the term from the *journées* of the old French Mysteries. The term *journée* was still in use in France in the seventeenth century, not for an *Act,* but for the several *Parts* of a play. Thus Hardy's *Histoire éthiopique* (*Theagenes and Chariclea* from Heliodorus) was

in eight *journées* of five acts each. Torres Naharro, who introduced the term into Spain (1517), divided his comedies into five
jornadas. But three became the rule with the dramatists of the
next generation.

l. 13. τὸ μυθος. So in all Edd., except for accent —τὸ
μυθὸς in B and C.

l. 16. *a late writer.* Ménage ? See below, note on l. 22.

l. 20. *Talkative Greeklings.* Cf. Ben Jonson, *Discoveries*
(under *Demosthenes*) : ' Which of the Greeklings durst ever give
precepts to Demosthenes ? ' ' Talkative ' is from Cicero, *De Or.*
i. 22. 102 ' Quid ? mihi nunc vos, inquit Crassus, tanquam alicui
Graeculo otioso loquaci, et fortasse docto atque erudito quaesti-
unculam de qua meo arbitratu loquar ponitis ? '

l. 22. *it was already known.* Compare the quotation from
Antiphanes the Comic Poet, in Athenaeus, Book vi. 1 (Meineke,
Com. Frag. iii. 106), which is probably the source, direct or in-
direct, of this passage of the *Essay*. Dryden might possibly have
had his attention called to it by Ménage, who quotes it in his
Osservationi sopra l'Aminta, p. 102 (Paris, 1654), and gives an
Italian translation :

Οἰδίπουν γὰρ ἄν φῶ
τὰ δ'ἄλλα πάντ' ἴσασιν, κτλ.

P. 47, l. 11. *Juno Lucina, fer opem.* Terent. *Andr.* iii. 1.
Quoted by Scaliger, *Poet.* i. 13, and vi. 3.

P. 48, l. 17. *Scaliger, Poet.* vi. 3 ; Dryden made good use of this
chapter on Plautus and Terence : ' Vasta inquiunt et hians atque
inanis Comoedia est : tota namque intercedit nox. Nam per
initia coenam curant : postea Chremes ait, *lucescit.* Sane igitur
abiit nox. Haec est illorum obiectio : quam sic diluimus, Datam
actamque fabulam ludis Megalensibus. itaque dimidium fabulae
actum vesperi : noctem transactam ludis : alterum dimidium
reliquum sub lucem.' Dryden, in the second edition, withdraws
his assent to this theory. It had before this been adopted from
Scaliger by Sidney : *Apologie*, ed. Arber, p. 14 : ' Yet wil some
bring in an example of *Eunuchus* [read *Heautontimorumenus*] in
Terence, that containeth matter of two dayes, yet far short of
twenty yeeres. True it is, and so was it to be played in two daies,
and so fitted to the time it set forth.' The question about the time
of the *Heautontimorumenos* was debated at length by many
scholars ; more especially between Hédelin and Ménage ; compare Hédelin (d'Aubignac), *Pratique du Théâtre*, p. 99 (l. ii. c. 2) :
' Beaucoup de Sçavans ont dit que la troisième Comedie de
Terence contenoit deux jours ; Scaliger, Muret, Vossius, le P.
Membrun, et d'autres l'ont ainsi pensé ; mais elle n'est pas seule-

ment de dix heures, comme je l'ay montré dans la premiere Dissertation du *Terence justifié.'*

P. 48, l. 19. *Euripides, Supplices,* 598–634. This is all from Corneille, *Troisième Discours.*

P. 49, l. 3. *C'est* assez *bien employer un tems si court,* Corneille, *loc. cit.* ; he goes on to discuss the time of the *Agamemnon,* and finds it more licentious than the *Cid.* The example from the *Eunuchus* is not in Corneille, but he gives a similar one from the *Andria,* a little further on in the same *Discourse.*

P. 51, l. 19. *universum triduum. Eun.* ii. 1. 18.

l. 27. ' *At vestri proavi Plautinos et numeros et Laudavere sales ; nimium patienter utrumque Ne dicam stulte mirati.'*   *A.P.* 270.

l. 33. *Multa renascentur quae jam cecidere,* &c.   *A. P.* 70.

P. 52, l. 7. *Mistaque ridenti,* &c. Virgil, *Ecl.* iv. 20.

l. 7. *Seventh Æneid. Aen.* viii. 91.

l. 11. *Ovid Metam.* i. 175 :

' Hic locus est quem si verbis audacia detur, Haud timeam magni dixisse Palatia caeli.'

Translated by Dryden in the Third Miscellany : ' the Louvre of the sky.'

l. 16. *et longas visent Capitolia pompas. Ibid.* 561.

l. 25. Cleveland. See note on p. 31, l. 12.

P. 53, l. 1. *Si sic omnia dixisset.* Juvenal, *Sat.* 10. 123.

l. 4. *For beauty, like white powder,* &c. Cleveland, *Rupertismus,* ll. 33–40 ;

' Strange ! That the Muses cannot wound your Mail ; If not their Art, yet let their Sex prevail. At that known Leaguer, where the *Bonny Besses* Supply'd the Bowstrings with their twisted tresses, Your spells could ne'er have fenc'd you ; ev'ry Arrow Had lanc'd your noble Breast, and drunk the Marrow : For Beauty, like white Powder, makes no Noise, And yet the silent Hypocrite destroys.'

White powder is 'such as is discharged without report ' : see Browne, *Vulgar Errors* ii. v. 5.

l. 23. *Omne genus.* Ovid, *Trist.* ii. 381.

l. 26. *Myrrha.* Cf. *Ann. Mirab.* Preface, above, p. 16, l. 4, and Preface to *Fables,* vol. ii. p. 247.

l. 30. *Troades.* The scene between Andromache and Ulysses in Seneca's Tragedy begins at l. 533.

P. 54, l. 16. *Juvenal. Sat.* 6. 195.

P. 55, l. 9. *Sum pius Aeneas raptos qui ex hoste Penates Classe veho mecum fama super aethera notus.*

Aen. i. 378.

l. 11. *Hector.* A character of *An Hector* was written by Butler ; printed in Craik, *English Prose*, ii. 523. *The Hectors* is the title of a comedy, 1656, 4⁰.

l. 19. *si foret.* Horace, *Sat.* i. 10. 68.

l. 26. Horace, *Ep.* ii. 1. 49 ' Miraturque nihil nisi quod Libitina sacravit.'

P. 58, l. 8.　　　　' media inter carmina poscunt
　　Aut ursum aut pugiles : his nam plebecula gaudet.'
　　　　　　　　　　　　　　Hor. *Ep.* ii. 1. 185.

l. 7. *the Red Bull* in St. John's Street, Clerkenwell. Pepys notes the unsuccessful attempt to revive old plays here ; he saw *All's Lost by Lust*, March 23, 1661 (' not one hundred in the whole house '), and *Doctor Faustus*, May 26, 1662 ; on April 25, 1664, he went to the *Red Bull* to see a prize-fight. See Collier, *Dramatic Poetry;* iii. p. 132 (1879), who quotes from Davenant, *Playhouse to be Let* (acted 1663) :

' Tell 'em the *Red Bull* stands empty for Fencers ;
There are no Tenents in it but old Spiders :
Go bid the men of wrath allay their heat
With Prizes there.'

It had been, before the Restoration, the favourite theatre for *Drolls* : see Francis Kirkman, *The Wits, or Sport upon Sport*, a Collection of Drolls and Farces, 1673 : ' I have seen the *Red Bull* Playhouse, which was a large one, so full, that as many went back for want of room as had entred.' Kirkman's frontispiece, showing a stage with a ' droll ' being acted, is supposed to be taken from the Red Bull.

l. 23. *Ex noto*, &c. Hor. *A. P.* 240.

l. 30. *Atque ita mentitur*, &c. *Ibid.* 151.

P. 59, l. 24. *perspective.* i.e. a telescope.

l. 28. *Quodcumque ostendis*, &c. *A. P.* 188.

l. 31. ἐτύμοισιν ὁμοῖα. Homer, *Od.* xix. 203 ; and Hesiod, *Theogonia*, 27 (the Muses speaking) :

ἴδμεν ψεύδεα πολλὰ λέγειν ἐτύμοισιν ὁμοῖα
ἴδμεν δ', εὖτ' ἐθέλωμεν, ἀληθέα γηρύσασθαι.

P. 60, l. 17. *Spanish plots.* The chief adaptations from the Spanish drama were *Elvira, or the Worst not always True*, by a Person of Quality [the Earl of Bristol], 1667, from Calderon, *No siempre lo Peor es cierto* : and the *Adventures of Five Hours*, 1663, by Sir Samuel Tuke, from *Los Empeños de seis Horas*, attributed to Calderon. Lord Bristol made two other versions from Calderon, which are not extant : *Mejor está que estaba* and *Peor está que estaba.*

l. 20. *Rollo.* The Bloody Brother, or the Tragedy of Rollo, Duke of Normandy, by John Fletcher.

P. 60, l. 30. *Oleo*, a medley, from Spanish *olla podrida* : see *Preface to Juvenal*, vol. ii. p. 54, l. 28 : ' *olla* or hotchpotch ' ; and *Rehearsal*, v. 1 :

> ' And we'll fall with our pate
> In an *ollio* of hate.'

l. 33. *Golias.* This reading (so also in Mr. W. H. Low's edition) is suggested by the *Golia's* of A, but *Golias* is rather too old-fashioned a form, and probably *Goliah* is to be read : the printer's error of *'s* for *h* is not too extravagant.

P. 61, l. 34. *protatic persons.* Characters appearing only in the introductory part of the play, see above, p. 45, l. 1. Donatus, in Terent. *Andr.* Prolog. 1, προτατικὸν πρόσωπον : Scaliger, *Poet.* i. 13 ' Protactica, sive prostatica ; cum quaepiam persona introducitur primo actu neque amplius usquam comparet.' Dryden probably took the phrase, as Mr. Arnold points out, immediately from Corneille, Examen de Rodogune : *personnage protatique.*

P. 62, l. 29. *a drum and five men behind it.* Compare *Henry V,* Act iv :

> CHORUS. ' When (O for pity !) we shall much disgrace,
> With four or five most vile and ragged foils,
> Right ill-disposed in brawl ridiculous,
> The name of Agincourt.

P. 63, l. 1. Compare Samuel Chappuzeau, *Le Theatre François*, Paris, 1674 : ' Estant à Londres il y a six ans, j'y vis deux fort belles troupes des Comediens, l'vne du Roy, & l'autre du Duc D'Yorc, & ie fus à deux representations, à la mort de *Montezume* Roy de Mexique, & à celle de *Mustapha,* qui se defendoit vigoureusement sur le Theatre contre les muets qui le vouloient étrangler ; ce qui faisoit rire, & ce que les François n'auroient representé que dans vn recit.' Corneille, in the third *Discourse* : ' C'est ce qui me donne lieu de remarquer que le poete n'est pas tenu d'exposer à la vue toutes les actions particulières qui amènent à la principale. Il doit choisir celles qui lui sont les plus avantageuses à faire voir, soit par la beauté du spectacle, soit par l'éclat et la véhémence des passions qu'elles produisent, soit par quelqu'autre agrément qui leur soit attaché, et cacher les autres derrière la scène pour les faire connoître au spectateur, ou par une narration, ou par quelqu' autre addresse. Surtout il doit se souvenir que les unes et les autres doivent avoir une telle liaison ensemble, que les dernières soient produites par celles qui les précèdent, et que toutes aient leur source dans la protase, que doit fermer le premier acte.'

P. 64, l. 25. *Segnius irritant.* A. P. 180–187.

P. 65, l. 12. *Magnetick Lady.* Act ii. sc. 2.

P. 66, l. 11. *The Scornful Lady.* Conversion of the Usurer alluded to later in the *Parallel of Poetry and Painting.* Compare Voltaire's note on Corneille's second *Discourse,* referring to the conversion of Felix at the end of *Polyeucte* : ' La conversion miraculeuse de Félix le reconcilie sans doute avec le ciel, mais point du tout avec le parterre.'

P. 67, l. 20. Velleius, i. 17. Read *Et* ut primo ; l. 23, *et quod* assequi. The clause omitted runs as follows : *et velut occupatam relinquens materiam quaerit novam.*

P. 68, l. 19. *The Liar* : Le Menteur, comédie, Paris, 1644 ; founded on *La Verdad Sospechosa,* published 1630 under the name of Lope, but afterwards claimed by Juan Ruiz de Alarcón, and printed among his works. Translated into English as *The Mistaken Beauty, or the Lyar.*

l. 23. *Mr. Hart.* Charles Hart (d. 1683), grand-nephew of Shakespeare, acted *Dorante* at the theatre in Vere Street, which was opened Nov. 8, 1660. See *Dict. Nat. Biog.*

l. 27. Corneille, first *Discourse (Du Poëme Dramatique)* : ' Ainsi dans les comédies, j'ai presque toujours établi deux amans en bonne intelligence, je les ai brouillés ensemble par quelque fourbe, et les ai réunis par l'éclaircissement de cette même fourbe qui les séparoit.'

l. 32. *Molière.* Molière (1621–1673) had published *L'Estourdy,* 1663 ; *Le Depit Amoureux,* 1663 ; *Les Precieuses Ridicules,* 1660 ; *Sganarelle ou le Cocu Imaginaire,* 1660 ; *L'Escole des Maris,* 1661 ; *Les Facheux,* 1662 ; *L'Escole des Femmes,* 1663 ; *La Critique de l'Escole des Femmes,* 1663 ; *Les Plaisirs de l'Isle Enchantée,* 1664 ; *L'Amour Medecin,* 1666 ; *Le Misanthrope,* 1667 ; *Le Medecin malgré-luy,* 1667. Two English plays were borrowed from him in this present year of 1668 : Shadwell's *Sullen Lovers (Les Facheux),* and Sedley's *Mulberry Garden (L'Ecole des Maris).*

l. 32. *The Younger Corneille.* Thomas Corneille (1625–1709) had written several comedies and tragedies ; acknowledging in his prefaces to the comedies his debt to the Spanish poets. See p. 145 and below, note to p. 76, l. 34.

l. 33. *Quinault.* Philippe Quinault (1635–1688) had written, among other plays, *Les Rivales* (1653, pr. 1661), which has some resemblance to the *Rival Ladies,* and *L'Amant Indiscret* (1654, pr. 1664), to which Dryden seems to allude further on in the Essay. See note to p. 76, l. 34. *La Genereuse Ingratitude* (1654) is a ' pastoral tragi-comedy,' in which one of the personages is a certain Abencerrage, ' sous le nom d'*Almansor.*' He wrote, later, the books of Lulli's operas ; *Atys, Roland, Armide, Amadis,* &c.

P. 69, l. 7. *Spanish Novels.* These had been used pretty early by the English dramatists ; Middleton's *Spanish Gipsy* is from Cervantes, and several of Fletcher's plots are due to Spanish novelists. The French, however, generally preferred the Spanish plays for adaptation.

l. 9. *Diego* is the comic servant in the *Adventures of Five Hours.* The *gracioso* is a stock character in Spanish comedy, and was no less indispensable in the French imitations. See p. 77, l. 14, ' this poor Philipin or French Diego ' : Philipin was a common name for him ; e. g. in *Le Feint Astrologue* of Thomas Corneille (1648), in Chappuzeau's *Dame d'Intrigue* (1663), Scarron's *Heritier Ridicule* (1649), and *Gardien de soi-même* (1655), and in the *Festin de Pierre* of M. de Villiers (1659), where Philipin is the servant of Don Juan : ' L'influence du *gracioso* espagnol est surtout visible dans les Filipin de d'Ouville et Bois-robert, dans le Crispin de Raymond Poisson, dans le Jodelet de Scarron. Jodelet en particulier répond tout à fait à ce personnage chargé d'égayer par ses bouffonneries les drames de Lope de Vega, de Calderon, de Moreto, de Tirso de Molina. Quant au Crispin que R. Poisson popularisa doublement, comme acteur et comme auteur, s'il ne le créa pas tout à fait, il rappelle son origine espagnole jusque dans le costume traditionnel qu'il garde encore de nos jours : fraise, épée, moustache, justaucorps à courte basque serré d'une large ceinture en cuir, livrée reproduisant à peu près l'uniforme de certains déserteurs de par delà les Pyrénées qui après avoir mené la vie de bandouliers dans la montagne étaient entrés dans la domesticité pour vivre.'—Victor Fournel, *Le Théâtre au XVIIe Siècle* (La Comédie), 1892, p. 118.

l. 10. *their humours are thin-sown.* Dryden does not seem to have read *Les Visionnaires* of Desmarests de St. Sorlin, the French *Every Man in his Humour.*

P. 70, l. 28. *Primum Mobile.* In the old astronomy, the Sphere beyond the Sphere of the Fixed Stars, which gives to the eight lower spheres their diurnal motion from East to West, round the centre of the Earth ; the ' natural ' motion being from West to East, as seen (*e. g.*) in the orbit of the Moon, and in the path of the Sun through the Zodiac. Compare Chaucer, *Man of Law's Tale* : ' O firste moeving cruel firmament,' &c. Bacon, *Essays (Of Superstition)* : ' a new *primum mobile*, that ravisheth all the spheres of government ' (i. e. forcibly reverses their movement). Ovid, *Metam*, ii. 72 :

> ' Nitor in adversum, nec me qui cetera vincit
> Impetus et *rapido* contrarius evehor *orbi*.'

Dryden also recognized the Copernican system : see p. 225, l. 37, and Preface to *Juvenal*, vol. ii. p. 103.

P. 71, ll. 30, 32. *Cinna, Pompey, Polieucte* of Pierre Corneille ; published, *Cinna*, 1643 ; *La Mort de Pompée*, 1644 (*v. sup.* p. 24, l. 8) ; *Polyeucte Martyr*, 1643.

P. 72, l. 1. *by the hour-glass.* The hour-glass was part of the pulpit furniture.

'As Gifted Brethren, preaching by
A carnal hour-glass, do imply
Illumination can convey
Into them what they have to say,
But not how much ——.' *Hudibras*, i. 3, 1061.

P. 74, l. 23. *Corneille's* Andromede : 'Andromede Tragedie representée auec les Machines sur le Theatre Royal de Bourbon.' (Rouen, 1651.) This was the first of Corneille's festival pieces brought out with elaborate scenery, &c. The *Toison d'Or* was the second ; called an *Opera* by Chappuzeau. See his Théâtre François (1674), l. i. c. 21, and L. Celler, *Les Décors* &c. *au XVIIme siècle* (1869), p. 119.

P. 75, l. 32. 'Il est facile aux spéculatifs d'être sévères ; mais s'ils vouloient donner dix ou douze poëmes de cette nature au public, ils élargiroient peut-être les règles encore plus que je ne fais, si tôt qu'ils auroient reconnu par l'expérience quelle contrainte apporte leur exactitude, et combien de belles choses elle bannit de notre théâtre.'

P. 76, l. 34. *one of their newest plays.* Thomas Corneille's *L'Amour à la Mode* (1651), A. iii, not quite accurately remembered. Scene, a street ; enter *Oronte* (the Lover *à la Mode*) and his man *Cliton*. *Lucie* talks to *Oronte* from the balcony, but withdraws as *Florame* enters (his friend) ; then (sc. 4) comes the break of which Dryden is speaking : *Dorotée* has an appointment with *Oronte*, in her father's house, and she and her maid *Lysette* are discovered in their room ; the change of place from the street to the room is to be understood from their dialogue. Enter *Eraste*, another lover, who has to be got out of the way ; then *Oronte*, wanting to know who the other man might be. *Lysette*, to pacify him, pretends a lover ; *Cliton* at the door overhears, and comes in jealous ; *Argante*, Dorotée's father, is roused ; his voice is heard within crying 'thieves ! ' And so forth. Dryden's recollection seems to have confused this with a similar scene in Quinault, *L'Amant Indiscret* (A. ii. sc. 4), where the servant is *Philipin*, and where he is heard 'drolling within' :

'*Lisipe.* Ha que ne tiens-je ici ce maudit Philipin !
Philipin. Je ne me vis jamais si proche de ma fin.
Lisipe. Qu'avez vous répondu, belle et chere Lucresse ?
Lucresse. J'ai trompé ce valet.

Philipin.   Ha la bonne traîtresse ! ' &c.

L'Amour à la Mode is from Antonio de Solis, *El Amor al Uso.*
Thomas Corneille's play was translated into English : *The
Amorous Gallant or Love in Fashion, A Comedie in Heroick Verse,
As it was Acted* (1675) ; in Act iii. there is the same incoherence as
in the original—no correction of the scenery. The play called
Love A la Mode (1663) is not in any relation to the French play
of this name.

P. 77, l. 28. *counterturns.* See above, note to p. 45, l. 10.

P. 78, l. 15. *Alexandrines.* More commonly in ' eights and
sixes,' or in doggerel.

P. 80, l. 15. *Quantum lenta,* &c. Virgil, *Ecl.* 1. 25.

l. 16. *Mr. Hales.* John Hales (1584–1656), Fellow of Eton,
1612 ; at the Synod of Dort 1618–1619 ; friend of Sir Henry
Wotton, who was Provost of Eton, 1623 ; dispossessed, 1640. See
Tulloch, *Rational Theology* (1872), vol. i. The *Golden Remains of
the Ever Memorable Mr. John Hales* was published in 1659. There
is a story of his being present when B. Jonson was speaking of
Shakespeare's want of learning ; see Rowe's *Life of Shakespeare.*

P. 81, l. 3. *Philaster,* acted probably in 1608, p. 1620 ; *The
Woman Hater* is an earlier play published in 1607.

l. 5. *Ben Johnson.* The *Case is Altered* (pr. 1609) appears to
be one of those earlier plays.

l. 28. *his dotages.* Dryden is thinking of Johnson's *New Inn*
and *Tale of a Tub.*

P. 83, l. 3. *his Discoveries.* See above p. 41, l. 10, and note.

l. 15. *Five Hours,* called also the *Adventures,* p. 69, l. 9, and
note to p. 60, l. 17.

l. 23. In the *Cid* the scenes are frequently broken, to the
grief of Voltaire, the commentator. E. g. on Act iv. sc. 3 he makes
his complaint : ' Toujours la scène vide, et nulle liaison ; c'était
encore un des défauts du siècle. Cette négligence rend la tragédie
bien plus facile à faire, mais bien plus défectueuse.'

Corneille apologizes for an irregularity in the fourth Act of
Cinna : ' Il est vrai qu'il s'y rencontre une duplicité de lieu particulier. La moitié de la pièce se passe chez Emilie, et l'autre dans
le cabinet d'Auguste. J'aurois été ridicule si j'avois prétendu que
cet empereur délibérât avec Maxime et Cinna, s'il quitteroit
l'empire ou non, précisément dans la même place où ce dernier
vient de rendre compte à Emilie de la conspiration qu'il a formée
contre lui. C'est ce qui m'a fait rompre la liaison des scènes au
quatrième acte,' &c.

Augustus goes out in sc. 3 ; Emilia enters in sc. 4 ; she is
supposed to be in a different room. There was a great restriction

of theatrical liberty between the *Cid* and *Cinna* : see Corneille's notes on the scenes of the *Cid* in his *Examen*, quoted above, *Introduction*, p. xlvii.

P. 84, l. 13. *instance in*, &c. This is the old logical idiom taken from the usage of Aristotle, with whom it means ' to prove an exception,' e. g. *Topica*, 157 b 2 : πρὸς δὲ τοὺς ἐνισταμένους τῷ καθόλου, μὴ ἐν αὐτῷ δὲ τὴν ἔνστασιν φέροντας ἀλλ' ἐν τῷ ὁμωνύμῳ.

P. 85, l. 19. *Ex homine hunc natum dicas.* Terent. *Eun.* iii. 2. 7. ' The one is the born image of the other ' : Parmeno's remark on Gnatho the parasite and his patron Thraso.

P. 87, l. 3. *Creditur*, &c. Hor. *Ep.* ii. 1. 168.

P. 89, l. 15. *ubi plura.* Hor. *A. P.* 351.

l. 22. *vivorum*, &c. Velleius ii. 36.

P.90, l. 34. *Julius Caesar.* Macrobius, *Saturn*, ii. 7 ' Favente tibi me victus es Laberi a Syro.' Cf. *Aul. Gell.* viii. 15 ; x. 17.

P. 91, l. 2. *Laberius.* The Prologue of Laberius was translated by Goldsmith in the *Enquiry into the Present State of Polite Learning*, 1759 : ' What ! no way left to shun th' inglorious stage,' &c.

l. 22. *says Aristotle. Poet.* 1449 a 23 : λέξεως δὲ γενομένης αὐτὴ ἡ φύσις τὸ οἰκεῖον μέτρον εὗρε, μάλιστα γὰρ λεκτικὸν τῶν μέτρων τὸ ἰαμβεῖόν ἐστιν. ' Nature discovered the proper measure, for the iambic is of all measures the nearest prose.'

P. 92, l. 9. *Arcades.* Virgil, *Ecl.* 7. 4.

l. 11. *quicquid conabar.* Ovid. *Trist.* iv. 10. 25 :
' Sponte sua carmen numeros veniebat ad aptos
Et quod temptabam dicere versus erat.'

P. 93, l. 19. *saying too much.* ' Ovide . . . qui est estendu iusqu'à l'excez.' (Chapelain, Preface to *L'Adone*.)

l. 20. *Seneca.* M. Seneca, *Controv.* ix. 5, quoting Ovid, *Metam.* xiii. 503–5 (Arnold).

l. 23. *Omnia pontus erat*, &c. *Metam.* i. 292.

P. 96, l. 4. *perpetuo tenore.* Cic. *Or.* 6. 21 ' isque [stilus medius] uno tenore, ut aiunt, in dicendo fluit nihil afferens praeter facilitatem et aequalitatem.'

P. 97, l. 3. The reference to ' Daniel, his *Defence of Rhyme* ' (1607) is added in the second edition. ' The universalitie argues the generall power of it : for if the Barbarian vse it, then it shewes that it swaies the affection of the Barbarian : if ciuill Nations practise it, it proves that it workes vpon the hearts of ciuill Nations : if all, then that it hath a power in nature on all. *Georgienez de Turcarum moribus*, hath an example of the Turkish Rymes iust of the measure of our verse of eleuen syllables, in feminine Ryme : never begotten I am persuaded by any example in *Europe* ; but borne no doubt in *Scythia*, and brought over

Caucasus and Mount Taurus.   The Scląuonian and Arabian tongues acquaint a great part of Asia and Afrique with it.   The Muscovite, Polacke, Hungarian, Germane, Italian, French, and Spaniard use no other harmonie of words.   The Irish, Briton, Scot, Dane, Saxon, English, and all the Inhabiters of this Iland, either have hither brought, or heere found the same in use.'

P. 97, l. 14. Dryden seems not to have known any of the regular Italian tragedies in blank verse (*versi sciolti*) ; it is strange that he should have neglected the blank verse of Tasso's *Aminta*.

P. 99, l. 19. ' *Temptanda via est qua me quoque possim Tollere humo victorque virum volitare per ora.*'

Virgil, Georg. iii. 8.

l. 24. *The Faithful Shepherdess*, acted in 1610 ; *The Sad Shepherd*, left incomplete at Jonson's death, 1637.

P. 100, l. 2. *Sandys his translation.* Published in 1636. See Preface to Ovid's *Epistles*, p. 230, and Preface to *Fables*, vol. ii. p. 247 : ' the ingenious and learned Sandys, the best versifier of the former age.'   His *Ovid's Metamorphoses, English'd by G. S.*, first appeared in 1626, and went quickly through many editions. *The Poetical Works of George Sandys* were edited by the Rev. Richard Hooper, in Russell Smith's *Library of Old Authors*, 1872.

l. 6. *Interdum vulgus rectum videt, est ubi peccat.* ' The People's voice is odd.' Horace, *Ep.* ii. 1. 63.

P. 101, l. 5. *heroic rhyme is nearest Nature.* See *Introduction*, p. xxiv.

l. 6. Read *Indignatur* item *privatis*, &c.   *A. P.* 90.

l. 9. *Effutire.   A. P.* 231.

l. 10. *too low for a poem.* Blank verse was little used for ' poems ' (not dramatic) between Surrey's versions from the *Aeneid* and the publication of *Paradise Lost*.

P. 101, l. 12. *an ordinary sonnet.* ' Sonnet ' in the general sense, for any kind of short poem.   The *Death song of Ragnar Lodbrok* (*Krákumál*) is called a sonnet by Sir William Temple in his Essay *Of Heroic Virtue*.

P. 103, l. 7.   ' *Pictoribus atque poetis Quidlibet audendi semper fuit aequa potestas.*'

Hor. A. P. 9, 10.

l. 9. ' *Nobis non licet esse tam disertis Qui Musas colimus severiores.*'   Martial. ix. 12.

P. 104, l. 29. *the Water Poet.* Dryden had been reading Jonson's *Discoveries* : ' The puppets are seen now in despight of the players : Heath's epigrams and the Skuller's poems have their applause. . . . Nay, if it were put to the question, of the Water-Rhymer's works against Spenser's, I doubt not but they would find more suffrages.' The works of John Taylor, the Water-poet, have been republished by the Spenser Society.

P. 105, l. 1. *Julius Cæsar.* ' qui etiam in magnis occupationibus quum . . . de ratione Latine loquendi accuratissime scripserit primoque in libro dixerit verborum delectum originem esse eloquentiae.' Cicero, *Brutus,* 72, 253.

l. 6. Seneca *Phaedra,* 871. N.B. *clusos* for *clausos* in all editions of the *Essay,* and in the references both of Dryden and Howard later in the controversy.

P. 107, l. 29. *Somerset Stairs,* ' a noted Place for landing and taking Water at', to the West of old Somerset House. See Strype's *Survey of London,* 1720, Bk. iv. p. 112.

P. 108, l. 4. The *Piazzas* on the North and East sides of Covent Garden. See *Survey of London,* Bk. vi. p. 87.

PROLOGUE TO THE MAIDEN QUEEN.

P. 109. This is the first of two Prologues ; it gives a summary of Dryden's critical ideas, agreeing generally with the *Essay.*

l. 7. *dead colours* ; or ' dead colouring ' to make the ground of the picture.

l. 12. *o'erseen.* Negligent ; according to the old idiomatic deponent) use of the past participle.

DEFENCE OF THE ESSAY (1668).

P. 111, l. 18. *Dimock.* The hereditary Champion of England, as Lord of the Manor of Scrivelsby, which was held by this service. See G. Neilson, *Trial by Combat* (Glasgow, 1890), p. 194 *sqq.*

l. 22. *one, who has the reputation of understanding all things.* This ' means mischief ' : see Pepys's *Diary* for this year, 1668, May 4 : ' and after dinner he and I to the Duke of York's playhouse ; and there coming late he and I up to the balcony-box, where we find my Lady Castlemayne and several great ladies ; and there we sat with them, and I saw *The Impertinents* once more, now three times, and the three only days it hath been acted. And to see the folly how the house do this day cry up the play more than yesterday ! and I for that reason like it I find the better too ; by *Sir Positive At-all,* I understand, is meant Sir Robert Howard.' *The Sullen Lovers, or The Impertinents,* was a comedy by Shadwell. See below, note to p. 133, l. 16.

l. 25. *Favorinus to Hadrian.* Cf. Aelius Spartianus, *Hadrian,* c. 15. Malone has further pointed out that the story is given in

Barclay, *Icon Animorum*, c. 10.   Dryden had been reading Barclay : see above, p. 6, l. 10.

P. 112, l. 20. *for the most part borrowed from the observations of others.* This very ample acknowledgement was not enough for Martin Clifford, late Master of the Charterhouse : *Notes upon Mr. Dryden's Poems in Four Letters,* p. 8 : ' I was about six years since a little acquainted with a Name-sake and Countreyman of yours, who pilfered out of Monsieur Hedelin, Menardiere and Corneille, an Essay of Dramatick Poetry, wherein he tells us another Tale ' &c.   This was not published till 1687, but apparently written in 1674.   ' Monsieur Hedelin ' is the Abbé d'Aubignac (1604–1676) ; his *Pratique du Théâtre* appeared in 1657.   *La Poëtique de Jules de la Mesnardière* was published in 1640.

P. 114, l. 24.   Horace, *A. P.* 361–364, 149, 150.

P. 115, l. 5. *Lazar.*   See Preface to *Annus Mirabilis*, p. 18, l. 18, and note.

P. 116, l. 29. *Reserate,* &c.   See note on p. 105, l. 6.

P. 117, l. 5. *Delectus verborum,* p. 104, l. 34.

P. 119, l. 16. *nullos habitura triumphos.*   Lucan, Phars. i. 12.

P. 120, l. 23. *My Lord L——.*   John Maitland, second Earl and first Duke of Lauderdale, 1616–1682.

P. 121, l. 29. *Ficta voluptatis,* &c.   Hor. *A. P.* 338.

P. 122, l. 5. *Sir John Berkenhead,* D.C.L., Fellow of All Souls, author of *Mercurius Aulicus,* &c. (1616–1679).   The reference here (given by Malone) is to his poem *In Memory of Mr. William Cartwright,* printed in *Comedies, Tragi-Comedies, with other Poems by Mr. William Cartwright,* 1651.   It is a vigorous piece of criticism, full of conceits, in praise of strength and purity of composition :
' For thy Imperial Muse at once defines
Lawes to *arraign* and *brand* their weak *strong lines* ;
Unmask's the Goblin-Verse that fright's a page,
As when old time brought Divells on the Stage ;
Knew the right mark of things, saw how to choose,
(For the great Wit's great work is to *Refuse,*)
And smil'd to see what shouldering there is
To follow *Lucan* where he trod amiss ;
Thine's the right Mettall, thine's still big with Sense,
And stands as square as a good *Conscience.*
No traverse lines, all *written like a man* :
Their heights are but the *Chaff,* their Depths the *Bran* :
Gross, and not Great ; which when it best does hit
Is not the *Strength* but *Corpulence* of Wit :
Stuft, swoln, ungirt : but thine's compact and bound
Close as the Atomes of a *Diamond.*' &c.

P. 122, l. 26. *Il.* viii. 267.

P. 124, l. 21. *my whole discourse was sceptical.* See note to p. 35, l. 22.

P. 126, l. 35. *Herculean.* Cf. Seneca, *Ep.* 87, 38 ' unus tibi nodus sed Herculaneus restat.'

P. 130, l. 26. *pag.* 44. Above, p. 75, l. 30.

P. 133, l. 16. *if I do not hereafter answer.* Pepys, 1668, Sept. 20 (Lord's Day) : ' . . . And so to dinner alone, having since church heard the boy read over Dryden's *Reply* to Sir R. Howard's *Answer*, about his *Essay of Poesy* ; and a letter in answer to that, the last whereof is mighty silly, in behalf of Howard.' Mr. Wheatley, in his note on this passage, gives the title of this ineffective letter, written by Richard Flecknoe : ' A Letter from a Gentleman to the Honourable Ed. Howard, Esq., occasioned by a Civiliz'd Epistle of Mr. Dryden's before his Second Edition of his Indian Emperour. In the Savoy, printed by Thomas Newcomb, 1668.' Dryden kept his promise, and, further, withdrew his *Defence* in the later editions of the *Indian Emperor*.

PREFACE TO ' AN EVENING'S LOVE, OR THE MOCK ASTROLOGER ' (1671).

P. 134, l. 16. *opiniatre.* ' An Opiniater ' is one of Butler's *Characters*.

P. 135, l. 22. *the zany of a mountebank.* Cf. Dryden's *Prologue to the Pilgrim*, 1700, l. 38 (in ' Quack Maurus ') :

> ' Our mountebank has laid a deeper train ;
> His cant, like *Merry-Andrew's* noble vein,
> Cat-calls the sects to draw 'em in again.'

P. 137, l. 25. *crambe.* Juvenal, *Sat.* vii. 154.

l. 33. *A . P.* 282.

P. 138, l. 3. *A . P.* 247, 248.

l. 14. *Ipse dixit* ; Αὐτὸς ἔφα ; said of the Master, in the School of Pythagoras.

P. 139, l. 5. Quintilian, vi. 3. 71.

l. 9. Quintilian, vi. 3. 2.

l. 27. Quintilian, vi. 3. 13.

l. 32. *Mr. Cowley.*

> ' Yet 'tis not to adorn and gild each part ;
>   That shows more cost than art.
>   Jewels at nose and lips but ill appear ;
>   Rather than all things Wit, let none be there.'
>   (*Ode—Of Wit.*)

P. 140, l. 17. *the Liar,* i. e. Corneille's *Dorante.* The *Chances, Wit without Money,* by Fletcher.

P. 143, l. 2. *Heinsius, before Horace his* Art of Poetry. Heinsius appears to have had no scruples such as Dryden here imposes on him. *Delectare enim ac docere est Comœdiæ* : Danielis Heinsii *in Horat. Notæ* (ad *A. P.* v. 270) Lugd. Batav. 1629.

P. 144, l. 17. *Et spes,* &c. Juvenal, *Sat.* 7. 1.

P. 145, l. 3. *El Astrologo Fingido* of Calderon. The anonymous English version of Thomas Corneille's play was published in 1668.

l. 15. *Wildblood and Jacintha.* ' *Wildblood* by Mr. Hart, *Donna Jacintha* by Mrs. Ellen Gwyn ' in the original cast.

P. 146, l. 6. *Romeo and Juliet.* Written in Italian by Bandello, not Cinthio.

l. 7. *Moor of Venice. Hecatommithi,* Dec. iii. Nov. 7.

l. 8. *Spanish novels.* These have been indicated by Langbaine, Dyce, and other scholars.

l. 9. *The Chances.* From Cervantes, *La Señora Cornelia (Novelas Exemplares,* x).

l. 9. *The Spanish Curate.* From *Gerardo, the Unfortunate Spaniard* (1615–1617), by Gonzalo de Céspedes. Translated into English, 1622. The play was licensed in that year ; a later edition, 1653.

l. 9. *Rule a Wife and have a Wife.* In part from Cervantes, *Novelas Exemplares,* xi, *El Casamiento Engañoso.*

l. 10. *The Little French Lawyer.* ' The plot is borrowed from Guzman in the Spanish Rogue, part ii. chap. iv : the story of Dinant Cleremont and Lamira, being borrowed from Don Lewis de Castro, and Don Rodrigo de Montalva.' Langbaine.

OF HEROIC PLAYS (1672).

P. 149, l. 25. *D'Avenant.* See p. 7, l. 27 ; p. 97, l. 26.

l. 31. *the Italian Operas.* For the history, see the essay of St. Evremond, *Sur les opéras,* 1677 (*à M. le Duc de Buckingham*), and L. Celler, *Les Origines de l'Opéra et Le Ballet de la Reine,* 1868. The first Italian Opera in Paris was the *Finta Pazza* (Achilles in Scyros) of Strozzi, 1645, represented at the Petit-Bourbon through the influence of Mazarin, who brought the stage-engineer Torelli from Parma to manage the scenery, &c.

For the relation of Opera to Tragedy and Heroic Drama, see above, the note on Corneille's *Andromede* (p. 74, l. 3). Chappuzeau, *Theatre François,* has some good remarks on the theatrical tastes of the Italians (l. 1, c. 21), and on Corneille's relation to the

Opera. *The Siege of Rhodes* on the English stage corresponds to the *Andromede* and the *Toison d'Or* in France.

P. 150, l. 2. *just,* i. e. regular.

l. 33. *and, consequently, that Love and Valour ought to be the subject of it.* The practice and theory of Tasso show how the classical form of Epic had been generally modified by the influence of the romances. Homer and Amadis are both authorities for the right conduct of Epic. The *Accademia della Crusca* went further and said there was no difference between Romance and Epic, except that the latter was tedious (*Difesa dell' Orlando Furioso,* 1584).

P. 151, l. 28. ' I cannot discern by any help from reading, on learned men (who have been to me the best and briefest Indexes of Books) that any Nation hath in representment of great actions (either by *Heroicks or Dramaticks*) digested story into so pleasant and instructive a method as the English by their *Drama* : and by that regular species (though narratively and not in dialogue) I have drawn the body of an Heroick Poem ; In which I did not onely observe the symmetry, proportioning five Books to five *Acts* and *Canto's* to *Scenes* (the *Scenes* having their number ever govern'd by occasion) but all the *shadowings, happy strokes, secret graces,* and even *drapery,* which together make the second beautys; I have (I hope) exactly followed,' &c. (Preface to *Gondibert.*)

P. 152, l. 4. *Petronius Arbiter.* This is quoted by almost every critic of the *Epic Poem* ; by Sir R. Fanshawe, in his translation of *Camoens,* by St. Evremond, Rapin, Bossu, &c., also by Coleridge, *Biographia Literaria,* c. 14. See above, note to p. 11, l. 28.

l. 19. *sting of an epigram.* Cf. p. 14, l. 35.

l. 28. *Appius. Pharsalia,* v. 65 *sq.*

l. 29. *Erichtho. Ibid.,* vi. 507 *sq.*

l. 32. This continues the answer to Davenant, who in the Preface to *Gondibert* had slighted the epic ' machinery ' : ' And more closely than Virgil waits on Homer doth Statius attend Virgil, and follows him there also where Nature never comes, even into Heaven and Hell ; and therefore he cannot escape such as approve the wisdom of the best Dramaticks ; who in the representation of examples, believe they prevail most in our manners when they lay the scene at home in their own country ; so much they avoid those remote Regions of Heaven and Hell ; as if the People whom they make civil by an easy communication with reason (and familiar reason is that which is called the civility of the stage) were become more discreet than to have their eyes perswaded by the descending of Gods in gay Clouds, and more manly than to be frighted with the rising of Ghosts in Smoke.'

Compare also Davenant on *Tasso*: ' Yet a Christian poet, whose
Religion little needs the aids of Invention, hath less occasion to
imitate such Fables as meanly illustrate a probable Heaven, by
the fashion and dignity of courts ; and make a resemblance of
Hell, out of the Dreams of frighted Women ; by which they continue and increase the melancholy mistakes of the People.'

    P. 154, l. 5. *Mr. Cowley's verses.*

      ' Methinks Heroick Poesie till now
      Like some fantastique Fairy-land did show ;
      Gods, Devils, Nymphs, Witches, and Giants race,
      And all but Man, in Man's best work had place.
      Then like some worthy Knight, with sacred Arms
      Dost drive the *Monsters* thence, and end the charms :
      Instead of these dost Men and Manners plant,
      The things which that rich soyl did chiefly want.
      But even thy *Mortals* do their *Gods* excell,
      Taught by thy Muse to Fight and Love so well,' &c.

    l. 22. *Segnius irritant. A. P.* 180.

    P. 155, l. 6. *Red Bull.* See p. 58, l. 7, and note.

    l. 17. *Almanzor*, the hero of the *Conquest of Granada* ; the
famous name of *Al Mansur* had already been used by Quinault in
a drama on the Wars of Granada ; see above, note on p. 68, l. 33.

    l. 26. *Artaban.* In the *Cléopatre* of M. de la Calprenède. See
Introduction, p. liv, for the relation of the French heroic romances
to the Heroic Poem.

    l. 26. *Calprenède* (1610–1663), author of *Cléopatre, Cassandre,
Pharamond* :

      ' Tout a l'humeur gasconne en un auteur gascon ;
      Calprenède et Juba parlent du meme ton.'

                      Boileau, *L'Art Poetique*, iii.

    P. 156, l. 7. *Homer's words. Iliad,* i. 225, 231, 194.

    l. 13. *Iliad,* i. 287.

    l. 17. *A. P.* 120.

    l. 26. *Venga egli,* &c. Tasso, *Gerusalemme Liberata* v 43 :
      Let Godfrey come or send, I will not hence
      Until we know who shall this bargain rue,
      That of our tragedy the late done fact
      May be the first, and this the second, act.

                              FAIRFAX.

    l. 31. *the Point of Honour.* Most of the Spanish plays turn on
the Point of Honour, and the French and English imitated them.
Compare the *Adventures of Five Hours*, Act v :

' *Don Henrique.* Why, were not you Antonio fighting with him ?
                Were you not doing all you could to kill him ?

Don Antonio.   Henrique, 'tis true ; but finding in my breast
An equal strife 'twixt honour and revenge,
I do in just compliance with them both,
Preserve him from your sword to fall by mine.
Don Carlos.   Brave man, how nicely he does honour weigh !
Justice herself holds not the scales more even.'
See also *The Rehearsal,* Act iii. sc. 2 (Prince Volscius) and Act v
(Prince Prettyman). The last great drama with this motive is
Hernani ou l'Honneur Castillan, 1830.

P. 157, l. 8. *Cyrus and Oroondates. Artaméne ou le Grand Cyrus,*
by Mlle. de Scudéry, was published under her brother's name,
1649–1653, and translated into English by F. G., *Gent.,* 1653.
Oroondates is the hero of Calprenède's *Cassandre,* which was translated by Sir Charles Cotterell, 1652, and became the favourite
romance of that kind in England. Cassandra, a name taken by
the heroine Statira at one point in the story, was adopted in many
English families.

l. 24. *Ben Johnson's* Cethegus. See *Defence of the Epilogue*
for criticism of some passages in Jonson's *Catiline.*

l. 27. *to destroy Nature. Catiline,* Act iii. sc. 1.

l. 28. *to kill all the Senate. Ibid.,* Act iv. sc. 3 :
' Would I
Had somewhat by myself apart to do ;
I have no genius to these many counsels :
Let me kill all the Senate for my share,
I'll do it at next setting.'

l. 29. *to look Cato dead.* Spoken by Catiline, not Cethegus,
ibid., Act iv. sc. 2.

P. 158, l. 5. *Their king.* Boabdil, called *el Chico (Boabdelin* in
Dryden's play). The history of Granada is the Spanish history of
the Zegries and Abencerrages (*Historia de las Guerras Civiles de
Granada*), which Dryden had probably consulted, as well as the
French works derived from it—*Almahide,* and Quinault's tragi-
comedy *La Généreuse Ingratitude.* See *Albion and Albanius,
Preface,* p. 272, and note.

l. 8. *in the* juego de toros. *Conquest of Granada,* First Part,
A. i. sc. 1 :
' Thus while he stood, the bull who saw his foe,
His easier conquests proudly did forego ;
And making at him with a furious bound,
From his bent forehead aim'd a double wound :
A rising murmur ran through all the field,' &c.

l. 15. *with a word* : ' una voce, qua Quirites eos pro militibus
appellarat.'—Suetonius, *Julius,* 70.

P. 158,l. 25. *Duke of Guise.* Cf. *Memoires de feu Monsieur le Duc de Guise,* Paris, 1668 (edited by the Sieur de Sainctyon, his secretary ; the time of the history is from Nov. 1647 to Ap. 1648). The *Éloge* describes his courage : ' Toute la Noblesse du Royaume de Naples l'a vu avec etonnement luy resister presque seul, et percer l'épée à la main tout ce qui s'opposoit aux efforts de son courage. . . . Il brava les vents et la mer, et luy quatriéme dans une felouque méprisa toute une Flotte ennemie pour aller secourir ses amis.' These Memoirs were translated into English (1669).

l. 35. *Verum operi longo fas est obrepere somnum.* Hor. *A. P.* 360.

DEFENCE OF THE EPILOGUE.

P. 163, l. 8. *Ingeniis,* &c. Horace, Ep. ii. 1. 88.

l. 13. *Lucilium.* *Sat.* i. 10. 50 :
' At dixi fluere hunc lutulentum, saepe ferentem
Plura quidem tollenda relinquendis.'

l. 20. *Si foret.* *Sat.* i. 10. 68.

P. 164, l. 19. *Quintilian.* i. e. in the Dialogue *De Oratoribus,* which was sometimes ascribed to Quintilian, and regarded as the book of which he speaks in *Inst.* vi. (*prooemium*) and viii. 6. 76 ' Sed de hoc satis quia eundem locum plenius in eo libro quo causas corruptae eloquentiae reddebamus tractavimus.' Cf. *Taciti Dialogus de Oratoribus,* ed. Peterson, Introd. i.

P. 165, l. 17. *Neque ego* illi *detrahere ausim.* Hor. *Sat.* i. 10. 48.

P. 166, l. 27. *acorns* are part of the stock of the Golden Age. Compare Virgil, *Georg.* i. 7 :
' Liber et alma Ceres, vestro si munere tellus
Chaoniam pingui glandem mutavit arista.'

l. 28. ἅλις δρυός. Cicero, *ad Att.* ii. 19 : ' Dices fortasse " dignitatis ἅλις, tamquam δρυός : saluti, si me amas, consule " : ' ' Enough of oak,' as the ancients said when they grew tired of acorns.

P. 167, l. 11. *Caedimus,* &c. Persius, *Sat.* 4, 42.

l. 30. *synchysis.* Cicero discusses the placing of words in *Orator,* c. 44 *sqq.* ; σύγχυσις is not found in this context, but is used in his letters, e. g. σύγχυσιν litterularum, *Att.* vi. 9.

P. 168, l. 1. *The preposition in the end of the sentence.* See above, p. xxvii, on the correction of this in the revised version of the *Dramatic Essay.*

l. 27. Ones, *in the plural number.* See above, pp. 32, 33.

P. 169, l. 8. *Well-placing of words.* See Dryden's remarks on Denham's famous couplet, vol. ii. p. 217, and for Mr. *Waller,* above, pp. 7, 14.

P. 170, l. 21. *Quem penes,* &c. Hor. *A. P.* 72.

P. 171, l. 10. *Dixeris,* &c.   *Ibid.* 47.

  l. 17. *Et vultus,* &c.   *Od.* i. 19, 8.

  l. 23. *curiosa felicitas.*   Petronius, *Satyr,* c. 118.

P. 172, l. 24. *Wit.* For the definition of Wit (in the sense of poetical genius) see p. 14, l. 22, and note.

P. 173, l. 4. *clenches.* See p. 31, l. 10, and note.

  l. 25. *sting of an epigram.* Cf. p. 14, l. 34.

P. 174, l. 2. *a famous Italian.* The reference is not easy to verify. The conceits of the Italian pulpits are treated with great spirit in the *Cannocchiale Aristotelico* (' the Aristotelian Prospect-Glass ') by D. Emmanuele Tesauro (ed. 5, Torino, 1670). The purpose of this great work is to justify conceits out of Aristotle, but it does not recommend them indiscriminately, and the following passage on facetious sermons is substantially the same as Dryden's citation. It is in the chapter *De' Concetti Predicabili* ; the context is invaluable for the history of style : ' ecco che alcuni, dimentichi del decoro, per dar gusto alla turba e fuggir fatica, incominciarono a buffonneggiar sopra i Pulpiti sacri, con mimiche rappresentationi e scede e motti scurrili, rinnovando la medesima corrottela deplorata dal Dante nel suo secolo di tutti i vitii fecondo.   Con molto maggior discretezza dunque alcuni Ingegni Spagnuoli naturalmente arguti, e nelle Scolastiche Dottrine perspicacissimi, trovarono non è gran tempo questa novella maniera d'insegnar dilettando per mezzo di questi argomenti ingeniosi detti vulgamente *Concetti Predicabili,'* &c. Conceits were handled more severely by Matteo Pellegrini, *Delle Acutezze,* 1639, and by the Cardinal Sforza Pallavicino, *Sopra l'Arte dello Stile,* 1646.

  l. 28. *Fletcher's Don John* ; in *The Chances.* The play was amended by the Duke of Buckingham, and acted at the King's House in 1667. See Pepys, Feb. 5.

P. 175, l. 21. *Black Friars.* Cf. Pepys, Oct. 16, 1668 : ' *The Queen of Arragon,* an old Blackfriars' play, but an admirable one.'

  l. 26. *Apollo.* See Jonson's *Works* for his *Leges Convivales* inscribed on the wall of his club-room at the *Apollo.*

  l. 26. *his sons.* The ' tribe of Ben ' included Herrick, Randolph, Cartwright, and many others whom he called his sons.

APOLOGY FOR HEROIC POETRY.

The *State of Innocence* is said by some authors to have been published in 1674, but I cannot find this edition. The book was entered at Stationers' Hall in 1674 (Masson's *Life of Milton,* vi. p. 710) ; it is recorded as a new book in the Catalogue for Hilary Term, 1676 (i. e. 167$\frac{5}{6}$) ; the earliest copy in the British Museum is dated 1677. Mr. Gosse thinks there was a surreptitious issue of the Opera in 1676, without *Epistle* or *Apology* ; ' many hundred copies of it being dispersed abroad without my knowledge or consent ' (p. 178, l. 11).

P. 178, l. 8. *a Princess.* Mary of Este, Duchess of York.

P. 179, l. 7. *my friend.* Lee :
> ' Something I would to your vast virtue raise,
> But scorn to daub it with a fulsome praise.'

l. 31. *A. P.* 351 : a favourite quotation, see *Essay*, p. 89.

l. 34. *Longinus.* Boileau's translation of Longinus appeared in 1674 : ' Œuvres diverses du Sieur D . . . avec le Traité du Sublime ou du Merveilleux dans le Discours.'

P. 180, l. 24. *says my author.* Longinus, c. 33.

P. 181, l. 6. *Heroic Poetry . . . the greatest work of human nature.* Rapin, *La Comparaison d'Homère et de Virgile* : ' De tous les ouvrages dont l'esprit de l'homme est capable, le Poëme Epique est sans doute le plus accompli : parce qu'il renferme les perfections de tous les autres.' So also in *Reflexions sur la Poëtique en particulier.* See *Dedication of the Aeneis*, the opening sentence.

l. 13. *Trojani belli,* &c. *Ep.* i. 2. 1.

l. 20. *cui mens divinior.* Hor. *Sat.* i. 4. 43.

l. 24. *the Italian commentators.* Rapin, *Reflexions sur la Poëtique en general* : ' Victorius Madius, Robortellus, et après eux Castelvetro et Piccolomini furent les premiers qui firent connoistre dans l'Europe les regles de la Poëtique d'Aristote, que les Grecs apporterent en Italie après la prise de Constantinople : et ceux-cy furent suivis du Beni, de Minturno, de Vida, de Gallutio, et de plusieurs autres.'

l. 26. *Rapin.* The Reverend Father Réné Rapin (1621–1687) ; his chief work in criticism is *Réflexions sur la Poëtique d'Aristote et sur les ouvrages des poëtes anciens et modernes,* 1674. His *Comparison of Plato and Aristotle.* &c., was translated by J. Dancer, 1673, two years after it was published in France.

P. 181, l. 25. *Boileau* (Nicolas, Sieur Despréaux, 1636–1711) was well appreciated in England. His first Satires were published in 1665–1667 ; one of them was translated by Butler. *L'Art Poëtique* appeared in 1674.

l. 30. *to instruct and delight* : as before, p. 36, l. 7, *supra.*

P. 182, l. 5. *the author of the* Plain Dealer : Wycherley. *The Plain Dealer* was published in 1677.

P. 184, l. 4. *tropes and figures,* discussed by Longinus, cc. 31, 32.

l. 6. *Catachreses* : see note on p. 31, l. c. 12.

l. 12. *Nec retia,* &c. *Ecl.* 5, 60.

l. 16. *Nocte natat,* &c. *Georg.* iii. 260.

l. 23. *Cleopatra. Od.* i. 37. 26.

l. 31. *Graditurque. Aen.* iii. 664.

l. 33. *Cowley* : in the *Davideis*, Book III.

P. 185, l. 5. *eighth* : by mistake for *seventh*.

l. 7. *Illa vel intactae*, &c. *Aen.* vii. 808.

l. 14. *Longinus quotes Herodotus*, c. 38.   Herodotus, vii. 225.

l. 34. *si vis me flere*, &c. Hor. *A. P.* 102.

P. 186, l. 4. *hyperbata* ; inversions of phrase, discussed by Longinus, c. 22.

P. 187, l. 14. *Nam certe ex vivo*, &c.   Lucretius, iv. 737 ; read *animalis*.

P. 188, l. 1. *these four lines* : in Act i. sc. 1 of the *Opera*.

l. 13. *Invadunt urbem. Aen.* ii. 265.

l. 16. *Mr. Cowley* : *Davideis*, Book I. *Nobis non licet esse tam disertis*, &c., Martial, ix. 12.

P. 189, l. 15. *Martial tells you* : a favourite quotation.   Cf. *Essay*, p. 103, l. 9, *supra*, and Rapin on *Homer and Virgil*.

l. 21. *Sir Philip Sidney and the translator of Du Bartas*. Compound epithets were in favour with Du Bartas, and Sir Philip Sidney was noted in his own time for following the example of the French poet ; so in Hall's *Satires*, vi. 1 :

> ' He knows the grace of that new elegance
> Which sweet *Philisides* fetch'd of late from France,
> That well beseem'd his high-styl'd *Arcady*,
> Tho' others mar it with much liberty,
> In epithets to join two words in one.' &c.

Rapin censures Ronsard and Du Bartas for this, and it was a common point for caricature ; the Poet in Desmarests' *Les Visionnaires* talks like Du Bartas :

> ' Je sors des antres noirs du Mont Parnassien,
> Où le fils poil-doré du grand Saturnien
> Dans l'esprit forge-vers plante le Dithyrambe,
> L'Epode, l'Antistrophe, et le tragique Iambe.'

Cf. Bouhours, *Entretiens d'Ariste et d'Eugene*, ii. (La Langue Françoise) : ' Le sommeil *charme-soucy*, le ciel *porte-flambeau*, le vent *chasse-nue*, l'abeille *suce-fleurs*, les fleurs *soueve-flairantes*, les Dieux *chevre-pieds*, sont des dictions monstrueuses dans le langage moderne.'

l. 27. *Pictoribus atque Poetis*. Hor. *A. P.* 9–10, 12–13.

P. 190, l. 5. Compare Dryden's letter to Dennis about ' machines,' quoted in the note on the Preface to Juvenal, vol. ii. p. 32, l. 1.

P. 190, l. 9. *Tasso*. Rapin does not appear to have censured Tasso, nor was Tasso open to censure, on this account. Rapin's chief remark on Tasso is that he dissolves the Epic with too much of the Pastoral and Lyrical element. See note on Preface to Juvenal, below, vol. ii. p. 27, l. 9.

l. 7. *Camoens.* Cf. Rapin, *Reflexions sur la Poëtique en particulier*, c. 13 ' le Camoens qui parle sans discretion de Venus, de Bacchus et des autres divinitez dans un Poëme Chrestien.' The *Lusiad* was translated into English by Sir R. Fanshawe, 1655.

l. 12. *Wit.* See Preface to *Albion and Albanius*, p. 270, and *Second Miscellany*, p. 258, and compare Dryden's *Life of Lucian* : ' If Wit consists in the propriety of thoughts and words, which I imagined I had first found out, but since am pleasingly convinced that Aristotle has made the same definition in other terms,' &c. The passage in Aristotle's *Poetics*, c. 6, was pointed out by ' the learned and ingenious Mr. Twining ' (Malone) : τρίτον δὲ ἡ διάνοια . τοῦτο δέ ἐστι τὸ λέγειν δύνασθαι τὰ ἐνόντα καὶ τὰ ἁρμόττοντα.

l. 16. *If our critics.* This sentence does not run smoothly and probably *or* has dropped out between the two *ifs* : ' if our critics will join issue . . . *or* if they will take it . . . it will be easy,' &c.

l. 17. *convenire in aliquo tertio* ; to find some means of agreement, in a third term, between the two opposites.

ALL FOR LOVE, PREFACE (1678).

P. 192, l. 20. *machine* : in the less common meaning of dramatic motive. Compare *Epilogue to Œdipus*, ll. 9, 10 :
' Terror and Pity this whole Poem sway
    The mightiest Machine that can mount a Play.'

P. 193, l. 19. *Montaigne* : *Essais*, l. ii. c. 17 : *de la presumption.*

P. 194, l. 16. *their Hippolytus* : in the *Phèdre* of Racine ; a new play, Jan. 1, 1677, at the Hôtel de Bourgogne.

P. 195, l. 4. *our* Chedreux *critics.* Cf. *Prologue to Albion and Albanius*, l. 32 :
' Then 'tis the mode of France, without whose rules
    None must presume to set up here for fools.'
Chedreux, a fashionable periwig, from the name of the inventor ; cf. Etherege, *The Man of Mode*, 1676, A. iii. s. 2, where Sir Fopling Flutter's periwig is *Chedreux* : ' he wears nothing but what are originals of the most famous hands in Paris.'

P. 196, l. 3. *a picture of Nature.* See *Introduction*, p. xxiv.

l. 16. *Rarus enim*, &c. Juvenal, *Sat.* 8. 73.

P. 198, l. 4. *that grinning honour.* Falstaff : ' I like not such grinning honour as Sir Walter hath ; give me life ; which if I can save, so ; if not, honour comes unlooked for, and there 's an end ' (1 *Henry IV. Act* v. sc. 3).

l. 28. *Crispinus.* Hor. *Sat.* i. 1. 120 ; 3. 139.

l. 28. *in the Holy Way.* Hor. *Sat.* i. 9 ; and Ben Jonson, *Poetaster,* Act iii. sc. 1.

l. 32. *Demetri teque,* &c. Hor. *Sat.* i. 10. 90.

P. 199, l. 5. *Saxum antiquum,* &c. Virgil, *Aen.* xii. 897.

l. 10. *Genua labant,* &c. *Ibid.* 905.

l. 14. *this rhyming judge of the twelvepenny gallery.* Dryden had been touched by Lord Rochester's (anonymous) *Allusion to the Tenth Satire* of the First Book of Horace, and chose to attribute it to some insignificant person. The *Allusion* begins with Dryden :

> ' Well, Sir, 'tis granted ; I said Dryden's rhymes
> Were stolen, unequal, nay dull many times :
> What foolish patron is there found of his,
> So blindly partial to deny me this ?
> But that his plays, embroider'd up and down
> With wit and learning, justly pleas'd the Town,
> In the same paper I as freely own,' &c.

l. 33. *Vellem in amicitia,* &c. Hor. *Sat.* i. 3. 41.

P. 200, l. 2. *a slow man hasty,* &c. Cf. Rochester, *op. cit.* :

> ' Of all our modern wits, none seems to me
> Once to have touch'd upon true Comedy
> But hasty Shadwell and slow Wycherley.'

l. 4. *Canibus pigris,* &c. Juvenal, *Sat.* viii. 34.

l. 8. *Lucretius.* Book IV. 1152 *sqq.*

l. 12. *ad Æthiopem cygnum.* Juv. *Sat.* viii. 33.

l. 23. *Vos exemplaria Graeca.* Hor. *A. P.* 268.

PREFACE TO TROILUS AND CRESSIDA (1679).

P. 202, l. 3. *Longinus :* on Aeschylus, c. 15.

l. 6. *Quintilian,* Inst. x. i. 66 : ' Tragoedias primus in lucem Aeschylus protulit, sublimis et gravis et grandiloquus saepe usque ad vitium, sed rudis in plerisque et incompositus.'

P. 203, l. 14. *one Lollius.* On Chaucer's mystification with regard to Lollius, his professed authority for *Troilus and Cressida,* see Ten Brink, *Chaucer-Studien,* and Skeat, *Chaucer* (1894), vol. ii. p. liii. *sqq.*

l. 18. *the name Cressida.* The name is from Boccaccio's *Griseida* (i. e. Chryseis), substituted for the *Briseide* of the French poet, who wrote the story of Troilus in his *Roman de Troie.*

l. 35. *and that there appeared.* A common use of *that* as a pro-adverb : see Kellner, *Historical Syntax,* § 448.

P. 204, l. 11. *to keep them all unbroken.* For *liaison des scènes,* see above, Essay, p. 40, l. 27, and note.

l. 33. *Mr. Betterton.* Thomas Betterton (c. 1635–1710), a member of the Duke's Company, which was organized by

Davenant in Lincoln's-Inn-Fields, 1661, moved to Dorset Garden (Salisbury Court) 1671, united to the King's 1682. There is a fine description of Betterton's acting in Cibber's *Apology,* c. 4.

P. 205, l. 4. *Amintor and Melantius* : in *The Maid's Tragedy.*

l. 6. *Iphigenia* : in Aulis.

P. 206, l. 10. *my friend Mr. Rymer.* Thomas Rymer (1641– 1713), Historiographer 1692, editor of the *Fœdera* 1704, &c., had at this time written a heroic play, *Edgar* (1677), and a critical Essay, *The Tragedies of the Last Age Considered and Examined by the Practice of the Ancients* (1678). Dryden's notes on this latter work were printed in an edition of Beaumont and Fletcher, 1711, and by Johnson in his *Life of Dryden.* In 1693 Rymer published his second Essay, *A Short View of Tragedy : its Original Excellency and Corruption, with some Reflections on Shakespeare and other Practitioners for the Stage.* Dryden's relations with Rymer were not constant ; ' For Tom the Second reigns like Tom the First ' in the Epistle to Congreve, 1693 ; and in the *Third Miscellany,* 1693, ' the corruption of a Poet is the generation of a Critic ' ; but in the Preface to the *Fables* he is ' our learned Mr. Rymer.'

l. 18. *Longinus* ; c. 13.

P. 208, l. 6. *Marriage à la Mode* ; printed 1673.

l. 8. *Œdipus* ; printed 1679.

l. 35. *Spanish plots* ; see the *Essay of Dramatic Poesy,* p. 60, l. 17, and note.

P. 209, l. 5. *The Slighted Maid* : a comedy by Sir Robert Stapylton, 4°, 1663 ; acted at Lincoln's-Inn-Fields. Pepys, Feb. 23, 1663 ; May 29, 1663 ; Aug. 28, 1668 ; ' but a mean play.'

l. 9. *Mustapha.* See above, p. 1 and note, and p. 63 and note.

P. 210, l. 1. *Rapin, a judicious critic. Reflexions sur la Poëtique en particulier,* c. 17 : ' Ce Philosophe avoit reconnu deux défauts importans a regler dans l'homme, l'orgueil et la dureté, et il trouva le remede a ces deux défauts dans la Tragedie.'

P. 211, l. 6. *Bossu, the best of modern critics.* The Reverend Father Bossu wrote a discourse, *Du Poëme Epique,* 1675, which was translated into English (1695) and had great favour among English critics. A summary of it was prefixed to Pope's *Odyssey.*

l. 14. *Rapin writes more particularly,* &c. ; *op. cit.,* c. 18.

l. 16. *fear and pity.* Compare the *Epilogue* to Œdipus, ll. 9, 10, quoted above in note on p. 192, l. 20.

P. 212, l. 28. *the mechanic beauties.* As distinguished from ' the living beauties of a play ' (Prologue to the *Maiden Queen,* above, p. 109).

P. 214, l. 9. *by complexion.* According to the old distinction of humours, for which see Ben Jonson, Prologue to *Every Man out of his Humour*.

P. 215, l. 13. *Notandi sunt. A. P.* 156. *Aut famam, ibid.* 119.

l. 14. *Servetur ad imum, ibid.* 126.

P. 217, l. 12. *Rollo, Otto.* The brothers, Dukes of Normandy, in Fletcher's *Rollo.*

P. 219, l. 23. *Plato.* According to the Platonic theory of Daemons, as explained by Apuleius and St. Augustine ; see below.

P. 220, l. 9. *that strange mixture of a man* ; Bessus.

l. 21. *to write pathetically, says Longinus, cannot proceed but from a lofty genius.* Longinus says what is rather different from this, that nothing in language is more lofty than noble passion, c. 8 : Θαρρῶν γὰρ ἀφορισαίμην ἄν, ὡς οὐδὲν οὕτως ὡς τὸ γενναῖον πάθος μεγαλήγορον, ὥσπερ ὑπὸ μανίας τινὸς καὶ πνεύματος ἐνθουσιαστικῶς ἐκπνέον καὶ οἱονεὶ φοιβάζον τοὺς λόγους.

P. 221, l. 18. *animadverts severely upon Æschylus. De Sublim.* c. 3 (after a quotation from the *Orithyia*) : οὐ τραγικὰ ἔτι ταῦτα, ἀλλὰ παρατράγῳδα . . . τεθόλωται γὰρ τῇ φράσει καὶ τεθορύβηται ταῖς φαντασίαις μᾶλλον ἢ δεδείνωται. Cf. *De Sublim.* c. 15.

l. 26. *a learned critic.* Bossu, *du Poëme Epique*, i. 348.

l. 35. Εὐφυοῦς, &c. This is from Rapin, *Reflexions sur la Poëtique en general*, c. 5 (t. ii. p. 120, ed. 1686) : ' Il est vray qu' Aristote reconnut quelque chose de divin dans le caractere du Poëte : mais il n'y reconnoît bien de furieux, selon que Castelvetro interprete ' : and Rapin quotes here, in the margin, εὐφυοῦς ἡ ποιητική ἐστιν οὐ μανικοῦ. Cf. Hor. *A. P.* 295 sq., and the commentators there. Arist. Poet. c. 17 (1455 a 32), διὸ εὐφυοῦς ἡ ποιητική ἐστιν ἢ μανικοῦ· τούτων γὰρ οἱ μὲν εὔπλαστοι, οἱ δὲ ἐξεταστικοί εἰσιν.

P. 222, l. 34. *Ovid. Metamorph.* xiii. 5 :
    '. . . Agimus proh Jupiter inquit
    Ante rates causam et mecum confertur Ulixes.'

P. 223, l. 15. *ibid.* 123 :
    ' Finierat Telamone satus vulgique secutum
    Ultima murmur erat.'

l. 19. *Mota manus,* &c. *Ibid.* 382.

l. 31. *sentences and similes.* Cf. *The Rehearsal*, Act ii. sc. 3 : ' you must ever make a *simile* when you are surprised ; 'tis the new way of writing,' &c. Cf. vol. ii. p. 140, l. 10.

P. 224, l. 10. *Sed nunc non erat his locus.* Hor. *A. P.* 19.

P. 225, l. 37. *'tis well there are no solid orbs to stop it on the way, or no element of fire to consume it* : the Ptolemaic system has been given up since Dryden last referred to the heavenly spheres. See above, p. 70, l. 28. In 1662 (*To My Lord Chancellor*) Dryden made use of both systems impartially.

P. 227, l. 18. *Bristol stone*, or *Bristol diamond* ; ' a kind of transparent rock crystal found in the Clifton limestone.' *N. Engl. Dict. s. v.* Cf. Ed. Benlowes, *Theophila*, 1652, *sig.* B 3 :
: ' Garnish no Bristows with rich Mine ' ;
i. e. do not set Bristol stones in gold.

P. 228, l. 27. *Rapin.* For this deduction of the rules of Poetry, compare J. Dennis to Walter Moyle in *Letters upon several Occasions*, 1696, p. 125 : ' Nothing can please in a Play but Nature, no not in a Play which is written against the Rules ; and the more there is of Nature in any Play the more that Play must delight. Now the Rules are nothing but an observation of Nature. For Nature is Rule and Order itself. There is not one of the Rules but what might be us'd to evince this. But I shall be contented with showing some instances of it, even in the Mechanical Rules of the Unities.'

OVID'S EPISTLES (1680).

I have not seen the first edition : the British Museum has none earlier than the third (1683).

P. 230, l. 4. *Mr. Sandys* ; see p. 100, l. c. 2, and note, and *Dedication of Third Miscellany*, vol. ii. p. 10.

P. 231, l. 5. *epigram.* Martial, *Epig.* xi. 21.

l. 10. *in that author's life* : the *Life of Horace* by Suetonius.

P. 232, l. 6. *Cur aliquid vidi*, &c. Ovid, *Trist.* ii. 103.

P. 233, l. 16. *his own life. Trist.* iv. *El.* 10. But Tibullus is there spoken of along with Virgil :
: ' Virgilium vidi tantum nec avara Tibullo
: Tempus amicitiae fata dedere meae.'

P. 234, l. 16. *Seneca's censure.* See above, p. 93, l. 20.

P. 235, l. 12. *Purpureus late*, &c. Hor. *A. P.* 15.

P. 236, l. 6. *Sabinus* : *Amores*, ii. 18. 27.

l. 9. *Arethusa to Lycotas.* Propertius, iv. (v.) 3.

P. 237, l. 1. *by divers hands.* Dryden translated *Canace to Macareus, Helen to Paris* (with Lord Mulgrave), and *Dido to Æneas.* The other hands are Mr. Cooper, Mrs. Behn, Mr. Rymer, Mr. Settle, Mr. Tate, and Mr. Butler.

l. 23. *to run division.* The common old term for executing variations on a musical theme.

l. 24. Mr. Cowley translated in his *Pindarique Odes* the second *Olympic* and first *Nemean* of Pindar, and Horace, *Od.* iv. 2 (*Pindarum quisquis*).

l. 29. *Nec verbo verbum.* Hor. *A. P.* 133.

P. 238, l. 1. *Sir John Denham.* Dryden has greatly improved his quotation by omitting four lines after the first couplet.

l. 17. *Atque iidem*, &c. *Heroid.* vii :
   ' Certus es ire tamen miseramque relinquere Dido
   Atque iidem venti vela fidemque ferent.'
P. 239, l. 3. *brevis esse laboro.* Hor. *A. P.* 25.
   l. 8. *Dic mihi Musa.* Hor. *A. P.* 141.
   l. 18. *Sir John Denham* ; in his Preface to *The Destruction of Troy, an Essay on the second Book of Virgil's* Æneis.
P. 243, l. 16. *the author, who is of the fair sex* : Mrs. Behn.

DEDICATION OF THE SPANISH FRIAR (1681).

John, Lord Haughton, eldest son of the Earl of Clare.
   P. 244, l. 6. *two plots.* Addison in his criticism of Milton, *Spectator*, No. 267, speaking of the two stories in *Paradise Lost* (the fall of Man and the fall of the Angels), says : ' In short this is the same kind of beauty which the critics admire in the *Spanish Frier, or the Double Discovery*, where the two different plots look like counterparts and copies of one another.' Johnson, in his introductory note to the *Merchant of Venice*, also refers to Dryden's play. Compare *Dedication of Third Miscellany* : ' Our audience will not be pleased, but with variety of accidents, *an underplot*, and many actors.' And the *Preface to Juvenal*, vol. ii. p. 102 : ' and though there be an underplot, or second walk of comical characters and adventures, yet they are subservient to the chief fable, and carried along under it and helping to it ; so that the drama may not seem a monster with two heads.'
   P. 246, l. 3. *Bussy d'Amboys*, by Chapman, 4°, 1607. The play was revived by D'Urfey (1691, 4°), who says that he saw Bussy acted by Hart about 1675.
   l. 4. *a fallen star.* This jelly is frequent in the poets ; cf. *Tyrannic Love*, Act iv. sc. 1 (Song of the Astral Spirits) :
   ' And lest our leap from the sky should prove too far
   We slide on the back of a new-falling star,
      And drop from above
      In a jelly of love.'
There is a simple and slimy plant (*nostoc*) which appears rather suddenly after rain in unexpected places as a little splotch of jelly ; it is called ' falling stars ' (F. W. Oliver).
   P. 246, l. 14. *a famous modern poet.* Malone traces this to Strada, *Prolusiones*, where it is told of Naugerius that he annually sacrificed a copy of *Martial* to the Manes of Virgil. Malone points out that the line quoted by Dryden from Statius a little further on is also quoted by Strada in the same prolusion.
   l. 32. *bubbles*, dupes.

P. 247, l. 3. *Quae superimposito,* &c. Statius, *Sylv.* I. i. 1, referred to again in the *Parallel of Poetry and Painting,* vol. ii. p. 149.

l. 14. *Sylvester's* Dubartas. *Du Bartas his Divine Weekes and Workes,* &c., first published in 1598, and frequently since. In the original it is ' perriwig with *wool.*' From *The Handicrafts,* i. e. the Fourth Part of the First Day of the Second Week. Referred to again in the translation of Boileau's *Art Poétique,* written by Sir William Soame, and revised by Dryden.

P. 248, l. 14. *the propriety of thoughts and words.* See p. 190, l. 12, and note.

PREFACE TO THE SECOND MISCELLANY (1685).

P. 251, l. 4. *History of the League* ; translated from Maimbourg, 1684.

l. 18. *Lord Roscommon's* Essay on Translated Verse, published in 1680.

P. 253, l. 14. *Ogleby's.* John Ogilby, 1600–1676, translated Virgil 1649 (second edition, ' adorn'd with Sculpturé,' 1654), Iliad 1660, Odyssey 1665.

l. 17. *many who understand Greek and Latin,* &c. Cf. Chapman, Verses *to the Reader,* prefixed to his *Iliads* :

> ' — But as great clerks can write no English verse
>   Because, alas, great clerks ! English affords
> Say they, no height nor copy ; a rude tongue
>   Since 'tis their native ; but in Greek or Latin
> Their wits are rare, for thence true Poesy sprung,' &c.

P. 254, l. 29. *a late noble painter.* Sir Peter Lely, died 1680.

P. 255, l. 30. *hand-gallop,* i. e. easy gallop, well in hand.

l. 31. *upon carpet-ground,* smooth and level ground ; so again, vol. ii. p. 85, l. 12.

synalœphas. See *Preface to Third Miscellany.*

P. 256, l. 8. *definition of poetical wit.* See p. 190, l. 12, and compare Lord Mulgrave's *Essay on Poetry* :

> ' So songs should be to just perfection wrought ;
>   Yet where can one be seen without a fault ?
> Exact propriety of words and thought,' &c.

l. 11. *Pleasure follows,* &c. Dryden is tired of the commonplaces about ' pleasure and instruction ' in Poetry.

l. 19. *Hannibal Caro,* 1507–1566 ; his translation of the *Aeneid* was meant as practice for an original heroic poem. See *Preface to Juvenal,* vol. ii. p. 29.

l. 24. *Tasso.* Not in a *Letter,* but at the end of the first of his *Discorsi dell' Arte Poetica,* 1587.

l. 25. *Sperone Speroni,* of Padua (1500–1588). Sometimes considered an enemy of Tasso ; there was a theory that he was meant to be satirised in the character of *Mopso* in Tasso's *Aminta*; see Ménage's note refuting this in his edition of the play.

P. 259, l. 33. *doubt of some eternal truths* : i. e. have doubts in their favour, be unable to reject them peremptorily like Lucretius.

P. 263, l. 5. *Essay on Poetry*, by Lord Mulgrave. Lord Roscommon's poem begins :

> ' Happy that author where correct essay
>   Repairs so well our old Horatian way.'

P. 264, l. 19. *translator of Lucretius* : Thomas Creech, Fellow of All Souls College. His Lucretius appeared in 1682.

P. 265, l. 26. *mai esce del bosco.* I have not been able to trace this piece of criticism. Whoever said it was probably thinking of Petrarch's address to his Ode *Chiare fresche e dolci acque* (Canzone xi) :

> ' Se tu avessi ornamenti quant' hai voglia
>   Potresti arditamente
>   Uscir del bosco e gir infra la gente.'

l. 31. *fond* = fund, store, supply : *fond* is the common spelling in Dryden's time ; *fund* in the eighteenth century. Swift has *fonde* (New English Dictionary, *s. v.*).

P. 267, l. 4. *curiosa felicitas* ; quoted above, p. 171, l. 23.

l. 5. *feliciter audet.* *Ep.* ii. 1. 166.

l. 11. ' Horat. Ode 29, Book III, Paraphras'd in Pindarique Verse ; and inscrib'd to the Right Honourable Lawrence, Earl of Rochester,' *Sylvae*, p. 127.

P. 268, l. 7. ' Now serpent like in prose he sweeps the ground.'

> Pope, *Imitations of Horace.*

l. 29. *hunc qualem nequeo monstrare et sentio tantum.* Juvenal, *Sat.* 7. 56.

P. 269, l. 8. *nearly related.* Dryden's son.

PREFACE TO ALBION AND ALBANIUS (1685).

Opera ; see p. 149, l. 33, and note.

P. 270, l. 1. *Wit* ; see note on p. 190, l. 12.

l. 13. *gods, and goddesses, and heroes.* Compare St. Evremond, *Sur les Opéras* (1677) : ' Après que la créance en a été perdue, les Italiens ont rétabli, en leurs *opéras*, des dieux éteints dans le monde, et n'ont pas craint d'occuper les hommes de ces vanités ridicules, pourvu qu'ils donnassent à leurs pièces un plus grand éclat par l'introduction de cet éblouissant et faux merveilleux. . . . Nous venons de prendre ce que les Italiens abandonnent ; et comme si nous voulions réparer la faute d'avoir été prévenus dans l'invention, nous poussons jusques à l'excès un usage qu'ils avaient introduit mal à propos, mais qu'ils ont ménagé avec retenûe. En effet, nous couvrons la terre de divinités, et les faisons danser par troupe, au lieu qu'ils les faisaient descendre, avec quelque sorte de ménagement, aux occasions les plus importantes. Comme l'Arioste avait outré le merveilleux des poëmes, par le fabuleux incroyable, nous outrons le fabuleux des *opéras*, par un assemblage confus de dieux, de bergers, de héros, d'enchanteurs, de fantômes, de furies, de Démons,' &c.

P. 272, l. 17. *Zambras*, according to the Dictionary of the Spanish Academy, are ' festivals of the Moors, with mirth, noise, and dancing.'

l. 19. *sortija* : in the Paris edition (1606) of the *Guerras Civiles de Granada*, c. 9, *juego de sortija* is rendered in the margin *course de bague* ; it was at this *running at the ring* that the feud between Zegries and Abencerrages broke out. See above, p. 158, l. 5.

l. 23. *Carousel*, a formal tournament, or display of horsemanship. A. Marvell in *Lachrymae Musarum*, 1649, *Upon the Death of the Lord Hastings*, ll. 33–36 :

> ' Before the Crystal Palace where he dwells,
> The Armed Angels hold their Carouzels ;
> And underneath, he views the Turnaments
> Of all these Sublunary Elements.'

There was a ' Carouselle ' at the Royal Manege in Edinburgh in 1768 ; the Duchess of Gordon presented the prize (see Fergusson's *Life of Henry Erskine*, p. 285, and *Scots Magazine* for the year).

P. 273, l. 7. *Pastor Fido*, 1585, produced at Turin for the marriage of the Duke Charles Emanuel with Catherine of Austria.

P. 275, ll. 21–4. *The Alchymist*, A. iv. sc. 3 (*Face* to *Sir Epicure Mammon*) :

> ' There will be perhaps
> Something about the scraping of the shards
> Will cure the itch—though not your itch of mind, sir.'

P. 279, l. 12. *Spanish plays*, in three Acts (*jornadas*). See *Essay of Dramatic Poesy*, p. 46, l. 4, and note.

P. 280, l. 8. *quem semper acerbum*. Virgil, *Aen.* v. 49.

l. 24. *Monsieur Vossius*. Isaac Vossius (1618–1689), Canon of Windsor ; called by St. Evremond his *Ami des Lettres*.